921279 $19.95

796
.332648 Green, Jerry
GRE   Super Bowl
           chronicles

WITHDRAWN

Freeport Public Library

Freeport, Illinoi

1 Books may be kept two weeks an
once for the same period, except 7 da
zines

2. A fine is charged for each day a b
according to the above rule. No book v
person incurring such a fine until it has

3. All injuries to books beyond reasonable wear and all
losses shall be made good to the satisfaction of the Librar-
ian

4. Each borrower is held responsible for all books charged
on his card and for all fines accruing on the same.

D1362227

SUPER BOWL
Chronicles

Also by Jerry Green

Year of the Tiger
Detroit Lions: Great Teams' Great Years

◆ ◆ ◆

SUPER BOWL
Chronicles

A Sportswriter Reflects on the
First 25 Years of America's Game

Jerry Green

Masters Press

Freeport Public Library
Freeport, Illinois

Published by Masters Press
5025 28th Street, S.E. / Grand Rapids, Michigan 49512

Copyright © 1991 by Jerry Green
All rights reserved

No part of this book may be reproduced, stored in a retrieval system, or transmitted, in any form or by any means, electronic, mechanical, photocopying, recording, or otherwise, without the prior permission of Masters Press.

Printed in the United States of America
First edition

Library of Congress Cataloging in Publication Data

Green, Jerry.
Super Bowl chronicles : a sportswriter reflects on the first 25 years of America's game / Jerry Green. — 1st ed.
p.   cm.
Includes bibliographical references.
ISBN 0-940279-32-0 : $19.95
1. Super Bowl Game (Football)—History. I. Title.
GV956.2.S8G73 1991
796.332'648—dc20   90-21431
CIP

Credits

Front jacket photo: Vernon Biever
Back jacket photo: Al Einstein
Photo of Joe Namath seated, poolside: Walter Iooss, Jr. / *Sports Illustrated*
All other photos: Vernon Biever

All excerpts from Jerry Green's columns reprinted courtesy of the Detroit *News*

In memory of
Frank Green, Chuck Hughes, Art Rooney,
and Roger Stanton

921279

Contents

Preface

The best thing about the Super Bowl is that it captivates America every year, unlike the Olympics, which cause us to fall in love only once every four years with a pubescent creature skipping around in leotards. The Super Bowl, and what happens in the months before it, provides us with our annual hearing test, courtesy of John Madden.

Some may remember that before John Madden jumped through paper hoops, sold thumbtacks and nails, and smeared wiggly lines with a grease pencil on your television screen, he was a football coach.

And somewhere at the end of the pageantry and promotion of every Super Bowl countdown, there is a football game. It's seldom a very good football game, but even if it were, how could it match all the hyping and touting and tub-thumping and partying and buying and selling that go on before?

"As much as I'd like to stay and have a Miller Lite," said Joe Montana, "I have to go." He was standing before an audience of cynical football journalists selective enough to attend only the classiest of free feeds at a luncheon sponsored by a certain brewery to honor the NFL's player of the year. This was midweek before Super Bowl XXIV, when Montana was rejecting notions that he was the best quarterback ever to float a football and while Terry Bradshaw was criticizing John Elway as a habitual loser with large teeth. Joe was so sorry he couldn't discuss the issues. He had to flee. His presence was necessary at football practice.

"Enjoy yourself and have a few for me," said Joe, spouting the Super Bowl oath.

It is important for America to have a midwinter belly laugh, which, in January 1990 was the most plausible *raison d'être* for the Denver Broncos.

"Did you hear how many Broncos it takes to fix a flat?"

"One. But it takes the whole team for a blowout."

It is important also, according to George Bush and General Norman Schwarzkopf, for us to have a time-out from the nation's more serious matters. The Super Bowl, sober and drunk, has gone on in war and peace, a genuine chunk of Americana.

Super Bowl week starts on Tuesday morning, early, in New Orleans or Miami or San Diego or some exotic palm-tree oasis in the vicinity of Los Angeles with Phil Simms or John Elway or Doug Williams or Jim McMahon surrounded by an elite regiment of 6,000 ink-stained wretches and 14,000 electronic media marvels. Pack journalism? All crunch forward together to hear the subject's response to the question posed by a society reporter from Dubuque: "If you were a tree, what kind of tree would you like to be?"

Straining to catch the answer for posterity on his micro-mini recorder, one newspaperman is heard to say to a TV guy: "Is that your bleeping boom microphone in my left nostril?"

"Yeah," is the response. "And if you don't like it, I'll stick it in a tighter place."

The Super Bowl, through the years, has evolved into a reflection of the American mood. The media interview the media about interviewing the media.

USA Today says that Brent Musburger says that Jim McMahon told John Elway that Terry Bradshaw never believed that Joe Namath once guaranteed that Vince Lombardi's gap-toothed grin was actually the product of an overzealous dentist in Canton, Ohio, immortalized for creating upper plates of false teeth.

But mostly, the Super Bowl is an annual slopfest in the dungeon of excess. And for me to have survived each and every one of them (to date) is a special honor and puts truth to the claim that those among us able to go the entire route rely mostly on cast-iron stomachs, unflappable psyches, and skinned elbows.

It all began for me one evening in June of 1966. I was a rookie about to embark on a brand-new, intriguing beat with the Detroit *News*. The beat guy before me had only one eye. Consequently, he was a cautious man. One day Joe Don Looney accosted him in the passageway of the Detroit Lions' charter plane and said: "Have you ever felt pain?" I inherited the beat. Now as the summer began, I started to charge myself up in preparation for training camp in July. This I did by taking my vacation in June. That's when the phone rang at home.

"This is your first call at home at night," said my predecessor, calling from the office and sounding gleeful. "You've got to come in. The two leagues are going to merge."

It's all been, as they say, uphill from there.

Through the years, I have been abused by Al Davis; amused by Joe Namath, Jim McMahon, and Garo Yepremian; astonished by the skills of Bart Starr, Terry Bradshaw, Joe Montana, Franco Harris, Jerry Rice, Francis Tarkenton, Jack Lambert, Lynn Swann, and Bill Walsh; bored by Chuck Noll and Dick Vermeil; fascinated by George Allen; intrigued by Don Shula and Tom Landry; ignored by Duane Thomas; gladdened by the pluck of Jim Plunkett; swarmed over by multitudes of revelers gripping plastic "go-cups" containing amber liquids on Bourbon Street; threatened by a riot in Miami; frisked by NFL security guards in wartime Tampa; awakened in the middle of the night by the frantic wife of a colleague who happens to have the same name; stung by the venom of Vince Lombardi; educated in the art of counting in roman numerals rather than on my fingers; and made to feel uncomfortable by what I might step in at Pete Rozelle's Houston Super Bowl party based on a cowboy/rodeo theme.

Also, through the years, I came into possession of 25 Super Bowl medallions or pins issued by NFL propagandists to press/media to distinguish them from autograph hunters and other jock lovers by NFL security specialists; 25 Super Bowl game programs; 25 Super Bowl briefcases; and 25 official ballpoint pens complete with Super Bowl insignia so that I might take only positive notes in my 25 Super Bowl reporters' notebooks about pro football's gala of galas. These articles are to be found in various places among my collected souvenir rubble of a quarter century. I throw nothing away. Particularly, the memories.

I
The Shotgun Wedding

Green Bay Packers 35, Kansas City Chiefs 10
January 15, 1967
Los Angeles Memorial Coliseum
Attendance: 61,946

Pete Rozelle squatted near the goal line, so close he could see the flames in quarterback Don Meredith's eyes in the huddle. Meredith called the play, and the Cowboys clapped hands and broke to step into their formation. It was dusk on New Year's Day 1967 in Texas, and rays of sunlight cut through the darkness to illuminate the men on the field of the Cotton Bowl.

Across the way, Vincent Lombardi paced, swearing through the gap in his upper row of teeth. The Packers were the reigning champions, the supreme powers of professional football. They were an ancient team, rooted in the tradition and history of the sport. And now their supremacy and what was so precious about Green Bay football were being threatened by this upstart team still in the boyhood of its franchise.

Tom Landry's Cowboys had one chance now. They were at the two. They had been rebuffed three times after reaching the two-yard line and once they had damaged themselves with a penalty in their overeagerness. They had made a game of it, all the way, unexpectedly, fighting back against a dominant team. Now it was fourth down with less than a minute to go, with the score Green Bay 34, Dallas 27. The Cowboys needed just two more yards and they could tie this game for the 1966 NFL championship—and force Lombardi into sudden-death overtime. Then it would be a crapshoot again, with the victor emerging to defend the pride and the

1

prestige and the honor of the NFL in what people were already beginning to call the "Super Bowl."

The force of all this drama surged through Pete Rozelle as he lowered himself onto the grass.

Then he looked up.

"Some game, isn't it?" he said, grinning to the man who had hunkered down next to him.

"It sure is," I responded. I was hoping to heaven I had found a sanctuary so that the guards who were shepherding the press to their proper vantage point behind the end zone would believe I belonged with the man next to me.

Together the commissioner of the National Football League and this rogue journalist heard Meredith bark his signals.

Dandy Don rolled to his right after a fake to Don Perkins up the middle. It was the option pass play. That was diagnosed immediately by Dave Robinson, who played left linebacker in Lombardi's defense. Robinson refused to be sucked in by the fake to the fullback, as had been the scheme in Landry's game plan. The bootlegging Meredith was prevented from running on his skinny stick legs.

From the invaded no-man's-land on the sideline, we could watch the expression on Meredith's face turn to panic. Finally, he heaved the ball toward the rear end of the end zone. The ball in flight resembled a dead duck. It was.

Tom Brown, the Packers' safetyman, did not fall for Meredith's fake either and stayed back in the pass coverage. He was guarding Bob Hayes, who had been the world's fastest human when he won Olympic gold in the Tokyo games in 1964. Now he was the world's fastest pass receiver. But he had nowhere to run. Brown was in front of him and neatly picked off Meredith's pass. We could read Meredith's lips: "Shit."

Across the way, Lombardi raised his arms. The final score was Green Bay 34, Dallas 27. It was another NFL championship for Lombardi, his second in succession, and his fourth in six seasons. Now the Packers could take care of the business of representing their 47-year-old league in this extracurricular engagement with the Other League.

Rozelle smiled, happy in the knowledge that it would be the established Packers representing the haughty NFL in two weeks' time. The commissioner strode up the ramp toward the Packers' locker room.

Inside, Lombardi grinned, and his players, bouncing around naked, acknowledged their just-won responsibilities.

"Hey, who won it in the other league?" asked Elijah Pitts, the running back, to a passing writer. "Who we gonna play?"

"Kansas City."

"Good, good," said Pitts, beaming. "We want to play them."

Three hours earlier, the Chiefs of dapper Henry Stram had polished off the Buffalo Bills, 31-7, for the championship of the upstart American Football League. Then the Chiefs sat watching TV in the drafty locker room of Buffalo's dowdy War Memorial Stadium. They kept cheering for the Packers. After all, the Dallas Cowboys had no more history or tradition than the Kansas City Chiefs.

"We've been pulling for Green Bay all along," Ed Budde, a Kansas City guard, told some writers. "All we ever hear is how good Green Bay is, how they're the best team in football; well, as long as we worked this hard to get into the Super Bowl game, we might as well play the best team in the NFL."

◆ ◆ ◆

Seven months earlier, in June 1966, two men held a clandestine meeting in a parking lot at Love Field in Dallas. One of the men was Tex Schramm, a reformed journalist who was now president of the Dallas Cowboys. Schramm had a nickname in NFL circles given him by William Clay Ford, the Detroit owner. The nickname was Loophole.

The other man was Lamar Hunt, young scion of Texas's oil-rich Hunts and something of a dreamer. He had been rejected for admission to the NFL when he tried to buy the Chicago Cardinals.

So Hunt's dream became another professional football league started from scratch. It was called the American Football League, and the teams started playing games in such towns as Oakland and Denver and Buffalo in 1960. Franchise owners referred to themselves as "The Foolish Club."

Pete Rozelle, from his perch in NFL headquarters on Park Avenue in Manhattan, disdained mentioning the AFL by its proper name. "The Other League," Rozelle called it whenever it was necessary to mention it. AFL owners seethed every time they heard this description.

From the very beginning, the AFL had to go to war for its survival. Hunt owned the Dallas Texans, founding them the same season the Cowboys began as an NFL expansion team. The Texans were formed to compete to the death with the NFL, but the Cowboys ran Hunt's Texans out of town in three years. Hunt took them to Kansas City.

In its early days, the AFL played games with NFL culls and rejects. Jack Kemp, who had drifted through the NFL, found a niche in the AFL. Tobin Rote, once a championship NFL quarterback for Detroit, resurfaced in the AFL. Len Dawson failed in the NFL with the Pittsburgh Steelers and Cleveland Browns, then drifted to the AFL. It was he who quarterbacked the Chiefs to their championship on the first day of 1967.

Still, to fight this war, the AFL had to develop its own young stars. It started waving huge bundles of cash in front of top NFL draft choices, and it began signing more of them than Pete Rozelle liked. Flashy collegians such as Billy Cannon, Fred Biletnikoff, Johnny Robinson, and Pete Beathard signed with AFL clubs. Sometimes they signed contracts beneath the goalposts moments after the end of their college bowl games. Indeed, Cannon had signed two contracts, one with each league. The man who had signed him for delivery to the NFL was Pete Rozelle, in person. Pete lost.

The NFL fought back with its money, history, and prestige. A "babysitter" plan was devised. The NFL would gather choice college players—all seniors, next year's pro rookies—at various hotels and other hiding places. Some of these would be wined and dined, and, well, suffice it to say they would all be watched carefully and protected from the AFL talent hunters.

One such player was a tall, talented pass receiver named Otis Taylor out of Prairie View in Texas. The Philadelphia Eagles had him secreted away, his room door under careful watch.

Taylor was in his room when there was a tap at the bathroom window. Taylor opened it. He crept out of the hiding place through a back door accompanied by Lloyd Wells, then a scout for the Chiefs. Otis Taylor signed to play for the Chiefs, another prize for the AFL in this war between the leagues. But this war could not be won in Kansas City, or Houston, or Denver.

◆ ◆ ◆

The AFL knew it needed New York to sell its goods to television, but the New York Titans were about to go belly up. Enter Sonny Werblin, rich and wise in the business practices of show business. He bought the club and renamed the AFL franchise the Jets. In essence, he declared himself at war with the NFL's rooted New York Giants. Quickly, Werblin dispatched an assistant coach named Chuck Knox to Alabama to keep watch over Joe Namath, Bear Bryant's prize quarterback. The Cardinals of the NFL, who had moved to St. Louis, had drafted Namath and figured that he would not want to use his talents in the Other League. They were wrong. Werblin offered Namath a contract for a then mind-boggling $425,000, 10 times the sums established NFL quarterbacks such as John Brodie were being paid. In this war, money was bullets and bombs, and the AFL was using its ammunition. NBC was paying the Other League to televise its games, and NBC didn't want minor-leaguers competing against the NFL and CBS.

The war between the leagues continued. It was expensive, but, then, war is hell.

That's when Al Davis started using his rocket launcher. An assistant coach in the AFL six years earlier when the league opened shop, Davis, then head coach of the Oakland Raiders, suddenly became commissioner of his league. It was April 1966.

"What we'll do is sign the NFL's best quarterbacks." That was the game plan Commissioner Davis put out.

John Brodie, a deprived $35,000 quarterback with the San Francisco 49ers, agreed to jump to the AFL for the Houston Oilers' promise of a million. The Raiders grabbed Roman Gabriel from the Los Angeles Rams. In addition, the AFL picked off the toughest of the Chicago Bears from George Halas, the NFL patriarch. This player was Mike Ditka.

The white flags fluttered two months later when Tex Schramm and Lamar Hunt met inside an automobile at Love Field, Dallas. They were cordial. They agreed that the two leagues were trying to destroy each other. They agreed that it would be wiser for the two leagues to cooperate and share the pot. They agreed to a merger of the NFL, established for 46 years, and the AFL, started from scratch six years earlier. They agreed there would be a common draft. They agreed that as part of the merger, the AFL would indemnify the NFL in New York and in San Francisco/Oakland.

Al Davis, a Raider in the truest sense, fumed with anger. The newly named commissioner had been sold out.

Sonny Werblin in New York wondered, "Why? In a year the NFL would have had to come to us."

But Schramm and Hunt had agreed on this merger and they agreed that it would be effective for the 1970 season, allowing three years to figure out the details. They agreed that Pete Rozelle would be the single lord-high commissioner once the leagues were merged.

They also agreed on one immediate matter—that the NFL and the AFL would play a world championship game the following January to determine once and for all which league was tougher. To be fair, each league would use its own football when on offense—the NFL its famed ball, *The Duke*; the AFL its own proud football.

♦ ♦ ♦

Back home, Lamar Hunt noticed his young daughter playing with a hard-shelled rubber ball. She'd bounce the ball and it would ricochet higher than his daughter, over her head. It was a new-fangled toy that was becoming popular with the kids.

"What's that called?" asked Lamar Hunt.

"It's a super ball," said his daughter.

"Aha!" thought Hunt. The thought just wouldn't go away.

♦ ♦ ♦

The first world championship football game named after a little girl's toy would be played in the Los Angeles Memorial Coliseum on January 15, 1967.

Years and years of acrimony tinged with wondering about the might of two leagues of football players would be reduced to one afternoon—to one football game. Maybe it wasn't pure hatred. But then maybe it was.

The NFL and its legions had scoffed at the AFL for so long. They had snubbed it, ridiculed it, and reviled it. The partisanship and emotion traveled beyond the rival players and the rival owners and Pete Rozelle versus Al Davis. It pitted network versus network. CBS, with powerful ratings produced by its marriage to the NFL, versus NBC, stuck with the leftovers, the AFL dross. The deal for this first match granted both networks the rights for television. Each would use its own set of announcers: Pat Summerall, Frank Gifford, Jack Whitaker of CBS; Curt Gowdy and Paul Christman of NBC—all partisan to the bone marrow.

But the poison of favoritism did not end at the soundproof window of the broadcast booth. The supposed uncompromising aggregation of neutral belief—America's sporting print journalists—arrived in Los Angeles masquerading as cheerleaders. The truth is we all—at least most of us, anyway—kept waving the flag of the league we had been covering. This small matter of surging blood did not prevent us from doing our jobs. But I have to confess that I didn't know if I could handle the terrible embarrassment I would feel if somehow, however small the probability might be, the Chiefs managed to beat the Packers.

"It'll be another 10 years before any AFL champion can beat the NFL," I proclaimed in the pressroom at the L.A. Statler Hilton, where the journalists established their digs. I said it with a sneer. Loudly. It was cockiness. It was arrogance. The AFL writers—Larry Felser from Buffalo, Dick Connor from Denver, Jerry Magee from San Diego, Will McDonough from Boston, Bob Valli from Oakland—were strangers, foreigners. In a few years they would all be friends, but now we writers formed into cliques. We went to dinner that way. You don't dine with the enemy. We might share a word or two, but what I said was what I felt. No pity. We weren't here to take prisoners. What I said and what I thought encapsulated the entire persona of the NFL.

I had covered a couple of AFL games, and I had gotten to know Jack Kemp. He had been a pudgy, crew-cut rookie nine years earlier with the Lions. They cut him and sent him on his travels, eventually to Buffalo and fame and fortune in the AFL.

Now I was in Los Angeles, and there was Hank Stram, a banty coach, preening in a waistcoat. The propaganda people had not arranged mass interview sessions around breakfast tables to interview the various players.

We went to the players' hotel rooms and sat on the bed or stood and asked questions and jotted down the answers. This was the first Super Bowl, and press relations were not yet that sophisticated. We were all called press. Nobody yet had taught us the word *media*. Writers disdained tape recorders and scribbled everything into notebooks.

The Packers were billeted in Santa Barbara, 95 miles up the coast. Lombardi was smart enough to keep the Packers out of Los Angeles. After practice, Lombardi relaxed with his assistants, flipping on the TV. Then the Great Lombardi, this Super Bowl week, watched cartoons—"Tom and Jerry" was his favorite.

Writers journeyed up to Santa Barbara, boldly signed Lombardi's name to drinks in the hotel bar, and listened to the pearls doled out by Bart Starr.

"We're concerned with winning and that's 40 people," Starr told us. "And there's no other way we could break it down. When you win, it's great for all 40."

Sure, Bart. Our passions are with you, but that's not what we're out here to put in our papers. The AFL has been saying it would beat the bejabbers out of the NFL, if they could ever get on the field together, and now we get this stuff. Platitudes.

So even the NFL writing contingent journeyed down to Long Beach, to visit the Chiefs in their marina-side quarters, near the oil wells.

"If you lie very still at night, you can hear those oil wells pumping," said the Chiefs' Fred Arbanas. "They make a strange noise that sounds like 'slush money . . . slurp money . . . slush money.' I lie there and think about all that stuff being pumped up and what you can buy with that money."

In keeping with the momentous nature of the occasion, each player on the winning side would be rewarded with the largest lode of money ever received in a team championship event—15 grand, twice as much as the losers' pot. The prize money itself was designed to create history.

And we clogged Freddie Williamson's room. He was The Hammer, and he was such a showboat he even wore white football shoes. Williamson vowed to destroy the Green Bay receivers with his hammer blows. "A karate blow having great velocity and delivered perpendicular to the earth's latitude . . . a lethal muthah."

Much better material.

"Jim Taylor, he ain't so hot," The Hammer informed the ink-stained wretches. "Jim Nance runs harder. Boyd Dowler ain't any better than Art Graham. You don't even know who Art Graham is. Art Graham plays for the Boston Patriots—once in a while.

"Taylor, Lombardi, we're going to whip their asses. All of them. And if Boyd Dowler or Carroll Dale or any of those other guys catches a pass in my territory, they're going to pay the price. Man, I'm going to lay a few hammers on them. And they're going back to the huddle with their heads ringing and their eyes full of stars and dots. Then they're going to tell old Bart Starr to throw the ball on the other side. Two hammers to Dowler and one to Dale should be enough."

This is known as great copy, even if it was loaded with one of The Hammer's favorite words, which was *bullshit*. Which was just what he was speaking. Gee, this Super Bowl stuff is going to be fun.

Los Angeles the blasé was hardly agog. Rozelle set the steepest price in history for a football game, 12 bucks. With a blackout set for the Los Angeles area unless there was a rush at the box office, the denizens of the city raised hell. The local papers provided instructions on the proper manner for rigging a bootleg TV apparatus by using a wire coat hanger as an antenna.

The odds makers were not afflicted with curiosity about what would happen in this first meeting of the AFL and NFL. The Packers were favored by 12 ½ points. The bookies solved this mathematical problem without the advantage of the primitive comparative score formula, always so helpful before.

Lombardi and Stram, friends once upon a time, did exchange three game films. "The Chiefs look fast," Lombardi decreed one day at Santa Barbara. "But how do I know," he said. "I don't know how fast the film was shot."

"It's the same for both teams," Stram said, bravely. "It's like playing on a muddy field."

The NFL continued to laugh and scoff, and The Hammer continued his hell-bent roar of braggadocio. But pro football was venturing into the deep unknown.

I was so stubborn about it, I went along with Pete Rozelle and refused to recognize this event by anything other than the official name—the AFL-NFL World Championship Game. Most people boiled that down to Super Bowl. But that was too carnival, too hokey, for me. And so it was on the day of the first Super Sunday in the history of mankind that the word *super* was never strained from my typewriter. Instead, I sized it up in this manner:

LOS ANGELES—A colossus or a resounding dud.

It could work either way, this first meeting of the football between the National and American Football Leagues.

The first competitive result of this shotgun wedding of pro football last June occurs Sunday after the loudest ballyhoo buildup in modern sports history.

... This is the ultimate world championship game after seven years of bitter expensive warfare. ...

According to those who deal with such information, this championship struggle—if it develops into one—has captivated the sports-minded populace of the nation. At least it has everywhere but in blacked-out Los Angeles.

Pete Rozelle, now commissioner of all he can see in pro football, hopes for a crowd of more than 70,000 in the Los Angeles Coliseum. Some 20,000 seats, therefore, would be empty.

... Even now with the teams meeting Sunday afternoon, the NFL, in the privacy of its own lodge, regards the AFL as nouveau riche.

..."It seems like a game should have some tradition before you can tell what it means," said Vince Lombardi, creator of the mightiest dynasty in pro football at Green Bay.

After filing that dispatch with a Western Union wire operator, it was party time for me. Pete Rozelle tossed his first Super B—, er, AFL-NFL World Championship Game party. It was held downstairs in the ballroom of the Statler-Hilton. A few hundred freeloaders attended. There was no difficulty wangling invitations. The NFL writers gathered in one cluster. The AFL guys stood around like wallflowers. Or so it seemed.

Just about the time the party broke up, Max McGee somehow escaped from the Packers' hotel, was seen at curfew, and was unseen again until the following morning. Max, after all, was near the end of his career. Legendary for his nocturnal exploits in Green Bay—he, it is said, once claimed intimacy with each and every one of a barful of women in that Wisconsin hamlet—McGee made his way into the night. Whereabouts unknown.

McGee figured he'd relax all afternoon on the Packers' bench. Lombardi had ignored McGee all season, and he had caught only four passes. He'd caught the pass from Starr for what stood as the winning touchdown two weeks earlier at Dallas. But that, McGee was certain, was his last hurrah in a distinguished career. Through the years, Lombardi, the despot, the total disciplinarian, had chuckled at McGee's frolics in the night.

"I sneaked out 11 straight nights after curfew," McGee had once said. "I must hold the NFL record."

Lombardi had devised an escalating fine scale for McGee. It started at $50 for a minor infraction and advanced by $50 increments to $500. Late one night Max was nabbed by the Wisconsin state police for speeding. The mess hit the papers. Lombardi singled out McGee in front of the entire club at a team meeting.

"Max, that'll cost you five hundred. If you go again, it'll cost you a thousand."

The Packers sat in shock. The coach was terribly upset.

"Max," said St. Vincent, "if you find anything worth a thousand bucks to sneak out for, hell, call me and I'll go with you."

Lombardi might have been a tyrant, but he was also a psychologist. He knew how to handle McGee. He knew how to handle all of them.

So the night before this first Super Bowl, McGee was in his room at curfew. And out of it a few minutes later.

"I knew I wouldn't play unless Boyd Dowler got hurt," McGee was quoted as saying in a biographical salute titled *Lombardi,* edited by Jerry Kramer, the famed Packers' right guard.

". . . I'd met some blond the night before and I was on my way to pay my respects. I didn't feel I was letting the team down any, because I knew there wasn't a chance in hell I'd play.

"I waddled in about 7:30 in the morning and I could barely stand up for the kickoff. On the bench Paul Hornung kept needling me, 'What would you do if you had to play?' And I said, 'There's no way I could make it.'"

Rozelle's planners made the pregame show a special event. A flyover of Air Force planes; astronauts whizzing over the football field on one-man jet-powered conveyances; the uncaging of what seemed like a million pigeons. The crowd—disappointingly small at 61,946—ducked in unison as Mike Mercer kicked off for the Chiefs: an historic era begun.

Moments later, as he slouched on the bench next to Hornung, McGee heard Lombardi's bark: "McGee." Max looked up and figured Lombardi had found out about the escapade of the night before and was about to sock him with a $5,000 fine.

"Get in the game," Lombardi commanded.

"I almost fainted," McGee said later.

Dowler had been struck down on the fourth play of the game, blocking on a sweep, damaging his shoulder.

Starr had the Packers driving early from their 20. They had reached the Chiefs' 37, third and three. Bart Starr was deadly, always, on third down. This time he passed, but was not quite on target. On the 19, Max McGee, just blinking awake, was running free. He reached behind him and seized the football, *The Duke* of the NFL. He was still free. He ran the remaining yardage on the 37-yard play for the first touchdown in the first Super Bowl. You wondered where The Hammer was.

"I reached my right hand back and the ball stuck," McGee explained later. "I was so surprised I expected to open my left hand and find a silver dollar."

But Len Dawson and the Chiefs moved the football more effectively than Vince Lombardi had figured. They could do this, and time and again they managed to cross midfield in the first half. The Chiefs tied it on Dawson's seven-yard pass with the AFL football to Curtis McClinton. Jim Taylor put the Packers up 14-7 with a 14-yard run. But before the half, the Chiefs' Mercer kicked a 31-yard field goal.

Lombardi raged as the Packers went off for halftime and TV America went off to do whatever it had planned. In truth, the grand Packers were being humiliated. Lombardi told his defensive assistant, Phil Bengtson, to change the concept for the second half. Bengtson ordered the linebackers to blitz more. The Packers were being held up by Dawson's play-action fakes and passes. Leonard, the NFL reject, completed 11 of 15 in the first half.

As the Packers changed plans, as the Chiefs felt they could win this football game, as America refreshed itself, an East Coast sportswriter left at home, and dismayed about it, rose from his seat in front of the TV. "C'mon," he said, grabbing the hand of his lady friend. The TV sound crackled into the bedroom as this journalist celebrated the championship game with an ancient ritual. But then he heard that the teams were returning from their own halftime respites.

"C'mon, hurry up," he said to the woman with him. "The Super Bowl's starting again."

"Super Bowl?" she said. "You're *in* the Super Bowl."

The rest of America settled down for drama in the second half.

Along with Max McGee, the Packers awakened. Lashed by Lombardi, they drove at the Chiefs. They trapped Dawson three times early in the third period as he sought to pass. Then he got one off. But Lee Roy Caffey, one of the linebackers now blitzing, ticked the ball. It wobbled, and upfield Willie Wood intercepted it. Wood streaked back 50 yards with the stolen AFL football to the Chiefs' five. Moments later, tackle Bob Skoronski led Elijah Pitts to a touchdown. The Chiefs were broken. McGee scored another touchdown on a 13-yard pass from Starr. Pitts scored again from the one.

Late in the game, with Lombardi in control, the Packers' scrubs were moving the ball. Donny Anderson went right on a sweep behind Gale Gillingham. There was a pileup, and at the bottom was a flattened figure in a white jersey and white shoes. He was out cold. The medics hovered around him, bringing him to. He arose woozily.

At the Packers' bench, somebody said: "What happened?"

Somebody else answered in a sweet falsetto: "Somebody got The Hammer."

So it was that the Packers had preserved the dignity and the honor and the tradition of the NFL. They dominated the Chiefs, 35-10. Once Woods intercepted Dawson, it was a cakewalk.

Lombardi strode down the tunnel and into the locker room, grinning.

"Nice game," he told McGee. Max had caught seven passes on the day he hadn't planned to play.

"Most any end could have done the same thing," said McGee.

"You're right," said Lombardi.

Lombardi then met the press, the NFL writers snickering in front of him. Vince was flipping a scarred football in his hands, trying to be restrained, diplomatic.

"That an NFL ball?" I asked, clearly able to see *The Duke* print on it. Lombardi didn't answer. So we asked again.

"This is an NFL ball," he said through his teeth, "and it kicks a little bit better, it throws a little bit better, and it catches a little bit better."

Next door, Hank Stram was sticking up for the AFL. "I don't think one game is any criterion to decide the strength of two leagues," Stram said.

But Vince wasn't finished.

"Their defensive backs are weak, weaker than I thought they'd be," he said. "That's where we beat them. They also didn't have enough depth."

Lombardi tried to stop himself. We egged him on.

"I don't think Kansas City compares with the top teams in the NFL," he said. "Dallas is a better team."

Vince looked at us with *The Duke* in his hands.

"There," he said, "you made me say it. Now I've said it."

I swore there was a flash of lightning shooting from between the gap in his teeth.

II
The Dynasty

Green Bay Packers 33, Oakland Raiders 14
January 14, 1968
Orange Bowl, Miami
Attendance: 75,546

G reen Bay played in the first professional football game I ever saw. I was 10, and the legendary names conveyed the romance of the game to me. On the field, playing the Giants at the Polo Grounds, was Don Hutson. I gripped his bubble gum card like a talisman. There was Arnie Herber—and Buckets Goldenberg, a name to enchant a youngster if ever there was one. I imagined Buckets as a beefy man with a craggy face beneath his leather helmet and mud-stained uniform. Cal Hubbard, the radio broadcasters told me, was the biggest, meanest, and most vicious lineman in captivity that fall. And in the summer he was a noted peacekeeper—as an American League umpire. I only wished the Packers still had Johnny Blood running for them, but there are always small disappointments when you are growing up.

Green Bay, I'd learned in geography class, was a small city in Wisconsin. I looked at the map and wondered why Green Bay had a team in the NFL. Then I learned that the Green Bay Packers had survived while other pioneers of the NFL, teams such as the Akron Pros, the Columbus Panhandles, the Rock Island Independents, the Oorang Indians, the Canton Bulldogs, and the Pottsville Maroons, had failed. They vanished along with teams such as the Boston Redskins, who transferred to Washington, and the Brooklyn Football Dodgers, who were a casualty of World War II.

It all flashed back to me when I, as a rookie reporter, again looked into the teeth of Vince Lombardi. The Lions, the team I covered, were in Green Bay for the opener of the 1967 season. The Packers were champions, winners of four NFL championships in the past five years. They were also the winner of the first AFL-NFL World Championship Game, a.k.a. the Super Bowl.

I stood at Curly Lambeau Field in Green Bay with Joe Schmidt. A decade earlier, Schmidt had been a hero for the Lions when they won three NFL championships of their own in six years, before the invention of the Super Bowl. Now he was a rookie again, the new head coach of the Lions, ready to confront Lombardi in his first game. Lombardi marched into the Detroit locker room and greeted Schmidt like a friend he hadn't seen in a while: "Joseph, how are you? Good to see you." The two coaches shook hands. Schmidt had played in the league for 13 years. He had played in some hellish, bitter games against the Packers and Lombardi. I mentioned to Schmidt that he and Lombardi seemed to have a deep friendship.

"That was the first time he ever talked to me," said Schmidt. The two teams tied 17-all that day, an indication that 1967 would not be a smooth, harmonious season in Green Bay. The Packers had grown weary. They were not fat; they were just aging. They had lost their last two games at the end of the previous season, to the Los Angeles Rams and the Pittsburgh Steelers. Lombardi was burning.

"This is a game for madmen," Lombardi would say. "In football, we're all mad. I have been called a tyrant, but I also have been called the coach with the simplest system in football, and I suppose there is some truth to both of those. The perfect name for the perfect coach would be Simple Simon Legree."

He was a dictator, a man of discipline and intimidation, and a perfectionist. And 1967 would be an imperfect season in Green Bay: 9-4-1, downright mediocre by Green Bay standards.

Inside, but still in the planning stage, Lombardi was considering retiring as a coach after the final game. He was thinking about cutting his workload in half, keeping the general manager's portion and handing the coaching to Phil Bengtson. But Vince would retire from coaching only if the Packers won another championship.

Though not a vintage team, Lombardi's '67 Packers won the division. But they had to beat some younger, hungrier clubs in the playoffs. First there were the Rams in a rematch. The Packers won, 28-7, setting up another Cowboys-Packers rematch for the NFL championship and the trip to the second Super Bowl. The Cowboys were a year smarter, and for a year they had smarted from their demise on the previous New Year's Day, when Dave Robinson forced Don Meredith to throw up the dead-duck pass that was intercepted by Tom Brown.

It was New Year's Eve 1967, the same two rivals, different venue. It was the heart of winter and the bay was frozen and the red line in the thermometer sank almost to the bulb. The night before, Saturday, the writers had partied at the NFL's freeload, as always. They'd spent the previous nights on their own, loading up at Chili John's, one of the famed haunts around the NFL. They told jokes about Green Bay's chief industry, other than pro football, as the toilet paper supplier to the nation. They bantered about how visiting players always liked to go to Green Bay when it was the opening of deer hunting season. That was when the town's husbands put on their plaid mackinaws to go off and shoot deer, and all the wives headed into town to visit the bars as singles.

The press stayed at the venerable Northland Hotel, where, once when the Lions were visiting, a naked woman jumped on an elevator crowded with players on their way to the team bus before a game. On the bus, the players decided it was a diversionary tactic dreamed up by Packers loyalists to take their minds off the game.

On this New Year's Eve morning, the writers awakened in the Northland—so well named—to see the windows thick with frost and icicles dangling from the eaves.

Jim Kensil, Pete Rozelle's number one hand, contacted Lombardi. It was 16 degrees in Green Bay—below zero.

"We were concerned whether we could play or not," Kensil would recall.

"What do you mean? The weather's beautiful," Lombardi told Kensil. "The sun is shining." Lombardi had prepared for just such an emergency. He'd had the turf at Lambeau Field dug up and miles of electric coils planted underneath to prevent freeze-up of the field. He took Kensil to show him a battery of dials and plugs and assured him the footing would be excellent despite the tundra conditions. Lombardi smiled his gap-toothed smile.

A few minutes later, Chuck Lane, his public relations man, had to tell Lombardi that the contraption had failed in the severe cold. The electric heating mechanism wasn't working. The field was frozen solid.

"His toy had failed and he was so sure it was going to work," Lane said. Lombardi fumed: "It's going to be known as Lombardi's folly." He worried that he'd be blamed for breaking the device on purpose.

Then, in another parry and thrust of the pregame psychological warfare, the Packers came out onto the field—and they weren't wearing gloves.

The temperature had soared to a balmy 13 below by the time the game started. It was another classic.

And this time it was the Packers who had to march late on offense to catch up. This time it was the Cowboys who had to protect their goal line as the clock ticked away.

Vapor pouring from their mouths and freezing in the air, these gladiators slugged it out as would two heavyweights for a championship. The Cowboys clung to a 17-14 lead as Don Meredith was a shining star in the icy cold. From 68 yards away, Bart Starr started the Packers' last drive. Chuck Mercein, a castoff runner out of Yale, bashed into the Cowboys' line. Jim Taylor was gone and Lombardi was left with pickups. Mercein, not good enough for the Giants and Redskins, cracked over the ice for seven yards, then 19, then eight. Starr, his fingertips numb, passed to Boyd Dowler, then Donny Anderson, the golden-boy successor to Paul Hornung.

Now the Packers were at the one with 20 seconds left and were trailing by three points. Starr called time out—his last one. Time for one play, possibly two. He went to Lombardi at the bench. He—and everybody frozen in the seats, and those going mad in front of their TVs—was certain the coach would order the field goal by Don Chandler. The Packers, for sure, would tie and try to win it in sudden death.

Lombardi ordered Starr back onto the field. More than that, he ordered a running play rather than a pass that would, if incomplete, stop the clock and allow a field goal on the next play.

Vince was gambling everything on his runner getting traction close in on the ground that had frozen solid.

Starr took the snap and tried a sneak to his right. There Jerry Kramer, the guard, drove as if his life depended on it into the Cowboys' Jethro Pugh. Starr rode behind Kramer, inches over the goal line.

At the bench, Vince Lombardi, emitting a gust of steamy breath, raised both arms aloft in victory. The Packers, 21-17 victors on the craziest gamble of Lombardi's career, were going back to the second Super Bowl.

"A lot of people said we were dead, but we rose," said Lombardi. "We were magnificent."

"Many things have been said by Coach and he's not always understood by those who quote him," said Jerry Kramer, who threw the block. "Perhaps this isn't Green Bay. Perhaps we're living in Camelot. Coach Lombardi, this is one beautiful man."

The Packers were to play the Oakland Raiders in the Orange Bowl, in Miami, in the second Super Bowl. It would be Vince Lombardi versus Al Davis. Davis was back running the Raiders after his brief tenure as AFL commissioner when he tried to destroy the NFL before the merger by kidnapping quarterbacks. His team wore silver and black and carried the motto "Pride and Poise." In the AFL championship game, the Raiders had toyed with the Houston Oilers, 40-7, for their 12th successive victory. They were 14-1, heading for the Super Bowl, and they were a team of violence.

Davis had the habit of picking up rogues and renegades who did not fit into the more sophisticated molds of other teams. One of these was Ben

Davidson, who had been accused of crushing Joe Namath during the season. He had played for Green Bay, but was not considered good enough for the NFL. Another was Daryle Lamonica, the quarterback with the spear thrower's arm. He had been drafted on the 13th round by the Packers, but he considered it an insult to be selected so low. Lamonica didn't want to play backup behind Starr, who just happened himself to have been a 17th round draft choice in the long ago. So Lamonica went to Buffalo and played backup to Jack Kemp until he was traded to Davis and Oakland.

The Raiders remembered Lombardi's forced words about the NFL's top teams being superior to the best of the AFL.

"A lot of people think the NFL is overrated because of weak teams like Atlanta, New Orleans, and Minnesota," said Al Davis when the Raiders arrived in Florida to set up camp. "But we don't think that way."

Davis was answering Lombardi's blunderbuss with a stiletto. This would be another mission for the AFL in Super Bowl II.

There, dammit, I said it. Finally. Super Bowl II, with the roman numerals. Such language was verboten in Pete Rozelle's lofty headquarters. How tacky, roman numerals! This, still, officially was called the AFL-NFL (1968) World Championship Game. That legend was printed on the 12-buck tickets and the one-buck program. It said that in all of Pete's press releases.

I myself, not such a purist, had yielded to temptation. In a couple of magazine articles, I had started using the terms Super Bowl I and Super Bowl II, as, I wrote, historians did when recording the Punic Wars in the ancient world. Referring to the games with roman numerals first in a magazine called *Sports Quarterly's Football,* published before the 1967 season, and then in Lou Sahadi's *Complete Sports* magazine, I staked a claim. It was sort of like claiming to be the first person to mush to the South Pole.

Of course, I remained staunch in my beliefs about the might of the NFL. But this time I arrived in Miami with a touch of humility.

A few months earlier, I had suffered with Alex Karras the night Denver beat the Lions in the first exhibition game between the leagues—only the second interleague confrontation—following Super Bowl I. Karras had boasted: "If we don't win, I'll walk home from Denver." After the Broncos beat the Lions 13-7—and the entire AFL cheered—I flew back to Detroit on the same plane with Karras. It was the quietest plane trip of my life.

But this was the Packers, not the Lions. I agreed that Al Davis knew something. I recalled my first meeting with Davis, when he was AFL commissioner for a few months the previous year. The AFL was meeting in Detroit, right after the merger, because Ralph Wilson, owner of the Bills, lived there. Rozelle's habit was to make friends with the press. He had been a public relations guy with the Rams before becoming commissioner as a compromise choice when the NFL ownership was deadlocked through 22 ballots. His style was to cater to us and answer our questions when we cornered him in hallways and hotel suites. He obeyed the Boy Scout oath.

Somehow I got through the door of Davis's suite at the Ponchartrain Hotel in Detroit during the AFL's meetings. I had a hunch that all commissioners were tuned to PR. I managed to get off a question.

Davis had a reputation for having been a street fighter in Brooklyn. The crooked edges were still stuck to his soul.

"Get the bleep out of here!" was the way Davis answered my simple little question. "Get out of my face."

He could smell an NFL rat in any alleyway, I surmised, although he might have seen the NFL branded on my forehead.

But in Miami, with his Raiders in Super Bowl II, he was congenial old Al. The Raiders themselves were billeted in Fort Lauderdale. They were available catch-as-catch-can for interviews at the hotel. It was open session, open season.

Davis made himself available to those writers who didn't particularly care to make that arduous trip all the way to Lauderdale, a few miles up the highway. He came to the press headquarters at the Doral on Miami Beach. Davis was a sun creature and he was out at the pool, surrounded by tough, enterprising journalists. I stood in the mob.

Al called the hype before the Super Bowl "the great snow job."

"I'm all for the merger," he said. "But I still think we could have licked the NFL.

"I've known Vince Lombardi since I was a kid in New York and he was an assistant coach. He's pretty smart. Who's called us a junior league except Lombardi? He's the one who started that line of thought, and everybody else picked up on it. It wasn't necessary."

Al Davis had made the Oakland Raiders into champions in his own fashion equally as much as Lombardi had created the Packers in the sixties. The Oakland team had been near death in the first years of the AFL. They played their games on a high school field. The second year the AFL was in existence, the Raiders won two games. The next year they were half as good, going 1-and-13. Davis, an assistant to Sid Gillman with the San Diego Chargers, arrived in Oakland as head coach in 1964. He was a man who bit his nails to the nub. When he shook hands, he spread his fingers so the shaker would think he'd grabbed a huge paw. He was preceded by his unpopularity.

The Raiders were operated by several owners and were in danger of folding. One of the owners, Wayne Valley, hired Davis as coach over the protests of his partners.

Valley would say: "I hired him because everybody hated his guts. Al Davis wants to win, and he'll do anything to win. After losing all the games we had lost in Oakland, I wanted to win some any way I could."

Al Davis brought in toughs, slicksters regarded as untouchables by other clubs in both leagues. Ben Davidson, dumped by the Packers, was one. "They say I'm a wild man, an animal, a bloodthirsty savage," Davidson, a towering six-feet-seven, his face adorned with a ferocious mustache, kept telling the writers—especially the NFL variety. "They say I broke Namath's cheekbone for no reason and that I enjoy hurting people. Now they keep nailing me with 15-yard penalties."

Davidson went on as his crowd of listeners became larger. "Myself, I'm looking for job security. So I won't put up with an offensive lineman holding me. He's using an illegal tactic to put my job in jeopardy. When a guy won't stop holding, you have to use illegal tactics yourself. Kick him. Next time he'll think twice."

Much of Davidson's conversation sounded like a prolonged growl.

Davis molded his contingent of roughnecks. He motivated them. He cajoled them. They became a team steeped in his personality. His first season in Oakland, the Raiders did their turnabout with pride and poise and went 10-4.

Now, three years later, Davis had been in the trenches with his own league and the NFL—and the Raiders were in Super Bowl II. He'd turned the onfield coaching duties over to Johnny Rauch. But these Raiders were Al Davis's. Rauch was hardly more than a figurehead on the sidelines. But he supplied interesting tidbits for the press, particularly the NFLers who were discovering new material.

"You won't believe this," Rauch said one day, "but I actually played in a game against one of my players." As Casey Stengel said, you could look it up. Rauch played quarterback at Georgia in 1948. The Kentucky quarterback he played against one Saturday was George Blanda. Now Blanda, leathery, gone from the NFL years before because he was so old, was the placekicker and backup quarterback for the Raiders.

The Raiders practiced on a field on the edge of a Florida swamp. Allegedly, there were alligators in the waters.

"I won't be running any sideline patterns," Fred Biletnikoff, the Raiders' top receiver, said one day during the week.

"If any team ever put together a nearly perfect season, it was ours," Lamonica said another day. "This team is superior to any team in either league and we'll prove it."

The NFL elitists in the press corps scoffed again. The Packers had been made 14-point favorites. We wondered why the spread was so small.

◆ ◆ ◆

Pete Rozelle was host to a Super Bowl II party on the Friday night before the game. It was held in the ballroom at the Doral and was an intimate affair. The conversation that night consisted of speculation that Lombardi would retire from coaching after the game on Sunday. The wise guys among us were certain Vince was done.

"He might even leave Green Bay and go back to New York and take over the Jets," said my friend New York, who believed in his sources.

"I think he'll stay, but won't coach again," said Washington, who worked the hotel hallways and perched close to the inner sanctums, befitting a prize reporter from America's capital.

The gossip went on. The Green Bay players themselves suspected they would be coached by Vince for the last time. In their minds, they thought they kept picking up hints. The reporters were not the only rumormongers at the Super Bowl.

"Coach Lombardi came to a meeting dressed in a business suit," Bart Starr said. "That was not at all characteristic of him. He was going to a reception and he told us how much he enjoyed coaching us and how proud he was of us. We all had lumps in our throats."

◆ ◆ ◆

On Super Bowl morning Jerry Kramer, who had thrown the block that had sprung the Packers to the sun and surf of Miami, jumped out of bed. "I put on my undershorts backwards," said Kramer, whose literary effort, *Instant Replay,* with writer Dick Schaap, would be destined for sports-book immortality. "And for the first time in my career, I missed a team meeting."

Kramer didn't realize he was supposed to be attending the meeting until he was sitting at breakfast. Scrambled eggs.

◆ ◆ ◆

Lombardi was solemn as he spoke to the Packers in the Orange Bowl before the game. "You are world champions. You are champions of the National Football League for the third time in a row; for the first time in the history of the league. That's a great thing to be proud of."

Nobody dared correct Lombardi in his retreat into NFL history. Actually, one other team had won three successive NFL championships, in 1929, 1930, and 1931. The team was—you guessed it—the Green Bay Packers, coached by Curly Lambeau. Ignoring this piece of history, Lombardi continued talking to another generation of champions about pride, the Packers' pride, and of glory and tradition. Then he sent his team out.

The pregame show was toned down from the extravaganza of Super Bowl I. There were two 30-feet-high rubberized figures, one dressed as a Packer and the other as a Raider, smoke pouring from the nostrils, confronting each other. Symbolic. But this time, full of wisdom, to the gratitude of a sellout crowd of 75,546, Pete Rozelle scrubbed the pigeon act.

Under the merger agreement, and an agreement with the pro football leagues' business partners, the TV networks, Super Bowl II was CBS's exclusive property. CBS stuck one of its 12 cameras into the Goodyear blimp. It rigged up four videotape machines so it could show replays—in slow motion. America was ready, and so were the Packers.

On the first scrimmage play, the Raiders sent the hulking Hewlett Dixon, one of those home-bred AFL stars, off to the left. Ray Nitschke, fangs flashing, met Dixon at the line of scrimmage. The collision was terrifying. Dixon was bowled over, bounced backwards, and set down in a heap.

I looked around at my colleagues and the smart aleck returned. "Well, this game's over," I said. Too loud.

But it was over.

The Packers scored on their first three possessions.

It started with a 39-yard field goal by Don Chandler. Junked by the Giants, Lombardi had rescued Chandler, balding and 33, and imported him to Green Bay. Lombardi had been an assistant with the Giants when Chandler was a young kicker. One day Chandler, frustrated, turned in his playbook and walked out of the Giants' camp. Lombardi fetched him back.

Now, years later, Chandler was repaying Lombardi for his faith. The second time down the field, Chandler kicked a 20-yard field goal.

The Raiders' defense—self-described as the Eleven Angry Men—remained a bit of a puzzle for Bart Starr. The running attack was brand new this season. It was made up of Donny Anderson, who, in true Green Bay fashion, was already building a small reputation as a playboy, and Ben Wilson, like Mercein and some of the other Packers, a player picked up as another team's reject.

But Starr's wizardry was not in how he handed off the ball to runners. It was in his agility in sidestepping the rush and snipping apart sections of the secondary. Ben Davidson and his stricken but courageous sidekick, Tom Keating, playing with a torn Achilles tendon, hounded Bart. But in the second quarter, Starr did his job on the secondary. He sent Boyd Dowler slanting across the middle. Dowler escaped by beating the bump-and-run of Kent McCloughan. Starr connected and Dowler went the distance for a 62-yard touchdown. It was 13 to zip.

Lamonica retaliated with a 23-yard touchdown pass to Bill Miller. But just before the half, after the Raiders' Rodger Byrd fumbled a fair catch on a punt, Chandler kicked another field goal. This third one went 43 yards.

Lombardi, as was his custom, chewed out the Packers in the locker room. They were only nine points ahead. He was worried.

Sensing the moment, the old-timers on the Packers gathered in the locker room—Kramer, Forrest Gregg, Nitschke, Starr, Dowler, Max McGee, Bob Skoroniski, Carroll Dale, Willie Wood, Henry Jordan, and Herb Adderley.

"We decided we'd play the last 30 minutes for the old man," Kramer said later.

And so they did. Chandler kicked a fourth field goal, 31 yards. Starr introduced the Eleven Angry Men and the AFL to his pet play, the third-and-one play-action bomb. There was Max McGee, back for his last hurrah, making one more critical catch in the Super Bowl. This one from Starr was worth a 35-yard gain. It set up a two-yard touchdown by Anderson.

McGee, though he didn't reveal any frolics about the night before Super Bowl II, did allow: "I really didn't expect to play. I told Boyd, kidding, to get hurt. Damned if he didn't. Damned if I didn't."

The Packers scored one more touchdown when Adderley picked off Mad-Bomber Lamonica and returned the intercepted pass 60 yards. The Raiders scored once more on Lamonica's second 23-yard pass to Miller.

As the game was ending, Lombardi again grinned at the bench. Kramer and Gregg hoisted him in the air. The Packers, beaten four times in their own league, had merely toyed with the Raiders, 33-14.

"This is the best way to leave a football field," Lombardi said as they rode him away in triumph. He had said it: He was giving up the coaching job in Green Bay, although he would confirm nothing about that after the game.

Camelot!

As Lombardi bounced atop the shoulders of his players, I walked across the end zone. Jerry Burns, Lombardi's defensive backfield coach, stepped with me. Burns's face was creased with lines and he had a way of saying things just properly—briefly but accurately.

"Horse shit game," Burnsie said to me. "Wasn't it?"

Another resounding dud!

But this time, Lombardi graciously volunteered that the AFL was closing whatever gap there was.

"The AFL is getting better," said Henry Jordan in the Packers' locker room. "If they improve as much each year, they'll be on a par with us soon."

Back in the pressroom at the Doral, the NFL writers gloated into the night as they mulled over Jordan's remarks. They figured the AFL had sliced the NFL's margin by six points in one year.

"Hey, they're getting closer," we agreed. "Three years from now they'll lose by only one."

III
The Guarantee

New York Jets 16, Baltimore Colts 7
January 12, 1969
Orange Bowl, Miami
Attendance: 75,377

While America's pro football journalists dined elegantly in Miami Beach, giving their expense accounts their first Super Bowl workouts, Joe Namath went to dinner in Fort Lauderdale.

It was the Sunday before the Sunday of the Super Bowl. Our stone crabs were excellent—just a dab of mustard sauce, a chaser of white wine. Football writers assigned to cover football games for their papers talk about trite things at dinner.

"I'd like to take the action he rejects," said Dallas, whose voice traveled slowly with a Texas timbre. "He's got a broad in his room every Saturday night before the game."

"Bullshit," said Newark, my skeptical friend from New Jersey. "I heard he drinks so much booze he can't do any broad much good."

One figure dominated the conversation this Sunday night of January 5, 1969. Joe Namath—with his braggart's mouth; his swagger; his cultivated drawl; his reputation for the fast, antiestablishmentarian lifestyle; his avant-garde arrogance; his insult-proof mentality.

John Unitas had just recently surrendered and given up his crew cut. Earl Morrall still had his. But Namath's hair was shaggy, his face was semi-covered by sideburns, his smile was quick, and his mouth was flapping.

"The Colts will murder him!" said Baltimore, who had covered the Colts the day Hoss Ameche crossed the goal line in overtime against the Giants.

23

Never would we see a team as good as the Colts of the fifties. Not according to my friend Baltimore, anyway. He kept reminding the rest of us that he'd played the game himself, in the trenches where football games are won and lost as in the ancient form of war. "He won't be able to carry John U.'s jock," said Baltimore. "The Greek's got it on the money this time."

Jimmy the Greek had said it first and America believed him. The Colts would beat the Jets by 18 points next Sunday. Too much Bubba Smith for Joe Namath. The writers, the bulk of us trained by watching NFL games with Unitas and Bart Starr and the Great Lombardi, believed it all.

But Joe Namath intrigued us. He had fascinated America with the Manhattan-woven tales of his exploits.

"Most of it's gotta be a crock," I told my colleagues from the towns around the NFL. "The old Manhattan merry-go-round. But you know something, we've had two of these Super Bowls and we've had two super snoozes. Lombardi might be a great coach, but he coached a bunch of robots. I thought Al Davis was gonna rip off my ring when we shook hands. I'm sort of eager to meet Joe Willie Namath."

My friend Dallas poured some more white wine. Newark took another two stone crabs. Then we split the bill and went back to the press hotel, the Hilton in Bal Harbour. The pressroom was still open, the bar busy with the usual sort of writer/lushes in what was becoming a familiar scene at the Super Bowl. A small woman with a weak chin and an official NFL Super Bowl III pin on her dress grinned at us as we walked into the room.

Couldn't be a writer—must be one of the new breed of Super Bowl groupies. Pete Rozelle is a man possessed of some sort of magic. The Super Bowl was starting to grab at America's psyche.

"Hey, even Pete Rozelle's calling this one the Super Bowl," I said. "About time. Must be the Madison Avenue influence. He's even using the roman numerals." You could look it up. The program, the tickets, all the propaganda out of Miami, were imprinted with a neat logo—Super Bowl III.

The Super Bowl had caught on so much that the sportswriters covering the game were now attracting their own groupies. But it was too early in the week to feel any stirrings about the woman with the weak chin and the press pin who kept leering at us from the couch. Super Bowl Sally, I called her. The Super Bowl had become both sexy and sexist.

We kept talking about Joe Willie Namath and the chances of having something better than another rotten football game at the Super Bowl.

We couldn't wait until we confronted this young man. Our press colleagues in New York had made Joe—Broadway Joe, they called him—a demigod. We yearned to inspect him, analyze him, and dissect his moods. And then, this done, our conclusions definitive, we yearned to flip him away, back among the defeated. Joe Namath and the $425,000 contract might have caused the NFL-AFL merger. But he was still AFL—and the AFL was riffraff. Nothing had changed.

We giggled about Namath. The man spoke arrogant junk. But we were covering the Super Bowl and there wasn't any better place to be than Miami in January.

Namath's boasts had been on the wires a week earlier, the day the Jets beat the Raiders in the AFL championship game. Namath had spoken in the locker room.

"There are five quarterbacks in the AFL who are better than Morrall," Namath said. He ticked off the names. Daryle Lamonica, who had played and lost in the Super Bowl the year before with the Raiders. John Hadl, the run-and-shoot man of the Chargers. Young Bob Griese of the expansion-created Miami Dolphins. Babe Parilli, the ancient number two quarterback of the Jets. And Joe Willie included himself, of course. "All better than Morrall," Namath said. The New York writers furiously scribbled his words on their notepads.

The message was flashed to the rest of America on the other side of the Great Divide, also known as the Hudson River.

"Can you believe that crap he speaks?" said my friend Chicago as we quaffed the free NFL booze in the pressroom.

"Man can pass, and he can win," said Buffalo. Not a bad guy, but he'd been covering the other league too long.

We were drawn toward Namath; we wanted to puncture him, turn him into another New York press myth. Shoot, my Princeton crew cut was shorter than Earl Morrall's.

This was 1969. Martin Luther King, Jr. and Bobby Kennedy had been shot dead only months earlier. America wept. America's cities burned. Vietnam burned. Draft cards burned. In upstate New York, organizers were planning a summertime concert that would be called Woodstock. Man would soon walk on the moon. A poetry-spouting champion boxer named Muhammad Ali had been stripped of his title and threatened with prison because he stood up and fought against the military elements of government. Joe Namath followed Ali into the political-sport arena. Namath had more fun, but he had become the role model for those who criticized or rebelled against The Establishment.

And in 1969, the august NFL of an imperious Pete Rozelle was the most visible symbol of The Establishment in polarized America.

Two months earlier, as the Colts dominated the NFL and the Jets struggled in the AFL, America had elected Richard Nixon, football fan supreme, as its next president. Nixon awaited inauguration during the week of Super Bowl III. Center stage was the property of Joe Namath.

That Sunday night, Namath strolled into Jimmy Fazio's place in Lauderdale. No socks, no coat, vintage Namath. He was a strange mixture of Pennsylvania mill town, Alabama adulation, and Manhattan image. Such chemistry, it could explode, it could enchant, it could vaporize. You could never be certain.

Namath walked in with Jim Hudson, his teammate. They had drinks. Namath preferred scotch, Johnny Walker Red. They were in a corner with gawkers all around. Among those gawking were Lou Michaels and Dan Sullivan of the Colts. Michaels and Sullivan ate their dinners, focusing now and then on Namath, as though he had been pinpointed by a spotlight. Dinner finished, Michaels and his teammate bellied toward the bar. Moments later, Michaels left Sullivan and walked toward Joe Namath.

"Namath," said Michaels as he approached, "Lou Michaels."

Namath said nothing. He barely nodded and took a pull on the liquor in his glass.

"You do a lot of talking, boy," Michaels said.

This time Namath responded. "There's a lot to talk about. We're going to kick the hell out of your team."

Michaels was a roughneck from the mill country of western Pennsylvania. His face contorted in anger.

"Haven't you ever heard of the word *modesty*?" Michaels asked.

Namath again was silent. Hudson steered him away from a potential fistfight to a table. A few minutes later Michaels and Sullivan joined them at the table.

"You still here?" Namath asked. He knew he had Michaels well-agitated.

"Damn right I'm still here. I want to hear everything you've got to say."

"I'm going to pick you apart."

"You're going to find it hard throwing out of a well."

"My blockers will give me time." Namath poked at his food.

"I never heard Johnny Unitas or Bobby Layne talk like that."

"I believe that."

Michaels didn't believe him. "Even if we do get in trouble, we'll send in Unitas, the master."

"I hope you do, because that'll mean the game is too far gone."

"Too far for what?" Michaels spurted.

Namath jumped up from the table without answering. "Excuse me, I want to say hello to a few friends of mine."

Hudson tried to soothe Michaels in Namath's absence. "Don't pay any attention to what Joe said," Hudson told Michaels. "You've got to understand him."

Michaels's face hardened into a scowl. He spoke as soon as Namath got back to the table.

"Suppose we kick the hell out of you? Just suppose we do that? Then what'll you do, Namath?"

Joe looked at Michaels like he was daft.

"I'll tell you what I'll do," Namath said. "I'll sit right down in the middle of the field and I'll cry."

The bill came and Namath grabbed it. He put Michaels's and Sullivan's drinks on his tab and flopped down a hundred-dollar bill.

"You guys got a ride back to the hotel?" asked Namath.

"No," said Michaels, "but we'll take a cab."

"Don't be silly, I'll drop you off," said Namath.

They drove off into the night. Namath dropped the two Colts at the Statler Hilton sometime during that Sunday evening.

"You know something," Michaels said to Sullivan in the lobby, "he's a helluva guy."

In Miami, we writers continued swapping stories in the pressroom. We were lost in our reveries. A story was breaking 20 miles away and we were in Miami drinking Pete Rozelle's scotch and gin.

I went up to my room, looking forward to the morning and the mass cavalcade to the Super Bowl camps. I phoned home and said everything was all right. The devil with the Colts. I was eager for my first contact with Namath in the flesh in Lauderdale the next morning.

It wasn't until Monday that we learned we should have been out snooping, not feeding our faces. Whispers, rumors, guesses drifted, then swept, through the pressroom in the Hilton. The New York writers, housed with the Jets at the Galt Ocean Mile in Lauderdale, broke the story. Namath and Lou Michaels, they nearly had a fight in Jimmy Fazio's. Namath sassed Michaels pretty good. Michaels almost punched Joe.

America's pro football writers—those not too hung over for the early wakeup call—poured out of the Hilton early the next morning. They were full of NFL muffins and NFL bacon and NFL coffee. They climbed aboard NFL buses. This was the Super Bowl and the NFL controlled the important things, the public relations. Synchronize your watches. The NFL had its army of sportswriters on the move. This was D-Day. Hit the beaches. The AFL flacks could chip in when they could.

The NFL's propaganda mission had become more and more sophisticated in handling the Super Bowl press, writers, photographers, and those television reporters who might also be covering. Independent sleuthing, personal digging, enterprising reportage were now mandated out at the Super Bowl, now and forever. Hadn't Rozelle even deigned, after a two-year battle of resistance, to call the event the *Super Bowl* this year?

The Jets' Super Bowl picture day was scheduled for 10 o'clock sharp at Fort Lauderdale Stadium. There was going to be a mob scene around Joe

Namath. Reporters pushed and elbowed. The first signals of print/TV hostility showed themselves. Television men with their huge cameras, burly cameramen tethered to soundmen with mike-bearing announcers, and print writers elbowed each other. It was a simple matter—of survival.

But at the center of this swirling knot there was no Joe Namath.

Next day in the Detroit *News,* I wrote:

FORT LAUDERDALE—Super Bowl week was officially underway with the lights and TV cameramen primed for action.

Ten o'clock yesterday morning and z-z-z-z-z-z-z.

Joe Namath, pride of the New York Jets and the American Football League, had his lengthy, well-coiffured locks snugly buried in a comfortable pillow. The "$400,000 quarterback," one reason there will be a Super Bowl Sunday, was sound asleep a few doors away at the Galt Ocean Mile Inn.

Namath's two running backs, Matt Snell and Emerson Boozer, also were sleeping beautifully.

The 37 other members of the Jets were in complete game uniforms for the benefit of the photographers. It was picture day for the Super Bowl and, of course, Namath was the feature attraction.

"We are taking appropriate action," said Weeb Ewbank, the Jets' coach.

It was learned that each of the three absentees was fined $50, just a pittance for Namath.

"I always sleep in the morning," said Namath, who has a record of having been fined before and has been seen staying out late once or twice.

"That's the thing to do, you've got to get rest."

Boozer and Snell are roommates and they left a wakeup call.

"We heard the phone ring," said Boozer. "But we figured it was just another call."

A special picture day was scheduled for Namath, Snell, and Boozer today. It was set for 3:30 in the afternoon, presumably by which time they will be awake.

Earl Morrall showed up live and in person at the Colts' photo day. Morrall was just folks. He was the original vagabond quarterback who had kicked around from the Steelers to the Lions to the Giants. He was a career backup, the essential journeyman every team must carry for the emergency when the starter goes down. In such a role, Morrall had gravitated to the

Colts quite late in his career. They had traded with the Giants for him in the last days of the 1968 exhibition season. Because the Giants had Fran Tarkenton, Morrall's value to them was only as trade fodder. They accepted Butch Wilson, a backup receiver, for Morrall.

But then John Unitas, his arm bad, went down during the Colts' final practice game. So Morrall had to take over for the great Unitas with the season about to start. He fastened on the famed helmet with the horseshoes painted on the sides and rushed to the huddle. He was vague about the Colts' offense, but he had been involved in so many offenses for so many years that he was able to figure out something about the system. With Unitas out for much of the season, Morrall assumed control of the Colts' offense. The engine didn't even cough. The Colts blitzkrieged through the NFL—the double-defending champion Packers, the Bears, the Lions, the muscular Vikings, and finally the Browns by a shutout in the NFL championship game.

"They are not nice people," said Joe Kapp, who played quarterback for the Vikings with the temperament of a linebacker.

But Earl Morrall, as flamboyant as a vanilla ice cream cone, was a nice person. He had heard Namath's comments about him a hundred times. "Joe's getting his newspaper space," Morrall told the writers at the Colts' photo session. The writers grinned. They knew that. "That's what he's after, isn't it?" Morrall said. "Look, any player on any team has information and opinions on other players that would send newspapermen running to their typewriters and get a great deal of newspaper space the next day. But players keep these opinions to themselves. At least that's the way it's been. Maybe Namath represents the new breed of athlete the coming generation wants. I hope not.

"When you've been playing football for 12 years as I have, you eventually come up against every kind of individual, from the quiet guy to the swinger and the loudmouth. Some guys never get their names in anything but the program. Other guys would do anything to get their name in the paper.

"Neither characteristic, as far as I'm concerned, has any effect on what happens on the football field."

On Tuesday morning, the press clogged the lobby of the Galt Ocean Mile. The Jets had promised that Namath would be available for interviews. He stayed locked in his room. The writers had to be satisfied with Ewbank and a bunch of the other Jets. Ironically, Ewbank had coached the Colts 10 years earlier. He won two NFL championships before there was a Super Bowl and before there was an AFL. He was the Colts' coach the frigid December day that Alan Ameche rumbled into the end zone at the climax of one of Unitas's precision drives against the Giants in the game for the

1958 NFL championship at Yankee Stadium. The Colts won that in sudden-death overtime. It was called the Greatest Game Ever Played. Back then, Ewbank was overshadowed by his own quarterback, too—John Unitas. He liked it that way. Four years after the Colts won the championship with Ewbank, they fired him.

At least the NFL writers had an angle when Namath continued to snub them.

Don Shula now coached the Colts. He could have something to say. He did. He delivered a rebuttal to Namath's comments about Morrall. "Namath hasn't been throwing against the defenses that Earl has been throwing against," Shula said. The words came out clipped, cold. It was Shula's way. His mind was jammed with X's and O's. Two years before he had lost a vital game to Lombardi and the Packers late in the season. It had cost the Colts a shot at playing in Super Bowl I. That day Shula had talked to the press for a few minutes and then had sunk back into his dressing room. I had known him when he was an assistant with the Lions in Detroit. I went in to offer my sympathy. Shula had his head bent over into his arms. I could hear him crying. I left without Shula ever knowing I had been in the room.

This was typical of Shula's intensity, and when he defended Morrall to the press, he meant it: "I don't know how Namath can rap Earl. After all, Earl was number one in the NFL. He's thrown all those touchdown passes. He's thrown for a great percentage without using dinky flat passes. He's Player of the Year. He's had a great season for us and we're proud of him. Anyone who doesn't give him the credit he deserves is wrong."

Shula looked over the mob of writers.

"But I guess Namath can say whatever the hell he wants."

◆ ◆ ◆

I expected an encore when I went to the Galt Ocean Mile on the Wednesday morning of Super Bowl week. We collected in a small room to listen to Weeb. But we wanted Namath. By now the mystique had grown. We were cursing him. We were berating him. He had us baffled.

Weeb finished talking and the press broke up into small groups around the other Jets. Gerry Philbin. Larry Grantham. George Sauer. Don Maynard. Winston Hill, who had once been drafted and cut by the Colts. Dave Herman. Who needs this stuff? I went into the shop to buy a new notebook. Super Bowls tend to gobble up the notebooks.

Just then a guy whose picture I'd seen in the paper wandered by. Joe Namath. He walked through the lobby and out to the pool. He took off his shirt and sat down by the poolside. I gawked. A bunch of us gawked.

Another writer, from the competing paper in my town, wandered over and asked Namath a question. Namath brushed him off. The guy got up and walked off in a huff. Namath sat there alone. Then Chuck Heaton of the Cleveland *Plain Dealer* went over. Namath greeted him. Somehow Heaton had made an appointment to interview Namath. We gathered around in a cluster. Namath said he was talking to Heaton alone.

But then he realized he had a captive audience. We surrounded him—young Brent Musburger from Chicago, Ray Sons out of Chicago, Heaton, Si Burick from Dayton, Dave Brady from Washington, and me, out of Detroit.

◆ ◆ ◆

Next day I wrote a profile for my paper, based on a semi-exclusive interview with Joe Namath, the most famous athlete in America:

FORT LAUDERDALE—The girl in the bathing suit cooed for an autograph. The young dark-skinned man with the sideburns and long, black hair signed his name agreeably.

He was sitting poolside in Bermuda shorts, lounging and talking and reading his morning delivery of mail.

It was mid-morning, not Joe Namath's time of day. But this was his type of scene. The swimming pool, Florida, people hovering over him. Others peering at him. It was one of his natural habitats.

Namath has been moody this week because of some incidents he was involved in which received special press treatment. He was disagreeable to strangers until yesterday morning.

"Somebody wrote I was fined for drinking J&B Scotch," said Namath with the sunlight glaring off his bare chest.

"Hell, I don't even drink J&B . . . unless they run out of Johnnie Walker Red.

"I was fined for missing the picture session."

This is one Joe Namath.

He has another natural habitat. It is a recent addition to our great Americana, a spectacle known as the Super Bowl. The third Super Bowl will be contested in Miami Sunday. . . .

Without Joe Namath, what he was and what he might do, there would not be a Super Bowl.

It was Namath who received $425,000 from owner Sonny Werblin to sign with the Jets and the AFL.

That payment, in 1964, turned pro football's rivalry for players into a complete war.

Because of Namath, and the appeal he had with all the publicity, the AFL was able to survive. The money war escalated until it reached a point where pro football's owners would have been foolhardy to perpetuate it.

So they agreed to merge the NFL with the AFL. Thus was created a game between the champions of the two leagues, the Super Bowl.

Namath tore open an envelope he lifted from his stack of mail. The stationery was burnt orange and Namath showed the piece to a friend. They both laughed. There was another letter in a lavender envelope.

This Super Bowl has been dominated by Namath. He is the central figure although his team is the projected loser by 18 points. The only way the Jets can win is if Namath wins it for them.

But all that has been secondary in the prelude to the Super Bowl.

Shortly after his arrival here, Namath downgraded his rival on the Colts, Earl Morrall, and said the AFL had four or five better passers.

Then a night later Namath was out in Fort Lauderdale and happened on some of the Colts. He supposedly had words with Lou Michaels, the kicker. They were harsh, fighting words and for a while a brawl was a possibility. But things settled down and Namath, very typically, picked up the tab.

Later he said he was only joshing the Colts when he told Michaels the Jets would kick the tar—or something—out of the Colts.

Then Monday morning Namath slept through the Super Bowl picture day as did two other Jets. They were fined $50.

"They've got 10,000 pictures of us, why do they need more than that?" said Namath.

Fines are nothing unusual for Namath. Money comes and goes and there is plenty—$10,000 for shaving off his Fu Manchu mustache, and income from a new restaurant in Miami Beach.

Maybe there even will be $15,000 for winning the Super Bowl. At least there will be a guaranteed $7,500.

All these amounts are but drops to Namath.

"The money in the Super Bowl doesn't mean a thing to me," said Namath. "My motivation is that it's the world championship game.

"Money's the last thing. It's not that much—unless it's tax free."

The interview ended. I felt the best I had all week. There was something worthwhile scribbled onto the pages of the new notebook. Joe Namath had been met, and we had been conquered. He dazzled us. He finally trusted us. Not a bad guy. Namath had brushed off the other writer from my town. I had it alone for my readership. You could hardly do that with the Super Bowl's style of pack-rat journalism. But . . . great.

That night Namath was chauffeured from the Galt Ocean Mile to Miami. He sat in the front right seat of the Caddy, sipping Johnnie Walker Red from a paper cup. It was the night of the Miami Touchdown Club's annual banquet. Namath was to be the honored guest, the Outstanding Player of the Year.

As Namath's car sped toward Miami, the Doral Hotel's ballroom was filling for a Super Bowl party. The writers and an assortment of other hangers-on were cocktail guests of Claude Kirk, Jr., the governor of Florida. Say nice things to the writers and they'll write nice things about Florida—the old tourism dodge. It was a decent party with a roast beef buffet. Norm Van Brocklin stood in the center of the room surrounded by a nodding audience. Van Brocklin had been a championship quarterback in the NFL with the Rams and the Eagles. Now he was coach of the Atlanta Falcons. Van Brocklin was known as "The Dutchman" in the NFL. He was known, too, for his opinions, which he delivered with sharp thrusts. His wisdom about pro football was unchallenged.

"On Sunday Joe Namath will be playing in his first pro game," Van Brocklin proclaimed. Those around him grinned, everybody in agreement.

Namath didn't hear The Dutchman's forecast across town. But when it came time to receive his award at the ceremonies at Miami Springs Villas, Namath stood up and spoke straight into the microphone.

"We are going to win Sunday," he said in the drawl he cultivated while playing for Bear Bryant at Alabama. "I guarantee you."

The next day's editions of the Miami *Herald* were out early. The headline on the front page said, simply: *Namath Guarantees Jet Victory*. Not many writers had gone to the Touchdown Club dinner. I was among the uninvited.

Next morning we sat befuddled in the pressroom at the Hilton as typewriters smashed out this brand new development.

"Damn," I said to a couple of guys. "Why didn't he tell us he guaranteed winning when we all sat down at the pool?"

Because of Joe Namath, most of us had been scooped twice in five days. We spent the rest of the week writing about Namath's audacity.

We giggled again about his nocturnal frolics. "When we won the AFL championship," Namath had said, "a lot of people thanked the wives. I'd like to thank all the single girls in New York. They deserve just as much credit."

Maybe more!

One of the writers had latched onto Super Bowl Sally.

◆ ◆ ◆

I still thought the Colts would slaughter Namath. We talked about it on Friday night down in the Hilton ballroom. The NFL was tossing its annual party. Pete Rozelle's bash was bigger than last year's, but it still was not a hot ticket. They could keep it in the hotel. The corporate folks didn't yet know how to score at this party.

It was the standard NFL feast; the main course was excess surrounded by ice statuary. Shoveling the food down, all talk was drowned out by the entertainment. The NFL had turned to show business and brought in the chorale group Up With People, the NFL's concept of being "with it." The group was made up of mostly college-aged kids with good voices. Most of them were blondish and blue-eyed. Most were white. They sang music from 20 years earlier at Joe Namath's Super Bowl.

When the singing ended, the kids left the ballroom. It was crowded at the exit. Toots Shor was having trouble getting down the steps and out of the ballroom. Shor was still in business then in New York, catering to the sports mob and its celebrities. The managers and coaches, the players and the writers, had to go to his joint whenever games took them in from out of town. Shor would sit there and drink with them past midnight and regale his listeners with tales about Hemingway and Stengel and DiMaggio. He was a fun guy.

But on this night he left Pete Rozelle's party with an angry look on his face. His exit was blocked by one of the Up With People singers. Shor flung the kid out of his way. It was a foreshadowing of Sunday.

◆ ◆ ◆

The Miami restaurants were too crowded for a decent Saturday night meal. We went to a party tossed by Dollie and Ed Cole; Ed was one of the bosses of General Motors back home. Nobody could understand Namath's generation. Nobody thought the Colts could lose.

While we partied on Super Bowl eve, Joe Namath slipped into a room for his customary night-before-the-game Saturday night. Those who knew him best said he had a young woman with him.

For our Sunday pregame stories, some of us contacted Vincent Lombardi for his opinion. Now a spectator, The Great Lombardi, the retired coaching conqueror of Super Bowls I and II, might have the final word about Namath's and the Jets' chances of beating the Colts.

"Infinitesimal," said Lombardi. You could see him breathing fire between the gapped teeth.

◆ ◆ ◆

Before the game Pete Rozelle had his usual pregame brunch in the Hilton. Bagels, lox, more ice statues. Pete threw it for a few friends: the entire press corps, families, friends, and anybody else who could look straight at another free meal.

Leaving the feasting room, I ran into Jack Kemp, who was now an old friend. I'd first met him right after the merger in 1966 at the AFL meetings in Detroit. Kemp was head of the AFL's players' association, a union boss. He had been rejected by three NFL clubs as a young player, then rescued from anonymity by the formation of the AFL in 1960. He was still playing quarterback for the Buffalo Bills, although he was getting on as a quarterback and was starting to envision himself in politics. The Bills were owned by Ralph Wilson, who lived in Detroit. On several occasions Kemp and I wound up as traveling partners on planes when he was returning from visiting Wilson. Kemp had been an arch-rival of Namath's with the Bills. He warned me not to underestimate the Jets, not to think that Namath couldn't create an upset.

♦ ♦ ♦

Pete Rozelle provided the transportation. I boarded the press bus early to go to the Orange Bowl. Not only can the NFL supply tons of food, but it also knows how to beat the football traffic.

Early in the press box by habit, I gathered around the New York writers. They had covered the Jets; they knew Namath the best. Only a few of them really thought the Jets would have a chance. Down on the field, Carroll Rosenbloom, the Colts' owner, stood talking to Don Shula when he spotted Weeb Ewbank. Rosenbloom graciously approached the man he had fired four years earlier. "We're having a victory party at my home after the game," Rosenbloom said. "You know where it is. I want you to come over."

Ewbank was never a man to display bitterness. He declined the invitation. "We've got a party of our own," he said. "I'd rather be there."

The game started at last.

Strange things started to happen. Shula, the arch-conservative, tried his pet trick play, the old flea flicker. Morrall took the ball and handed it off to Tom Matte. Matte lateraled it back to Morrall, who then ran to his left to pass. Far downfield at the Jets' five, Jimmy Orr, the party-loving little receiver, waved his arms in frantic signals. There wasn't a defender near him. It was a sure touchdown. But Morrall never saw him. He could not see on the field what we could see so easily from the double-tiered press box.

"Look, look at Orr," we shrieked.

Morrall, in desperation, flung the football down the middle toward fullback Jerry Hill. Jim Hudson intercepted the pass.

Upstairs, it gradually dawned on me. The Colts were not annihilating the Jets. They had had three chances to score touchdowns and had failed. Lou Michaels had missed a chipshot field goal. Joe Namath was guiding a controlled offense. Bubba Smith wasn't killing him. Matt Snell was moving the ball. The Jets had scored a touchdown.

Already story leads started flipping through my brain, and I was to write this one later:

MIAMI—It happened. Space has been conquered and the New York Jets are the professional champions of the universe.

Joe Namath, the Broadway loudmouth, is king of the quarterbacks and the American Football League is equal.

The quality gap between the AFL and the NFL has been closed. Listening to the Jets, there remains a gap—and someday the NFL might even catch up with the AFL.

It happened, and at 5:50 yesterday afternoon, as darkness shrouded the Orange Bowl, the Jets finished bullying and burying the Baltimore Colts, the team supreme of the NFL.

The score was 16-7, and today there are those who call this the greatest upset in the history of team sports.

Maybe so.

"The only people going for us were the New Yorkers," said Namath. "The rest of the world was against us. A whole lot of people were wrong.

"Eighteen-point underdogs . . .

"How bad did you pick us to get beat? How bad did you pick us to get beat?" Namath kept yelling the question to the strange faces as the crowd descended upon him.

Namath, the "$400,000 quarterback," savior of the AFL, the man who said and repeated that Baltimore's Earl Morrall was inferior to several AFL quarterbacks, had every right to gloat, and he did.

He had guaranteed that the Jets would win this third Super Bowl—and they did.

They had been given no chance.

They had been downgraded and snickered at, and Namath had antagonized people with his bragging.

They won—and the Colts, supposedly the mightiest team in football, groped, erred, and collapsed.

Thus, the world-champion Jets were enriched by $15,000 per man. The Colts received $7,500, but that is hardly balm for the embarrassment suffered as the first NFL team to lose in the Super Bowl.

Super Bowl III, watched by 75,377 in the Orange Bowl, for the first time was an interesting, exciting, climactic football game. In the first two, the Green Bay Packers crushed Kansas City, 35-10, and Oakland, 33-14.

Only a few days ago, in the prelude to the Super Bowl, the Packers' Vince Lombardi had described the Jets' chances as "infinitesimal."

"You've got to have confidence in yourself," said Namath as the yards of tape were unraveled from his fragile knees. "You've got to have it to win.

"We had confidence in ourselves. They had confidence in themselves. We won. They lost. It's a crazy game."

The Colts had the great, crushing defense, the varied and successful offense—the power and strength to defeat every team in pro football.

The Jets had Namath and some receivers—and two complexes. They had the standard AFL inferiority complex plus the complex of being miniature Baltimore Colts.

"A lot of teams in our own league said we had no business being here," said Randy Beverly, the Jets' right cornerback, who was supposed to be a pigeon, but excelled on pass defense.

"We didn't get credit for our defense in our own league."

In their buildup from a comical team on which the paychecks were bouncing only six years ago, the Jets forged themselves largely from rejects from the Colts.

Six of the world champions had played on the Colts or gone to training camp with them.

They were dropped by the NFL and found refuge on the Jets.

"I went to Pete Rozelle after the game and said to him, 'Welcome to the AFL,'" related mustachioed Bake Turner, who is one of the rejects. "He was mad."

The AFL, of course, regards the pro football commissioner as NFL oriented. Rozelle was NFL commissioner before the 1966 merger with the AFL.

There was one other ex-Colt with the Jets—Weeb Ewbank, the roly-poly 61-year-old head coach. Twice Ewbank had had NFL champions in Baltimore.

"Don't forget I've never lost a championship game," he reminded us after his players flung him into the showers with his clothes on.

The Jets won because Namath passed with great marksmanship, completing 17 of 28 passes for 206 yards.

They won because their offensive line handled the Colts' pass rush.

They won because Matt Snell was given holes to travel through.

They won because their secondary covered the Colts' receivers and intercepted four passes. Each of the four—two by Beverly and one each by John Sample and Jim Hudson—stopped a potential touchdown drive by the Colts.

They won because their pass rush was sufficient to negate Morrall and later old, aching-arm Johnny Unitas.

And they won because the goof-proof Colts, who had won 15 of 16 games in the NFL, made too many tragic mistakes. The Colts gave up the ball five times on the four interceptions and a fumble.

"We moved down there and didn't score when we got there," said Morrall, who had found stardom as Unitas's emergency successor after 13 nondescript years in pro football.

"That's what we had been doing all year."

"Namath beat our blitz more than it beat him," said Don Shula, who succeeded Ewbank as head coach in Baltimore in 1963. "I don't think we did anything right.

"We didn't play defense the way we did through the year. We had a lot of opportunities through the year and (today) our offense didn't get the key play."

On the first series, the Colts advanced to the Jets' 19, but Lou Michaels was wide on a field goal attempt.

On the third series, the Colts were on the Jets' six, but Morrall's pass to Tom Mitchell was deflected and changed course.

Mitchell's hands were low and the ball bounced off his shoulder pad and halfway across the end zone and Beverly intercepted it.

Namath then marched the Jets 80 yards to a touchdown. Snell scored it on a left-end sweep, outrunning Rick Volk and Dennis Gaubatz.

Three more times the Colts almost scored in the first half. Michaels was wide again on a 48-yard field goal attempt. After Tom Matte ran 58 yards, the Colts reached the Jets' 15, but Sample dived in front of Willie Richardson and intercepted a pass by Morrall at the two. Then Sample tapped the ball off Richardson's helmet, just to agitate.

On the next series, the Colts resorted to trickery that had been tried and proven with a touchdown during the season at Atlanta. This was the key play of the afternoon—the boomeranging play after which the Colts were no longer the better team.

It was the old flea flicker. Morrall handed off to Matte, who started on a right-end sweep. Matte suddenly stopped and lateraled overhand back to Morrall.

Morrall glanced downfield and passed to fullback Jerry Hill going over the middle.

At the five, unnoticed, was Jimmy Orr, waving his arms frantically for attention. The Jets did not have a defender within 25 yards of Orr.

"I caught the ball facing in and saw Hill open in the middle," said Morrall.

"I didn't see any movement in the corner. I missed Orr down there when he was wide open. I didn't see him. If I had seen him, I'd have thrown to Orr." Jim Hudson cut in front of the pass and intercepted it at the Jets' 12.

"It was bad judgment," said Shula. "We got a touchdown on that against Atlanta and this time we went to Hill when Orr was wide open for a touchdown."

"He knew where I was against Atlanta," said Jimmy Orr. "I was wide open."

The 7-0 lead preserved, the Jets added to it with three field goals by Jim Turner in the second half. Namath kept the Jets marching against the tiring Colts' defense with passing and Snell's running through the left side.

Turner's field goals were 32, 30, and 9 yards, and the Jets had a 16-0 command by the second minute of the final quarter. By then Unitas was trying to rally the Colts.

It wasn't until the last three and a half minutes that the Colts could score and then it required three shots from the one. Hill finally barged in to prevent the Colts the ignominy of a shutout.

Recovering an onside kickoff, the Colts went to the Jets' 19 with two and a half minutes left, but then Unitas threw three incompletions and the Jets were world champs.

Snell ran for 121 yards in 30 carries, most of them on inside thrusts. "I ran the off-tackle option maybe 10 or 11 times," said Snell. "It's called the 10 straight play. It goes left or right. It goes to daylight."

The blockers ahead were Winston Hill, one of the rejects from Baltimore, and Bob Talamini, who blocked Fred Miller.

"We felt we could handle their defense after the first couple of series," said Talamini, who has been in the AFL since its inception in 1960. "They had used up their repertoire and we were blowing them out."

Teams in the NFL feared the Colts' blitz. Namath handled it, actually exploited it.

"He beat our blitz more than it beat him," said Shula.

Namath would pass quickly and accurately as the Colts' linebackers rushed—and there would be needed gains.

"Joe was fabulous," said Ewbank. "He called a great game.

"The running game was going good, so we stuck with that. It went on ball control and the fact that we didn't make any errors."

The 80-yard touchdown drive in the second quarter proved to the Jets that they could move the ball against the Colts' supposedly gruesome defenders. It took 12 plays to go to the end zone.

Snell ran six times on the drive for 35 yards. He carried on the first four plays, all on the left side. Then Namath started passing.

Twice he hit George Sauer for 13 and 11 yards. Then he passed 12 yards to Snell. Snell carried on the next two plays and on the second he scored.

Standing in the bedlam of the victorious locker room, Ewbank kept approaching his players.

"Make sure you show up on time for the All-Star game," said the beaming Ewbank to each player.

That's the Jets' next game—against the College All-Stars in August. New York will be the first AFL representative in the All-Star game.

Joe Namath will show up, it is certain. But it might take some doing. A couple of hours after the Jets became world champions, Namath left the Orange Bowl accompanied by two female companions and escorted by two policemen with leashed police dogs.

"I hope the dogs know who to bite," said Broadway Joe.

I felt good. I had gotten to interview Namath again, in semi-private, when he was lying, almost naked, on a rubbing table in the trainer's room. The black goop was still beneath his eyes. Grime from the field covered his face. As he talked, the trainer was unbinding his legs from the tape wrappings that held them together. Namath had quieted down some by this time, but his face was aglow despite the black smears of the eye shadow.

"I told you so," he said. He had earned that very, very rare right—the right to gloat.

John Sample was one of those who had been dumped by the Colts and resurfaced in the AFL with the Jets. Sample had Hammer-like tendencies.

"It's gonna take the NFL 20 years to catch up," he yelled at Namath, grinning with glee.

◆ ◆ ◆

I sat upstairs, fiddling with my copy, molding it, hoping only to capture the drama, the mood, of this momentous upset that could change the course of pro football for the rest of the century.

Late that night the lights in the press box continued to blaze as the last writers struggled for their own special words to describe how Joe Namath had guaranteed victory and delivered. It was then that the protagonist of their stories was leaving the Orange Bowl in the far corner, across the way, with the two women, the two cops, and the two attack dogs. He was, at that moment, more than myth, more than conqueror, more than a champion. He was, I supposed, what Everyman dreamed he himself could be.

Bobby Layne, to the NFL-trained mind, might have been the greatest scorer to remove his pants one leg at a time. Babe Ruth's 714 home runs were chronicled one by one, but his lusty exploits were never listed in the guidebooks. It wasn't until Joe Namath hit Broadway that an athlete's sexual passes were recorded along with his touchdown passes.

IV
The Chinese Fire Drill

Kansas City Chiefs 23, Minnesota Vikings 7
January 11, 1970
Tulane Stadium, New Orleans
Attendance: 80,562

I met Jimmy Cannon right after I checked into the Roosevelt Hotel in New Orleans and went to the pressroom. They had cut the interval between the championship games and the Super Bowl to a week and I was hard up for a story. Jimmy's Irish mug was full of gloom, more so than usual.

"This is the end of football," Jimmy said. "It's finished."

I looked at him, waiting to hear the punch line. He was serious. Grave, talking rapidly in that New Yorkese he had perfected.

I'm not generous with my use of the adjective *great*. TV is not my medium. I do not waste the word frivolously on the merely good or the simply excellent.

Jimmy Cannon was a great sports columnist. In Korea, he had been a great war correspondent.

I had read Cannon when I was a schoolboy, and I marveled at his command of English and the staccato tempo of his sentences. He had been a columnist with the New York *Post.* Sometime in the fifties, he had switched to the New York *Journal-American,* where I had established my journalistic roots as a copyboy for $29 a week.

The *Journal* had merged with the *Herald Tribune* and the *World-Telegram & Sun*—seven dignified New York newspapers melded into one

42

giant glob—and then the entire mess collapsed into a tub of wrong-colored ink. Jimmy Cannon was writing out his great and distinguished career for a syndicate without a New York outlet.

"Tell me about this guy from Detroit," Cannon said in his brusque fashion. "What guy?"

He told me. NBC-TV was out with a report that a gambling scandal had hit Super Bowl IV in January 1970, the very day the hype and hoopla were beginning. Len Dawson was one of the names listed in the report, which centered on a Detroit figure named Donald "Dice" Dawson. Dice Dawson had been arrested in a federal gambling raid on New Year's Day, several days earlier. According to NBC's Bill Matney, a reporter I had known in Detroit, the two Dawsons, namesakes but not related, had talked occasionally on the telephone. Leonard, the report said, would be subpoenaed by the grand jury. Several other NFL/AFL quarterbacks were also fingered by NBC, including Joe Namath and the Lions' Bill Munson. The story would break nationally in a few minutes on "The Huntley-Brinkley Report," and whether truth or fiction, it had all the ingredients it needed to shock the world. Because it was the start of Super Bowl week, a very black cloud covered Len Dawson, who in five days would be a starting quarterback for the Chiefs versus the Minnesota Vikings in a football game that was gradually developing into the most powerful sporting event in America.

"So, who's this guy from Detroit?" Cannon kept asking me. By now a dozen other writers had surrounded us. I was suddenly considered an oracle about a guy I had met once, when he had stopped by our table at a restaurant/inn he operated in a Detroit suburb. All I knew about Dice Dawson was that he had come out of a prominent Detroit auto-dealer family and liked sports. I didn't know a thing about any gambling activities and connections with pro quarterbacks.

But I did know one helluva story had hit this Super Bowl, that Pete Rozelle had better come up with his best verbal adagio—and that I'd better get myself to wherever Len Dawson was at this very minute.

◆ ◆ ◆

The taxi barreled down Tulane Avenue, a stretch of seedy bars advertising Dixie beer in flickering neon, to the Fontainebleau Hotel. The driver, sympathetic to my urgency, circled around a garish fountain in the driveway and dumped me at the front door. I tossed some bills at him and dashed inside.

"Where's Dawson?"

The guy at the desk told me the eighth floor. I rode up to eight. Paul Zimmerman of the New York *Post* and Ken Denlinger of the Washington *Post* were standing in the dimly lit hallway outside Number 858. One of us tapped. The door opened and Len Dawson peeked out. He was somber, and a look of deep pain covered his face. He stepped into the hallway, and we asked him a question. He talked for a few minutes, slowly, softly. Jim Schaaf, the Chiefs' PR guy, appeared. He said there would be a press conference and we should wait. Schaaf then called room service. He ordered a batch of shrimp and another batch of crabmeat. Pro football knew how to handle any emergency: aim for the writers' tummies.

The press conference was packed; it started as midnight approached, deadline time. I batted out the story as fast as I could to be transmitted to the office. The Super Bowl had became a major local story.

NEW ORLEANS—Len Dawson, implicated in a gambling probe just five days before he is to play quarterback for Kansas City in the Super Bowl, says, "I am completely innocent."

Dawson answered a knock at the door of his hotel room last night and spoke of the bombshell that has cast a pall over pro football's championship game.

"I just heard about it," Dawson said in response to a televised report that he would be subpoenaed with four other pro football players to testify before a grand jury in Detroit regarding a federal gambling investigation.

"I don't appreciate it at this time. I want to think about football."

The 34-year-old veteran of 13 pro seasons was remarkably composed as he spoke to a small group of reporters.

Dawson, annually the top percentage passer in the American Football League, said he did not see last night's TV report linking him to the investigation.

"I heard about it from our publicity man," said Dawson.

The Chiefs, who play the Minnesota Vikings in Sunday's Super Bowl, appeared shaken by the events. Coach Hank Stram reportedly called a team meeting and told them to remain mum on the subject.

"I don't think it will have any effect on the situation," said Stram when asked if the Dawson story would affect the Chiefs' outlook on the game. . . .

Stram said Dawson would not be sheltered from interviewers in the days before the Super Bowl, but he said he hoped the questions would involve football.

"Officially, no comment," said Jerry Mays, a co-captain of the Chiefs. "It's the most freakish thing in the world how this came about.

"It's not going to bother us. I don't know what it'll do to Lenny. This afternoon [Tuesday] he didn't seem to react to it. He's got ice water in his veins, anyway. None of us believe this can be true."

After his brief conversation with the reporters, Dawson said he wanted to confer with Stram.

Stram said there would be an announcement in five minutes. Two hours later Dawson read a mimeographed statement in which he admitted casual acquaintanceship with Donald Dawson, of Detroit, who was arrested last Friday in the investigation.

Len Dawson said he had spoken with Donald Dawson three times during the 1969 football season and had known him for about 10 years.

"Gentlemen," said the quarterback, reading his statement to a news conference: "My name has been mentioned in regard to an investigation being conducted by the justice department. I have not been contacted by any law enforcement agency or been apprised of the reason my name has been brought up.

"The only reason I could think of is that I have a casual acquaintanceship with Mr. Donald Dawson of Detroit, who I understand has been charged in the investigation.

"Mr. Dawson is not a relative of mine. . . . My only conversation with him in recent years concerned my knee injuries and the death of my father. On these occasions, he contacted me to offer his sympathy. His calls were among the many I received.

"Gentlemen, this is all I have to say. I have told you everything I know."

Pro football commissioner Pete Rozelle, who was not due here until today from his headquarters in New York, also issued a statement regarding the disclosures.

Rozelle's statement: "We have been advised by the Justice Department that no decision has been reached as to whether any athletes will be called before a grand jury.

". . . We feel the act of some individual or individuals in involving certain professional football players with this investigation by unattributable comments to news media representatives is totally irresponsible.

"More than a year ago during the 1968 season, rumors were circulated regarding Dawson. At that time, Dawson . . . cooperated fully with our office and Dawson volunteered to take a polygraph [lie detector] examination to establish his innocence in regard to the rumors.

"The test and our independent investigation proved to our satisfaction that the rumors were unsubstantiated. . . ."

There would be no touring Bourbon Street post-midnight this Wednesday morning. In a few hours, we would have to march off to the camps of the Vikings to see Joe Kapp and of the Chiefs, kept in proper step by the NFL's drummers. This was press day, and Leonard Dawson, unlike Joe Namath a year ago, would not be sleeping in. How could he sleep at all? Restrict your questions to football! All of us had the spirit of Jimmy Cannon bursting inside of us. The corps that marched would be a corps of America's harshest cynics.

Joe Kapp wouldn't talk about his scars. Word was he'd received them in a bar fight up in Canada when he played football there. The other guy broke off the bottle neck of one of those magnificent Canadian brews and went for Kapp's face. Joe arrived in Minnesota with a croaking voice and a worn mackinaw that had yielded its belt years before. Kapp was the embodiment of the Vikings. While Vikings coach Bud Grant, out of Canadian football himself, stood on the sidelines, hands in pockets, face frozen without expression, never a flicker of emotion, Kapp rumbled across the Minnesota football landscape without any evident battle plan. He rediscovered the ancient jump pass and returned it to the NFL. Kapp played minus the grace of Bart Starr and Joe Namath—or Len Dawson. His passes fluttered. Some of them seemed to travel end over end. But they got there, eventually.

Kapp did not hold the football in the orthodox way, by the strings, in the manner of classic quarterbacks.

"I just don't believe I have to get the ball by the strings," he said. "It's not necessary to do that to get the job done."

He'd rather run himself than stand back in the pocket. "I look at running as a salvage job," he said. But his favorite play, it seemed, was running at linebackers, then running them over. Three days earlier, in the NFL championship game in Minnesota, he had flattened the Browns' Jim Houston. That turned the ball game. Joe Kapp carted the Vikings into the Super Bowl with a 27-7 victory. Kapp himself had scored one touchdown by busting over people on a broken play. When it ended, Kapp wobbled through the tunnel of the Minnesota stadium, supported by two beefy teammates.

"We're gonna be the best," Kapp croaked, as he weaved from side to side. He'd been roughed up more by the joyous fans than by the Browns. They pounded his helmet until the two players rescued him and dragged him into the tunnel.

In the locker room, Kapp croaked again: "Give me some juice." Carl Eller, a leader of the staunch Minnesota defense known as The Purple Gang, handed Kapp a bottle of champagne. Kapp guzzled. He had gone out in the beltless mackinaw the night before and bought all the champagne himself.

"Guarantee we'll win?" he asked, repeating the question about the Super Bowl. "I think it'll be a few days before I decide what I'll say about it."

He and Eller shared the bottle. Blood trickled from Kapp's nose and into his mouth, mixing with the champagne.

"Blood, blood . . . is there blood?" asked Kapp, the croak now mocking.

Now America's corps of football journalists bounded around Joe Kapp at the Airport Hilton in New Orleans. Kapp had been upstaged by rare hard news at a Super Bowl. Now we were looking for the quaint feature touch, before trekking to Rozelle's press conference that afternoon.

"Joe," my friend San Francisco inquired, "you're here where Starr and Namath played, you're not the classic quarterback . . . "

Kapp cut off the questioner.

"Classics are for Greeks," he said. "Who's a classic quarterback? I think I can play some ball."

♦ ♦ ♦

Pete Rozelle's idea was to play the Super Bowl in the South. In warm weather. Let the writers, the fans, soak up the sun, escape from the snow for a week. Enjoy.

The NFL's press bus drove back toward town from the Vikings' camp. We were all bundled up on this morning at Rozelle's warm-weather site. The bus rolled around the fountain of the Fontainebleu. Ice covered the statues. The fountain was frozen. It was 27 degrees this morning in New Orleans.

♦ ♦ ♦

That morning, the Chiefs were hit by another mob of invaders. Hank Stram was ready to switch all conversations to football, if possible. He still burned from Vince Lombardi's jibes in the moments after the first Super Bowl. Lombardi had scoffed at the Chiefs. He had scoffed at the AFL. Stram had been an AFL original. He had been insulted and he sought redemption. He had devised a radical offense that utilized his quarterback, rolling in what he called a moveable pocket. He originated several unorthodox sets. Stram felt his strategy opened up the game. Preening, boasting about his system, Stram called it the "Offense of the Seventies." The decade was just beginning and other coaches, he was sure, would ape him and his offense.

"I'm not trying to sell our offense," Stram insisted. "I definitely feel the trend in the sixties was a simplicity trend with a basic 4-3 defense and one or two formations on offense. I do think the seventies will have a variety of formations. We'll use as many as 15 to 25 formations in a game. And we put in something new for every game."

Stram was sitting at a large table with a red tablecloth in a restaurant with a Polynesian motif. He prided himself on his ability to remember names. Three years after the merger, the leagues still divided, some of us NFL writers had become familiar. We weren't still the enemy—not after Joe Namath's victory of the year before and the manner in which it had changed the geography of pro football. But this game versus the Vikings was going to be the AFL's last chance and Stram personally wanted it to be a last hurrah.

"In the first Super Bowl, the players were motivated," Stram said. "Then afterwards there were some stories about how they played. Very frankly, we weren't impressed with things that were said then."

Hank Stram said this with soft caution. He was not a man to allow his emotions to blister in front of the press. But his eyes tightened to slits as he recalled the scoffing words of Vince Lombardi.

♦ ♦ ♦

On the Wednesday afternoon of Super Bowl week, Pete Rozelle walked into a large room that was packed with reporters. He stood at a microphone, and we squeezed and shoved to get as close to the man as we could. Rozelle was the most urbane of commissioners. He could take a delicate subject and polish it, refine it, make disaster seem a victory. Now he addressed the Dawson Affair—the reports regarding Len Dawson and his gambler-acquaintance just before the Super Bowl.

"This is the end of football," Jimmy Cannon said one more time, right in front of the commissioner.

Rozelle exonerated Len Dawson—and the other players. "I have the utmost confidence that he has done nothing that would lead us to take any action against him," Rozelle said.

Suddenly, there was a flare-up in the press mob. Moe Siegel, the wonderful jokesmith from Washington, uttered something about gambling. Pat Livingston of the Pittsburgh *Press* snarled at Siegel. "I've known Len Dawson for years since he played in Pittsburgh," Pat said. "He's the cleanest athlete I've ever known." Siegel, who had pipelines into the government, responded with words of doubt. Ordinarily, Livingston was a mild-mannered man. He moved toward Siegel, and I was in between. The words were loud. But ultimately these two men, long-time friends, tamed down before staging Super Bowl Press Conference Fistfight I. The passions burned themselves out.

"We have no information that any pro football player has bet on a professional football game," Rozelle said.

Rozelle had one additional bit for me. Seven years earlier he had banned Alex Karras along with Paul Hornung for gambling and had fined several of the Lions for making small wagers. He was attuned to gambling. For my Detroit readers, he now cleared Bill Munson with grand Rozellean flair: "Bill Munson is a cross between Fran Tarkenton, Bart Starr, and Christ."

Rozelle had killed the issue. My story ran across the top of the front news page of the Detroit *News*.

And that night I was free at last. Dinner at Commander's Palace. Gumbo. Gulf shrimp. Then I hit Bourbon Street. The Old Absinthe House was crammed around the bar and in the back room with writers, football owners, GMs, and probably a player or two out after curfew.

This was how a Super Bowl was supposed to be.

◆ ◆ ◆

Pete Rozelle did not concern himself with the gambling in the pressroom of the Roosevelt. A lot of us had gone cluck-cluck in condemning the Super Bowl when the gambling issue dominated the news before Rozelle cleared Dawson. Now we fished out dollar bills to participate in the press pool.

Paul Zimmerman had tacked a sheet of lined legal paper on the bulletin board. We picked our favorite, guessed at a reasonable score, and gave Paul a buck to participate in the pool.

True to my NFL blood, I figured the Vikings would handle the Chiefs by two touchdowns.

The Vikings might have been NFL, but they weren't any older than the Chiefs of the AFL, and they didn't possess any more tradition. The Minnesota club was formed in the NFL in 1960, as Lamar Hunt was building his AFL with a bunch of adventurous dreamers. The NFL went into Minneapolis-St. Paul for one selfish reason: to prevent the AFL from capturing the territory. The AFL had planned a franchise in Minnesota, but when the NFL, with conniving strategy, captured the Twin Cities territory, the AFL evacuated the area—and put a club in Oakland.

◆ ◆ ◆

It was the half-century season for the NFL, and the old league sent the new Vikings into Super Bowl IV with considerable pride. The league had meager roots. George Halas and the other founders sat around on the running boards of the vehicles in a Hupmobile dealership in Canton, Ohio. These pioneer players were paid 10 bucks a game. Halas coached, played for, and owned the Decatur Staleys. He moved his team to Chicago and renamed it the Bears. Even in the twenties, pro football knew it had to be marketed. Halas found time to write the press releases and deliver them to the papers.

The Vikings were a throwback football team. Their strengths were defense and the quarterback/leader, Joe Kapp. The defense—Alan Page, Carl Eller, and companions—had one motto: "We meet at the quarterback." The press called the Vikings' defense the "Purple People Eaters."

"I hate that, Purple People Eaters," Page once told me in a falsetto tone. I thought of some other words to use.

Joe Kapp, in his roughneck fashion, had provided the Vikings with another motto: "40 for 60." "Forty guys playing like hell for 60 minutes," he said. Kapp would shriek it in his coarse voice. Then he'd go out and drink with his teammates. Sometimes one of them felt it necessary to punch him out. Once Kapp and Lonnie Warwick, a tough linebacker, brawled outside a saloon in the snow.

Bud Grant taught the team to play in his image. The Vikings were icy-tough, stolid. Bud Grant filled America's TV screens with his stoic image, hands in purple pockets, headphones strapped to his head like moose antlers. A chunk of ice statuary. The Vikings froze their opponents to death.

The NFL, to celebrate its half-century season, placed patches on the shoulders of all its players. The patches said simply: NFL-50. The message was understood: Stick it in your nose, AFL!

◆ ◆ ◆

Henry Stram swaggered through New Orleans. The Vikings might be throwbacks to the era of Neanderthal football. Hank continued to boast that his brand was the football of the future, that Offense of the Seventies.

"They've never played anybody with our quickness and speed," Stram said of the NFL champions.

The Chiefs had finished second in their division, behind Oakland in the AFL West. They had lost twice to the Raiders during the season, 27-24 and 10-6. They had been losers to the Raiders in seven of the prior eight meetings before the two bloodied rivals played each other again in the 10th, and last, AFL championship game.

Kansas City had managed to eliminate the reigning champion Jets and Joe Namath the week before, 13-6. Then, playing for the AFL championship and advancement to Super Bowl IV, Stram sent the Chiefs' defenders whipping in on Daryle Lamonica, still the Raiders' quarterback. They trapped Lamonica four times behind the line when he intended to pass. And when he did pass, they intercepted him four times. Meanwhile, Lenny Dawson steered the Offense of the Seventies, its moveable pocket, its Tight-end I, its variety of tricky shifts, with neat skills. The Chiefs upset the Raiders, 17-7. Al Davis bit his fingernails to the nub.

Hank Stram was back in the Super Bowl, yearning for revenge. It was fitting for him. Through the 10 seasons of the AFL, Hank Stram was the only original coach to remain with his team from beginning to end.

There would be ample motivation. But these Vikings, 14-point favorites, flaunting those NFL-50 patches on their shoulders, were another of these invincible NFL teams.

Sure, thought Hank Stram.

◆ ◆ ◆

Pete Rozelle did not wear an NFL-50 patch on his gray flannel suit. He should have. Though he was commissioner of the entire realm of pro football, Rozelle bled NFL blood. It ran thicker than Johnnie Walker Red.

Two months after Joe Namath had delivered on his guarantee in Super Bowl III, the 26 club owners gathered in Palm Springs. They were there to put together the last parts of the merger. There was a Super Bowl between the league champions. There had been a common draft. The NFL owners, condescendingly, were talking to the AFL owners. And the NFL owners were asking the AFL guys, "Why don't you keep your own identity?" Rozelle was hunting for loopholes to keep the NFL separate from the AFL, with an interlocking schedule in a major-league-baseball-type establishment.

"By 1970, there would be 10 years of publicized rivalry built up between the AFL and NFL," Rozelle said. NFL purists said Amen.

Led by Paul Brown, who had formed the expansion Cincinnati Bengals, the AFL owners battled the NFL's plan to keep them from joining the 50-year-old league as full-fledged partners. Brown had his private motive. He had been forced out by Art Modell in Cleveland, cashiered from the franchise that carried his name. He wanted to be in the same division with the Browns. He wanted two shots at them every season. So he suggested that the AFL and NFL should be mixed into a massive cocktail shaker, and the 26 clubs rearranged by geography.

The two leagues caucused in separate rooms at the El Mirador Hilton in Palm Springs. The NFL had the larger room because it had more teams. Rozelle kept flitting across the carpet between the two meeting rooms, in search of accord.

"I keep crossing the DMZ," Rozelle told the writers at one of his briefings during the stalemate. America was raging at the Vietnam War. And in Vietnam, the warring sides were separated by a Demilitarized Zone—DMZ to the headline writers far from the "toy departments" of the daily press.

The AFL had 10 club owners and 10 teams; the NFL had 16 owners and 16 teams. There was imbalance, and those AFL owners who could count beyond 10 realized they could be outvoted at meetings—unless they all joined up in a single, greater NFL conglomerate. They had paid the

NFL $18 million in indemnities and considered that a proper initiation fee. Besides, when Paul Brown had paid $7 million to join the AFL, his money also went to the NFL.

The writers, perhaps wiser, had long before declared peace with each other. We were all football writers, and stories, not NFL pride or AFL sensitivities, were most important. Dick Connor and Bob Valli had become friends of mine.

We scratched to cover these Palm Springs meetings in March of 1970. Connor, out of Denver, had a pipeline into the Broncos. Valli, from the Oakland *Tribune,* was tight with the Raiders. We all had lunch the third day of the meetings at a patio restaurant in Palm Springs.

"We need a guy with good NFL connections," they told me.

"I'll try," I told them. We made a pact.

"The NFL is unanimous in wanting to keep the identities separate," William Clay Ford, the Lions' owner, told me in a hallway at the hotel. The totality of the NFL's stubbornness was duly reported in three newspapers—in Denver, in Oakland, and in Detroit.

The NFL then suggested, with Rozelle carrying the message across the DMZ to the AFL, that pro football retain a status quo for a few more years. In other words, the NFL sought to delay the merger. Denver, Oakland, and Detroit readers knew this the following day.

Al Davis was rattling sabers inside the AFL's caucus room. He managed to obtain 4 of the 10 votes, his own and proxies from Kansas City, Buffalo, and Boston.

"This is not untrue," Davis said. This development, and Davis's confirmation, were reported in Denver, Oakland, and Detroit.

Then Davis had a brainstorm. A secret solution that would eliminate the 16 to 10 imbalance.

"Let three NFL clubs join us," said Davis, going for the NFL's jugular. The idea was so simple: form two 13-club groups to be known as the National Football Conference and the American Football Conference, in competition under the giant banner of the National Football League.

Only three newspapers printed Davis's secret peace plan the next day—in Denver, Oakland, and Detroit.

But peace was months of haggling in the distance.

The owners of the two sides met three more times in New York. Three volunteers were needed from the old NFL to move over and join the AFL clubs in the new AFC. The franchise proprietors battled in Rozelle's office and carried over their conflicts to the bar at Toots Shor's.

Art Modell typified the NFL owners' establishment. He turned defiant when asked if he would transfer the Browns to the group with the AFL upstarts.

"There is no way the Cleveland Browns will move over," said Modell, indignant. "We're not going to emasculate the NFL."

Rozelle finally had enough. He made the owners captive in his headquarters at 410 Park Avenue. In essence he locked the front door.

"Oh, I've been taking naps on the floor," said the patrician Lamar Hunt when asked how he combated fatigue in Rozelle's prison.

A few blocks away the writers locked themselves into the NFL's pressroom at the St. Regis for the night. We kept getting tips that the owners would have a settlement in 30 minutes. In an hour. Soon. It dragged on through a Friday night and well into daylight Saturday. Writers fought with photographers who wanted to capture the drama by shooting pictures of their sleeping comrades.

At last there was a puff of white smoke. They had hammered out a solution. Art Modell broke open the stalemate. He told his friend, Pete Rozelle, he would move the Browns into the new AFC, in the best interests of pro football. The venerable Art Rooney agreed, reluctantly, to switch the Pittsburgh Steelers. Carroll Rosenbloom had a special reason for transplanting the Colts. He could get his revenge twice a season against the Jets. They'd be in the same division.

Now Rozelle had to convince the remaining 13 club owners of the future NFC to agree on an internal realignment plan. The battling continued. Finally, Rozelle hit upon the solution. He drew up five different division schemes and stuffed them all into a vase on his secretary's desk. Then Thelma Elkje, the secretary, drew out one scrap of paper.

Thus, the NFL got its merger finished—in a raffle.

◆ ◆ ◆

Len Dawson tossed most of Saturday night and Sunday morning in Room 858 of the Fontainebleau. His stomach churned with nausea. In a few hours he must prove his innocence to a dubious America.

◆ ◆ ◆

It rained on Super Sunday in New Orleans. The scalpers on the walkways outside rickety Tulane Stadium got themselves soaked. Tickets were up to $15, and they were selling for half that.

In the press box, Jim Finks was confident. He was general manager of the Vikings. He had built a club from an expansion patsy to NFL champions—40 for 60, NFL-50. He was the one who had brought Joe Kapp and Bud Grant down from Canada. He was the one who had traded Francis Tarkenton to the Giants. "With Francis we're nothing but a 7-7 club,"

Finks had said. With Kapp, the scattershooting quarterback who maintained that classics were for Greeks, the Vikings were champions.

In the Chiefs' locker room, Stram soothed Dawson. He reminded those players who had been beaten by the Packers in Super Bowl I of the words of Vince Lombardi. He reminded them of their responsibility to the AFL. The Chiefs put on their blood-red uniforms, with a special little something extra just for this last game. Buck Buchanan and Jerry Mays, who had been AFL players for the duration of their careers, had deep memories.

"What Lombardi said doesn't bother me now," Buchanan told people. "He should have looked around his own league, at the Steelers and St. Louis. They never won any championships. What bothered me was people called me a sorry football player.

"After the first Super Bowl, nothing was pleasant for six months," Mays recalled. "I never had any love for the NFL. I had a worse grudge against the NFL than the others on this team. I was run out of my hometown, Dallas, by the NFL."

◆ ◆ ◆

The pregame show featured two hot-air balloons floating over the field, one marked *Chiefs*, the other *Vikings*. Suddenly, one balloon crashed into the grandstands, near the end zone. It was the balloon etched *Vikings*. I stifled a chuckle in the press box and felt a touch of déjà vu. Ominous.

Then Pat O'Brien, the actor, recited "The Star-Spangled Banner" to the toots of Doc Severinsen's trumpet.

Something odd was happening on the field. Again. The classic Len Dawson was moving the football against the monstrous Vikings. Joe Kapp was stuck against Mays and Buchanan and the Chiefs' defense. The Chiefs had one of the early soccer-style placekickers, Jan Stenerud. Stenerud had come to America from Norway to study at Montana State on a skiing scholarship. The football coach discovered a booming kicker.

Stenerud scored the first nine points of Super Bowl IV on field goals of 48, 32, and 25 yards. On the next kickoff, the Vikings' return man, Charlie West, let the ball hit him on the thigh. The Chiefs recovered. Dawson passed to Otis Taylor, wide, to the five. On the next play, the Vikings were suckered by the trap scheme devised by Stram. The left-side linemen pulled and allowed Page to charge dead ahead. Little Mike Garrett waltzed through the vacated area for a touchdown. By halftime, Minnesota was being beaten 16-0.

◆ ◆ ◆

The NFL always has been acutely aware of history. So the halftime show of Super Bowl IV was a recreation of the Battle of New Orleans, in which

General Andy Jackson's Americans were superior to the British in the War of 1812. Dressed in their period costumes of early 19th-century British and American troops, the actors fired musket blanks at each other and unloosed cannons. Cavalry men rode prancing horses into the mock battle. But alas, the horses upon hearing the booming reports of the cannons bolted and reared. Riders fell. War was hell.

Bud Grant and Joe Kapp were spouting similar thoughts.

The Vikings scored on Dave Osborn's four-yard run early in the third quarter. They now had a chance if Kapp could fire his end-over-end flutterballs near his targets. But Buchanan, Mays, Aaron Brown, and Curly Culp harassed him with their pass rush. The Vikings couldn't figure out the stacked linebackers, Stram's concept, so different than it was in the NFL.

The Chiefs moved again with Dawson fooling the Vikings with a flanker reverse to Frank Pitts on a third-and-seven situation. Pitts barely made the first down. Then at the Vikings' 46, the defense sent two blitzers at Dawson. He calmly passed short, six yards, to Otis Taylor on a sideline pattern. Taylor beat, then broke away from Earsell Mackbee, crunched over safety Karl Kassulke at the 10, and pranced into the end zone for a 46-yard touchdown. Another favored NFL champion was done.

On defense, the Chiefs continued to confound and befuddle Kapp, ultimately driving him from the game. The Vikings just could not figure out Hank Stram's schemes.

Stram had been wired for sound for this game. He yelled into the microphone when the Vikings tangled up in their own inertia: "They can't figure it out, they don't know what they're doing. It's like a Chinese fire drill out there."

Super Bowl IV ended 23-7 in favor of the Chiefs. By game's end, Dawson was already in the locker room.

◆ ◆ ◆

We fought our way through the mobs, down the ramps, and into the tight locker rooms of Tulane Stadium. Len Dawson was in the center of the Chiefs' locker room. He had a hand covering one ear so he could hear the speaker on the phone connected to the other ear. His caller was President Nixon, who had watched the Super Bowl at the White House.

"The world looks up to pro football players for courage," said Richard Nixon, a one-time pass receiver for Whittier College.

"Thank you, Mr. President," said the quarterback.

Dawson had thrown only 17 passes, completing 12. He had been masterful—in the classical mode of Starr in the first two Super Bowls and of Joe Namath the year before. It was total vindication.

"I don't have to answer to anybody again about any gambling unpleasantness," he said. "No one can appreciate how much torment I endured all week, answering the questions about my supposed friendship with unsavory characters."

We crushed closer to him.

"Now, it's no disgrace to lose to us," said Len Dawson.

Dawson picked his small son, Lenny, from the floor and brought him up to the podium with him.

"Dad," said the boy, "you done good."

◆ ◆ ◆

At its very end, the AFL had matched the NFL in victories in the Super Bowl. Two for each side. It would never be the same again.

While listening to Dawson, I looked across the small room. Jerry Mays was grimy, grinning. He pulled off his Kansas City jersey. I immediately noticed what the equipment man had added to it especially for Super Bowl IV: a small, shield-shaped patch was sewn onto the shoulder. It said, simply: AFL-10.

We left the locker room to write some more history.

◆ ◆ ◆

While the Chiefs celebrated their victory, somewhere in New Orleans, some unknown person celebrated his good fortune. The wallet containing the many dollar bills of the press's pick-'em pool was gone—into the light fingers of a pickpocket.

V

The Ultimate Interview

Baltimore Colts 16, Dallas Cowboys 13
January 17, 1971
Orange Bowl, Miami
Attendance: 79,204

Pete Rozelle brought us back to Miami Beach for the first Super Bowl after the realignment of two proud leagues into a greater NFL, without any NFL-51 patches. This would be Super Bowl V, and something was missing. Indeed, plenty was missing from this business concoction that was tickling the American psyche more and more each January.

Now the two leagues were gone. The purpose for playing a Super Bowl was gone. It had been designed as the gauge of quality between the NFL and the AFL—one the establishment, the other the upstart; one proud and cocky, the other new and a symbol of the unrest and the bitterness of the 1960s. Just a few years earlier, Vince Lombardi had crunched the AFL and then insulted it with his words. Then Joe Namath had slapped the ancient NFL across its cheek with his guarantee and his victory.

"Welcome to the AFL," Bake Turner had told Pete Rozelle. It was marvelous vindication.

Now all this was gone forever, legislated out in the conference rooms of Palm Springs and Park Avenue. The Super Bowl had become merely another football game; for a championship, of course; captivating a nation, of course; giving the members of the sporting press a week of midwinter warmth, of course; sometimes even giving them something worthwhile to write.

The purist within me ached. The purist within me also wondered when this Super Bowl championship would produce a football game that was competitively super.

There had been four Super Bowls, and in two the Packers had been dominant; the other two produced revenge and satisfaction for a group of belittled athletes and their owners and fans. History was made and tradition smashed.

But none of the four Super Bowls had been decided by a late, late score. None had possessed the elements of drama that make pro football a special creation. Not once had there been any doubt in the fourth quarter as to the victor.

Now we were back in Miami Beach, back where the Super Bowl gouge was invented, our reflexes conditioned for the obligatory insults from the hotel staff.

The Super Bowl teams were the Dallas Cowboys and the Baltimore Colts. The Cowboys had finally made it as champions of the NFC, although I arrived in Miami with a steadfast belief that they had been quite lucky. The Colts were back, Carroll Rosenbloom, the owner, vowing revenge for what had struck him at Super Bowl III. But as my friend Normie Miller out of New York put it: "They've got two NFL teams playing in the Super Bowl, for Pete's sake." For Pete's sake, indeed. The AFC sent forth into the Super Bowl a club it had annexed so pro football could merge. The two clubs playing each other would be two clubs with NFL roots. The ghost of the AFL, for the sake of the purists, did not have a team in this Super Bowl.

◆ ◆ ◆

Tex Schramm, a.k.a. Loophole, with a position deep in the inner sanctums of the NFL, wandered across the ball field in Fort Lauderdale. He had never figured he'd be there on this Super Bowl V press day in January 1971. Nearly five years earlier, Schramm had plotted out the merger with Lamar Hunt in their clandestine meeting in the parking lot in Dallas. A Super Bowl championship game was the first dramatic product of this meeting. Schramm's team had been close to qualifying for this Super Bowl twice. Painfully close, inches and seconds away. But it was Vince Lombardi and the Packers who won and advanced to Super Bowls I and II. It was the Cowboys, Tom Landry, and Schramm who suffered the agonies.

Steve Perkins, my lanky, sardonic writer friend from Dallas, had called the team he covered "Next Year's Champions." The description fit the Cowboys as snugly as a pair of dung-smeared cattle boots.

And now, a decade after they had begun as a 0-13-1 expansion club, the Cowboys were in decline. They had missed just barely and were on that backward slide that afflicts all decent football teams when the players start to age.

Don Meredith had retired. He had been the only quarterback the Cowboys had ever had, a brash rookie the first year when the club could not win even one game. He had been their quarterback through the years of gradual improvement until they became almost as excellent as the Packers. Next Year's Champions. But then, envisioning this slippage, Meredith accepted a job offer and made a radical career move. He joined the group broadcasting a new television creation on ABC called "Monday Night Football." Meredith, with a Texas-spun sense of humor, was there as a foil to Howard Cosell.

On a Monday night in November, the Cowboys played the Cardinals in the Cotton Bowl, at home. The Cowboys lost, 38-0. The home fans chanted for Meredith. "There's no way they're going to get me to go down there," said Meredith.

The Cowboys had already been beaten, 54-13, by the Vikings. Landry was in a quandary trying to replace Meredith with either Craig Morton or Roger Staubach. Now after the blowout loss to the Cardinals, a rival in their own East Division of the new NFC, the Cowboys were 5-4 for the season. Shocked, Tex Schramm figured his team was dead, done.

Funny, the Cowboys won the remaining five games on their schedule. They beat the Redskins, the Packers, the Redskins again, the Browns, and then the Oilers. Landry had appointed Morton his number one quarterback for the duration. Morton was neither the polished passer nor the bravura quarterback Meredith had been, but Landry solved half of the problem by electing to think for Morton. The coach would call the plays from the sideliness and message them into the huddle—an unorthodox plan.

Most of the plays Landry would call for Morton were running plays. They featured Duane Thomas, a rookie runner out of West Texas State. Calvin Hill, the distinguished Yale man, was injured. Thomas was a slashing runner. But he had been bypassed by 21 clubs in the pro football conglomerate because of his difficult moods and occasional defiance of authority. The Cowboys had become a contender via the wise draft suggestions of Gil Brandt, who dared to pick athletes other scouts avoided. Schramm/Landry accepted Brandt's suggestion. They drafted Thomas 22nd in the first round.

So it was that the Cowboys reached the playoffs with a 10-4 record. On the day after Christmas 1970, they played the Detroit Lions.

Here was the team I covered on a daily basis for the Detroit *News*. And it was a fun year, because the Lions also were 5-4 in November. They had lost shockingly to the expansion New Orleans Saints, 19-17, on Tom Dempsey's field goal at the gun. Dempsey's kick was flat, low, and straight. He was so far from the goalposts, on the goal line, that Alex Karras and the Lions didn't bother to rush. They stood there, laughing at the impossibilty of the field goal attempt. It went 63 yards and just scratched above the crossbar.

But the Lions, like the Cowboys, won their final five games to finish 10-4. Detroit did not win its division. But in their realignment measures, Rozelle and his owners were left with some odd numbers, such as three first-place clubs in each conference, so they elected to include the best second-place club in the playoffs. They would call this team the wild card. Putting second-place teams into the playoffs offended the purists. Pro football was developing the playoff mentality of hockey. But the mathematics of the merger made it necessary.

Even as the wild card, I reckoned, without much prejudice, that the Lions at the end of the season were the best team in the NFC. In their five-game winning streak, they had to beat four clubs that were in first place. They did that, including the Oakland Raiders on Thanksgiving. They spotted the Raiders a 14-0 lead in the first quarter and then won, 28-14, as Al Davis gnawed away at his nervous fingers and sought reasons. Davis, an avid reader of my newspaper, found his reason a couple of weeks later. I had written an article the day before Thanksgiving based on an interview with Davis, and he didn't like it. After covering one of those Raiders-Chiefs bloodbaths in Oakland, I ventured into the locker room. Davis was flushed with victory. He spotted me and spoke into my ear.

"You cost us that game in Detroit," Davis told me in his normal whisper. It was a terrific compliment.

So here were the Lions versus the Cowboys, with America watching on Saturday afternoon TV. Both teams had resorted to the traditional method when floundering in midseason—they switched quarterbacks. Tom Landry had gone to Morton. Joe Schmidt had gone to young Greg Landry for Detroit. Greg, not related to Coach Tom, had personally spirited the Lions into the playoffs with their five emotional victories.

In the emotion of the playoffs, these two unexpected rivals battered each other with inertia. Duane Thomas managed some decent running and led the Cowboys to a field goal in the second half. The Cowboys trapped Greg Landry in his own end zone for a safety. They Lions needed just one touchdown to advance in the Super Bowl playoffs, but they couldn't get it. The Cowboys won by a score of 5-0.

The next week they defeated the San Francisco 49ers, 17-10, three days after New Year's 1971. Next Year's Champions were in the Super Bowl.

◆ ◆ ◆

"I never thought we'd be here," said Tex Schramm as I greeted him in Fort Lauderdale on the Monday before Super Bowl V with some sarcastic remarks about the 5-0 aberration. "Not this year, after all we've gone through."

It was fine, sunny. The NFL had produced a decent supply of danish pastry back at the Americana, where we were billeted on Miami Beach. Then with the red, white, and blue NFL flag flapping alongside Old Glory on the flagpole in front of the Americana, the propagandists synchronized their NFL watches. In step, we were marched to the press buses.

I read my Miami *Herald* on the ride up to Lauderdale. I felt fortunate that the Americana's newsstand had sold me the paper for merely double the street sale price.

"What the hell," I told my friend Newark on the bus. "I'd rather get gouged than insulted like I was by the bellboy when I checked in. 'Deeet-roit,' the kid said, 'ain't nobody comes from there.' Newark, in Miami Beach they think you're not happy if they don't insult you. Just like New York."

"Bleep you," said Newark. "Read your paper."

◆ ◆ ◆

I approached Duane Thomas as soon as I finished insulting Loophole Schramm in the Dallas camp. Most of the press, and the enlarging group of TV guys, were surrounding Tom Landry and asking questions about how he felt finally making it to the Super Bowl. They gathered around Bob Lilly and asked the same questions. And around Craig Morton, who was in the Super Bowl as a robot quarterback.

Duane Thomas sat on the grass in short left field. He was pretty much by himself. I bottomed out on the grass and faced him. Milt Richman, the astute national sports editor for UPI, also plopped onto the grass. Thomas talked in a soft, polite voice. His head was bowed. I asked him a question, his feelings about being a rookie and playing in pro football's ultimate game. He looked at me and responded and I wrote the following story for my paper:

FORT LAUDERDALE—Duane Thomas is known by the Dallas Cowboys as Othello the Regal, the brooding Moorish character created by William Shakespeare.

Thomas . . . is not at all impressed that he is the Cowboys' most prolific scoring weapon for Sunday's Super Bowl game with Baltimore—even though he is a rookie.

This is a strange young man, who discussed football and life in a slow, cautious voice.

"My philosophy is not to be excited," said Thomas. . . .

He is not excited about his record—803 yards as a rookie, plus 278 as Dallas finally managed to win a semifinal playoff game and the National Football Conference championship. His total of 1,081 yards would make him the second most productive rookie runner in the 51 years of pro football. Cookie Gilchrist gained 15 yards more his first season with Buffalo.

"How happy can I get?" repeated Thomas. "It's unlimited. Everything about me is unlimited." There was no bravado in Thomas's voice as he said this.

Dallas uses a very complicated offense with a variety of formations. It is difficult for a rookie to absorb, although in Thomas and Calvin Hill, the Cowboys have had two rookies-of-the-year in succession.

"It's not complicated," said Thomas in his matter-of-fact way. "It's technical."

Those who have watched Thomas realized the Cowboys' offense should not have befuddled him. He tends to run where he pleases anyway. Sometimes he follows his blocks, sometimes he goes in another direction. Either way, he is effective in gaining yardage.

"To me, nobody ever reaches the ultimate," Thomas said.

Certainly, playing in the Super Bowl, especially in his first pro season, must be the ultimate for a football player.

"Playing in the Super Bowl is the ultimate as far as the establishment is concerned," said Thomas in his soft voice. "But for the individual, no. You never are going to reach the ultimate point, because you're going to make mistakes, even in the Super Bowl. And if the Super Bowl were the ultimate, it wouldn't happen again next year."

I jumped on the NFL bus for the ride to the Colts' headquarters at Miami Lakes Country Club. I had Duane Thomas's metaphysical musings captured in my notebook, words only heard by a smattering of us. Thomas had drifted away after placing this holy, Rozellean Super Bowl in its non-ultimate perspective.

We've had Fred Williamson, The Hammer; Joe Namath; Joe Kapp; and now Duane Thomas talking a different kind of stuff. Who wanted to hear the twanged platitudes of Tom Landry?

At this moment, riding the bus to the Colts, I loved covering the Super Bowl. Even if it meant Miami Beach, the Americana, the clawing on press day, the mass interviews, being held captive by Pete Rozelle's propaganda minions. There was the rare time when you got lucky. I felt so fortunate about the semiprivate interview with Duane Thomas.

It would be impossible to manage anything different out of the Colts. Everybody had the same angle. It was obvious, in your face. The Colts were back. Two years earlier they had been 18-point favorites to lick the Jets. Joe Namath had guaranteed that he'd lick them, and he did. He was devastating. They were devastated. Now they had an opportunity for redemption.

"The Jets stole our pride and everything else," said Billy Ray Smith, the defensive lineman. "We have to get it back."

"The mood the last time?" said Bubba Smith. "There wasn't any mood. We walked out of the hotel that morning like the Jets were going to be too scared to show up. I think we even got to believing what the papers said—that we were going to win by 17, 18 points. It was a shock when the Jets got in front of us. When I thought it over later, that was a bad day all around. Even our team bus followed the Jets' bus on the way to the Orange Bowl."

Earl Morrall, the consummate backup quarterback, still ached about the misfired flea flicker. He was back, the goat of Super Bowl III, in his career role as the supporting actor behind Johnny Unitas.

"I still get flashbacks about what happened," Morrall said, a small, painful smile on his face. "A few passes hitting shoulders. The interception on the flea flicker when we might have had a touchdown. John Sample reaching around Willie Richardson for the interception near the goal line. You remember the mistakes.

"I've replayed that whole game over and over in my mind. I've wished thousands of times to do that game over again, because what went wrong was my fault."

But Earl Morrall, age 36, still wearing his Michigan State crew cut, 15 years a pro vagabond, member of five teams, was a realist about a hero's redemption. He knew he was along at Super Bowl V only for the emergency, lest John Unitas go down in action.

And then there was Mike Curtis, the linebacker known as The Animal, the player who once flattened with a sharply directed forearm a fan who'd run onto the field in a drunken stupor.

"No one knows the despair, the abject humiliation we felt that day," Curtis said, encircled by writers at Miami Lakes. "The 1968 Baltimore Colts, the perfect football machine that crushed every opponent in a tough schedule. The Colts, the first National Football League team to lose a Super Bowl. I felt great anger inside me that day. . . . "

The ultimate game? Mike Curtis believed it.

◆ ◆ ◆

Duane Thomas went for a walk, a solitary man on the beach outside the Cowboys' hotel in Lauderdale. His feet touched the sand, and he could hear the thunder of the breakers as the salt water splashed onto the beach and became glowing foam in the moonlight.

"I like the ocean, the water," Thomas said the next day when reporters found him. "I think about being on the beach. Far away. I think about being on the beach in New Zealand."

Covering this Super Bowl was hardly a day at the beach for us. Pete Rozelle had come up with a vanilla Super Bowl. Other than Duane, we had Tom Landry, Don McCafferty, Craig Morton, and John Unitas, who remained tight and stiff with the press into his dotage. We had two football teams that lacked glamour at an event demanding glamourous treatment. We had two teams full of flaws.

Besides, the NFL had gone back to the two-week gap between the championship games and the Super Bowl. The press was commanded to report on Monday. That meant that on Tuesday, Wednesday, and Thursday we were buslifted to the camps for interviews. It meant an added day of squeezing out something creative from a series of mumbles.

Plus, we were in Miami Beach for the third time in five years. Some of the guys liked the place. I didn't. I didn't dislike Florida. I hated it. There was no Bourbon Street in Miami, only Collins Avenue. I never could comprehend jai alai, and dog racing didn't turn me on. And if I'm going to be forced to wait an hour on line at a restaurant, when I finally eat I'd rather it be Galatoire's in New Orleans than Joe's Stone Crab down the Beach, although once you negotiated your way in those stone crabs were wonderfully good.

The pool at the Americana was all right, but you had to fight the tourists for your share of the sun. Al Davis wasn't there to enchant you with his conspiratorial whisper. The Colts, joining up as part of the AFC, took care of that.

You'd write whatever material you'd managed at the camps in the morning, hit the pool for a bit, make some dinner plans, hit the bar in the pressroom, go up and shower, meet back in the pressroom, and head out for dinner at Joe's or The Forge. Then you'd stop back at the pressroom in the hotel. In Miami, it was always crowded at 10 o'clock after dinner. The NFL called it the Hospitality Room, which was OK by me, admission by official Super Bowl pin only. Wives, girlfriends welcome. It was here that the best rumors were polished, honed, stretched, made better.

And it was here that Super Bowl Sally, with an official, NFL-minted Super Bowl V pin, had beckoning smiles for everybody. Sometimes even those with wives on their arms.

◆ ◆ ◆

The Super Bowl had become the showcase for premier quarterbacks, even if it had never become the football colossus advertised for four years.

We had Starr and Dawson and Namath and Lamonica. We had the charisma of Morrall and Kapp, even if they busted out. Now the Cowboys were in Super Bowl V with Craig Morton. What were we supposed to say about a Super Bowl quarterback whose coach was afraid to let him pass? For me, he supplied a negative fascination.

At midweek, I joined the buslift to the Cowboys' morning interview session in hopes of being able to figure out what made Craig Morton tick. If, indeed, he did tick.

You could feel sympathy for the guy. He was tall with the ideal physique for a quarterback. He should have been the classic quarterback. But there was none of the swagger of Namath and Kapp, none of the calm assurance of Starr and Dawson, none of the flair of Lamonica. In the two playoff games, Morton had thrown the ball only 40 times—and he had completed 11. Only 11.

Morton had an available alibi if he wanted to use it—trouble with his receivers. Bob Hayes, the burner with the Olympic-sprint gold, had feuded with Tom Landry most of the season. Landry benched him, a naughty boy. Lance Rentzel played with flair and fervor and was the best true receiver on the Dallas club. But he had been a very, very naughty boy. The dashing Rentzel, husband of the more dashing singer Joey Heatherton, had been busted on a morals rap at midseason and left the ball club. Lance had been caught exposing himself to a young girl.

The Dallas quarterback might have said he didn't have anybody to pass to if he had been free to throw the ball. But to his credit, he didn't say that.

"You know what the figures are, but they don't bother me," Morton said at the Fort Lauderdale base. "If I can hit a couple of third-down plays to keep ball control, that's all I care about. As long as I'm doing my job, I'm not worried about it.

"Coach Landry says adversity brings success. I kind of believe in it. They've booed me a lot in Dallas. They don't like me much. But here we are.

"I think they expected qualities I don't have. Don Meredith was flamboyant. He made jokes. He was the ideal quarterback. He kicked them around, and I couldn't do that. I'm not rah-rah. I want to lead by example."

There was a certain pathos to Craig Morton. It was a strange mood for a Super Bowl in Miami. I went back to write, hoping I could make Craig Morton into a sympathetic figure. This Super Bowl was going to be the ultimate game in Craig Morton's life.

◆ ◆ ◆

The Colts' loss in Super Bowl III remained a deep, personal insult to Carroll Rosenbloom. His ego had been punted. Losing to Weeb Ewbank, a coach he had fired, and to John Sample and a number of other players he had cashiered, Rosenbloom had bristled for two years. Revenge would be his only satisfaction. He had taken the proud Colts into the AFC, joining with enemy clubs, just to get back at the Jets. The switch was sweetened by a $3 million transfer pot awarded to each of the three clubs joining the AFC, but Rosenbloom's moods could not be sweetened.

"I can't sleep, all I can think of is revenge, vindication," Rosenbloom had said. "When we get even it's going to be awfully sweet, and we will get even."

His anger was heightened by the loss of his coach. Rosenbloom had tapped Don Shula, a young, obscure assistant coach in Detroit, and made him head coach in Baltimore. Now, Shula broke his deal with Rosenbloom and skipped to Joe Robbie's Miami Dolphins. Rosenbloom could not have been more pissed off. He demanded and received a draft choice from the Dolphins as balm for losing Shula.

"I have not talked to Robbie or Shula since this happened," Rosenbloom said. "I will not talk to Robbie or Shula ever again. One stole something from me. The other allowed himself to be stolen."

Rosenbloom screened 28 applicants for the coaching job and rejected them all, including George Allen. Then Rosenbloom appointed towering Don McCafferty, a career assistant, as Shula's successor. The Colts' players cheered. Shula had been brilliantly successful, but his intensity made the players uptight. They loved McCafferty's approach. They nicknamed him The Easy Rider.

His soft, patient style worked. In their first season playing with the old AFL clubs, the Colts dominated the new conference. They went through the season with an 11-2-1 record. They won with John Unitas in control, with late rallies. They won games by two, four, three, and one point(s). It always helped to have a kicker they could trust and they'd found one in Jim O'Brien, a rookie with the quaint characteristics of a true placekicker. In the playoffs, the Colts dominated the Bengals, 17-0, in the first game. Then they killed off Al Davis's Raiders, 27-17, in the championship game.

"That kicks the genius coach theory into a cocked hat," said Rosenbloom. "Mac took a team that looked like nothing last year, a team riddled with dissension, and turned it into a champion. Here is a man who has no inner sanctum, no pretensions, no assistants—only associates. Everybody gets the credit except McCafferty. He is just a splendid man. What's more, he brought the fun back into the game of football for me."

The Colts took turns bashing Shula.

"He even called plays for me," complained the great Unitas.

"I'm not supposed to talk about Shula," said Bubba Smith. "But I wouldn't have cared if he went to Brazil. I didn't like him personally. He was always yelling at somebody and a lot of guys didn't like that. Mc-Cafferty is a different kind of guy, a quiet leader."

Rookie Jim O'Brien showed up with long hair and a kicker's style. "This is the age of Aquarius," said O'Brien. "I'm an Aquarius."

In his first pro game he kicked three field goals, the last with 56 seconds left. The kick beat the San Diego Chargers, 16-14. The Colts hugged O'Brien, patted his long hair, and named him Lassie.

Some kickers have fits of nerves and don't sleep much. O'Brien was able to sleep before football games. He even dreamed.

Jimmy the Greek had gone for the risk again. The Cowboys had been made one-point favorites, despite their flaws.

◆ ◆ ◆

I looked down at the field of the Orange Bowl from the upper tier of the dual-decked press box. Down there was where Joe Namath delivered on his guarantee and altered pro football history. He did it, and now we had the Cowboys and the Colts playing in the Super Bowl two years later.

We'd been partied out by Pete Rozelle and his now-fashionable bash at the Americana. The NFL had developed the skill of taking ice statuary to the highest, dripping art. Which chunk of ice would melt first, the one molded to spell AFC, or the slab carved to form NFC? Would it be an omen? I retired to my room before the final results were in.

Now, stuffed with lox from Pete's pregame brunch, we stood for "The Star-Spangled Banner." "O, say can you see . . ." Rozelle looked into the wild blue yonder. Where are they? ". . . and the home of the brave." Where were they?

Four minutes later, roaring through the heavens, the four Air Force jets arrived, buzzing the field, trailing white plumes in their display of American might. They flew off toward the horizon. No plummeting hot-air balloon this time. But the planes had been four minutes late. The pattern for Super Bowl V had been established.

In the first quarter, the Cowboys' Chuck Howley intercepted a pass by Unitas. Howley returned the football to the Colts' 46. Morton took over. Three plays later the Cowboys were on their 31. They'd gone backwards for 23 yards. The Cowboys punted. The Colts' safety, Ron Gardin, fumbled the kick. The Cowboys' Cliff Harris plopped on the free football at the Colts' nine. This time the Cowboys didn't retreat. They got a field goal, a 14-yarder by Mike Clark.

In the second quarter, after Morton had been penalized for throwing a pass to Blaine Nye—a guard—Clark kicked his second field goal, 30 yards. The Colts tied it, 6-6, when Unitas fired the ball upfield and it ricocheted to John Mackey, who ran for a 75-yard touchdown. The Cowboys protested that it was an illegal play, that defender Mel Renfro had not really flicked the ball before Mackey caught it. The argument was futile.

Then Lassie O'Brien missed the extra point because blocking back Tom Nowatzke missed the block.

Next, Unitas fumbled the ball away at the Colts' 28. This time Morton got the touchdown, on a seven-yard pass, of all plays, to Duane Thomas.

A few moments later, Unitas was intercepted by Renfro. He was hit after throwing the ball by George Andrie. Unitas writhed on the field, his ribs crushed. At the Baltimore bench, Earl Morrall snapped his helmet tight and started to warm up. This was Morrall's role, the emergency backup, and in this emergency he was back in the game, on the field, where two years ago he had suffered ignominy and ridicule.

His brain filled with memories and thoughts of redemption. Morrall hit two passes just before halftime, advancing the ball to the two. McCafferty shunned the field goal. Morrall passed again toward Tom Mitchell in the end zone. The ball fell, uncaught.

No mock warfare and soldiers in period uniforms this time. Anita Bryant roused American patriotism with her songs.

Then the Colts' Jim Duncan fumbled the second-half kickoff, and the Cowboys moved to enlarge their 13-6 lead. Duane Thomas struggled for the end zone. He tried too hard and fumbled the ball ahead of him. Duncan squared things by recovering the fumble.

In the fourth quarter, Morrall threw a pass and Howley intercepted again. But Morton couldn't move the ball and the Colts got it back.

It was time again for the pet flea flicker. Morrall tossed the ball to Sam Havrilak. Havrilak was supposed to flip it back to Morrall. The Colts loved trick plays. But Havrilak's view of Morrall was blocked by the rushing Jethro Pugh, six-feet-six. Havrilak spotted John Mackey alone, so he threw the ball that way. Eddie Hinton cut in front, caught the ball, and headed for the end zone. But oops, the ball was ripped from his hands and the bouncing fumble rolled through the end zone and automatically into Dallas's possession.

Now the Cowboys faced danger. Morton had the football and he passed it. Duncan deflected it. Rick Volk intercepted it and ran it to the Cowboys' three. From the two, Tom Nowatzke, cut by the Lions as too-slow, crashed in for the touchdown. O'Brien made the kick, and for the first time a Super Bowl was tied in the fourth quarter with the issue still up for grabs. The score was 13-each.

Two minutes remained. Morton had the ball again, back on the Cowboys' 27. There was plenty of time for the Cowboys to move, to win. Morton passed toward a back coming out of the backfield, a heady athlete with a coach's mind named Dan Reeves. The ball failed to reach Reeves. Mike Curtis intercepted Morton's throw and took it to the Colts' 28.

Norm Bulaich powered the ball twice to the 25. With five seconds left, Morrall called time out. McCafferty sent the rookie, Jim O'Brien, out to try to win it. The Cowboys jeered and hooted O'Brien. O'Brien looked at them and heard them with his heart thumping. "Don't worry about it," the veteran Morrall told the rookie O'Brien. "Concentrate."

The time-out over, the TV commercial finished, Morrall spotted the snapped football. O'Brien kicked it with his swinging right foot. The ball went dead solid perfect through the goalposts on the goal line to the right of the press box, and the Colts won it, 16-13.

Bob Lilly, who had suffered all the pain through the years when the Cowboys were scoffed at as Next Year's Champions, removed his Lone-Starred helmet and fired it straight up, 50 feet above the field. The helmet landed and rolled and stopped.

◆ ◆ ◆

You wondered whether you had just been witness to a classic football game with a great finish or a slopfest in which two "cheese champions" couldn't play the game straight. Between them, the Colts and Cowboys had managed six interceptions and four lost fumbles. But they also had managed to hold TV's largest audience in history: 64 million American homes by NBC's count, to the bitter end.

"I had a dream a week ago Saturday, after the club got down here, that the game would be won by a field goal," O'Brien said in the joy of the locker room as Carroll Rosenbloom's ego burst. "But I couldn't tell who kicked it, me or Mike Clark. I couldn't see the number and the dream was in black and white, so I didn't know which uniform it was. I said I'd have to wait until Sunday to see who won."

Billy Ray Smith, the Colts' roughhouse defensive tackle, stripped away his uniform. He had carried the agony of Super Bowl III with him for two years.

"It's all over now," Smith said. "I just won $15,000, and see this blood on my pants? You ask whose blood this is? It's my blood. This is my last game. What can I possibly do after this?"

The commentaries on a strange piece of history etched in my notebook, I dashed beneath the stands to the Cowboys' locker room. What would Duane Thomas say about the fumble that cost Dallas a touchdown, the fumble that turned this screwball game? I looked all over. Duane Thomas had vanished. He had been correct. This could not have been the ultimate game. They would play it again next year.

VI
The Ultimate Silence

Dallas Cowboys 24, Miami Dolphins 3
January 16, 1972
Tulane Stadium, New Orleans
Attendance: 81,023

The marvelous thing about being a sportswriter is that we get to make judgment decisions as to what news is—and isn't. For example, when an individual becomes stone silent and refuses to utter one syllable into our delicate and discreet ears, we have news copy worthy of long treatises and hey-wow headlines. The guy is snubbing us. He refuses to talk to the press, and that becomes a bigger story than if he stood among us at a mass interview and babbled nonsense for an hour.

So it was that Duane Thomas was the most vital, most critical, most intriguing, and most appealing story as America headed into Super Bowl VI. Duane had refused to utter a mouthful since he had portrayed Tom Landry sometime back in training camp as "a plastic man . . . no man at all." He called Tex Schramm, who refused to renegotiate his contract, "sick, demented, and dishonest." Those words uttered, Duane shut up voluntarily.

The Cowboys reacted by dumping Thomas as far away as they could: They traded him to the New England Patriots. At his first practice, Thomas got into a flap with Coach John Mazer about the way to squat in his stance. Mazer booted him off the field. The Patriots sent him back to Dallas. After missing three games, he rejoined the Cowboys, silent, morose, stuck within the system. The story increased in importance as the season dragged along and the Cowboys advanced ever onward to their second Super Bowl.

70

We were back in New Orleans, and Duane, in his silence, had upstaged Richard Nixon, the former reserve receiver out of Whittier College. There was no silence from Nixon. He was blabbing—from his vantage point at the TV set in the White House. He recalled a tricky play from his own playbook and sent it in a message to Don Shula, care of the Miami Dolphins. Nixon drew the X's and O's in his personal presidential penmanship. The down-and-in with Paul Warfield slanting through the Cowboys' secondary was worth six, according to Nixonian logic.

Yippie. We all arrived in New Orleans for Super Bowl VI in full wonderment whether Duane Thomas would decide that maybe this would be the ultimate game after all. We thought perhaps he would tell us: "I'd rather be in New Orleans than in New Zealand."

The tension was awesome as the NFL propagandists trooped us out of the Roosevelt Hotel for the annual press/photo/deep-question day. The Cowboys were assembled at the New Orleans Saints' practice facility just outside of town.

And there was Duane. He plopped himself into a bleacher seat alongside the field. Thirty, fifty writers plopped themselves all around him. I was planted, turned around, in the row below this explosive, most prominent news figure of Super Bowl VI. I was almost in his face. Will Grimsley, the dignified columnist from the Associated Press, was in the seat next to Thomas.

What happened over the next half hour or so would become historic. We all stared at Thomas, waiting for one word, perhaps even a sentence. Nobody said anything. The silence was of the deafening sort. As we stared at him, Duane stared out onto the field where reporters with notepads and microphone guys attached to two other guys with video cameras and sound recording doohickeys scrambled among the Cowboys, picking up pearls.

What fools! The story was over here on the bleacher seats, in the silent vacuum.

Then it happened. Duane Thomas leaned forward toward me and looked at my left wrist. Suddenly, unpredictably, he broke his season-long silence. He spoke. Words. In the English language.

Armed with Duane Thomas's first quotes in five months, the cream of America's football journalists rushed for their writing machines. We had our Super Bowl scoop.

NEW ORLEANS—Duane Thomas sat on a splintery bleacher seat, contemplating who knows what, while his audience sat at his feet.

They call the Dallas Cowboys' superb and silent running back "The Sphinx." He sat in the sunshine yesterday at the annual Super Bowl picture day and as usual said almost nothing.

Thomas has not spoken a word for public consumption since last summer, when he failed to have his pro contract renegotiated. At that time he called Coach Tom Landry a "plastic man . . . no man at all," and club president Tex Schramm "dishonest."

Finally, Thomas returned to football a brooding, baleful man. He spoke to no reporter, seldom talked with teammates. Yet he is a major reason the Cowboys have won nine straight football games and are in Sunday's Super Bowl against Miami.

Thomas did appear in a picture with the Cowboys' offensive 11 yesterday. He even took one step to the right at the request of a photographer. Ten Cowboys were smiling as the pictures were taken. Thomas remained impassive.

As the Cowboys broke off and were sidetracked for individual interviews, Thomas slipped over a rope and onto his bleacher throne. A group of newsmen surrounded him. "I don't feel like being bothered now," Thomas said. That made seven words.

Then there was silence for several minutes. Thomas rubbed his face with his right hand and looked around him.

"Do you have the time?" he said finally. That made 12 words—all he said for the day.

"Duane, are you happy to be back in the Super Bowl?" he was asked. Silence.

"Last year at the Super Bowl you said you'd walk along the beach and dream of being in New Zealand. Do you still dream of going to New Zealand?"

Silence.

"Have you refused to talk this year because somebody misquoted you?"

Silence.

It was futile. . . .

The Cowboys put up with Thomas because he has helped them to the Super Bowl two years in a row. The other day Tom Landry fined Thomas because he failed to go to practice.

Yesterday Thomas did all that was required of him—he was present at picture day.

"The whole situation is that if the team accepts his actions, then I accept them," said Landry.

The story hit the wire services. It made every paper in America. Back on the press bus, I offered to show guys my wristwatch. I was glad I didn't own a Mickey Mouse. Duane Thomas had talked—to me. I gloated.

"Think I'll donate it to the Pro Football Hall of Fame," I told my friend Philly, shaking the ticking timepiece in his face.

"Creep," he said.

◆ ◆ ◆

Sunday evening is when the games of Sunday afternoon are replayed. The players are out carousing, working off the week of stress and near captivity, the despair and joy of their game, the physical pain. But Sunday night, for the millions who have spectated on any given Sunday, is reserved for reflection. Before a crackling fire, the privileged who wore bulky snowmobile suits to observe in dank stadiums, or the multitudes who watched from living room easy chairs, all become analysts. All are professorial in their knowledge, all concluding haughtily that they know exactly what went wrong. Or right.

On the Sunday evening after the Dolphins and Cowboys qualified to play each other in Super Bowl VI in New Orleans, one particular and knowledgeable fan reflected about his day of watching games. He sat behind his large desk where great decisions are made. The fan doodled out a play that seemed workable. The pass receiver would dash downfield, fake the cornerback outside, and then smartly cut in and catch the football. It seemed so clear, so effective.

The play diagram completed, the doodling fan placed a telephone call. It was one o'clock in the morning. In Miami, the telephone rang in the residence of Don Shula, coach of the local team. Shula drowsily was watching a tape-delayed television showing of the game his team had won the afternoon before.

"Don," said the late-hour caller, "this is President Nixon. Congratulations on the Dolphins' victory."

The nation's number one pro football fan and the coach of the new AFC champions conversed for some time. The president mentioned that although he was number one a fan of the Washington Redskins, he had a feeling for the Dolphins because he spent his fun times in Key Biscayne. The men talked about the game and discussed some technical aspects of the sport. Then the president delivered his coup de grâce, his plan for a Miami offensive in the Super Bowl against Dallas.

"You know," said Nixon apprising Shula of the master play he had diagramed, "I still think you can pass to Warfield down and in against Dallas."

Shula thanked the former wide receiver from Whittier College for his suggestion and returned to his drawing board.

◆ ◆ ◆

Don Shula stood up before the Super Bowl press mob and splashed us all with matter-of-fact footballese. We yearned to be entertained.

"All I want to be is 50-50 in the Super Bowl," Shula told us. "We'll try to overcome our lack of experience with aggressiveness. This one will be won with hitting."

Shula did not send me dancing to my typewriter. We were in Cliché College.

I'd known Don Shula for 10 years, since he'd been a very young and very smart assistant with the Lions and had gone off to become a very young head coach in Baltimore. He'd worked in Detroit for George Wilson, a powerful, tough, loyal man who'd played powerful, tough football for the Chicago Bears when they were the Monsters of the Midway.

I knew how Shula ached when his team lost. And at Super Bowl VI, I knew he was bearing the painful stigma as Super Bowl loser the day of Joe Namath's crushing victory. He transported that pain with him. It was obvious.

Occasionally, he would loosen up, just a bit. A favorite question at the Dolphins' show-and-tell sessions was about the presidential phone call.

"I thought it was some kind of nut," Shula said of his first thoughts when the phone rang.

The Dolphins stayed at the same Fontainebleau where Len Dawson had suffered through his week of suspicion during Super Bowl week two years earlier. Now, outside, two real dolphins splashed in the fountain pool.

The human Dolphins were unexpected guests. They were an expansion franchise, formed within the AFL six years earlier. Their original coach happened to be George Wilson, who had chucked the head coaching job with the Lions out of his sense of loyalty. William Clay Ford, the Lions' owner, fired all of Wilson's assistant coaches, and the head coach opted to go, too. In Miami, Wilson used all his expertise to build a new team from scratch. Four years later, he was fired. Two years after that, the Dolphins won the AFC championship and went to the Super Bowl, young, impressionable, and resourceful.

Shula had jumped out of Baltimore when Joe Robbie offered him the coaching job of the young Miami club. George Wilson's sense of loyalty had been scarred by the firing/hiring. He had groomed Shula to become a head coach and had recommended him to the Colts and Carroll Rosenbloom in 1964. He condemned Shula for not notifying him when Robbie went coaching/seeking in Baltimore. And Wilson said he had built the Dolphins to the verge of a championship before Shula replaced him.

"Any Joe Doakes could have coached them into the Super Bowl," Wilson said.

At last Shula managed a touch of humor. He stepped to the microphone to begin one of his daily press conferences and said: "Just call me Joe Doakes." I finally danced to my typewriter.

How I made it was a matter of tremendous mystery. This was not a Super Bowl for pins and needles and worry that a momentous story involving sin or gambling might break any midnight. Bourbon Street beckoned. What I had missed in my devotion to scrambling for the story, sniffing around outside Len Dawson's room two years earlier, I was determined to compensate myself for during the week of Super Bowl VI. That meant a fine New Orleans dinner as a prelude to the rest of the night at the Old Absinthe House. It was Moran's one night, Aranud's the next, the Court of the Three Sisters the following night.

The Absinthe House was jammed every night with writers, owners, and visiting players. We exchanged tidbits, told stories, drank beer, and ogled the ladies. The strip joints down the street were for tourists. Pat O'Brien's and those tall hurricanes were for the folks from Yonkers. This was football people and football talk. Tom Dempsey, the placekicker, stood at the bar one night and told me how he kicked the 63-yard field goal that had crushed the Lions a couple of years earlier. He still existed on that one kick.

About 11 o'clock, I'd wander around the corner and down Royal Street to another bar, which the Players Association had adopted as its headquarters for the week. I went to check Greg Landry, the Lions' quarterback. He was nearing his free agency, on May 1. His agent kept tipping me that he'd already had a couple of offers from other NFL clubs. There was even a code system arranged. The GM of one of the pursuing clubs was code-named Blackie. The Lions were set to claim tampering violations. It was a story I had to write daily, upstaging the Super Bowl in my own paper. And by the end of the week, Greg Landry, Lions' GM Russ Thomas, and the agent had a contract meeting in the Royal Sonesta in New Orleans. It would be settled soon.

And there was terrible sadness.

Greg Landry, one night, called me over and said: "This is Sharon Hughes." Chuck Hughes had died on the field in Detroit during a game against the Bears that season. He went out on a pass route and collapsed in a heap. Dick Butkus waved frantically for the medics, who tried to revive Chuck but couldn't. He was pronounced dead an hour later in the hospital, but he died right on the grass in front of all the people in Tiger Stadium during a football game.

Sharon Hughes was his widow—and the NFLPA had invited her to New Orleans. We stood there in the bar and talked about Chuck. She said, "I can't believe it happened. Every night when I go to bed, I still reach out for Chuck."

I strolled back to the Old Absinthe House, and on the way I had a good cry.

It was three o'clock in the morning, same as it was every night that week—Monday, Tuesday, Wednesday, and Thursday—when I left the Absinthe House to walk back to our hotel headquarters at the Roosevelt. Yet, somehow, when the NFL sounded reveille in the morning, I was up and out and on my way to hear plastic Tom Landry and his comments that packed all the imagination of supermarket coupons.

The NFL's buslift out to the Cowboys' quarters at the Airport Hilton was full of red-eyed passengers, fellow sufferers of the same self-torture techniques.

◆　◆　◆

If Don Shula carried with him to New Orleans the burden of losing a Super Bowl he should have won, Tom Landry arrived cursed with the most defamatory stamp that could be applied by the press in sports: *Choke-up!*

That was the precise translation of the phrase "Next Year's Champions." Landry knew he lugged that stigma into the room every time he stood up at his press conferences in the days before Super Bowl VI.

"You'd like to think this was just another game," he said at his Thursday media session. Bob Griese and some of the other Dolphins had strangely referred to the Super Bowl in that manner, strange because they could not have known what they had not endured.

"But it's not. It is the ultimate." Tom had to feel that way. Even if Duane Thomas didn't.

Tom was tormented by the Cowboys' narrow losses to the Packers at the thresholds of the first two Super Bowls when Lombardi was the ruling despot of the NFL. But in the following two seasons, when the Cowboys were matured, battle-tested, and ready logically to replace the Lombardi-less Packers, they had fallen to the Browns in the playoffs. Both times the Cowboys were expected to win. Both times they were disgraced. Then, when at last the Cowboys did reach Super Bowl V, they fell again to the Colts in the game decided with five seconds to play. That was five consecutive years of broken hearts. And you could read the pain in Landry's words and spot the jittery moods of the Cowboys as Super Bowl VI week slipped by.

"We have been looking forward to this game since last year at Miami when we walked off the field as losers," Landry said.

Bob Lilly, who had thrown his helmet sky high at the losing climax of Super Bowl V, spoke with uncharacteristic bravado. He had suffered through the five near misses and now he said of the Dolphins assigned to block them: "They might have to haul them away in a meat wagon."

Then Lilly told Steve Perkins: "It's kind of scary. I don't see how we can lose." But only Joe Namath had the nerve to guarantee a victory three days before a Super Bowl.

The Dolphins came to the Super Bowl with a swagger. They were a team of no-names, coached by a Joe Doakes, molded out of culls, castoffs, and rejects—and some very excellent draft choices. Put together, they were unexpected champions. Bob Griese and Larry Csonka were picked out of the draft; Paul Warfield, Nixon's favorite, had been acquired via trade from the Browns. But the shook troops had been free agents or cuts from other clubs or guys who had been in the semi-pro leagues. Guys such as Larry Little, Manny Fernandez, and Bob Kuechenberg, a circus clown's son who had been playing for the Chicago Owls in the Continental League when summoned by the Dolphins.

And then there was Garo Yepremian, the left-footed, soccer-style placekicker who had been booted off the Detroit team.

Only one Joe Doakes could have coached this misfit collection into the Super Bowl: Don Shula. And he did it in a 10-3-1 season, together with some amazing dynamics in the playoffs.

◆ ◆ ◆

While Richard Nixon's play diagram drew most of the attention this Super Bowl week early in the 1972 election year, the Democrats played with a political football, too. Tom Landry waved a telegram from Lyndon Baines Johnson, former president, lifelong Texan.

"My prayers and presence will be with you in New Orleans, although I don't plan to send in any plays," LBJ messaged Landry.

"I think the president kind of hedged a bit," Landry said, "because he picked a play Warfield runs in every game."

Mel Renfro would be the cornerback assigned to break up the play Nixon suggested be sent into the huddle. The resulting hubbub annoyed Renfro.

"Suppose he scores a touchdown on it?" Renfro said with a feeling of hopelessness. "What happens? Everybody knows he beat me on the president's play."

"We run that play a lot," Warfield said poolside at the Dolphins' camp. "That's one pattern I've been particularly successful on. . . . I'm surprised the president knows the maneuver. But it doesn't mean we're going to use the pattern the president diagramed. But it doesn't mean we won't. Just because the president suggested it doesn't mean there'll be extra pressure on me if it's called."

By Friday, everybody in New Orleans was talking about Nixon's play. Everybody except Duane Thomas.

♦ ♦ ♦

Roger Staubach was the anti-Namath. Out of Annapolis, a veteran of the war in Vietnam, Staubach had finally become entrenched as the Cowboys' quarterback at midseason. Until then, Landry had played again with alternating Staubach and Craig Morton. They alternated starts, they alternated halfs. At times Landry was so thoroughly frustrated, he alternated his quarterbacks play after play after play.

The system was a terrible failure. The Cowboys reeled to a 4-3 record to the midpoint of the season. Landry was forced to make a decision, or else. Roger Staubach, the former Naval lieutenant, would be his number one quarterback from now on.

"Roger Staubach is potentially a championship quarterback," Landry said. Nobody believed him. Roger, at 29, was tender and inexperienced. A warrior perhaps, but a pro quarterback? Staubach responded by winning and winning again and winning again. The Cowboys finished their schedule with seven victories, no losses, ex-lieutenant Staubach in command. They were 11-3. They clubbed the Vikings, 20-12, in the playoffs and then dumped the 49ers again, in the NFC championship game, 14-3. Staubach had them in Super Bowl VI riding a nine-game winning streak. He went to the game with less pro experience than any previous Super Bowl quarterback.

I was always enchanted by the Quarterback Mystique, the allure these athletes had, their hellish lifestyles, their charisma. New Orleans was built for these quarterbacks—Bobby Layne, Billy Kilmer, Sonny Jurgensen, Joe Namath, Joe Kapp. The carousers, the night owls. Their best games were played on Sunday afternoons when their eyes were blurred from Saturday night.

For sure, the Cowboys were spotted on Bourbon Street this week. But not Roger Staubach.

"Oh, I'm not a Bourbon Streeter," Staubach, a square, explained to a circle of writers who had trouble staying awake. "I'm not night-oriented. I did go into town one night to have a shrimp dinner. But the other nights I stayed in my room and had a cheeseburger. Then I watched a movie on TV, *Night Stalker*. Then I studied game films. By watching the films I can keep my adrenaiin going. I can sit in my room and concentrate on football. But don't get the wrong idea. They're not putting food under the door for me."

Somebody asked Staubach what kind of officer he had been in the war in Vietnam.

"I had 140 men under me," Staubach said, "and I imagine more than a few will be pulling for Miami on Sunday."

Not so square, Staubach.

◆ ◆ ◆

New to the Super Bowl, the Dolphins came with a tad of arrogance, an attitude well-earned.

"Last year I was back in California," said Manny Fernandez, one of the rushers on the Dolphins' No-Name Defense. "I got drunk the night before and slept it off the next day. I turned Dallas-Baltimore on in the third quarter. It looked crummy, so I turned if off. I just wasn't interested."

As the buildup intensified, Fernandez could not bring himself to respect the Cowboys, favorites by five points. Perhaps it was false bravado. I didn't believe so.

"How could we be awed by Dallas," Manny said, "after beating Kansas City? I can't imagine a team with better personnel than Kansas City. And the Colts were defending world champions and this year they were stronger than last year, and we beat them."

The Dolphins, this collection of rabble and finery, had waltzed through the season to their 10-3-1 record. They drew the Chiefs, mighty Kansas City, in the first playoff game on Christmas Day 1971. It was a bloody battle between a veteran club that had won a Super Bowl and the upstarts formed out of expansion. After four quarters, they were tied at 24-24. It was sudden-death. And neither club could win it in the fifth quarter. A game advanced into a sixth quarter for the first time in pro football history. Then with 7:40 gone in the second overtime, the Dolphins won it. Garo Yepremian, the little kicker booted out of Detroit as unreliable, kicked a 37-yard field goal for the victory.

Miami moved on. They played the Colts for the AFC championship on January 2. Griese started the Dolphins off with a 75-yard bomb to Warfield. There was sudden inspiration on Pennsylvania Avenue in Washington. The Dolphins won the game, humiliating the Colts, 21-0. Carroll Rosenbloom was infuriated by the loss to Shula. And that night, Richard Nixon phoned Shula in Miami with his executive play.

"We may not be as big as some and we may not be as fast as some," Manny Fernandez told us. "We're just a bunch of humpties plugging along. Give us some credit."

◆ ◆ ◆

Pete Rozelle's party on Friday night at the Roosevelt was a wonderful relief. Early to bed at last. The ice statues dripped, and as always there was no room to sit down and you had to freeload standing up. Gripe. Gripe. And Saturday would be a busy day.

The fight mob had descended on New Orleans. Joe Frazier would be defending his world heavyweight championship on Saturday night in the new Convention Center. An opponent named Terry Daniels was picked to fall for Joe. Daniels was the son of a Cleveland millionaire. With all the press in town, the promoters figured they had a captive audience and could get tons of publicity. So we had to work on Saturday night. But not for long. Frazier punched Daniels into pulp in four rounds. Bourbon Street was a madhouse at midnight.

◆ ◆ ◆

It was chilly again in New Orleans on the sixth Super Sunday in the history of creation. Thirty-eight degrees. We huddled in the press box at Tulane Stadium to watch the pregame extravaganza. The Tyler, Texas, hot-stepping marching band performed with the Apache Belles giving us some more Dixieland. Then it all turned military. The Marine Corps' silent drill team performed. The Army, Navy, and Coast Guard formed ranks in front of an enormous American flag. Then, as the Air Force Academy choir sang "The Star-Spangled Banner," 20,000 balloons were released—as the fans praised Rozelle for forgoing the pigeon bit. Then eight Air Force F-4 Phantom jets streaked over Tulane Stadium. One peeled away, to symbolize the Missing Man, the American men missing in Vietnam. It was a display of America's fighting might. A fitting environment for Lieutenant/quarterback Roger Staubach.

◆ ◆ ◆

And again funny things started to happen. Larry Csonka, the muscular rusher, had not fumbled once in 235 carries for the Dolphins through the entire season. Early in the Super Bowl, he dropped a handoff from Griese. Chuck Howley, again thriving on enemy errors, recovered. Staubach took the Cowboys downfield and Mike Clark put them ahead with a nine-yard field goal.

With the ball again, Griese dropped back searching for a receiver. Bob Lilly slammed his blocker into the meat wagon and started in pursuit of Griese. Griese dodged and scrambled, retreating, zigzagging. Lilly finally nailed him—for a 29-yard loss.

It was time to launch the presidential pass. Griese dropped back. Warfield raced from the line and slanted across the secondary. Griese passed the football. Mel Renfro had spoken a few days earlier of the pressure of being involved in this scenario. He batted the pass away from Warfield. Cliff Harris, the safetyman next to Renfro, said: "Nixon's a great strategist, isn't he?" Renfro smiled.

The Cowboys scored again. Duane Thomas, silently, effectively, kept pounding at the Dolphins. The drive reached the Miami seven. Now Lance Alworth stepped into the huddle. Alworth—known as Bambi—had been an AFL original, one of the fine heroic symbols of the disenfranchised league with the San Diego Chargers. Now in this postmerger mix, he had been traded to the Cowboys, standard-carriers of the old NFL. Alworth heard the signal, dashed into the end zone, and Staubach hit him with a nifty pass in the left corner.

Dallas went in at halftime up 10-3. Yepremian got a 31-yard field goal for Miami just before the half.

Any hopes Shula had were squelched by the Cowboys' first drive in the second half. This one belonged to Duane Thomas. He burst around the end for 23 yards. Then Bob Hayes went 16 on a flanker reverse. Thomas went in for the touchdown from the three. In the fourth quarter, Staubach flipped another seven-yard touchdown pass—this one to an old tight end who was ending his career, Mike Ditka.

The final score was 24-3 for Dallas, a thorough whipping for the young Dolphins. And victory at last for Tom Landry.

NEW ORLEANS—Never more can the Dallas Cowboys be ridiculed as Next Year's Champions, the team that chokes up in the big game. . . . "I don't think any one who has won it could feel as great as we did," said Bob Lilly, the magnificent defensive tackle who has played through the horrors of the last six years as the Cowboys kept losing in title games.

"We've been in championship games so long—and it has been frustrating so long. I don't think anybody can understand.

"Finally . . . we finally got here."

I batted away as fast as I could at my old Olivetti portable. There was so much to write. Warfield had caught just four balls, only one of 23 yards worth any damage. Renfro had to fit high in the story:

"Everybody had me set up all week on that down and in to Warfield," Renfro said. "All I heard was Warfield, Warfield, Warfield—that was going to be the key to the game. I was bugged by it and it put a lot of pressure on me. I don't think I ever felt this good."

And then I had to write about Duane Thomas. He had come into the locker room with Jim Brown, the great runner from the Browns. Jim Brown was about the only guy Thomas would ever talk to. Tom Brookshier asked Brown if Duane could be interviewed on the postgame show on CBS. Duane agreed.

Brookshier stuck the microphone in Thomas's face and said: "You have a lot of speed for a big man."

At last, Duane Thomas spoke, aloud, listened to by the television watchers across America. Thomas responded to Brookshier's statement: "Evidently," he said.

Tom Landry was struggling with a static-clogged phone line across the room. He could hardly decipher President Nixon's congratulations on the bad line. As he listened to Nixon, Landry looked up and spotted Thomas speaking his word to Brookshier. Landry's face popped in astonishment.

VII
The Flimflam Man

Miami Dolphins 14, Washington Redskins 7
January 14, 1973
Los Angeles Memorial Coliseum
Attendance: 90,182

Every time I fly across the United States I marvel at the splendor of our land. Perhaps this was Pete Rozelle's message on the Sundays when the Super Bowls were played. The spectacle tugged at our patriotism—the fighter flyovers, the military nature of the pregame and halftime shows. The Super Bowl was very American, and on the Sunday one week before Super Bowl VII, I flew across the continent again. We passed over the Rockies, cut to our left, and flew over the burnished red rock of the Grand Canyon. In my reverie, I discovered a chain linking the six Super Bowls I'd covered.

The Super Bowls had become a continuous story of personalities, even if the quality of the football competition did not reach Rozelle's aesthetic specifications. Give us Tom Landry, Don Shula, Don McCafferty, and the Super Bowl becomes vanilla. Give us Joe Namath, Joe Kapp, Vincent Lombardi, Al Davis, even Duane Thomas in silence, and the Super Bowl experience is full of flavor.

I was going to L.A., back to the original Super Bowl scene and the original dud, to meet up again with George Allen. The first time I encountered Allen on the beat, he was the head coach of the Los Angeles Rams. It had been a Monday night game and had ended late. George finished off his postgame platitudes by saying: "I'm going home and watch some films and have a bowl of ice cream."

My imagination sent me a message that the ice cream would be chocolate, or perhaps tutti-frutti. Joe Schmidt, in Detroit, had discussed fellow coach Allen with me one day. "He's a cheat and a con man," Schmidt had said.

Daniel Reeves owned the Rams and was enchanted by Allen's methods when he hired him as head coach. The Rams started to win. Allen traded away stockpiles of high draft choices for athletes who were ancient on other clubs, but just properly aged for his purposes. He motivated them, gave them direction. They listened to his speeches: "The future is now." And they won games.

Nevertheless, Reeves fired Allen. "I had more fun losing than I did winning with George Allen," Reeves explained. But Allen's method was to coddle, pamper the fossil athletes, treat them so much better than they ever had been before. In undermining his owner/boss, Allen created fierce loyalty among the players. When Reeves fired Allen, the players rallied behind their coach. It was a revolution and Reeves capitulated and kept him. But that only meant that Reeves would fire Allen for a second time from the same job.

The chain connecting the Super Bowls, from the first onward, was now attached to George Allen. Allen would not have gone to the Washington Redskins if Vince Lombardi had not died. Soon after Lombardi gave up his coaching role in Green Bay, he realized how dreadfully he missed the work. So he went to the Redskins to coach for Edward Bennett Williams, the famed Washington trial lawyer. In Washington, as coach of the Redskins, the Great Lombardi died, his stomach ravaged by cancer. Then Williams hired the out-of-work Allen.

Allen was annointed with total control. One of his early acts was to build an isolated compound outside Washington and the halls of government, in rural, remote Virginia. It did not seem too much of a coincidence that the CIA was also headquartered there. Allen wanted the Redskins' training facility to be secure, impregnable to all the football spies that filled his imagination. He had two practice fields built, one real grass, the other artificial turf. Next to the fields, inside an enclosure as guarded as the Berlin Wall in 1972, Allen put up a cinder-block structure containing meeting rooms, training rooms, locker rooms. Every espionage-foiling measure was taken—except for tunnels underground. And perhaps, those, too. I would never have been permitted inside the gate.

Edward Bennett Williams saw what Allen had done with the carte blanche he received and said: "I gave George an unlimited budget and he spent it all in one day."

Allen had embarked on a crusade. The Redskins had not won an NFL championship since 1942. "Losing is worse than death," Allen said. After every victory, Allen led his players in a raucous singing rendition of "Hail to the Redskins."

Allen worked contrary to the orthodox NFL replenishment practices of dumping worn goods for promises. In Washington, Allen proceeded to make 19 trades. He stripped the Redskins naked of premium draft choices for years ahead. He traded away so many draft choices that the Redskins did not have a draft choice in the '72 draft until the eighth round. In his biggest deal, he peddled some of his most valued draft choices to the Rams to get six of his precious ancient players—among them Jack Pardee and Diron Talbert—back together with him in Washington. On the team he named the Over the Hill Gang.

And as with Schmidt, his fellow coaches regarded Allen with suspicion, if not outright distrust. In May of 1972, before Allen's crusade to reach Super Bowl VII, Pete Rozelle fined him $5,000 after he had been caught fleecing two other clubs in trades. Allen had blithely traded draft choices he had previously traded to different clubs. But trading the same draft choice twice was part of George Allen's style. He would do all he could to win, and ethics and giving the other guy a fair shake were totally foreign to his losing-is-worse-than-death philosophy.

The writers would rush toward George Allen this week of Super Bowl VII. He was fast copy, he was there vulnerable to be ripped, criticized, castigated by us wondrous media moralists. But no matter what, despite the con and the blarney he fed us, I liked George Allen. There was a devilish charm to his catch-me-if-you-can mentality. And I always had a respect for winning.

I knew this: Allen and the Redskins would upstage Don Shula and the Dolphins during the annual prelude to the Super Bowl. The young Dolphins were in this Super Bowl striving for perfection. They arrived at Super Bowl VII 16-0 for the season and the playoffs. There had never been an unbeaten, untied champion in the 53 years of the NFL's history. Once before there had been a perfect champion in pro football, Paul Brown's 1948 Cleveland Browns. But those Browns, 15-0, played in the All-America Conference. Thus their accomplishment was ignored by the NFL's historians even after some AAC clubs were merged into the NFL in the pre-Super Bowl year of 1950.

Now Shula was back, twice a Super Bowl loser, and I knew he knew how devastating it would be should his team lose again. It would be a strange scene: Shula, shooting for the perfect season, attempting to defend a controversial quarterback decision under the barrage questioning of the curious mob, still the second story to George Allen. And George would make a show about how he wished he could duck the press and all the Super Bowl distractions.

◆ ◆ ◆

I rented a car and drove south from LAX, where my plane had landed. The NFL, without checking the road map, booked the press into Newport Beach. That was terrific. There were good restaurants, fine people-watching, picturesque scenery. The problem was logistics. Our otherwise delicous Newport Beach settlement was 25 miles from Long Beach, base of the Dolphins, a journey north through the smog on the clogged San Diego Freeway. Our place was 36 miles west of Santa Ana, where the Redskins were put up. If, as good reporters, we wanted to cover both camps, our daily journey would involve crooked hauls up and across the greater Los Angeles freeway network. Always in thick traffic. Not as the crow flies. We would log more than 100 miles a day on the buslifts if we intended to interrogate both Allen and Shula before we ever started to write our daily stuff. And if we intended to sample the nocturnal joys of L.A. after work, it was another 50 miles away.

◆ ◆ ◆

Eight months before Super Bowl VII, Don Shula was organizing for the 1972 season. He placed a phone call. Some of the trauma remained from the loss in Super Bowl VI. Shula realized his young champions needed a blending of wisdom and experience. An insurance policy.

Earl Morrall was located on the course at the Detroit Golf Club and called to the telephone in the clubhouse. Don Shula was on the phone. He had some simple questions for the 38-year-old quarterback. Did Morrall plan on playing another season? Morrall told Shula that he had played 17 seasons and that now he was considering retirement. The Colts had placed Morrall on waivers, and he had been claimed by the New England Patriots. A losing club did not appeal to Morrall. Shula asked Morrall if he'd consider playing for the Dolphins. Morrall thought about his plans, his future out of football—and then told Shula, yes, he could accept playing for the Dolphins, a championship team. He'd be the backup to Bob Griese, just in case.

The Patriots dropped their claim to Morrall. He went to the Dolphins for the sum of $100, the standard waiver price. Morrall had spent the bulk of his career responding to the alarm of a frantic coach who needed a veteran quarterback in an emergency. That had been his role when Shula traded for Morrall in Baltimore. Then Earl had been pressed into service to replace the great John Unitas. In that capacity, Morrall started Super Bowl III and became the goat. In that capacity, Morrall replaced Unitas partway through Super Bowl V and became a hero.

Now Morrall had been summoned again. And Shula's clairvoyance benefited the Dolphins early in the '72 season. Griese went down with a busted ankle in the fifth game with the Dolphins undefeated. Morrall started the next nine games and the Dolphins won all of them and finished 14-0 with a quarterback that cost Shula the price of a long-distance call and a hundred bucks. Morrall took the Dolphins into the playoffs. He beat the Browns, 20-14, in the first round. Next up for the Dolphins were the Steelers, who had defeated the Raiders in their first-round game on Terry Bradshaw's deflected pass that Franco Harris caught in midair, as he trailed the play, and ran for the winning touchdown. The Immaculate Reception.

The Dolphins, 15-0, and the Steelers were square at 7-7 at halftime. Griese's ankle had mended, and Shula put him out in the second half and benched Morrall. The Dolphins won on two touchdown runs by Jim Kiick, 21-17, and advanced to the Super Bowl.

Clearly, Earl Morrall's quarterbacking had gotten the Dolphins to the Super Bowl. Clearly, they had remained unbeaten because of Morrall. Clearly, Morrall had earned the start in Super Bowl VII against the Redskins. Clearly, Shula had a terrible decision to make in the two-week gap between the championship game and the Super Bowl. Shula did not dally. He killed off the suspense that might have been created in the daily press about his ordeal in determining his Super Bowl quarterback. Before the Dolphins flew out of Miami for L.A., Shula called Griese in.

"How's the ankle?" asked Shula.

"I feel fine," said Griese. "The ankle feels the best it has since I hurt it."

"Good enough to start in the Super Bowl?" Shula asked next.

"I'm ready to play if that's your decision," said Griese. Together they went out to find Earl Morrall and tell him what they'd decided.

Now the buslift from Newport Beach unloaded its cargo of press questioners at the Dolphins' practice site up the freeway in Long Beach for the yearly picture day rituals. We raced for Morrall, this additional connection in the chain linking the Super Bowls. We raced for Shula.

"In this game you try not to let emotions, personal feelings, get involved," Morrall said, the trooper mouthing the team line. "Of course, I don't agree with the decision, but I'll abide by it. I thought I had a good year and deserved the start. Coach Shula told me the staff had a meeting and agreed we'd be stronger with Griese starting. I'll be ready."

I marched over to Shula. He said, "I didn't have a decision to make until Bob came off the bench in Pittsburgh and proved he was 100 percent."

It was just another epsiode in the life story of Earl Morrall. And Shula had made himself wide-open vulnerable to this batch of second-guessers, if Griese came back flat, if Morrall couldn't rescue him again, if the Dolphins lost this ultimate game.

◆ ◆ ◆

It was a jaunt over the freeway to Anaheim, where we did not expect friendly greetings from George Allen and the Redskins. We were reluctantly admitted to Anaheim Stadium. Helmeted cops checked and double-checked the Super Bowl VII pins the NFL ordered us to wear so we would not be mistaken for KGB.

Allen had abided by the request of Rozelle's department of propaganda. He had his players on the field, available for conversation and the like, although he griped about the intrusion.

There was worse still than the press invading the confines of Allen's practice field. The NFL, attempting to combat the blasé moods of the citizens of Los Angeles, had invited the public to witness the picture day spectacle. Of course, the taxpayers and other curious mortals would be confined to the grandstands. Punctually, the flacks led the members of the media through the stands and through the barriers and onto the field. Three thousand school kids and some hooky-playing adults jeered at us, harping at our privileged status.

George Allen's topic was total preparedness for the Super Bowl. "If I had my way," Allen said, "we'd have practiced until Friday in Washington. We have fine facilities at home. All the fanfare and everything hinders the players in their preparation. When you take the players out of their own environment, it hurts them."

As Allen delivered his discourse on Super Bowl distractions, a teenage boy in a yellow jacket scrambled over the fence and darted brazenly across the field. There were cheers, then boos, as the Anaheim cops chased and then corralled the intruder.

And suddenly, another 2,000 youths clambered over the fences and onto the field. The Redskins were hurriedly evacuated to safety beneath the grandstands. Somewhat out of breath, Allen continued his discourse in the vacant clubhouse of the California Angels.

"See," he said, "there are distractions out here. I thought they were going to break a few arms and legs of my players. It's a little scary."

The rabble's field raid had succeeded in gaining us admission into the Redskins' locker room, to the additional chagrin of Allen.

My passion for the Quarterback Mystique took me to Bill Kilmer. Now, here was a player who fit the mold of swaggering personality quarterbacks. He couldn't throw a pass worth a hoot. Those he did get off knuckled or fluttered or turned topsy turvy. He croaked his signal calls. He had been passed around by a couple of clubs. As a young quarterback with the San Francisco 49ers, Kilmer had spent a night out on the town. Driving home, his car had careened into a ditch, shattering his leg in the crash. The bone had protruded into the stagnant swamp water. Kilmer, pinned inside the car, almost drowned. He was fished out and fought off the danger of gangrene. The doctors doubted he would ever walk again without a limp. But a year later, Kilmer was back in the 49ers' camp, trying to take away John Brodie's job.

Allen, in his wheeling and dealing, had gotten Kilmer for little in exchange from the New Orleans Saints. In Washington, Allen made Kilmer his number one quarterback, ahead of Sonny Jurgensen, the hugely respected pure passer who had lasted through a number of presidential administrations. And Jurgy, with his paunch, happened to fit my idea of what a quarterback should be, also.

But it would be Kilmer, the 34-year-old roustabout, who would start against the perfect Dolphins in Super Bowl VII. He had taken Allen's Redskins to an 11-3 season and then a 16-3 playoff victory over the Packers and a 26-3 rout of the reigning Cowboys for the NFC championship.

I approached him in front of his locker. "You remind me of Bobby Layne," I said to this man with the florid face. Kilmer looked back at me and grinned.

"Do I really?" he said.

"Yeah," I said. "I mean that as a compliment. In Detroit, we still gauge all quarterbacks against Bobby."

"I know, thanks," said Billy Kilmer.

◆ ◆ ◆

On Tuesday and Wednesday mornings we made the circuit to Long Beach to visit the Dolphins, then across to Santa Ana to drop in on the Redskins, then back to Newport Beach. The NFL provided all the amenities for the trek except care packages and pith helmets.

In Long Beach I joined the throng that had Larry Csonka encircled during the Dolphins' interview session. This blithe spirit had posed for the cover of *Sports Illustrated* at midseason, during the Dolphins' drive toward perfection. Running was their mightiest force, and Csonka was their mightiest runner. He had run for 1,117 yards during the season, most of the yardage gained in three-, four-, or five-yard thrusts straight ahead. In this age of O.J. Simpson and the Redskins' slasher Larry Brown, Csonka ran the old-fashioned way. Like Bronco Nagurski, he was sheer power. He weighed 237 pounds and his size overwhelmed us as he answered our questions.

But Csonka was charming as he told us about his boyhood on a farm in Ohio with a stern father. "I grew up in a small town playing sandlot football and driving cows, which gives you an urge to get out of a small town. . . . I did typical farm work, pitching hay and milking cows. You notice the way farmers are always the butt of jokes, the farmer's daughter and things. It always ticked me. I made 90 cents an hour for my farm work. I wanted to get out and now I miss it."

We asked Csonka about the new sociological debate begun by some former players who wrote books about football being dehumanizing. It was portrayed as a game played by dopes.

"I don't like people to come up to me and make me feel I have a dumb animal image," Csonka said. "People say I can run through a brick wall. When you come down to philosophies, why would you run through a brick wall? It's a compliment in one sense and a putdown in another sense."

Throughout the long interview, I kept watching Csonka's face. He seemed to be wearing a permanent smirk, just a tiny one, what is referred to as a shit-eating grin.

It was the identical expression Csonka wore in the *Sports Illustrated* cover shot when he posed beneath the goalpost with running colleague Jim Kiick. Amazingly, Csonka faked out the *SI* photographer and the magazine's corps of meticulous checkers and editors. He appeared on the cover—on newsstands everywhere, in America's mailboxes—in full grin, with the middle finger of his hand extended in a certain way down the pants leg of his Miami uniform. America grinned with him.

◆ ◆ ◆

The ring the Super Bowl champion is entitled to wear is placed on a different finger. "I just want that ring," had become an awful cliché among the players in the interview sessions during the Super Bowl prelude. But George Allen played to this motivation for his aged athletes. Long ago at training camp he had obtained a large photograph of a Super Bowl ring and plastered it onto the wall of the Redskins' training room.

"George told us he was going to get us the biggest diamonds in the world for that ring," said Diron Talbert. "He told us that during the year when we began to hurt, limp, and drag. We had to come back into the trainer's room to get put back together again. George told us we should stop and look at that picture. He told us it might make us forget those pains.

"Well, man, I hurt and I've been hurting all year. Both my shoulders are sore and my leg hurts and sometimes I limp a little. I ain't slept the whole season, because every night when I turn over in bed, the hurt starts all over again. But I look at that picture and I can take the hurt for another game. I want that ring, man."

◆ ◆ ◆

Garo Yepremian gave me a necktie he had sewn, and I thanked him. He was a personal favorite and had been since the day I met him. That was in the fall of 1966 in Tiger Stadium, Detroit. I was the only reporter covering the Lions' practice that day. The entire ball club was gathered on the field in a semicircle watching what looked like a placekicking exhibition.

"Watch this," said Pat Studstill, the Lions' best receiver, as I crossed the turf from which I was strictly forbidden. "I've never seen anything like it. He's some guy from Cyprus."

A little bald-headed guy was swirling his left foot soccer-style at the football and drilling kicks 50 yards through yonder posts. It was a phenomenal exhibition. The opposition writer had taken the day off. I knew I had lucked into a terrific story all alone. The kicker finished the tryout and went to the locker room with another man and Russ Thomas, the Lions' general manager. Thomas tried to shoo me away, but I refused to budge. Thomas and the other man went to the corner of the locker room and engaged in a discussion. I thought it must be contract talk. I approached the kicker.

"Can I ask you some questions?" I said. The kicker looked me over.

"I don't speak English," Garo Yepremian said, in a language that was not Phoenician.

I backed away. Soon Thomas and the other man completed their discussion. The other man was Krikor Yepremian, Garo's brother. I was given leave to interview Garo, one-on-one. He told me he had played soccer in Cyprus, then moved with his family to London. He said he had played soccer in Hyde Park and worked as a haberdashery salesman. His brother had come to America and started watching football on television. Soccer-style placekickers were just coming into fashion in the NFL, and Krikor brought Garo to the States with a grand plan to get him tryouts with some NFL clubs. The Lions signed him on the spot.

I asked him if he knew anything about American football. He said he had seen some on TV. But he had never seen a real game. Three days later the first action he ever saw in a real NFL game was of his own left foot kicking off for the Lions against the Colts. He booted the ball downfield. Then he turned around, bent over, his rear end directed toward the onrushing Colts' return team, and retrieved the kicking tee.

He could kick. A few weeks into his career he kicked six field goals, matching the NFL record, in a game against the Vikings. "They ought to tighten the immigration laws," said Norm Van Brocklin, then the Vikings' coach.

Alex Karras and Garo would yap at each other in Greek during practices. Karras hated quarterbacks and kickers. "He keeps dancing and yelling, 'I keek a tawchdown,' " Karras said.

Joe Schmidt, the Lions' head coach, lacked faith in Garo, and after a couple of seasons, the Lions released him. The Dolphins, still building in Shula's new regime, signed him. They needed a placekicker.

For Miami Garo kicked the field goal that beat the Chiefs in the longest game ever played. Now, a season later, he was in the Super Bowl for the second time.

We kicked over old times at Long Beach as the Dolphins awaited Super Bowl VII. Garo laughed about how he told me that first day he didn't speak English, in perfect English. And then he told me how much he disliked playing in Detroit.

"The coaches didn't treat me like I was on the team," he said. "All they ever had me do at the meetings was turn off the lights when they showed the game movies. They never treated me like a football player."

♦ ♦ ♦

The most devastating thing that can happen in the career of a journalist is to be locked up somewhere else when a major story breaks on your assignment. In 1967, I had been late going to Super Bowl I because the Lions were hiring Joe Schmidt as head coach. It had been my story and I covered it.

Now I was in my room in Newport Beach on the Friday two days before Super Bowl VII when the phone rang. It was the office. "Joe Schmidt just quit," I was told. The words clunked me in the head. To paraphrase George Allen, it was worse than death. I was out in California and back in Detroit a story had broken and other guys on the staff would have to handle my beat for the Friday afternoon paper. What lousy timing. I felt sorry for myself. All I could do was make the phone calls to Schmidt, William Clay Ford, and Russ Thomas and write a follow-up column for Saturday's *News*.

Schmidt had been the original great middle linebacker on championship teams in the fifties, a monstrous competitor. As a coach, he had been funny and he had been angry. Every Monday after games, he was forced to endure hours of grilling from Ford/Thomas. Lots of times the vote tallies were 2-1 and Joe lost. Joe called them "How come?" meetings. He became an expert on the hire-fire practices around pro football and he coined a phrase to sum up the firings of fellow coaches: "the ziggy." We'd sit in his office, two guys discussing the state of the NFL, and Joe would say: "Van Brocklin got the ziggy." Then he'd go "heh, heh, heh," not that he believed the firing of a poor man was funny, but that the entire system was slapstick. Now Joe Schmidt had delivered a self-ziggy. He had told his bosses to stuff it.

"It had gotten so there were things more important in life than winning football games," Joe told me over the phone as I felt rotten in this Super Bowl atmosphere. I mentioned that George Allen, whom Schmidt had criticized as a con man, had told us he'd sacrifice a year off his life to win Super Bowl VII.

"Not me," said Joe. "Maybe I don't want to sacrifice those things to win a Super Bowl. There are certain goals you want to reach in life, there are a lot of things you have to sacrifice. I'm not willing to make the sacrifice that George Allen is. That's a big statement to make. I love winning and I love doing those things like everybody else. I want to win as bad as George Allen. It's pretty hard to compromise."

I called Ford and Thomas. They kept guffawing and joking. Joe Schmidt was gone and they seemed glad. Now they had been spared the pressure of giving the ziggy to a local hero.

◆ ◆ ◆

The Super Bowl prelude went on this crazy day. As was the routine on the Friday preceding Super Sunday, the coaches were required to travel to the media headquarters for press conferences. All their ideas had been picked, all their complaints were old fodder, all their jokes were pale. For George Allen this press briefing to which he had to be driven the 36 miles from Santa Ana, then back to practice at Anaheim, was an unwarranted distraction.

"Because of these distractions, yesterday we had the worst day of practice we've had," Allen told the media. "And now because I had to come out here on Friday, I'm missing a team meeting for the first time in 23 years of coaching."

After his press session, Allen took note of Schmidt's resignation from coaching.

"How old is Joe?" asked Allen, coach of the Over the Hill Gang. Maybe he could still get Schmidt to suit up on Sunday.

Shula suspected Allen of spying on the Dolphins' practices from tall buildings overlooking Blair Field in Long Beach. Shula was asked if the Dolphins were filming their practices to catch mistakes, as the Redskins were doing.

"No," said Shula, "George Allen is taking them for us. We're thinking of moving our last practices to Tijuana. I say that now so George can start scouting the area for our new practice field."

But at Long Beach, the Dolphins detected that Shula, loser twice in the Super Bowl, was becoming uptight.

"Can you imagine what Don will be like if he loses another Super Bowl?" asked Jim Mandrich, the tight end.

"As a coach, it would be selfish of me to say I would take a place in history if we win, in light of my previous Super Bowl record," Shula said.

◆ ◆ ◆

Pete Rozelle had been under criticism for the lack of drama in Super Bowl after Super Bowl. "The Super Bowl has not had an aesthetic interest for several years," Rozelle confessed.

It was party time, at last. Rozelle's party had become such a hot item that the NFL decided to move it away from the ballroom of the press headquarters. That way sponsors, network officials, button-downed martini guzzlers from Madison Avenue, politicians both in office and running, and owners' friends, families, and creditors could all freeload at the party with the media folk.

So, Rozelle, in keeping with his obsession for cultural betterment, rented the Queen Mary. The dowager ship was tied up in Long Beach as a tourist curiosity now that it had been retired from transatlantic service. For one gala evening it became pro football's own showboat.

They bused us up to the docks and we climbed the gangplank into a swirl of humanity. All of Washington seemed to be there, except for Dick Nixon, fan of both teams. It was so crowded it turned the art of freeloading into a match of sharp elbows and saintly patience. Damn the torpedoes, batten down the hatches, hoist the party pennant from the yardarm, full speed ahead.

◆ ◆ ◆

It was Super Sunday at last. Now for the most aesthetically interesting Super Bowl, in the delicate words of Pete Rozelle, since Super Bowl III. It would be Allen and his fossils after a week of wailing about distractions versus the would-be perfectionist Dolphins, that team with "little fishies on the helmet," as the great Jim Murray wrote in the Sunday L.A. *Times,* and Don Shula, twice a loser in this ultimate football game.

Rozelle, for the benefit of the eastern bloc of NBC's television audience, had scheduled the show to start at 3:30 p.m. in New York. Three time zones west, it would begin shortly after noon, and the January sunshine rays would be flat and low. It was a situation that caused George Allen pain. The sun might be a factor. So Allen had slipped one of his emissaries into the Coliseum at 12:30 two days earlier to scout the sun. The sun scout sat there through the afternoon charting the angle of the sun through the smog.

"Can't overlook anything," Allen said.

Shula thought: The whole season has come down to one game. The season-long success, the records, the 16-0 mark, all are hanging in the balance. If we lose, the whole season will be a bust. Nobody would remember the 16 victories. They would all point to the one loss.

And Jimmy the Greek was at his Super Bowl finest. Allen's Redskins were established as the favorites, by three points. I followed the line. I made my dollar pick in the pressroom pool: Redskins by three.

◆ ◆ ◆

It was L.A. and Rozelle was back to launching pigeons during the pregame festivities. Also 20,000 balloons, and keeping with the in-the-air mode, the Apollo 17 crew, returned from the moon, was featured. The Little Angel Singers from Chicago's Holy Angel Church sang "The Star-Spangled Banner." The blaring University of Michigan Marching Band pranced through its routine. Hollywood was represented by Sammy Davis, Jr. and Andy Williams. The traditional Air Force jets buzzed the Coliseum.

Then Allen, Shula, Csonka, Kilmer, and Griese were permitted to play a football game.

It was not exactly aesthetic football. The Dolphins went up 14-0 in the first half. At the end of a fine march, Griese passed 28 yards to Howard Twilley, who twisted the Redskins' Pat Fischer into a 180-degree spin at the five. Twilley stepped into the end zone. Before the half, Nick Buoniconti intercepted one of Kilmer's passes and ran it back 32 yards to the 27. Csonka and Kiick hit the line. Griese hit his tight end, Mandrich. Then Kiick blasted through the Over the Hill Gang for a touchdown from the two.

The Redskins had not crossed midfield in the first half. The game turned into a defensive slugfest. Kilmer was intercepted three times, twice by the scooting Jake Scott. Shula tried to protect the lead with a conservative offense. Finally, after Scott had returned an interception 55 yards, the Dolphins had the chance for an insurance score. A bit more than two minutes remained.

Shula sent Yepremian in to attempt a 42-yard field goal. Earl Morrall held the ball down and Yepremian kicked it. The ball hit the Redskins' Bill Brundige squarely in the torso, and the blocked football bounced over the grass. Yepremian picked it up. "I keek a tawchdown, I keek a tawchdown"— he had been hounded by his words for years.

Garo pulled his arm back with the ball, trying to pass, and the ball squirted from his fingers. He reached for the ball and batted it right into the hands of Mike Bass, the Washington cornerback. Bass grabbed the football and ran along the sideline, in front of the anguished face of Don Shula, all the way for a touchdown. The Redskins had scored and were a touchdown from overhauling the Dolphins.

Allen ignored the onside kickoff maneuver, figuring it would fail, and that ample time remained to get the ball again. He was wrong.

LOS ANGELES—They are obscure journeymen, the nondescript athletes who toil on defense for the Miami Dolphins.

They are a potpourri with names such as Nick Buoniconti, Manny Fernandez, Jake Scott, Vern Den Herder, Dick Anderson, Lloyd

Mumphord. As a unit they call themselves the No-Name Defense. Mostly they are made up of rejects, former free agents, and lower draft choices.

"We're the greatest team ever to play the game," said Nick Buoniconti, elder spokesman for this motley crew. "We don't get the credit. Maybe if we win five Super Bowls in a row we would. . . ."

The 14-7 victory over the Washington Redskins yesterday in Super Bowl VII made the Dolphins unique. No team ever before in the 53-year history of the NFL has won the world championship with a perfect record.

"We're 17-0 and we're still getting rapped," said Don Shula, his solid jaw defiant.

"This team has gone into an area no other team has gone before. We won all our games in the season, then both in the playoffs, then the Super Bowl. And when you're first to do something the team has to be given credit. . . . The thing I'm going to do is relish this game. I've been through a lot of frustration and disappointment in my young life.

"You always point to the ultimate. I've been here three times and failed twice—and a lot has been said about my failures. We accomplished more than the 1966 and 1967 Packers."

"Shula is an egotist," said Buoniconti. "He has an ego that is very large and he passes it on to us. . . ."

Little, bald Garo Yepremian stood prayerfully in the center of the champions' locker room. His gaffe might have cost the Dolphins their perfect season.

"I'll never be a quarterback," he said as we clustered around him. "I felt I could throw downfield and complete it for a touchdown. I was hoping I could get it to Larry Csonka." Larry Csonka, the farmboy fullback, grinned.

"Garo thought he was a quarterback," said Csonka. "He thought he was six-six like Roman Gabriel, with hair down to his shoulders."

Yepremian's pass became etched as my favorite highlight in seven Super Bowls.

VIII
The Abominable Snowman

Miami Dolphins 24, Minnesota Vikings 7
January 13, 1974
Rice Stadium, Houston
Attendance: 68,142

II, IV, VI, VIII, who do we appreciate? And now, one goal drove Don Shula. He had ripped the monkey of defeat off his back, and he reflected into history and yearned to emulate the noblest of Romans, Vince Lombardi. Lombardi had been the victor in Super Bowls I and II with the Packers. Since then, five different teams had won the five Super Bowls. Five different coaches won. Parity had afflicted the pro football conglomerate. Dynasties were dead.

Throughout the '73 season, Shula was haunted by Lombardi's accomplishment of winning two Super Bowls in succession. His Dolphins were playing in their prime. They were reigning champions and they were dominant and brilliantly coached. The usual grumbles of champions had begun to flare up, but the Dolphins were good enough to play over their discontent.

Imperfect this time—they had lost two games on the repeat trip to Super Bowl VIII—the Dolphins nonetheless considered themselves the best team in the history of pro football. Shula's ego, as Nick Buoniconti had said the January before, dripped over onto his entire ball club.

This was the drama as we headed off once again to Pete Rozelle's Circus Maximus. Were the Dolphins the best ever? And could Don Shula match Lombardi?

The Dolphins would be playing the Minnesota Vikings. Bud Grant at the Super Bowl again. Could we break his crust of Minnesota ice? No Joe Kapp this time. Rather, the eminent Francis Tarkenton, the original scrambling quarterback. When he was chased out of Minnesota for exile in New York with the Giants, Francis was described as the consummate 7-7 quarterback. Now in his 13th professional season, Francis was involved in postseason football for the first time.

I looked forward to the week, even though the rich men who vote on the Super Bowl locations had awarded this one to Houston, Space Age City, hometown of Mission Control. The game would be played in Rice Stadium. I swallowed my cynicism pills on the Sunday before Super Sunday and headed for the airport.

There are times I am able to write on airplanes. I jot out the words longhand on a scrap of paper, maybe an envelope, then copy my scribble into something legible on my still trusty Olivetti portable typewriter. On this Sunday, the inspiration for a column struck in the air and I went to work.

A Funny Thing Happened on the Way to the Super Bowl
(A Contemporary Playlet)

Characters

Emperor Peter, head of state
Marcus Delectus, prime minister
Flackius, minister of public relations
Maximus, deputy to Flackius
Minus, deputy to Maximus
Several Legionnaires and Slaves

Scene: The throne room of Emperor Peter at Super Bowl VIII, an ancient sacred ritual, celebrated annually. The emperor, a man of great wisdom, is seated on the throne, his acolytes seated below him in a semicircle. Legionnaires guard the dooorway. Slaves serve the emperor and his acolytes and occasionally fan them with plumes.

Emperor Peter is attired in a toga. A laurel wreath encircles his head. The acolytes wear togas and leather sandals. . . . Flackius carries a spear to indicate his rank as the emperor's spear carrier.

A huge red, white, and blue banner hangs behind the emperor's throne. It bears the legend NFL. Each acolyte wears a sundial on his wrist with the insignia NFL emblazoned on the timepiece. The emperor is conducting his forum on preparations for Super Bowl VIII. . . .

All but the emperor: Hail Peter.

Emperor (in an imperious voice): The countdown has begun. VI more days until it is again Super Sunday. . . . All, I trust, is in order.

Marcus (in a firm voice): All is in readiness, Our Emperor. The combatants arrived last night. The coliseum is being cleansed, and our sacred symbol, the NFL, will be painted at the center of the arena IV days hence. The chariots to transport the faraway visitors have been hired. A site has been commandeered for our annual Super Bowl orgy and invitations have been dispatched to all the guests from around the domain. Flackius and his staff have seen to it that the countdown will be orderly.

Emperor: Fine, splendid. The state runs smoothly as usual, I see. Emperor Bowie and his ministers can again be envious. The Super Bowl orgy, the details, please. Last year it was on that barge we hired, the . . .

Flackius (in an eager voice): The Queen Mary, Our Emperor. The barge was overladen with visitors.

Emperor: Yes, I thought I was attending the Circus Maximus. It will be different this time, I pray. Where is it?

Maximus (in an eager voice also): We have arranged to hire the Astrodome, Our Emperor. Our visitors from far away should be impressed.

Emperor: Fine, fine, the Astrodome, the eighth wonder of the world, I am told. Was it impossible to transport the pyramids for the orgy? Have you spoken to Hannibal, our general in charge of such logistics? The pyramids would be most impressive. I thought, perhaps, Cleopatra herself would come.

Marcus (in a concerned voice): Cleopatra, no, Our Emperor. She cannot delight us with a visit to the Super Bowl at this time. Indeed, I have brought from home my, er, no Our Emperor, Cleopatra declined our invitation. I delivered it to her personally on my last journey.

Emperor: The Astrodome, I like that, indeed. The eighth wonder of the world for Super Bowl VIII. It is poetry. What have you arranged for the combatants?

Minus (in a low-keyed voice): We have run it up the flagpole—I learned that in my travels—and again have decided this year to award the standard $\overline{XXV}$ [25,000] dollars to the victors. The vanquished again will be rewarded with $\overline{VIID}$ [7,500] dollars.

Emperor: The combatants . . .

Marcus: Yes, Our Emperor, the Dolphins. They are the champion gladiators, as you may recall. From a city to the south, Miami.

Emperor: Ah yes, the Dolphins . . . with that little Cypriot who thought he would like to fling the projectile.

Marcus: And the Vikings, from our province in the far north, Minnesota.

Emperor: Vikings? They are brutes and the Ides of January do approach. Fine then, the Dolphins and the Vikings are the combatants VI days hence. I am certain you have made arrangements for the annual flyover of doves.

Flackius: We have pigeons, Our Emperor. It is less demanding on the treasury.

Emperor: And the arrangements for the midpoint of the contest?

Flackius: It will be the best, Our Emperor. The subjects from Carthage have obliged us with their cooperation. We shall reenact the second of the Punic Wars at halftime. The spears will be blunted so as not to create wounds. I am told it will be a most extraordinary sight for all our citizens in our territories.

Emperor: And certainly, there is a large contingent of scribes present as always to record the festivities to enlighten our fellow citizens in the provinces.

Flackius: Hundreds, Our Emperor, from all our major cities. I am seeing personally to their whims and wishes.

Marcus: I have a cup of hemlock for one.

Emperor: Not during the countdown to the Super Bowl, Marcus. Afterwards you may throw him to the lions. But not now, this is the Super Bowl and how could the lions ever get here?

All: Hail Peter.

(Curtain)

The NFL had selected the new Hyatt Regency, with its flowing jungle in the lobby, as its press headquarters. I filed the playlet column in the pressroom, found the media poll on the bulletin board, picked the Dolphins by a XXI to XVII score and paid Paul Zimmerman my buck. I was set for another Super Bowl prelude, listening to Shula's platitudes, watching Bud Grant melt.

Bud Grant came out of the great white North with a frosty, stolid image, and his team played that sort of football. Roman Gabriel, the tall, dark quarterback for the Rams, said once after another loss in Minnesota on a gloomy, miserable night: "The Vikings take advantage of their weather. You have to have a little bit of luck to beat these guys."

"George Allen gets a lot of mileage out of emotion with the Washington Redskins," Grant said of the hysterical gang the Vikings beat in the first round of the NFC's Super Bowl playoffs. "They're always cheering and singing. We don't do that."

The picture of Bud Grant was frozen in my mind. His football teams dominated the NFC Central. They played the fiercest defense in the league. They were unspectacular on offense, a power team. No matter what was happening on the field, Bud Grant stood on the sidelines, a statue of white ice. His hands were stuffed into the pockets of his purple jacket, his purple cap flecked with snowflakes was on his head, his headset-antlers fixed on the cap. Grant was the original Abominable Snowman, outfitted in this purple. To me, purple is the ugliest color in the spectrum—and the Vikings, in my opinion, played ugly football.

But within the division, their ugliness was combined with a brutalizing efficiency. They crushed their opponents, the Lions in particular, year after year.

Grant never smiled. He put on a terrific act.

The Vikings won the NFC championship on the next-to-last day of 1973. After upending Allen's Redskins, the defending conference champions, the Vikings had to play in Dallas. It would be the Cowboys or the Vikings returning to the Super Bowl. Minnesota's galling loss to the Chiefs in Super Bowl IV, the AFL's last stand, remained an indelible memory. The Dallas fans taunted the Vikings.

One of them hung a banner in large, clear letters at the mouth of the Vikings' locker room tunnel: *Losers.*

The Vikings could see the banner from the field as they played the championship game. It wasn't close. The Vikings beat the Cowboys, 27-10, to qualify for Super Bowl VIII.

When the game ended, Gary Larsen dashed for the *Losers* graffiti. Larsen was not a demonstrative man. He was the least-publicized of the Vikings' front four. He played with Alan Page the lawyer, with Carl Eller the actor, with Jim Marshall the outdoorsman. Larsen ripped the sign off the grandstand facing. He shredded it and flipped the confetti to the artificial turf of Texas Stadium.

"I saw it when we came out to warm up," Larsen said. "It just made me a little mad. I made sure it went down, but I wanted to wait until the end of the game. There are no losers on this club."

Bud Grant was a fraud, an insidious con artist who had hoodwinked us for years with his glacial front. The stuff about the Vikings lacking passion was a myth we had come to trust.

After Larsen tore down the *Losers* sign, the Vikings burst into bawdy song in their victorious locker room. Just like the Redskins.

The Vikings arrived in Houston the Sunday before Super Bowl VIII, and two buses rolled onto the airport tarmac to lug them to their hotel. Their cavalcade was halfway across Houston when smoke began to pour from one bus. It stopped and some of the players jumped off. The second

FREEPORT PUBLIC LIBRARY

bus continued. The lighting system had short-circuited on the first bus. It was fixed and the trip resumed.

The first bus finally arrived at the hotel and the passengers/players went into the lobby. They looked for the guys who had taken the second bus. They weren't there. At last the second-bus riders arrived an hour behind schedule. The driver of the second bus had taken a wrong turn and gotten lost.

Welcome back to the Super Bowl, Bud Grant.

◆　◆　◆

The Dolphins swaggered to this Super Bowl. There was romance to this team that was the first to qualify for its third Super Bowl. But the Super Bowl prelude, the daily press sessions, had become a drag. It was routine, it was boring, it was the same worn-out questions.

It had been another sensational season on the field. The Dolphins weren't invincible this time, in the '73 season. The first of their two defeats had been versus the Raiders, long ago in September. But the Dolphins got even. They played the Raiders again in the AFC championship and won, 27-10. Larry Csonka scored three touchdowns. The Dolphins' record was 14-2 as they went off to Houston for Super Bowl VIII—and every one of the Dolphins reflected, with their coach, on the Green Bay Packers and Vince Lombardi and history. "Best ever?" The Dolphins believed they were.

That was on Sunday afternoons, when they were displayed in public. They were spiffy, precisioned, disciplined. They exuded solidarity and comradeship. They emitted an aura of machined perfection. On Sundays.

Yet there were different vibrations transmitted when they were not actively engaged in running and passing footballs. They had become a crabby team.

Somehow Shula managed to unite factions to play games as a team and to win. The Dolphins, like the bickering Oakland A's in baseball, were a reflection of the strained, violent times. They won despite anarchy in the locker room, acrimony within.

"Fifteen guys will be jumping to the World Football League next year," said Doug Swift, the Miami linebacker who was educated at Amherst.

The new WFL was wooing Larry Csonka, Jim Kiick, and Paul Warfield. Kiick had been turned into a part-timer so Mercury Morris could run with Csonka. "I got to think of myself," said Kiick.

Csonka and Kiick wrote a book with Dave Anderson and ripped Shula for being too strict, too implacable.

Mercury Morris continued to sulk and blast the coach, as he had when Shula did not play him in Super Bowl VI. Jim Mandrich griped that he wasn't playing enough. Jake Scott and Dick Anderson were among the squawkers, having held out in tandem for better contracts. They remained in a funk throughout the championship season, and both again made All-Pro despite their disenchantment.

Now, at the Super Bowl, the bachelor Dolphins complained that owner Joe Robbie refused to bring girlfriends or mothers to Houston. Only the wives.

Shula himself often battled with Robbie. At an off-season banquet in Miami, Robbie noticed that Don Shula and his wife were late and were not yet seated at the table.

"We've got a thousand people waiting on you," Robbie said to Shula, according to Morris Siegel, the Washington raconteur, who was to be master of ceremonies. "Let's get up there."

"Don't ever yell at me in public again," Shula bristled, "or I'll knock you on your ass."

◆ ◆ ◆

On Monday morning, the ticked-off Dolphins were not the only grousing team in the Space Age City. The buses made it, with their cargo of Vikings, to Delmar Field, a field used by local high schools. Affable, easy-going, icy Bud Grant took a gander at the facilities where the Vikings were to train for Super Bowl VIII. Bud stopped being affable, easy-going, icy. He steamed.

"This is shabby treatment," Grant growled when the press hordes rode up for the annual press day pageantry. "This is the Super Bowl, not some pickup game."

The locker room did not have lockers. The Vikings had to hang their jeans and double knits on nails pounded into the walls. There was no special changing room for the coaches, where they could have the privacy to discuss situations away from the athletes. There were no rooms for the meetings that are so vital to football coaches. Most of the shower heads had rusted and could only trickle water. A family of sparrows had nested in the shower room. Grant felt the Vikings were being dumped on. Literally.

Meanwhile, the Dolphins were fixed in comparative luxury at the Houston Oilers' practice facilities.

Grant blamed Emperor Peter Rozelle's sophisticated Super Bowl staff for screwing up the logistical arrangments. And he said so, as the press gathered around him, grabbing the shreds of controversy that boost the writing job from the deadly routine of the Super Bowl prelude.

"The NFL sets up the practice facilities and they had a year to do it," Grant said.

"Go look for yourself. We don't have any lockers. Our seven coaches get to share one table for spreading out our clothes. And we have to go back to the hotel for our meetings instead of having them here right before practice. The facilities definitely give the Dolphins an advantage."

The writers scribbled as fast as they could in their brand-new Super Bowl VIII notebooks with their brand-new Super Bowl VIII pens.

◆ ◆ ◆

Bud Grant's complaints reached Pete Rozelle's ivory tower on Park Avenue, Manhattan, with the speed of tom-tom signals. A Super Bowl coach is not permitted the right of normal bitching. Rozelle sent a message back that Bud had better shut up. Or else, he'd be fined.

I stopped off at the Dolphins' media day and muscled my way into the group around Garo Yepremian.

"How's your arm?" I asked.

"My arm is stronger," said Garo. "It's stronger because I've been wearing my Super Bowl ring. I've been working on my passing."

Nearby, Don Shula discussed the same subject with a bunch of writers.

"He'll never throw the ball again," said Shula, uttering a Magyar oath. "Of that I'm certain." That revealed how much Shula knew.

One of the photographers had happened to uncover an official NFL football complete with Pete Rozelle's autograph. Garo grabbed the ball and cocked his arm. He threw. The football drifted away in a semi-spiral and somebody caught it 20 yards away. As a scholar of seven prior Super Bowls, I had seen less artistic passes thrown in these annual epics.

And Shula had thought he had nipped Garo's lust for passing long before in training camp.

"Coach Shula had boxing gloves for me to wear at training camp in case I wanted to pick up the ball," said Yepremian. "I'm going to wear my boxing gloves Sunday."

We went out for dinner at Brennan's, a branch of the famed New Orleans restaurant. I guess we missed Bourbon Street. There were a bunch of us in the restaurant. A friend of mine offered something he had stashed in his pack of cigarettes.

"Go on, take one," he said. I declined and then decided what the heck, I'm a reporter, I hear so much about this marijuana stuff I ought to have the enlightening experience. I took it back to my room at the Hyatt. There, I held the cigarette for a long time before touching a match to it. It grated my mouth, it scorched my throat. It didn't do a thing for me. I tossed it into the toilet and took the elevator down to the pressroom.

I had a beer to cleanse my soul. The card game was just starting up in the corner. I kibitzed for a few minutes and then went upstairs and read Dan Jenkins's *Semi-Tough*.

◆ ◆ ◆

We piled over to the Vikings' hotel for the Tuesday press briefing to hear what Bud Grant had to say now that he'd been gagged by Pete Rozelle. We were led, sheep-fashion, to a dining room on the top floor, the penthouse restaurant.

Bud went up to the microphone.

"I've been threatened with a fine by the commissioner," Grant said. "He took a dim view of my observations."

His gripes about the one-room facility with nails on the walls and birds in the john had made headlines across America.

"I know we went from where we were the other day," Grant said, "right to the penthouse here."

Nick Buoniconti ran into Fran Tarkenton at dinner time in a place in Houston.

"If I have to explain one more time how we plan to stop your scrambling, I'll be climbing walls," said Buoniconti, chieftain of the No-Name Defense. "You know how we're going to try to stop you. We hope enough of our guys slide off blocks and finally catch up with you."

Three years of Super Bowl hype made the champion players feel like victims.

Pete Rozelle was informed by his acolytes about Bud Grant's penthouse comments at Tuesday's press session. Rozelle phoned Grant and told him the fine would be $5,000.

◆ ◆ ◆

The nightly card game started as scheduled in the pressroom of the Hyatt. It was a hot game, and as the hours went by the spectating writers drifted off to their rooms or out of the hotel to the joints in town. It was long after midnight when the pressroom was suddenly busy again.

The Houston cops had arrived in the pressroom. "It's a raid." The poker players looked at the cops.

"No one moves until we finish this hand," said Rick Talley, the Chicago columnist.

◆ ◆ ◆

Grant and Shula went to the Hyatt for the traditional Friday final press conferences.

"The league told us we could have one workout at Rice on Saturday," said Grant, now twice-rebuked. "They told us the Dolphins would be there at two and when did we want to work out. The Dolphins worked out at Rice on Wednesday. The league never told us we could go there a second time.

"One of our players said, 'This isn't the Super Bowl. It's the Dolphins' bowl.'"

♦ ♦ ♦

The NFL had selected Rice Stadium for Super Bowl VIII, even though it was uncovered and lacked amenities. Rice Stadium had more seating than the Astrodome. Rozelle could squeeze 72,000 ticket holders into Rice. He could squeeze his Super Bowl orgy into the Astrodome. So the Astrodome was rented for party purposes and the floor was covered with dirt. The pro football establishment and its ladies took off their stuffed shirts and mink and dressed up in . . . whoopeee, cowboy. The NFL went cowboy complete with cattle, fiddlin' music, chili, and barbecued beef.

It was the best Super Bowl party yet, if you were careful you didn't step into any pasture pies. Wide open spaces.

To celebrate Super Bowl VIII, the NFL purchased $3,000 worth of balloons. The 17,000 balloons floated out of Rice Stadium to climax the pregame extravaganza, and the Dolphins crunched methodically through the Vikings on a 68-yard drive on the game's first series. Csonka crashed for the touchdown from the five. They got the ball back and crunched 66 yards on the second series. Kiick scored from the one. The Dolphins had set the pattern for Super Bowl VIII, and America collectively yawned. Next Yepremian came on—no boxing gloves, but no pass—and the little guy booted a 28-yard field goal. The score was 17-0 Miami by halftime and 24-0 entering the fourth quarter following another march finished by Csonka's second touchdown from the two on a broken play.

Finally, the Dolphins permitted a score. Tarkenton made it in from the four. It was the most one-sided Super Bowl of the VIII played so far with a final score of 24-7 that did not reflect how superior the Dolphins were. Csonka gained 145 yards. So dominant were the Dolphins on the ground that Bob Griese threw only seven passes. He completed six of those. There was no other way to document what the Dolphins had accomplished with their 32nd victory in 34 games over two seasons, but:

HOUSTON—Somebody with a touch of poetry in his soul and a piece of chalk in his hand etched a simple message on the blackboard in the Miami Dolphins' locker room: *Best Ever*.

So now we are left a subject for great debates. . . . Are these spiffy, polished, precisioned, awesome Dolphins superior—or even equal— to the domineering Packers of Vince Lombardi and Bart Starr?

"I don't know who wrote *Best Ever* there," said Manny Fernandez
. . . "but I concur wholeheartedly."

This tanned, mustachioed Latin athlete then switched his voice to
biting sarcasm.

"Nobody's as good as that ole Pack," Fernandez said with mocking
delight for those enchanted with the eternal superiority of the dynastic
Green Bay clubs of the 1960s.

"Nobody would have beat the Miami club the way it played in this
game," said Jim Finks, the general manager of the vanquished Vikings,
"whether it was the Packers or the '27 Duluth Eskimos."

"I'm not going to talk about it any more," said Shula, sipping a can of
beer outside Rice Stadium. . . . "I'm going to let other people compare.
This team did everything anyone ever asked of it. . . .

" . . . I can't tell you how much this means, going back-to-back in
the Super Bowl. . . .

"It is an honor to be compared with Vince Lombardi. . . . I coached
against him—and I admired him as a coach and a man."

Best ever?

Bart Starr is a football intellectual. He was the most valuable player
in Green Bay's two Super Bowls. . . . Yesterday Bart Starr was a
television analyst. I sought his opinion an hour after Miami finished
dismembering the Vikings.

"I can't compare, it's impossible," said Starr. . . .

"I'd be disappointed if the Dolphins didn't think they were better
than we were. And I think they'd be disappointed if they thought we
didn't think we were better.

"The Dolphins are sensational. They excel at every phase of football. No one can ever appreciate the pressure on a team trying to
repeat and it's a credit to them. It would be more of a credit to them
if they could do it again next year."

Starr escaped my safety blitz. He was tactful. But examine his
words. They proclaim his esteem for the Dolphins.

They also reveal this Packer's greater esteem for his own football
team. The Dolphins have matched the Packers with victories in two
straight Super Bowls.

But Bart Starr recalls that the Packers won an NFL championship
the year before the inaugural Super Bowl. He recalls that the Packers
won two earlier NFL championships in the sixties—a total of five in
seven years.

. . . "We won 32 games in two years," said Nick Buoniconti.
"Without any braggadocio, I have to say we handled three teams in
the playoffs with no problems. I was with Boston when the Packers

had their dynasty and I didn't see them much. I was an AFLer then. I still am. I'm an AFLer all the way."

. . . "We consider ourselves now comparable to the Packers," said Larry Csonka. Ours was as great an accomplishment as any team that ever played."

You write columns to a conclusion and mine, on this day, was:

"I'll take Bart Starr, the nonpareil quarterback, over Bob Griese now and the Packers' defense over the Dolphins'. Best ever? The Dolphins are super. The Packers of Lombardi and Starr, though, were the best ever. And still are.

That old NFL blood still coursed thick within me.

IX
The Grand Old Man

Pittsburgh Steelers 16, Minnesota Vikings 6
January 12, 1975
Tulane Stadium, New Orleans
Attendance: 80,997

Back in 1933, when Depression I was at its worst, Art Rooney plunged $2,500 into a pro football club in Pittsburgh. This sum, according to the story, amounted to Rooney's winnings on a particularly fortunate afternoon at the racetrack.

Rooney, in those old days, had better luck in games of chance and with the horses than he did with his new football team. He was the proprietor of such Pittsburgh establishments as the Allegheny Sportsman's Club and the Lotus Club. Those permitted entrance could participate in such recreation as blackjack, dice, and roulette. One afternoon in 1937, Rooney dented the bookmakers at picturesque Saratoga. The legend grew through the years. Rooney won in a single swoop a sum once reported at $108,000 and later said to be a half million. No matter, it was a tidy piece.

Art was always charitable. He staked the bookies with cab fare to the Grand Union Hotel, where the actress Lillian Russell and the Civil War general and later U.S. president Ulysses S. Grant had taken the soothing Saratoga Springs waters. Then Rooney dispatched the leftovers to his brother Dan, a Franciscan missionary in China.

The pro football team, first named the Pirates after the local baseball club, then renamed the Steelers after the city's heartbeat industry, was a struggling also-ran. There was scant profit to be made in pro football. The team was Art's hobby.

As pro football carried onward into the 1970s, Rooney was one of the NFL's old-guard owners. With gray hair and dimming eyesight, always with a cigar in his hand and a wonderful story on his lips, he was the most beloved man in pro football. The other owners, bicker as they did, all loved him. The players loved him. The fans loved him. And we, the writers who chronicled this sport, loved him more than all the others. He told stories. He was kind. He was friendly.

He would sit in Toots Shor's in New York during the lengthy league merger meetings, sip Vichy water and lemon, and regale us with his tales.

"You know, I would have been in the league longer than I have," Rooney would say, "but we had those blue laws in Pennsylvania that you couldn't play on Sunday. We played anyway. You paid the constable 25 bucks and he looked the other way. But you couldn't be sure enough to make a schedule. So we didn't get in a league.

"I had a team we called the Hope Harvey's. Harvey was the doctor and I didn't have enough money to pay him, so I named the team after him. That and hope, because we were always hopin'."

So as writers, we turned the wonderful stories about his football franchise and its failures, its disappointments, into love stories, quaint and compassionate. Anybody else, we would have ripped him.

In the old days, the Steelers had a runner named Fran Rogell. The team was coached by Jock Sutherland or some other old block of immortality, and there wasn't much variety to the offense. Every week at Forbes Field the Steelers would start the game with a plunge into the line by Rogell. The fans, the few who bought tickets, chanted: "Hi diddle diddle, Rogell up the middle."

The Steelers' history with quarterbacks was, well, strange. Sid Luckman was originally a Pittsburgh draft choice, but he emigrated to the Bears. Bobby Layne was a draft choice and was traded away before his first game. Johnny Unitas was a ninth-round draft choice, but was cut in training camp and returned to the local sandlots before moving on to ultimate immortality in Baltimore. Len Dawson was with the Steelers, but they traded him. Jack Kemp, then a crew-cut kid, was cut.

The club operated out of a room in the Fort Pitt Hotel. Rooney kept it open 24 hours a day. The card game was perpetual. Actors, athletes, politicians, grifters stopped by as their whims decreed.

Bobby Layne was exiled back to Pittsburgh after he had been used up in Detroit. Layne once came down bleary-eyed but sharp for a breakfast interview years after he had retired.

"They had a little ole bitty office in a hotel," Layne told me. "Mr. Rooney was great, but nothin' was first class. Their scoutin' system was somethin'.

They subscribed to all the newspapers around the country. They'd read how the colleges came out on Saturday. That's how they drafted."

The Steelers took this system—the newspapers supplemented by the *Street & Smith Yearbook*—into the 1960s. Once, with the aging Layne as their quarterback and Buddy Parker as their coach, the Steelers almost won their first division title in 1963. They missed on the final Sunday. "There'll be another year," Rooney said to his sympathizers.

But pretty soon there was expansion and merger. Fancy new franchises came in with dollar-sign birthmarks. The newcomers started to dominate the pastime established decades before by craggy sportsmen pioneers. Pro football became a sport of merger, conglomerates, tax shelters, computers, television, agents, jurists, politicians.

Then in January 1975, pro football unexpectedly dipped back to its roots. Art Rooney was 74 years old and his team qualified for Super Bowl IX.

We were headed back to New Orleans. But what intensified the pleasure was that Rooney would be there. A team with a ne'er-do-well history covering four decades would be there.

The Steelers were in and they would be playing one of those teams born out of expansion with the $$$$ insignia—the Minnesota Vikings, twice defeated in Super Bowls, back again for another shot.

◆ ◆ ◆

Fran Tarkenton was the scrawny son of a southern preacher. He threw with a crooked arm and skittered about the football field like a frightened matador.

"He will lose games he should win and win games he should lose," said his first coach with the Vikings, a man of foul disposition. "And so he will always be a 7-7 quarterback."

Francis Asbury Tarkenton fit well this description for an eternity or so. Erratic was Tarkenton's style—flashy, dedicated, and flighty so that the total came up 7-7. Again and again.

But that was in the past, a history that was now obscured by success and a dazzling array of huge numbers. Tarkenton, in 14 seasons with the Vikings, the Giants, and the Vikings a second time, was now approaching Johnny Unitas's records for the most pass completions and most touchdown passes in the NFL book.

Sam Baugh, a passing legend before there was a Super Bowl, once said: "The best passer I ever saw? Norm Van Brocklin."

Van Brocklin? In 1961, he coached his first game after his career as a marvelously stylish artisan. His quarterback in that first game was Fran Tarkenton, a freshly drafted rookie from Georgia. That first game, for an expansion team that had never played a league game before, Tarkenton beat the Chicago Bears. And Van Brocklin was a coaching winner. Years later, when he was fired, Van Brocklin would type Tarkenton as the quarterback who would lose games he should win, win those he should lose, and stay at 7-7 forever.

Tarkenton lugged that stigma for years. In New York, where the Giants had touted him as their answer to Joe Namath. Back to Minnesota, when the Vikings suddenly lost Joe Kapp and struggled and brought Francis back. His style was totally different. He was not Starr, not Unitas, not Namath. He didn't drop back into a pocket, set up, stay there, and throw. Tarkenton scrambled. He flitted. Hither and yon, wherever his feet went.

And then, in the mid-seventies, the team he quarterbacked started to win. He was 34, and in January 1975, he was with the Vikings for the second time. He was still typecast as a loser, despite the mighty statistics accumulated over the seasons.

We hit on him on the day the NFL tub thumpers took us to the camps for the annual picture day. The mobs gathered around him with their mikes and television cameras and Super Bowl pads and pens. Francis loved the scene. He loved to talk, he loved to preen.

"Every quarterback has got critics," Tarkenton said. "That's why quarterbacks are able to do more after 30. Before that, if you win it's nice, if you lose it isn't. And when you lose, people criticize you.

"When you're younger, you're wondering why people don't like you. You hear that you can't throw deep. You can't read defenses, you can't lead the team. Look at the young quarterbacks—Dan Pastorini with Houston, Jim Plunkett with New England—quarterbacks who are struggling along. I doubt if Pastorini and Plunkett are going to win with the teams they're with now. They're going to be caught in the same syndrome.

"It's historic. I've always busted my butt, but it happened to me. Look at Sonny Jurgensen, he never won until recently. Billy Kilmer. Y.A. Tittle was the classic example of that. They were all traded around and didn't start winning until they were in their thirties. Not many quarterbacks stay with their teams throughout their careers.

"I've seen a lot of quarterbacks beaten down. It happens to a lot of kids who never play after their twenties. Look at Earl Morrall. There never has been a passer more abused than Earl Morrall when he was in his twenties."

Tarkenton had an audience, and he was preaching. The emotions hissed from him, and there was a bizarre mixture in Minnesota because Bud Grant was his coach. Bud's staunch belief was that offensive tackles, their faces hidden behind cage-masks, deserved as much recognition as quarterbacks.

Once, after a stunning running play produced a 41-yard gain and led to a victory, Francis was asked if Grant had sent the play in from the bench. Francis glowered at the reporter. "What did you say?" he asked.

The reporter repeated his question, "Was the play sent in from the bench?"

Tarkenton looked straight at his interrogator and said: "Baby, no one sends in plays for Francis."

The relationship was such that Bud Grant said: "Quarterbacks can't be God Almighty."

It was another lovely installment of my favorite topic, the Quarterback Mystique. The historical data from the mouth of Tarkenton was put to print. I agreed with his theory, that quarterbacks must age and mellow before they can become winners.

Then I suddenly thought—of Terry Bradshaw. Terry Bradshaw was 26, and sometimes he would run in circles behind the offensive line, in the manner of a coltish Francis Tarkenton. Bradshaw lugged a stigma with him, too, to New Orleans to Super Bowl IX. He was suspected of being shallow of intellect; bluntly, people declared that Terry was plain ole dumb.

We strolled the French Quarter at night and talked about Terry's head. I recalled that months before my friend Cleveland had said, quite loudly: "If Terry Bradshaw is a Super Bowl quarterback, I'm a Hong Kong tailor." This had been before the '74 season. Now I suggested as we stood three deep in the Old Absinthe House that he scour New Orleans searching for a sewing machine at a bargain price. "Terry wears size 44," I said. And ducked.

◆ ◆ ◆

When the owners and the general managers of the pro football establishment needed something to tickle their funny bones, the Pittsburgh Steelers were always there. Even the functionaries on the Lions laughed at them. "The Steelers? What can you say about them?" I was told out at the Lions' camp one day in the early seventies. "They haven't done anything for 40 years." I should have told the guy, "Go look at your own highlight films." But I'd been taught to be polite. Besides, you don't mouth off that way to guys who used to play pro football in leather helmets.

In 1968, the year of Joe Namath, the team Namath used to watch in western Pennsylvania was going 2-11-1 and finishing last in what was then called the Century Division of the NFL. The Steelers needed a new coach. Art Rooney and his son Dan thought about George Allen. Then Danny went off to Baltimore to talk to Chuck Noll, one of Paul Brown's disciples on Don Shula's staff with the Colts. Noll was an old blocker with a football brain. Dan Rooney, with snappy judgment, hired Noll.

Going high in the draft, the Steelers used their first-round pick on Joe Greene, a defensive tackle from North Texas State. He was an obscure player, and again those on the other clubs thought of the Steelers' draft history and snickered.

For sure, the giggles were warranted. In Noll's first year the Steelers went 1-13. No genius here. The Chicago Bears also had a 1-13 record. Pete Rozelle fished a coin out of his pocket and flipped it heads or tails. The Steelers won the right of picking first in the 1970 draft.

"You know the Steelers had a history of bad first-round draft choices," Art Rooney would recall. "We wound up discarding them, the way we did with Johnny Unitas. We missed so many good players over the years. Then we won the coin flip when the Bears tied us as the worst team in professional football. We'd agreed that Terry Bradshaw was going to be our number one draft choice and that we were going to go with him."

So the Steelers picked Bradshaw first off the board. Again there were the snickers. Terry's dumb. He's from a tiny school, Louisiana Tech. The Steelers did it again, screwed up the draft.

And that 1970 season, Terry Bradshaw, Mean Joe Greene, and Chuck Noll didn't team up to do much of anything. It was the first season in the AFC, and the Steelers managed to go 5-9. A year later they managed to improve by a game, at 6-8. In three seasons, Chuck Noll had amassed 12 victories.

In 1972, the Steelers selected Franco Harris, a massive running back from Penn State. They got Jack Ham from the same school in the same draft. Bradshaw was no longer an apprentice quarterback. Joe Greene was the most dreaded pass rusher in pro football. Harris was a muscle runner as a rookie. There was a squad of football players around them—L.C. Greenwood, Mel Blount, Ernie Holmes, Dwight White, Ray Mansfield, Andy Russell, Frenchy Fuqua, Rocky Bleier, who had returned from Vietnam shot up in the war. For the first time in nine years, the Steelers managed a winning record.

They did more than that. They went 11-3. They finished first in a division for the first time in their 39 years of existence. They were in postseason playoffs for the first time. They made Art Rooney's eyes tear.

The Steelers went to the playoffs and played the Raiders, and this was the game won by the Immaculate Reception. Bradshaw threw the ball up in desperation. Fuqua and the Raiders' deadly Jack Tatum collided as the ball reached them. The ball ricocheted back to Franco Harris, who caught it and ran for the touchdown that won the game.

But this was the year the Dolphins were perfect, and they went to the Super Bowl. The next year they went back, and the Steelers gained a little more maturity, and a little more impatience.

Meanwhile, they were building a vicious rivalry within the conference with the Raiders. The rivalry was fraught with charges of dirty tricks—this was the era of Watergate—and dirty play. At last, the Steelers managed to win their first championship for Art Rooney in 1974, beating the Raiders

24-13 in a bloody game. Bradshaw produced the vital score in the fourth quarter on a six-yard pass to Lynn Swann.

This franchise, which had been a league joke for so long, was in Super Bowl IX. But it had been a year of hell for Terry Bradshaw.

Back when my friend was delivering his slice of folderol about the fine art of Hong Kong tailoring, Terry Bradshaw was agonizing over his professional death. He had been fired as the number one quarterback of the Steelers. Noll, the evolving genius, had manifested his displeasure by making Joe Gilliam the starting quarterback beginning with the '74 season. Bradshaw was a mite irreverent.

"I'd love to be traded," said the deposed one. "I'm just tearing my guts out knowing I'm not going to be starting. I heard I might be traded to San Francisco and that would just delight me. I even went into the locker room singing 'I left my heart in San Francisco.' Nobody laughed or said a word."

Now we gathered around Bradshaw at Super Bowl IX, digging for pearls of wisdom. Bradshaw had recaptured the job he forfeited to Gilliam after six games on the bench. Noll, bright as always, made the change. The Steelers continued onward—they had been doing all right with Gilliam—to finish 10-3-1.

"If I have a good game, we're going to win the Super Bowl," Bradshaw told us. We scribbled his words down as though they had been spoken by a scholar. After all, that black helmet he wore seemed to be the largest in the NFL.

◆ ◆ ◆

It was another killer week in New Orleans. Dinner—Antoine's or Arnaud's—washed down by the beverages served at the Old Absinthe House, baseball talk in the back room with Reggie Jackson, then back to the Roosevelt and not much sleep. We could always catch our zzz's during the discourses by Chuck Noll every morning.

Noll knew more football than the writers, and he made sure we knew it. We'd ask questions, and he'd respond by letting us know how dumb we were. He'd finally gotten things pounded into Bradshaw's head. Now he was working on us. Most of us couldn't tell the difference between a mousetrap and a punt. Therefore, we were a bunch of dopes.

"Chuck," said a questioner, "ever since the Jets won at the Super Bowl, a team playing in it for the first time has lost the game. Is there a way to tell how your team might respond since it's their first time?"

Noll, connoisseur of fine wine and fine art, looked at the guy as though he had been removed from his contemplations by a begger asking him for a quarter.

"I can't tell if the players are ready to play emotionally," said the coach. "Can you? I've given up trying. You win this game with good, basic, fundamental football. There's a lot of hoopla to the Super Bowl, but it all comes down to blocking and tackling."

It's a good thing my good friends Scoops Brannigan and Cubby O'-Switzer arrived at Noll's press conference, flashing their credentials. Noll was explaining how Dwight White was taking deep-breathing exercises to cure the flu by Sunday when he was double-teamed by Scoops and Cubby.

"About Terry Bradshaw, is there a correlation between head size and intelligence?" mused Scoops, identifying himself as from the *Daily Steamer*.

Chuck Noll looked like he'd gag. He'd been in dull midsentence.

"We haven't heard any scoops," said Scoops Brannigan. "But we've heard some dangerous rumors and we've passed along some hearsay. Hearsay and innuendo. That's our motto."

The reporters in the room immediately recognized we had tough competition at this Super Bowl IX. Scoops had come in wearing a press card in his wide-brimmed fedora. A lot of the others of us were wearing Super Bowl IX caps, emblazoned with the NFL crest. Except for the guy in the Massey-Ferguson cap. Scoops had on his pinstriped suit and a florid bow tie and black-and-white wing tips. He was quite de rigueur in this group of guys in blue jeans with bags under their eyes. Scoops was lugging his typewriter.

"It's my old Underwood," said Scoops. "Forty years old."

Cubby next to him had started popping pictures with his Speed Graphic. He was dressed in a faded green cap, a brown tweed suit, and a mismatched vest. Already I was outdressed and behind the competition.

Six NFL flacks rushed into the room in horror and yelled for their rent-a-cop security guards with the large muscles.

"We're going to mooch as much as we can," said Scoops. "And we have our dumb questions."

The security guards unhanded them. They had spoken the magic words to prove they were authentic Super Bowl media.

"We're bloodhounds," piped in Cubby. And he stalked over to Franco Harris and asked a difficult question.

"Franco, how many quarters in the game?"

Franco thought about this before answering: "Four?"

The buses came, and it was time to leave the Steelers for the Vikings' press briefing. Scoops and Cubby got on a bus. When they reached the Airport Hilton, they immediately headed for Francis Tarkenton.

"Strictly off the record," Cubby asked, "is this just another game?"

"When I was a kid, it was something I always wanted to do," said Francis. "I'm just so happy I'm going to kick Joe Greene's butt."

Scoops grabbed Bill Brown, the Vikings' fullback with the World War II crew cut. "Will you be up for the game?" Scoops asked Brown.

I could see I was getting clobbered in the interview room.

"Yes, I think I'll be up by twelve or one o'clock," said Brown, and Scoops jotted down the answer and a couple of snoopy guys also mooched the response for their own stories.

I have always felt somewhat nauseous about the media interviewing the media. But I hadn't seen Cubby or Scoops in the press hospitality room at the Roosevelt before, picking off the gratis pretzels and beer. They hadn't even been in the throng at the Absinthe House the night before. I knew most of the reporters, I knew my competition. I was forced to interview the media this one time. The Super Bowl press had gate-crashers. These guys from the *Daily Steamer* turned out to be Lance "Scoops" Rentzel and Fred "Cubby" Dryer, from the Rams, masquerading as workers.

"Where'd you get the outfits?" I asked.

"From NFL Properties," said Dryer, and I jotted in my notebook. It was certainly better stuff than I got from Chuck Noll.

♦ ♦ ♦

Bud Grant did not object to the Vikings' facilities. He found them decent and pleasant. Instead, he trashed us for concentrating on Tarkenton and Bradshaw.

"The media make a big thing out of quarterbacks," Bud said one morning. "We don't."

Although he had once said that quarterbacks can't be God Almighty, in reference to Francis, Bud now told us: "Quarterbacks have better hunches than coaches."

It was not great material. But Bud, 0-2 in Super Bowls, did not have a great team. The Vikings had gone 10-4 for the season and then lucked out over Rentzel, Dryer, and the rest of the Rams to win the NFC championship, 14-10. The Vikings won because the Rams jiggled at the one-yard line after a 99-yard march. The Vikings won because the Rams could not scoop up a simple fumble that bounced through their mitts and back to Minnesota.

"This team is not as good as our other two Super Bowl teams," said Alan Page, the defensive tackle/lawyer. "It is my opinion, just a feeling I have."

♦ ♦ ♦

The steelworkers arrived from Pittsburgh late on Friday and then came the purple-clad blond hordes from Minnesota, lugging strange-looking Super Vikings helmets with horns protruding from the sides. The multitudes came together on Bourbon Street. The mobs tramped through fragmented plastic and puddles of spillage. The symbol of the Super Bowl is not the silver trophy, the NFL's memorial to Vince Lombardi. It is the plastic cup, semi-filled with amber liquid. Tons of plastic were ground underfoot. The Super Bowl had become a commercial toot.

It was bonanza time for the souvenir hawkers. The horny Vikings helmets cost four bucks; a knitted Steelers hat sold for seven. Bourbon Street offered an intricate study of the species. Football had become an excuse for uninhibited carnival behavior.

I milled through the Super Bowl IX celebrants, trying to figure out an answer. Roman numerals and Bourbon Street. People. The plastic cup, with the moveable drink, had become the trend of our times. I imagined that it must have been like this during the disintegration of Roman civilization centuries ago. Only the Romans, who exulted to the savage spectacles at the Coliseum, drank from goblets. Not plastic.

Pete Rozelle's Super Bowl orgy took place at the new Rivergate Convention Center on the banks of the Mississippi. Some jazz, some creole food, some conversation. I ran into Lamar Hunt, who was responsible for so much of this: the merger between the leagues, the Super Bowl that resulted, the naming of this slice of Americana. I mentioned some of my thoughts to Hunt. He put the week-long shell game into some perspective.

"This is the battle of cocktail parties," Hunt said. "ABC. NBC. CBS."

◆ ◆ ◆

Back at the Roosevelt, I repeated Hunt's philosophy to Morris Siegel, my friend the Washington wit. Moe had just returned from a tour of the battleground of Bourbon Street.

"You can tell who the Pittsburgh fans are," said Moe. "They're the ones with the bent noses. Those coal miners are big enough to beat their own football team."

◆ ◆ ◆

It was wet, cold, and gloomy on Super Sunday, 44 degrees and gray skies over Tulane Stadium. As always, America paused with great expectations for Super Bowl IX. As always, the game produced comic relief and missed these expectations.

At halftime, Pittsburgh was snugly in command, by the score of 2-0. The Steelers spurted to their score when Tarkenton turned to hand off the ball and, seeing a lineman crashing, dropped it. The ball bounced off L.C. Greenwood and rolled five yards. Tarkenton dove for it and skidded into the end zone with possession. The scoring highlight occurred after the Steelers failed in their first opportunity on Roy Gerela's errant field-goal try from 37 yards. The next attempt went awry when Bobby Walden, the holder, scooped up the bouncing center snap and tried to run. He lost seven yards. The Vikings had a shot after Rocky Bleier fumbled the ball away. Fred Cox missed the field-goal kick from 39 yards. Just before the half, the Vikings' John Gilliam was hit on a pass catch and the ball popped out for an interception at the Steelers' five.

This was one show that did not need canned laughter.

There had been one other feature to the first half. Bradshaw put on a skittish display in which he streaked left and right, then left and right again into a mass of Vikings at the NFL crest at midfield. Somehow he escaped and continued to run until he eventually fell out of bounds. As he concluded his adagio act, a young woman streaked in the other direction, clad lightly against the chill. Two cops pursued. One cop yanked off his overcoat. The woman was more adroit than he, and he tumbled to the sodden turf. The cops, pleasant chaps, finally captured the lass, but instead of ejecting her, they held her so she could be photographed. It could have been a highlight for NFL Films.

Later, reports that Pete Rozelle had hired the young woman to distract the crowd from what else was happening on the football field were denied.

The Steelers managed a touchdown in the third quarter, at last, on Franco Harris's nine-yard run. Then the Vikings managed a touchdown. The Vikings fumbled. The Steelers recovered but could not move. They had to punt. The Vikings' Matt Blair blocked the punt, and Terry Brown recovered the bouncing ball in the end zone for the TD. But Cox blew the extra point. Of course.

Then Bradshaw passed four yards to Larry Brown for a touchdown, and this revival of vaudeville finally ended: Pittsburgh 16, Minnesota 6. Four times the Steelers had batted away Tarkenton's passes, three times by Greenwood. On one of those, the ball ricocheted back to Francis. He caught it, receiver of his own pass, and threw again, 41 yards to Gilliam—neat, but illegal.

So now, Bud Grant held the distinction of being the losing coach in three Super Bowls, fraught with sparrows, lost buses, and quarterbacks who told us classics are for Greeks or who believe they are godly. Art Rooney was a winner for the first time away from the racetrack at age 74; his first championship came 42 seasons after his $2,500 investment. Rooney had gone to the locker room before the game ended so he could greet his team.

"I came down early to make sure my hair was combed," Rooney said.

X
The Graceful Swann

Pittsburgh Steelers 21, Dallas Cowboys 17
January 18, 1976
Orange Bowl, Miami
Attendance: 80,187

A colossus or a resounding dud? We were stuck on the original question as we headed toward Super Bowl X. Scrape away the pomp and pageantry, and there never had been a Super Bowl worthy of the name.

Every year in mid-January, the nation trembled with great expectations. We journalists had seen a series of lopsided football games; eaten dozens of char-grilled slabs of beef; trudged miles through shattered plastic cups along America's tackiest thoroughfare; sat in awe of an athlete who refused to speak; heard the wails of supposedly genius coaches; battered our bodies with nightly wassails; turned into aching insomniacs; been poked, shoved, smacked by hard metal TV cameras; been imprisoned by NFL security creatures; watched tons of ice carvings melt; ridden hundreds of choking miles on fume-filled press buses; had several colleagues busted for engaging in a friendly card game; gagged on grass; been told we were nothing but distractions and nuisances; written millions of excited words about what should happen and thousands more about why it didn't; watched pomaded TV spielers make believe they were journalists; and guffawed at the slapstick antics of some of the world's highest-paid professional athletes at the climactic moments when they were expected to perform at their ultimate finest.

In 10 years, professional football had become the glitziest, most captivating, most profitable sporting activity in our country. Pete Rozelle had been able to cajole and sway Congress. NFL merchandise from Super Bowl wristwatches to books to bedsheets to kids' sports paraphernalia glutted the marketplaces of America.

We heard Rozelle tell us: "The Super Bowl is like the last chapter of a hair-raising mystery. No one would think of missing it."

But Rozelle, this man of Machiavellian insight, had not been able to produce one colossal Super Bowl football game. And Rozelle himself had become more and more concerned about America's dozing habits during the Super Bowls.

"We've talked about it a lot," Rozelle said, "but it's something that's impossible to change as much as we'd like to. The game doesn't have the electricity, I agree. The coaches go into it with conservative game styles. Certainly we'd like to see more exciting games like some of our playoffs."

The Super Bowl had become so lucrative to the players and teams, it had been so overdramatized beforehand, that it had caused its own artistic destruction.

Such were the blasphemous notions I lugged back to Miami, to Super Bowl X—this confrontation between the Steelers and the Cowboys, between Bradshaw and Staubach, between Noll and Landry, between quality and excess.

Before taking off for Super Bowl X, there was a personal letter on NFL stationery, mailed from 410 Park Avenue, New York. The letter was signed, simply, "Pete," and below the signature the identifcation, "Pete Rozelle, Commissioner."

Dear Jerry:

As of Sunday, Jan. 18, 1976, you will have taken perhaps your most significant step since puberty: formal induction into the most exclusive sports society in the known civilized world—The Super 10 Club.

You have already been certified as a member of the club by virtue of having been among that elite group of media people who were fortunate enough to experience the exhilarating thrills and pleasure of all the Super Bowls past. . . .

There were only a few of us survivors in this select lodge. Only 42 of the most hardy. On Thursday night, Pete would be tossing a special party in our honor.

◆ ◆ ◆

The orange ball of flame popped from the horizon in the Atlantic, and the NFL's platoon of flacks synchronzied their identical watches. Outside the Americana, our headquarters again, the NFL emblem snapped smartly in the ocean breeze. On the next mast, the American Bicentennial banner fluttered with 13 stars on the blue field and the number 76. Left, right, left, right. Get in step, you raggedy-asses. Full of Florida orange juice and NFL danish, we marched onto the waiting buses. Off to take Terry Bradshaw's IQ; or learn if Roger Staubach was still a square, or had four years in the NFL stretched him into a rectangle? Super Bowl X week was officially under way. Time for America to stop and salute.

One hour and 50 minutes after the majestic sunrise, the punctual Pittsburgh Steelers appeared on their practice field for photo day. Mean Joe Greene marched in the lead. He lifted an 8-millimeter movie camera to his eyeball. A 35-millimeter still camera dangled from his neck on an Indian-design strap.

The Steelers, defending champions of the universe, showed up with their own cameras. While the photographers shoved and whizzed and snapped at them, the Steelers snapped back at those taking their pictures.

◆ ◆ ◆

Tex Schramm, ole Loophole, stood at the Cowboys' familiar practice ground in Fort Lauderdale, again in wonderment. The Cowboys, once the team vilified as "Next Year's Champions," had made it back to the Super Bowl in the midst of a rebuilding program. They hadn't planned on going to the Super Bowl so soon again. They had stripped the club of their aging veterans, athletes who had All-Pro memories and decrepit bodies. Pro football is a sport of cycles. Clubs rise, some reach the pinnacle of excellence, then drift back to the pack and mediocrity. If they have sharp managements they assemble new players good enough so they can rise again. Some clubs never make it, but the cycle syndrome hits even the best. "If you had told me we'd be here when I saw you last October," Schramm said, spying me, "I'd have laughed in your face."

The Cowboys had made it to Super Bowl X with 14 rookies on their roster of 43. Gil Brandt, the most astute personnel talent man in the business, had supplied this fresh lode for the Cowboys. Tom Landry, the plastic man, twanged in disbelief.

"Our rookies are the reason we're here in the Super Bowl," Landry said, typically without a smile or a tear. "Our veterans said, 'Our All-Pros are gone.' But our guys said, 'We're not through.'"

Bob Lilly, Cornell Green, Calvin Hill, and Duane Thomas were gone. Meshing such rookies as Randy White, Burton Lawless, Thomas Henderson, and Bob Breunig with a bunch of 30-year-old gaffers, the Cowboys became a 10-4 club. It was just good enough to qualify for the NFC playoffs as the wild-card team. A team didn't have to win its division title in the NFL's playoff mentality. Granted entrance into the four-club playoffs, the Cowboys proceeded to whip two 12-2 clubs—the Vikings, 17-14, on Roger Staubach's 50-yard Hail-Mary pass to Drew Pearson, and the Rams, 37-7, for the NFC championship.

"The veterans saw we had good rookies and played better, and that's the influence our rookies had on this club," said Landry, his logic proven.

◆ ◆ ◆

America's sports journalism was undergoing a sociological change. Not all the ink-stained wretches and electronic media marvels assigned to Super Bowl X coverage were men. We had drifted from the glacier age. There were women sportswriters now, many of whom were very talented and very probing. Someday they might even be sufficiently qualified to be granted entrance into the NFL's sweatiest sanctuary, the NFL locker rooms.

During the season, Betty Cuniberti, a Washington writer, had somehow obtained the information that the NFL closeted three gay quarterbacks. Her story caused a national sensation.

Later in the season, I was watching a pro game at home on television, in deep concentration. I was staring at the Cyclops absolutely enthralled with a brilliant touchdown play. It was so sensational I almost applauded.

"Did you see that?" I said aloud, unaware that I had been observed turning up my enthusiasm.

"I sure did," said the curious Nancy Green, a woman whose interest in football ranged from the amours of Joe Namath to what Carrie Rozelle would be wearing to the next Super Bowl party. "How come they are patting that one guy on the fanny? Is that part of the game or something?"

Now, I could explain a safety blitz or a shotgun formation to my dear wife. But for once I was stumped. She said something about my responsibility to know everything about this exercise of football.

"They sure wear tight pants when they play football," said she.

Baffled, I took my lack of knowledge to the Super Bowl, where I would be sure to solve the mystery because the Steelers and the Cowboys had to be the two teams that led the league in fanny patting.

I conducted an unscientific survey. "What do you want me to do?" said Mean Joe Greene. "Hit them in the head? I'm not a psychologist, and I don't dig those people digging into our heads."

He patted me on the shoulder as he commented.

"I think it's because all football players feel left out of something," said L.C. Greenwood. "Nah, nah. It's a form of congratulations for an achievement. A sack. A nice tackle. It's something that's been handed down by athletes through the ranks."

"It's tradition," said Jean Fugett, the Cowboys' bright tight end out of Amherst.

"It's a natural reaction," said Mel Renfro, "the old pat on the behind when somebody's done a good job."

"It's part of the game," said the Cowboys' Drew Pearson. "Your team-mates have been together all year. If your rear is there, pat it. It's no big deal, not homosexual."

"Maybe that's the one spot that doesn't get hit, so it isn't sore," said Lynn Swann. "That's a helluva question to ask. Tradition, tradition."

"That's been going on for years," said Terry Bradshaw. "Then that story came out about three fag quarterbacks. Then they came out with a picture in the paper of Franco Harris and me coming off the field, me patting him after a touchdown and his arm around me, and I said, 'Oh, gee.' And they put the picture up on the board in the locker room."

"It's a type of congratulations," said Ernie Holmes. "A news editor might come up to you and pat you on the head if you wrote a good story. A type of appreciation. I never thought of it as anything else. It's, 'thank you, I wanted to get the quarterback, but you did.' Why, what do you think?"

I thought I'd tell the delightful wife who was so curious about football that's what you call a touchdown.

I did not broach the subject to Roger Staubach. Roger was again a championship quarterback, still studying films, still avoiding the Super Bowl nightlife. When he was the MVP at Super Bowl VI, he had asked for a station wagon as his prize rather than the usual sports car. He was the square quarterback, the anti-Namath. Then, during the season as the Cowboys somehow were advancing to their surprise Super Bowl appearance, Staubach was interviewed on television by Phyllis George, the erstwhile Miss America, who had made it to the ranks of Brent Musburger and Jimmy the Greek. She, too, was fascinated by the amours of Joe Namath and asked Staubach his opinion.

Staubach said on the air that he enjoyed sex as much as Namath. Then he added: "But only at home with my wife."

"That really hit the country," said Staubach, now, as he was interviewed by the rabble at Super Bowl X. "My wife, Marianne, was sitting with me during the interview and she about fell off the couch laughing. I've always thought I had a family image. We have four kids. That's why I preferred the station wagon to the sports car.

"I guess until now I had such a square image that people thought I don't even take a drink. Well, I don't smoke. I don't swear, and I don't mess around."

Half of the writers blushed.

◆ ◆ ◆

In the days before the Super Bowl, as we went around and around and asked the players the same questions over and over, it was impossible to figure out the moods of the teams. There is no gauge to provide advance information about how the players might perform on Sunday. During the morning interviews, the Cowboys were giddy. They were there, and the Vikings weren't, and form had been kicked for an upset.

The Steelers, meanwhile, were crabby and bored at their digs at Miami Lakes. They were excellent and they knew it and you could see them swagger and preen. This was a team of guzzlers and renegades. They had waltzed through the AFC season with a 12-2 record. Then they had pasted the Colts in the playoffs and then their blood enemies from Oakland in the AFC championship game.

They had gone through the Super Bowl hoopla before. It was fresh and fun for them once, but now it was distasteful and superfluous.

"Let's get this over with and go home," said Ernie Holmes, who at times would carve his haircut into a stubby arrow resting on an otherwise shaven skull.

Holmes was no guy to fool around with. A couple of years earlier, during the off-season, he had turned sniper on an overpass of the Ohio Turnpike, taking potshots at a cop in a helicopter.

"I'm so mad I can eat these palm trees," Holmes said. "I don't like this place. It's for people with arthritis. They come here to play golf or die. All that's out here are these mosquitoes and space. This is no place for champions.

"As a champion, I'd like to have some hip-hip hooray going into another championship game."

"We're not as emotional as last year because we're better," said Bradshaw.

♦ ♦ ♦

The NFL had a crisis. It had sold the 80,187 tickets to the Orange Bowl months before. Corporations had discovered the Super Bowl as a terrific place to wine and dine their clients for a few days. The ticket price was now $20, and ersatz tickets were popping up and being purchased as genuine. A guy bought 18 of the bogus tickets for $30 apiece. When the ink began to smudge, he yelled copper.

"We could see right away they were counterfeit," said Jim Kensil, Rozelle's top aide. "But it was an expensive counterfeit job. These have different row and seat numbers. Usually, the numbers are all the same because it's cheaper."

The NFL couldn't give the the money back to the guy who paid $30 for the phony tickets. But it did give him a letter so he could prove his business expense to the IRS.

♦ ♦ ♦

Pete Rozelle tossed a very nice, semiprivate party for all the guys of his Super 10 Club, although it could not be classified as our biggest thrill since reaching puberty. A few speeches, some food, some drink, lots of memories tossed around with Super-Bowl-hardened perennials such as Edwin Pope, Dave Klein, Mel Durslag, Jerry Izenberg, Dick Connor, Will McDonough, Normie Miller, Pat Harmon, and others.

♦ ♦ ♦

Chuck Noll apparently had spent the past year at charm school to prepare for his encore at the Super Bowl.

"All teams who get to the Super Bowl are good on defense," he told us at the Friday press conference. "In order to win, you first don't lose it." Most of the media experts in his audience agreed.

"An expert," said Noll, "is a person who can make a statement and not have to prove it."

♦ ♦ ♦

Pete Rozelle rented the Hialeah Race Track for his Super Bowl X party on Friday night. On the stately grounds, amid the pink flamingos, the Super Bowl press and selected NFL guests freeloaded al fresco. We stood around and talked about Pete's class and why couldn't he have a football game to match the party? We munched his seafood and vittles. Bands played and, as luck would have it, the stables nearby were unoccupied, and the prevailing winds blew away from the party.

♦ ♦ ♦

The California papers headlined: *Florida Freezes for Super Bowl!* Pete Rozelle's concept of the warm-weather site, the fun and game, had turned to junk. On Sunday morning, as we lined up for the brunch at the Americana, Miami Beach shivered.

Lynn Swann woke up at the Steelers' headquarters wondering if there might be a bounty on his fragile head. He had been crunched and KO'ed in the AFC championship game by the Oakland safeties, Jack Tatum and George Atkinson. Chuck Noll barked about dirty football, saying, with clear accusations, that there was a criminal element in the NFL. Swann went to the hospital with a concussion.

Two weeks later, he was barely prepared to play in the Super Bowl. He had missed the critical workouts. The doctors had warned at midweek that another severe knock to the head could result in permanent damage. Swann mulled over the decision, his choice, whether to play. Then he read the newspaper, the quote from Cliff Harris, the Dallas safety. "I'm not going to hurt anyone intentionally," Harris had said. "But getting hit again while he's on a pass route must be in the back of Swann's mind. I know it would be in the back of my mind."

Swann made his decision as he read the statement. "The hell with it, I'm gonna play." The thought ripped through Swann's battered head, and he told his coach and his teammates he would play.

The announcement was relayed to us. "I'm still not 100 percent," Swann said. "I value my health, but I've had no dizzy spells. I read what Harris said. He was trying to intimidate me. He said I'd be afraid out there. He needn't worry. He doesn't know Lynn Swann. He can't scare me or the team."

◆ ◆ ◆

Super Bowl X began with the customary pomp and circumstance. Up With People provided a trendy rendition of "The Star-Spangled Banner." The jets streaked through the sky. The Goodyear blimp lumbered above the Orange Bowl. We did not know that it was being used as a Hollywood prop and we were all extras in the film *Black Sunday*. In the terrorist movie, all the 80,187 spectators at Super Bowl X were targeted for death by darts fired from the blimp. Thank heavens quick thinking saved us all.

In the early moments of the real-life game, Super Bowl X looked like a replay from the Super Bowl of the year before. Same script. On the first series, Bobby Walden, the Steelers' punter, reached for a low snap. He couldn't get his foot up to the football, and he was tackled at the 29. Staubach needed one play to put the upstart Cowboys, underdogs by six, in front. He fired to Drew Pearson on a crossing pattern for the touchdown.

The Steelers came back. Bradshaw sent Swann streaking up the sideline to the right. The pass drifted high, in an arc, and as the ball came down Lynn Swann seemed to take off and glide. He caught the ball, twisting to keep his feet inbounds, at the 16. Moments later Bradshaw tied the score at 7-7 with a five-yard pass to Randy Grossman.

In the second quarter, Dallas regained the lead. Toni Fritsch, the bald Austrian import, booted a 36-yard field goal. Back came the Steelers, and Bradshaw again dispatched Swann streaking upfield. With a leap, Swann tipped the ball away from the defender and caught a 53-yarder, flipping onto his back. The Steelers reached the 13. But then, just as time expired, Roy Gerela was off on a 39-yard field goal attempt. Dallas had a 10-7 lead at the half.

In the press box, we nodded sagely at each other. We had a football game to cover, and we started to polish up our superlatives.

The Steelers got close again in the third period. And again, Gerela flubbed the 33-yard field goal that would have tied it. As the ball missed the posts, Cliff Harris barged into the kicker and twisted him and wrestled him. Jack Lambert, his face flaming, his eyes pinpoints, seized Harris and tore him away from the kicker. Then Lambert, the angry Pittsburgh protector, fired Harris to the ground.

Until then, the Steelers on defense—Holmes, Greene, Greenwood—had been lethargic. Lambert, despite his youth and newness to the defense, had become its spirit leader.

The game continued with the Cowboys clinging to their three-point lead into the fourth quarter. The Steelers trimmed it to one point nearly four minutes into the fourth. Reggie Harrison blocked Mitch Hoopes's punt and the ball bounced through Dallas's end zone and out for a safety. Dallas 10, Pittsburgh 9.

Now Gerela redeemed himself. The Steelers got the ball on the free kick after the safety and marched again. Gerela was good on a 36-yard field goal, making the score Pittsburgh 12, Dallas 10. Next, Mike Wagner intercepted a pass by Staubach and brought the ball back to the Dallas seven. Gerela kicked an 18-yard field goal. Pittsburgh 15, Dallas 10.

Six plus minutes remained for the Cowboys to score a touchdown and win. They couldn't move and the Steelers started at their 30. Terry Bradshaw dropped back, and again Lynn Swann was streaking far upfield. Bradshaw escaped the Dallas blitz and threw it. Swann kept running and crossed over toward the center of the field. Mark Washington, the Dallas cornerback, ran step for step with him. Then Swann tooled into overdrive. At the five, Swann reached and grabbed the pass with the tips of his fingers and kept right on running for the touchdown. The play went 64 yards, and America watched agog because plays like that had not happened before in the Super Bowls. The Steelers missed the point after, but it didn't seem to matter with 3:02 to play. Pittsburgh 21, Dallas 10.

But on any Sunday, three minutes is a load of time. The Cowboys scored again, Staubach leading his young team and then passing 34 yards to Percy Howard with less than two minutes left. Pittsburgh 21, Dallas 17.

Still time. The Cowboys' onside kickoff did not work. But the Steelers could not run out the clock. The Super Bowl reeked with drama. The Cowboys had the ball back on their 39 with 1:22 to play. Staubach ran for 11 yards, then passed for 12 to Preston Pearson. Now the Cowboys were at the Steelers' 38. Staubach, the Hail-Mary passer, threw one toward the Pittsburgh end zone that was too far for Drew Pearson. Staubach threw another for Howard and it, too, dropped incomplete. He threw a third and Glen Edwards intercepted it at the three. And only then did Super Bowl X end. Pittsburgh 21, Dallas 17. The Steelers, as had Green Bay and Miami, had won successive Super Bowls.

In the locker room, Chuck Noll's reaction to matching Vince Lombardi and Don Shula as a double winner was quite predictable. He flexed the fingers of both hands in front of his face as if to say, so what? Then Noll said it. "It's nothing special," he said, and he seemed to mean it.

Lynn Swann had made four acrobatic catches for 164 yards, and the touchdown that won the game—the game he might not have played in if it weren't for a dare, and a threat, by the Cowboys.

"I never had a day when I felt so loose," said Swann. "No one hit me hard enough to hurt me, just hard enough to make me want to get up and catch another."

It was nasty in the Dallas locker room. Nasty toward Jack Lambert, who had turned the game by flipping Cliff Harris to the ground.

"I come from back East and all the time I lived in Baltimore I always thought of Pittsburgh as a dirty city, a crude city, and a blue collar town," said Jean Fugett, the Cowboys' articulate tight end. "And that's exactly what I think of their football team, the way they behaved out there.

"This is a team in love with themselves. My thoughts are that the wine of success has intoxicated the Steelers. There were a lot of incredible cheap shots taken out there."

"They had a middle linebacker I didn't care too much for," said Randy White of Lambert. "He was hitting late and big-mouthing out there."

MIAMI—The long face below Jack Lambert's blond hair turns scarlet when the emotions surge—and the words run rapidly and the language is scarlet, too.

Lambert is the youngest and the most volatile of the Pittsburgh defenders. Now it was the victorious aftermath of yesterday's colossal Super Bowl and Lambert's face remained flushed from hairline to lantern chin.

"I feel we were intimidated," spewed the second-year middle linebacker. "Pittsburgh is a team that should intimidate."

It was a super Super Bowl for the first time. Because of the quaint strategy of bomb-burst plays, and because of the hostility of the combatants. It became an epic the way a savage championship fight does or a dazzling, free-scoring baseball game in the extra innings of a World Series.

Pro football has lacked this aesthetic quality in its Super Bowls. But yesterday it gained the drama and the suspense and the theater because the influence of intimidation changed in midgame.

"Everybody had talked about how dull the Super Bowl was, how bad," said Lambert. "Well, the fans finally got one."

XI
The Pink Elephant

Oakland Raiders 32, Minnesota Vikings 14
January 9, 1977
Rose Bowl, Pasadena
Attendance: 100,421

He stood in front of us, huge, leaning forward, patting his beefy palms, bellowing at us, shrieking, getting louder and louder in a hypertense voice that grated our eardrums. But as I sat there, I realized there was a special intelligence in the words he was speaking.

John Madden!

Who the devil was he? I had seen him lots of times on late Sunday television, after the Lions were finished for the day, when I wanted to watch a football team with appeal. He had red hair, and he wore short-sleeved shirts, and he stalked the sidelines as his team, dressed in pitch black, would explode with a bomb-like pass.

The Oakland Raiders fascinated me more than any other team in pro football. This was Al Davis's team, and the Raiders were built with his imprint. Ten years after the AFL fought to get the merger truce, Davis still hated the NFL. He still detested Pete Rozelle and all of us who had once carried NFL megaphones.

The Raiders maintained their sinister facade. Davis was the street fighter out of Brooklyn, and the Raiders played street football. The enemy—all other teams, the league, the press, were the enemy—called them the dirtiest team in football. The criminal element, in the words of Chuck Noll.

They played the cloak-and-dagger game better than all their enemies. They were the most secretive organization in sport.

As he hit Los Angeles for Super Bowl XI, John Madden remained an enormous secret. Davis had made him the Raiders' head coach at age 32, in 1969. Just from television, I developed the impression that John Madden was a monumental oaf. The great Jim Murray wrote that Madden resembled one of those blown-up, filled-with-air, bouncing pink floats you see in the Macy's Parade on TV every Thanksgiving morning.

And darned if that wasn't the perfect description. Until the air exploded out of the float, until Madden spoke.

"We had talk going about us all year," Madden told us. "It started with the opening game against Pittsburgh and the talk about roughness. Then there was the Chicago game when the referee inadvertently stopped a play. We had to live with the fact that we were called lucky because that probably cost Chicago a touchdown, and we won by one point. Then there was the talk that we would lie down and lose to Cincinnati so that they would qualify for the playoffs and eliminate Pittsburgh. Then everyone said, 'Omigod, they didn't.'

"Then there was the talk about the rematch with New England, which had beaten us so badly during the regular season, and then the talk about more roughness and the penalty against the Patriots at the end of the game. And after that we heard about having to play Pittsburgh again when it had won 10 straight games, and how the game would be World War III. But we won, and it wasn't that rough.

"Sure, we've been lucky when we had to be. But a lot of our games had been surrounded by talk about luck and controversy, and the talk hasn't affected us."

This man speaking was not an oaf. Somebody new had joined us at the Super Bowl, and we had a football coach who wouldn't drone on as we fought our urges to snooze during the daily briefings that had become so much a part of the Super Bowl routine.

"Man," I said to my friend Minneapolis, "an articulate football coach."

♦ ♦ ♦

I steered the rental car into the parking lot at the Los Angeles Marriott, the press headquarters, and unloaded all the stuff I had tossed, casually, into the trunk. I had been in California for nearly two weeks over the holidays covering Michigan in the Rose Bowl. Pete Rozelle had selected this same august stadium as the site for Super Bowl XI. So what I did was check out of Michigan's hotel five minutes from the Rose Bowl and drive from Pasadena to Los Angeles to check into a hotel so I could cover another football game in Pasadena.

No wonder newspaper auditors sometimes get funny ideas that the writers are tinkering with their expense accounts.

And from the headquarters in L.A., out near the airport, we had to ride the buslift every morning soon after sunrise to visit the teams down the San Diego Freeway in Costa Mesa and Long Beach.

No wonder newspaper writers sometimes get ticked off when newspaper editors get funny ideas about what great times we have covering events out in California. Sometimes they don't even understand that we writers from the Eastern Time Zone forfeit three hours off our deadlines every time we squat down to write.

Bah humbug! Double bah humbug!

The Vikings were back. They had lost three of these ultimate games— losses as lopsided as Finland versus Russia in World War II—and now here they were again. They had scored at the rate of one touchdown per Super Bowl loss. Now they were on their fourth trip. Before the week ended, I figured, we would be part of captive audiences for Bud Grant for nearly one month of our lives.

The Los Angeles papers had party time. Jim Murray mused in the *Times* that the Vikings never should have been granted their visas to enter California. He appealed that the Vikings must be protected under the Geneva Convention and by the Red Cross. All Oakland touchdowns should be worth only four points, he wrote, and Pete Rozelle should limit the Raiders to 10 players on the field at any time—and Kenny Stabler should be forced to pass right-handed.

Minnesota is a rather provincial place, and its citizenry took some umbrage at the reaction of the Californians.

"Negative," said my friend Minneapolis, a man of purple passions and purple undergarments.

But then California is a provincial place itself. And Californians took umbrage when the Florida papers covering the Super Bowl headlined: *Super Bowl Swamped by Daily Rains.*

♦ ♦ ♦

I yearned to write a definitive piece about the Raiders. I wanted to capture the essence of this team that wore black, that played with the motto of "Pride and Poise," this team that Al Davis operated in the shadows, in the netherworld of football, even after all these years censoring the initials NFL from his club's press guide. In an era of high-profile propaganda and tub-thumpery, the Raiders were the only organization in professional sports that did not have a functionary designated as public relations director—translation: press agent, flack, propagandist. Putting on my fedora and stuffing my press card into the band, I set out on my mission. I stopped at a phone to call my old pal Al Davis. The switchboard operator put me on hold. "You're under surveillance," she said. Then the line went dead.

Never to be rebuffed, I smeared charcoal across my face at dusk one morning, dressed in my camouflage suit, snipped the barbed wire, and then scaled the wall into the Raiders' encampment. Al LoCasale apprehended me as I hit earth on the other side. I had known LoCasale for maybe 20 years, ever since he had done the scouting circuit on the college campuses, looking for prized prospects. Now he was the top henchman of Al Davis. He waved a newspaper in my face. Somehow the Raiders have put together a network that enables them to obtain newspapers in all the enemy cities around the NFL as soon as they come off the presses. LoCasale had a copy of the Detroit *News* from the other day, when I had written a column about the Raiders' KGB secrecy. He wore a grin that indicated he thought I was a smart ass. He also wore a cap with the Raiders' shield on the front and scrambled eggs on the visor.

"I see they've promoted you to commander," I said, snapping a smart salute.

"Apparently our German shepherd didn't pick up the scent, and you got in," LoCasale said to me.

"How come the Raiders bill themselves as the Good Guys?" I asked LoCasale, figuring to shoot while I had the chance.

"Black is bad," LoCasale told me. "You know, the good guys wear the white hats. Black connotes evil. It's dirt. It means crime. It's bad. Well, the Raiders wear black shirts, and our fans realize the guys in black shirts are the good guys. It's that kind of image that's part of the mystique of the Raiders.

"The Good Guys. They talk about how Chuck Fairbanks improved New England. That was nothing. When Al Davis got to Oakland in 1963, we were the trash can of the American Football League. The club was moving to Portland one day, somewhere else the next. It played home games in three stadiums in three years. It had no money and no draft choices. Al Davis took it from 1-13 to 10-4 in one year. We haven't been down since."

Since I was his prisoner, LoCasale felt safe enough to pass along some of the Raiders' lore. He told me about the mighty defense the Raiders would be throwing at Fran Tarkenton on Sunday. It was a defense that consisted of code names: Mad Stork, Matzoh Ball, Dr. Death, Whiskey Man, Trunk, and Tooz. LoCasale blabbed out the program names of these agents of devastation and defeat: Ted Hendricks, Monte Johnson, Skip Thomas, Willie Brown, Otis Sistrunk, and John Matuszak.

"Ahh, Otis, guy with the shaved head and the heavy lids," I said back to LoCasale. "From the University of Mars."

"That's him." Then he told me that Bud Grant would never be able to decode the offense, the passes from the Snake to Blinky and the Ghost. He clued me in on their true identities: Snake Stabler, Blinky Fred Biletnikoff, and Ghost Dave Casper.

"Yeah," I said, "but Bud Grant has got you guys on Super Bowl experience."

"Hah," said LoCasale, "but the Pink Elephant has never lost a Super Bowl game."

"Pink Elephant?"

"John Madden to you," said my informant. Then he told me the nickname for the team doctor: Needles.

I tried to wiggle free, but he had me trapped. "Here's another," he said and told me about the Raiders' annual ritual when they arrive at training camp in Santa Rosa in July. The Raiders put on a parade to announce their return to the townsfolk and proclaim that their annual club air hockey, bar bowling, and ping pong tournaments would soon be in full swing. Phil Villapiano, the linebacker, was in charge. He commandeers a fleet of convertibles, LoCosale told me, decks them out with bunting, and converts them into parade floats.

"I presume they wire-jump the engines on the cars," I said, and LoCasale threatened me with an electrified wand.

He continued by telling me the rules for the air hockey and other tournaments, strictly enforced by Commissioner Villapiano:
1. Drinking is mandatory. Urine tests will be given to all competitors after events to make sure they have been drinking.
2. Cheating is encouraged. The most inventive cheaters will be awarded prizes.
3. Verbal abuse of all opponents is encouraged.
4. But physical abuse won't be allowed.

"We don't condone violence," LoCasale told me. Then he surprised me because I presumed I would be led away to a cell and miss the Super Bowl party and everything until the game was over.

"We're going to let you go," LoCasale said. "We think you'll spread the Good Guys Gospel. And remember, I'll have your paper here tomorrow."

◆ ◆ ◆

I filed the column back to Detroit and went out to dinner, privileged to be in august company. I was invited to join a group with the great, great Red Smith, still writing phrases of brilliance, along with the renowned Jack Murphy from San Diego and the renowned Blackie Sherrod from Dallas. We went to a small Italian ristorante with red and white squares on the tablecloths. I didn't utter a peep. Just listened to the conversation. It was priceless.

Next morning, early, I went out to the Vikings' camp to hear what speech Fran Tarkenton had prepared this time. He was a personal 0-and-2 as a Super Bowl quarterback. The Vikings had added a comic element to this Super Bowl XI; the piety of the event had been stripped away by our uproarious laughter. Memories flashed. We had giggled, too, eight years ago at Super Bowl III when we finally caught up with Joe Willie Namath, poolside.

"We want the whole world to know this time we're going to win the Super Bowl," said the quarterback of the Super Bowl's only triple loser.

He looked at us squarely, speaking with his scrambler's run-off-at-the-mouth bravado. Again there was the connection from one Super Bowl through the years to another. This was Super Bowl déjà vu. Francis avoided use of Namath's choice word, *guarantee,* the guarantee that the Jets would beat the Colts, but he had delivered the same boast. The Vikings weren't the heavy 18-point underdogs the Jets had been eight years earlier; the betting spread arranged by Jimmy the Greek was a mere four points in favor of Oakland. Still, the Vikings were in California with the stigma and shame of three Super Bowl defeats.

"There's an obsession with this team to win this game," Tarkenton said. He was pressing 37 and had etched the fanciest passing records in football's archives. Most completions, most touchdown passes, most yardage. More than Starr, Luckman, Baugh, Layne, Otto Graham. But fewest world championships.

The Vikings reached this Super Bowl with victories over a collection of lightweights and the ill-starred. They had survived through the season with remarkable use of the occult. Perhaps they had a pact with the devil. Teams get lucky, and this Minnesota team had been chock-full of good luck through the '76 season. They kept rolling sevens while their opponents came up craps. I wrote:

If they were playing this Super Bowl in Las Vegas, the Vikings would break the town. . . . The football bounces for them better than any other team in creation. It hits Sammy White in the head, rolls down his arm and across his tummy and into his hands for a touchdown. The other team scores what should be a tying touchdown, but the holder juggles the PAT snap in his concrete fingers and the Vikings still lead.

The Vikings' most potent weapon was the blocked kick. One blocked kick might be skill. Two might be the result of better talent. But during this season, the Vikings blocked 15 kicks. That had to be sheer luck. Fifteen inopportune breakdowns by the opposition.

Football can be a funny game. The Vikings discovered that at Super Bowl IX, when they spent the day following the bobbled ball. Now they were in the Super Bowl because the Rams went for a field goal after reaching the six-inch line in the NFC championship game. Tom Dempsey, who had once kicked the 63-yard field goal, missed the 19-yard field goal. It was blocked. It bounced. Bobby Bryant scooped up the ball and ran 90 yards with it, and the Vikings had a touchdown rather than the Rams. The Vikings won the game, 24-13. That play typified the season. The Lions goofed up the extra point that would have produced the tie; the Bears screwed up two extra points. The Vikings had an annual feast in their own division, the NFC Central. No rival in the group—the beloved Lions, the Bears, or the Packers—had been able to put together a winning record during any of the previous four seasons. The Vikings had a softer trip to the playoffs than any other qualified team in pro football.

In this season, they were 11-2-1 for the regular schedule and then bumped off the Redskins in their first playoff game. The Rams, on Chuck Knox's decision in the first quarter to shoot from inches for the field goal that backfired, succumbed due to their own flaws, not due to the Vikings' dubious skills.

Two or maybe three other clubs in the NFC were more generously talented than the Vikings. The Cowboys and the Rams, for certain, and perhaps the Cardinals. The AFC had become the dominant half of Rozelle's conglomerate. AFL/AFC clubs had won seven of the previous eight Super Bowls, the legacy of Joe Namath and months of negotiating across the DMZ. And now the Raiders, Steelers, Bengals, and perhaps the Colts and Patriots, were superior to the Vikings.

Despite Tarkenton's bleatings, I chalked the Vikings as perhaps the number eight or number nine team in the entire NFL.

"The Raiders have the best personnel in football," Grant insisted. Abominable Snowman Bud also took notice of the daily rains and told us: "Baby, you don't have to shovel this, it runs off."

◆ ◆ ◆

I thought I wrote good stuff about the Raiders. No way did I want to be responsible for costing the Raiders a Super Bowl and having Al Davis stuffing me in a vendetta years later.

So I wrote that the Raiders were very happy, finally, to be back at the Super Bowl after all these years. I wrote that they had been in the AFL/AFC championship game six times in the previous eight years and had lost those six games due to an assortment of misadventures. Such as a pox placed on them by Pete Rozelle. Now they had smashed his hex and beaten the violent, archenemy Steelers, and Al Davis was back at the Super Bowl where he belonged. I wrote that the Raiders had been brilliant all season with Kenny Stabler and their code-named athletes in posting a 13-1 record. I wrote that despite all the complaints by the Patriots that George Atkinson bashed Russ Francis's nose in the playoff game and that the officials goofed on a New England penalty that led to the Raiders' winning touchdown with 10 seconds left, the 24-21 victory was justified. I wrote that they turned the Steelers to cream puffs in the 24-7 victory in the AFC championship, and contrary to what everybody else said about injuries keeping Franco Harris and Rocky Bleier out of the game, that they didn't play because they were scared.

I figured I'd get a cap with scrambled eggs on it and a medal from the Raiders. Instead I got a call from my office asking me how I'd been brainwashed.

◆ ◆ ◆

We'd spent the entire week of the Super Bowl prelude commuting to Irvine and Long Beach and Costa Mesa, all the other direction from Pasadena. Now on Pete's party night, we were buslifted on the clogged freeway 25 miles to Pasadena to the Convention Center. It was noisy, crowded, and forgettable, and I wished Pete had been able to arrange for the Queen Mary again. It took an hour each way to get to the party and back to the Marriott. Which meant I was riding the buses twice as long as I stayed at the party.

The rains stopped for Super Sunday. It was time to can the frivolity and get serious. I took the first bus for the long haul to Pasadena and munched Pete Rozelle's free box lunch that had been distributed to my seat in the press box. I awaited this match-up between two teams with reputations for being incapable of winning—pardon this phrase—the Big One.

Super Bowls past flashed through my washed brain.

Only three of the Super Bowl XI Raiders had played on the club Al Davis brought to Super Bowl II that had lost to the Packers in Vince Lombardi's coaching farewell to Green Bay. One of those players was Pete Banaszak, who had started in the Oakland backfield in the 1968 game. Nine years later he would be starting Super Bowl XI.

"I remember coming out of the huddle on the first play and looking at them," Banaszak had recalled during the week. "The Ray Nitschkes. Henry Jordans. Herb Adderleys. Willie Davises. They were guys I collected bubble gum cards of when I was a kid. I grew up near Green Bay.

"On the first play, I was supposed to block Dave Robinson, and Hewritt Dixon carried the ball. I didn't even touch Robinson and Nitschke came over and got Dixon for no gain. I had spike marks all over my back. I thought after that Super Bowl we'd be back the next year. It took nine years. Now it's so much bigger. It's a circus."

◆ ◆ ◆

Vicki Carr banged out the words to "America the Beautiful." She sang with the purple mountains visible to the north of the Rose Bowl, and the sun out at last in the spacious skies.

The pregame festivities ended at last, and—and after last year's colossal Super Bowl, we were back in the rut. The teams shoved at each other for a while. Then the Vikings might have struck. They had the Raiders pinned back. Ray Guy was the best punter in pro football. He was so good Al Davis once used a first-round draft choice on this punter. In four pro seasons, Guy had never had a punt blocked on him.

But these were the Vikings, and the punt block was their foremost weapon. Fred McNeill broke through and took Guy's punted football in his chest. The ball was at the three. But these were the Vikings and this was the Super Bowl. They couldn't score from there. Rather, they fumbled the ball back to Oakland.

Quickly, the Raiders marched 90 yards before halting and Errol Mann, dropped by the Lions during the season, kicked a 24-yard field goal. Madden chewed out Stabler because the score should have been 14-0, not 3-0. "Don't worry, we'll get a lot more points," Stabler told the gesturing coach.

Soon it was 16-0, Raiders. Stabler, passing to Ghost Casper, took his team downfield. The touchdown came on a one-yard left-handed flip to Casper. A few minutes later, the Raiders scored again, with a 17-yard pass to Biletnikoff advancing the ball to the one. From there, Banaszak powered in and heaved Pete Rozelle's football to the customers in the seats.

Halftime was a relief. Pete Rozelle had gone to Walt Disney's studios to provide the entertainment. We had Mickey Mouse, live and in person.

Mann kicked a 40-yard field goal to up Oakland's lead to 19-0. Then Tarkenton managed a touchdown on a seven-yard pass to Sammy White. Stabler brought the Raiders back, connecting with Biletnikoff on a 48-yard pass. Banaszak scored his second touchdown from the two and again flipped the ball into the stands.

Tarkenton tried again and Willie Brown grabbed his pass and returned the interception 75 yards for another touchdown. Grant removed Tarkenton then. Francis squatted on his purple helmet, his hide bruised, his ego scraped. The mark of defeat could not be removed. Minnesota managed one more touchdown, exceeding its usual Super Bowl allotment, on reserve Bob Lee's 13-yard pass to Stu Voigt. The final was Oakland 32, Minnesota

14—another laugher, lifetime immortality for Bud Grant as an 0-4 Super Bowl coach.

The Raiders, Super Bowl champions at last, hoisted grinning, gesturing, bobbing John Madden, the Pink Elephant, and tried to carry him from the field. He looked just like a float in the Macy's Parade. But his bulk was too much for Tooz and the Mad Stork. They dropped him.

"We had tougher games than this in the AFC," said Madden.

Pete Rozelle brought the gleaming Vince Lombardi Trophy into the locker room beneath the stands of the Rose Bowl. He waited out NBC's commercial and then stepped onto the podium to present the prize to Al Davis. Archenemies, together in a moment of ceremony.

"I'm sorry the trophy isn't silver and black," said Rozelle, the trooper, bravely carrying on the show. "But it's close. Your victory was one of the most impressive in Super Bowl history."

The men had to shake hands, Davis responding with his loose-handed, splayed-fingers grip.

"Hey," said Gene Upshaw, the left guard who had been with the Raiders from the AFL days on, "we made you shake hands with the commissioner." Davis laughed at that.

"I felt if we could win the Super Bowl, all these myths would disappear," Davis said. "It's like when Joe McCarthy was manager of the Yankees. He got the credit, and the guy in the front office was unknown. We had to win the Super Bowl to bring that to the organization and to John Madden. Now John will be recognized as one of the great coaches of all time."

In the other locker room down the passageway, Francis Tarkenton presented a tragic figure. His numbers in ink on paper were superior to the numbers of all those who had been champions. But the stamp on his stuffed hide was that of *Loser,* three times in three Super Bowls.

"The Oakland Raiders are a better football team than us," Francis said to those of us swarmed around him, feeling sorry for him. "But that doesn't make them better people or make them live a better life.

"What we're trying to do is run through all the AFL clubs to see if there's one we can beat."

XII
The Devil's Overcoat

Dallas Cowboys 27, Denver Broncos 10
January 15, 1978
Louisiana Superdome, New Orleans
Attendance: 75,583

Free drinks. Free pretzels. Free gossip. The mixture can be deadly. And if the Super Bowl media mob made up the largest collection of freeloaders in the history of mankind, the same group formed the world's largest gaggle of gossipmongers. We fuel on all of this stuff, and the Super Bowl is fertile territory for rumor and speculation.

There are a thousand writers with a thousand ideas elbowing for a tiny bit of something different. We come from every city in the country and cover every club in Pete Rozelle's domain. And the timing is beautiful, the middle of January. All the coaches who are going to be fired have been fired, the final ruins of the previous season. But all the coaches who are going to be hired for the following season have not yet been interviewed, not yet had their brains dissected by discriminating owners who have no concept of the proper way to don a jockstrap.

The result is we stand in Rozelle's pressroom helping ourselves to NFL refreshments and trying to impress the guys we are swapping rumors with that we are very smart and very well-connected.

Such was the situation as I arrived in New Orleans for Super Bowl XII between the Dallas Cowboys and the Denver Broncos.

The Lions were, for the third time, about to undergo a coaching change in the midst of Super Bowl week. They had given Tommy Hudspeth the ziggy—Joe Schmidt's ancient description—right after the '77 season had ended in devastation. Actually, they had already hired his replacement, but tried to keep their choice a secret. For some reason, they thought it would hold for a month.

I happened to have a friend who dealt at the same Grosse Pointe establishment that William Clay Ford frequented. Ford happened to discuss his Detroit football team with the proprietor of this place and happened to drop the name of the next coach. A few days later my friend happened into the same place of business. The proprietor whispered to him: "Guess who the next coach of the Lions is gonna be. Bill Ford was in here the other day and . . . " My friend phoned me.

"Monte Clark's going to coach the Lions," he told me.

"Balderdash," said I.

"Yeah, Bill Ford goes to the same shop as I do and he said it to the guy and the guy told me and I'm telling you, but protect me," said my friend.

"You're a good friend," I said, and fumbled around for a bit, searching for Monte Clark's phone number in the California mountains. I got him on the first ring.

"Where'd you hear that?" Clark said.

"Well, I heard it," I said.

Clark wouldn't confirm that my source was right, but then he didn't say he was wrong, either. We talked about football for a bit, what he'd been doing since he'd been unjustly fired by the San Francisco 49ers. I wrote the story. My paper splashed it across the front page of the news section.

Everybody laughed and said I was dead wrong.

My competition was proclaiming that Chuck Knox, still head coach of the Rams, was going to the Lions. Knox had been an assistant in Detroit under Joe Schmidt. He was itching to escape from the Rams and get back to the Lions. He had almost succeeded a year earlier in a plan he masterminded with help from Schmidt, the old coach. Ford wanted Knox at that time and made a hard pitch for him. But Carroll Rosenbloom, who had traded his franchise in Baltimore for the team in Los Angeles, demanded a number of Detroit players to free Knox.

"They're trying to steal my coach," Rosenbloom said.

Now, a year later, Rosenbloom was trying to get rid of Knox after the Rams had failed to reach the Super Bowl. He begged the Lions to take him. Knox phoned Ford. Ford refused to take the call. Ford had been embarrassed by the Knox affair the previous year. Besides, he had already hired Clark.

None of this had been announced. Talking to Schmidt, I was told Knox was going to Buffalo, where Jim Ringo had been fired. Still, my competition was touting Knox as the next Lions' coach.

And Jimmy the Greek went out on CBS with his exclusive prediction: "I have learned that Chuck Knox will be going to the Detroit Lions, and Monte Clark will be the next coach of the Buffalo Bills. My sources are unimpeachable."

At Dallas, two nights before the Cowboys played in the NFC championship game, I encountered the Greek in the pressroom. He walked in with Brent Musburger.

"It's the other way around," I said to them. "Ford won't have Knox. He's already hired Clark. And I've been told Chuck Knox is going to Buffalo."

"You're wrong," said the Greek. "You got it backwards. You're full of it."

Now it was 10 days later, in New Orleans. The Super Bowl media mob stood in the NFL's hospitality room in the new Hyatt Regency. We were drinking the free drinks, munching the free pretzels, exchanging the free gossip. It was the eve of the annual photo day, a Monday evening.

"Who you guys gonna believe?" I said, polishing the official Super Bowl XII media pin on my sweater. "Jimmy the Greek or me?"

"You're full of crap," said my friend New York.

We went out to dinner at Arnaud's and then over to the Old Absinthe House. The gossip got deeper and deeper as the night got later.

Tuesday morning, we were off to the Broncos and then the Cowboys. I stood on the field at Tulane in a group talking to Red Miller, the Denver coach. Miller had a face that looked like a broken fist. He was keeping us interested, and when the guy holding the TV camera shoved me, I decided it was time to hold my turf. The TV guys, traveling in triplicate with cameras, sound doohickeys, and mikes, were getting thicker and pushier. I was standing there, and they were encroaching. Now a foreign hand tried to force me out of the way. So I shoved the TV cameraman back. We exchanged a couple of bleep-yous. But fortunately—probably for me—that was the end of it. We both had work to do.

We knew Tom Landry and could predict what he would say all week long. But Miller was somebody new, with new thoughts, as John Madden had been the previous year.

"I'm here for one reason—to help the players play better on Sunday," said Miller. The Broncos had forced Miller's predecessor, John Ralston, out of his job with constant bitching. Lyle Alzado, the bearded terrorist/pass rusher, was ringleader of the mutineers.

"I appointed a bitch coach," said Miller. "It's Randy Gradishar, our linebacker. I want them bitching to improve during the week. If they're not complaining about something, something's wrong.

"The bus driver took a wrong turn and we were on the freeway another 10 minutes. That was a good bitch. We didn't have any grits served at breakfast. Rubin Carter, he wants some grits. He bitched a little. Otis Armstrong found a cockroach in his room. That was real good. Otis did a good job of bitching on that."

Miller had been a heavyweight boxer in his youth, fighting in the Golden Gloves. I should have asked him for a lesson and taken on the TV guy.

◆ ◆ ◆

I wasn't in a great mood on the buslift to the Cowboys' session. We were back at the scene of Duane Thomas's Great Silent Scenario. I glanced at my watch and figured it belonged in Canton, at the Pro Football Hall of Fame.

It was cold and boring. More Tom Landry. Roger Staubach, the square, had become the premier quarterback in football.

The quarterback match-up provided one element of intrigue for those of us desperate for an angle. The Denver quarterback was none other than poor Craig Morton. It would be Staubach versus Morton, a retreat in history, to the Dallas quarterback rivalry after Don Meredith fell for the blandishments of television. You wanted to hold a pity party for Morton. Morton was the Dallas quarterback who had thrown the ball somewhere toward Dan Reeves and had it intercepted in the waning moments of Super Bowl V. Baltimore kicked the field goal to win that weird football game. Morton was the guy who alternated with Staubach the following year as Landry went bonkers. Tom finally settled on Staubach, a decision of brilliance it turned out, and won Super Bowl VI. Morton had drifted away. Now he had resurfaced in the Super Bowl, on the other side. His old Dallas teammates were overjoyed.

"I think he won't finish the game," said Cliff Harris, who had once failed to scare Lynn Swann out of a Super Bowl.

Harris was a balding safetyman for Dallas. He looked more like the bartender at the Old Absinthe House than an athlete. He had come out of mighty Ouachita Baptist to become an intimidator in the NFL. He had nearly caused a riot in Super Bowl X when he went clubbing into Roy Gerela. This was the guy Jack Lambert had body-flipped to the grass. Now after giving us a geography lesson—Ouachita Baptist could be located in Arkadelphia, Arkansas—Harris was taking a contract out on Morton.

"Craig has a bad hip," Harris said. "I think he won't finish the game. Any time you have a guy hurting, he might not finish the game. With him out, it'll be a different game.

"I think anybody can be psyched. That's part of my own philosophy of football. But Craig knows me. He might be less prone to being psyched.

"It's a physical game, but a great receiver, you tell him you're going to drop the next pass, and he might drop the next pass.

"There are legal ways you can get cheap shots on guys. Not that I would do it. Technically, if a receiver doesn't catch a pass, he's a blocker. Intimidation makes the game fun and interesting for me."

"Do you like the safety blitz?" I asked the man who looked like the barkeep at the best watering spot on Bourbon Street.

"I love it," said Harris.

"Favorite play?"

"Yeah."

"Why?"

"It gets me close to the quarterback."

"Doesn't Craig know your act?"

"I wouldn't try to psyche Craig," said Harris, and the sarcasm dripped. "It's not important. It's just the Super Bowl."

◆ ◆ ◆

I went back to the hotel, wrote, filed the column, and called the office in Detroit. The editor told me the Lions had called a press conference for Wednesday morning. Here I was once again at the Super Bowl, out of town, and the story was breaking back home. But not all of it. The Bills had called a press conference in Buffalo, too.

This was one night I did not stay out late on Bourbon Street.

I was awake early at the Hyatt. I hopped the bus downstairs and rode out to the Broncos' headquarters. I was hopped-up myself. I headed for a pay phone in the lobby. The office confirmed the details for me. Monte Clark was the new coach of the Detroit Lions. Chuck Knox had been hired by the Buffalo Bills. How smug could I be!

"Stop preening, showboat," my friend New York yelped at me.

"Is the Greek in town yet?" I muttered.

I called the Lions' office in Detroit to talk to Clark. He would be my column subject today—no Cowboys, no Broncos.

"Thanks for not denying the story when I called you last time," I said to Clark.

"I tried to help you as best I could," Clark responded. "I'll be going down to New Orleans and see you there."

I floated, gloated back into the Broncos' interview room, just to listen.

The bloody Lions couldn't get to play in one, but once again they'd upstaged the Super Bowl.

◆ ◆ ◆

This time Pete Rozelle had really come up with a gimmick for his Super Bowl: the Broncos!

My mind dug back into the history of the American Football League, vanished years earlier in the merger. The Denver Broncos were the symbol of the AFL, to those of us with NFL roots. They came with the AFL's charter—a team of culls and rejects, athletes who could never qualify for NFL clubs such as Detroit and Philadelphia. They were imports who had played in Canada and kids such as Gene Mingo, who wrote a letter while he was still a sailor in the U.S. Navy, begging for a tryout. The owners dressed their Broncos in gold jerseys and brown pants. Their socks had thick vertical stripes. Not even Pete Rozelle had ever seen a football team wearing socks with up-and-down stripes. The NFL establishment giggled at Denver. So did most of the AFL.

The club did not have a playbook. It could barely afford a football.

The 1960 schedule called for the Broncos to play in the first game ever contested by the AFL, on a Friday night in Boston. The Broncos showed up in their grotesque regalia, and everybody laughed. The football players looked like they'd emerged from old tintype photographs from the 1920s. The Broncos were 16-point underdogs. Mingo ran a punt back 76 yards for a touchdown. The Broncos defeated the Patriots, 13-10. The AFL had been launched.

Within a year, the club was nearly bankrupt. The team was about to be moved to San Antonio. Some local Denver money was plunged into the franchise, and the AFL kept it in the Rocky Mountains. The Broncos played through the sixties with a series of 2-11-1 and 3-10 seasons. When the NFL annexed the AFL as part of the merger, the Broncos trailed along. As full partners, the Broncos of the early seventies, now dressed in bright orange and blue, had improved their standards to five victories in a season. It was 1973 when the Broncos, at last, finished a season with their first winning record. They were 7-5-2 under John Ralston.

Ralston went on TV and promised the Denver people: "twelve and two and on to the Super Bowl."

The Broncos skidded backwards.

Three years later Ralston was dumped in a revolt by his players. Ralston had come out of Stanford to coach in the pros with a Dale Carnegie approach. The players mocked Ralston. He had spent 13 years in the off-season teaching motivational theory for the Dale Carnegie organization. But he wasn't able to teach motivation during the season.

"Everybody laughed at us," the bearded, angry Lyle Alzado told the writers. "People in restaurants would come up to us and say, 'twelve and two and on to the Super Bowl,' and laugh.

"When we were on the field and looked to the sidelines for leadership, there was nobody to give it. Our coach was running up and down the sidelines cheerleading. Nobody was coaching."

I started taking notes.

"Our offense was a predictable ballet," said Billy Thompson, a veteran defensive back. "One, two, three, kick. One, two, three, kick."

A dozen anarchists met in secret after the 1976 season—Alzado, Armstrong, Thompson, Tom Jackson, Haven Moses, and Gradishar among them—and drafted an anti-Ralston statement, despite an improved 9-5 record. They leaked it to the press.

It said: "We don't believe it is possible to win a championship under the guidance of John Ralston. He has lost the respect of the players and we don't believe he is capable of leading us to a championship."

"That Dale Carnegie stuff was all bullshit," said Alzado at Super Bowl XII, slipping into falsetto. "'Hey man, we're gonna do better today than yesterday.'"

And Red Miller became the coach.

◆ ◆ ◆

It is not known for sure if Pete Rozelle emitted a mighty cheer when the Cowboys qualified for Super Bowl XII on New Year's Day 1978. Bud Grant put that thought in our craggy heads. Pete wanted theater in his Super Bowl, not purple patsies.

The Cowboys went click, click, click with typical precision through the NFC season with a 12-2 record. They didn't have to breathe hard. They reached the playoffs for the 11th time in 12 seasons, a remarkable feat in a bang-up sport with a draft aimed toward producing artificial parity. They had their Staubach, and he was playing with veteran's brilliance now. But the root of their success was their wisdom in the draft. Now again, with Gil Brandt's input, Loophole Schramm and Smilin' Tom Landry had come up with a coup. They had gotten Tony Dorsett, the Heisman Trophy runner, by jumping all the way up the draft rotation. Dorsett was worked into Landry's complex scheme slowly, efficiently. He was prepared to use his slippery skills in the playoffs.

So the Cowboys polished off the Bears, 37-7, in the first playoff game. They would play the Vikings in the NFC championship game.

The NFL was confronted again with—ugh—the possibility of the Vikings going back for their fifth Super Bowl. The simple mathematical fact was, for the Vikings to go 0-4 in Super Bowls, they had to go 4-0 in NFC championship games.

Bud Grant told us at Dallas before the NFC championship game: "I'm not sure the league is particularly happy that we're in the playoffs. They'd rather have the glamour teams. I don't think we have the charisma as a team that some of the other clubs do."

Nobody could tell for sure if Bud had his tongue in his cheek. But the world was spared from having to stuff down the Vikings at another Super Bowl. The Vikings had peaked a game early versus Dallas. They fumbled the ball away a couple of times and their defense went plop. The Cowboys won it 23-6 to qualify for their own fourth Super Bowl.

In Denver, there was a new insanity known as Broncomania. The townspeople displayed a permanent extended finger to the rest of Pro Football America. It was not the finger folks customarily use for such gestures, but rather the index finger. Number one. The people clad themselves in orange—orange fools' caps, orange drawers, orange T-shirts, orange nightshirts. The defense, led by Alzado and Jackson and Gradishar, was referred to as the Orange Crush.

And crush it did. The Broncos crashed through the AFC season with a 12-2 record.

"Broncomania is more than just something happening in Denver and Colorado," my old AFL friend Denver told me as we hit Bourbon Street one night. "Broncomania now covers Wyoming and Utah and Idaho."

"Shoot, man," I responded. "Broncomania right now is native America— as much as the Wild West, Manhattan Island, and the Golden Gate Bridge. People can identify with the Broncos. With the downtrodden."

In the postseason playoffs for the first time ever, the Broncos beat the muscle of Pittsburgh, 34-21. Then they played the Raiders for the AFC championship. In the third quarter, Rob Lytle, Denver's top runner, coughed the ball up. It was an obvious fumble. Mike McCoy recovered it for the Raiders as John Madden floated for joy on the sideline and Al Davis clenched a happy fist in the press box. But on the field, Ed Marion, the head linesman, waved off the fumble recovery. He had blown his whistle before the ball popped loose. The play was dead; Denver retained possession. The TV replays clearly showed a fumble, but there was no rule allowing a reversal. The Broncos went on to score a touchdown; they went on to win the AFC championship game, 20-17; they went on to Super Bowl XII. Denver went crazy. So did Al Davis. People said there ought to be some way to review disputed calls by reviewing TV replays. Others said that would be folly and would never be included in Pete Rozelle's rules.

Billy Thompson had played through the terrible years with the Broncos. He was a nine-year veteran, and now he was at the Super Bowl surrounded by writers from across America.

"Everybody said it would be a cold day in hell if the Broncos got into the playoffs," Thompson told us. "Everybody said it would be a cold day in hell if we won a game in the playoffs. Everybody said it would be a cold day in hell if we got to the Super Bowl."

Thompson grinned at the whole bunch of us. "Well, we made the devil wear an overcoat."

The Broncos possessed some sort of dirty-faced appeal. What was it? They made you laugh. They tugged at your sympathy strings. They were life's clobbered souls risen for their hurrah, at last.

If only all those orange-clad bumpkins didn't tag along.

The Broncos came to the Super Bowl banking on a reformed mugger and barroom bouncer, a mortician, a refugee from the Pottstown Firebirds and World Football League, and a born-again quarterback.

Lyle Alzado was the onetime mugger and bouncer. He now led locker-room coups.

The mortician was named Godwin Turk. He said: "I like funeral homes and always have. I just started as a kid. I learned from the bottom up. I started washing hearses, making runs, and picking bodies up. I was in the 10th grade before I started putting my hands on them." Turk planned to use his Super Bowl earnings as a partial payment on a funeral home in Houston.

Jack Doblin, a receiver, had gone from the Pottsdown Firebirds of the sandlot leagues to the Chicago Fire of the short-lived World Football League to the Broncos to the Super Bowl. That was better than his real-life job of cracking bones as a chiropractor.

And the born-again quarterback was Craig Morton, now 35, who had been chased at Dallas years before by Staubach. Morton had been excellent in the season and the playoffs, beating Oakland with a very sore hip that further limited his limited mobility. Poor Craig, he was at the Super Bowl with the IRS safety blitzing him for payment of back taxes.

He was told that Cliff Harris, his supposed friend, had put a bounty out on him for the Super Bowl. Morton replied: "That's a stupid thing to say."

◆ ◆ ◆

It was broad daylight as I pushed my way down Bourbon Street. The crowds were thick, and everyone carried the now traditional plastic cups in their hands. Football had become America's excuse to get drunk. And it seemed as if all of Denver was clogged into this street—the yahoos in their orange cowboy hats, their orange sweatshirts, their orange pants, their orange skins. Monte Clark was at the Royal Sonesta, ready to meet the émigrés in the Detroit press who had skipped town early to cover the Super Bowl.

Jimmy the Greek was in the lobby. He was talking about 300 million dollars being bet on the Super Bowl. I approached him with a nickel-full of tact.

"I guess I was the one who had it right," I said. "Clark to Detroit, Knox to Buffalo."

"Hmmmmph," responded the Greek.

◆ ◆ ◆

Pete Rozelle's party was held on the banks of the Mississippi at the Rivergate Convention Center. The theme, as expected in New Orleans, was jazz. The food was Cajun.

Rozelle's party planners really missed it. King Tut was in town this Super Bowl week. I had gone to the Treasures of Tutankhamen at the New Orleans Museum of Art for guidance in making my prediction for the dollar Super Bowl press pool. Looking at King Tut's mummified face amid his 3,000-year-old Egyptian playthings, I said: "How do you see it, Tut?"

I heard a deep voice respond, I think: "Don't believe the books, lad. Take the Cowboys and give the points."

The Greek had made the Cowboys five-point favorites.

"Most of all, beware of Greeks bearing gifts," the deep voice seemed to tell me.

King Tut's tomb might have been the best Super Bowl party scene ever. Pete's planners blew it.

◆ ◆ ◆

The sun appeared on Sunday after another cold, dreary Louisiana Super Bowl week. But climate did not matter. Super Bowl XII was staged indoors, in the monolithic Superdome. No blimp. No Air Force flyovers. No bus rides, either. We walked over a bridge from the Hyatt to the football game.

Tom Landry started Super Bowl XII with a gimmick. A double reverse put the ball into the hands of Butch Johnson, a wide receiver. Butch dropped it and got it back as Tom Jackson and the orange-suited Broncos dove for it. Lucky for Dallas, the play lost only nine yards.

But again the trend of the Super Bowl had been established. Dallas punted. Denver moved to the Cowboys' 33, and Morton was tackled for an 11-yard loss. Denver punted, and Tony Hill tried to field it at his one, rather than letting it bounce harmlessly into the end zone. Hill fumbled. Three Broncos dove for the ball. Hill recovered it. Then Dorsett, a touchdown hero in his first playoffs, fumbled. The Cowboys recovered again. Then they punted.

Now Morton had the ball. He stepped back to pass, and Harvey Martin and Randy White rushed in on him for the line. Craig threw. Randy Hughes intercepted at the 25. Staubach is death when given the opportunity. He took the Cowboys in for a touchdown, scored from the three by Dorsett.

Moments later Morton was intercepted a second time, by Aaron Kyle. This time Staubach got the Cowboys a field goal, a 35-yarder kicked by Efren Herrera. The Broncos were down 10-zip in the first quarter.

In the second quarter Herrera kicked a 43-yard field goal for a 13-0 lead.

Red Miller ordered Morton to throw the bomb to the streaking Haven Moses. Moses beat the cornerback, Bennie Barnes. Morton underthrew the ball and was intercepted a third time. Dallas had to punt. Downfield, John Schultz waited to field the football. The ball hit him in the head, on the helmet with the bucking bronco etched upon it. Dallas recovered. The Cowboys failed to score more.

Morton connected on a pass to Doblin, the escapee from the Pottstown Firebirds and WFL. Doblin fumbled the ball. Dallas recovered. The Orange Crush halted Dallas. Morton connected on a pass to Riley Odoms. Odoms fumbled the ball. Dallas recovered.

Just before halftime, Morton passed again. Mark Washington grabbed it, and Morton had been intercepted for a fourth time.

At last the clock ran down, and it was finally halftime. Denver had been lucky to be down only 13-0 after seven turnovers. Herrera had missed two field goals, and the Cowboys also had fumbled the ball away, at the Denver 12. Miller told Morton in the locker room he would be starting the second half, but if the Broncos failed to move, he'd be yanked.

The Broncos moved, slightly. Morton got them into field-goal range. Jim Turner, point scorer in Super Bowl III for the Jets, kicked a 47-yarder. But then Staubach, on a pass play he made up in the huddle, hit Butch Johnson 45 yards downfield. Butch dove and caught the ball at the goal line. Dallas was up 20-3.

Morton tried again. He threw. Too Tall Jones reached for the pass and missed it, nearly interception number five. That was it. Miller benched his quarterback—true to the words of Cliff Harris that Morton would not finish the game. Norris Weese took over and guided the Broncos to a touchdown in four more plays. Lytle scored from the one. Denver was behind by 10 again, and the Broncos had been a fourth-quarter team. But then Weese fumbled the ball away.

Landry went to the halfback pass, and Robert Newhouse fired a floater that Golden Richards caught to produce a 29-yard touchdown.

That was it and Pete Rozelle's 12th Super Bowl showcase ended with two quarterbacks who came out of the WFL circus—Weese and Dallas's Danny White—rolling around, groping for bouncing footballs. The final was Dallas 27, Denver 10; the Cowboys had broken the AFC's string of five consecutive Super Bowl victories.

As it ended, a Dallas linebacker named Hollywood Henderson crumpled an orange cup in his fist, thrust it at the crowd, and yelled: "There's your orange crush."

◆ ◆ ◆

Tom Landry had been immortalized with his second Super Bowl victory, joining the Great Lombardi, Don Shula, and Chuck Noll.

Landry was plastic when asked if he was proud to be joining the legends. "Not really," he twanged. "I don't have goals like that."

Perhaps it was a reaction to the quality of the football. Between them the Super Bowl teams managed 10 fumbles, four pass interceptions, 20 penalties, and three missed field goal attempts.

NEW ORLEANS—This was the Super Bowl, honest injun!

I know that to be a fact, because at halftime Pete Rozelle recreated the Follies Bergeres for the millions tucked away in their living rooms across America. Once before Pete had recreated the Battle of New Orleans and the cannon went off and the horse bolted tossing the cavalryman into the end zone.

One of these years Pete ought to recreate a pro football game at the Super Bowl—just to provide something different.

XIII
The C-A-T

Pittsburgh Steelers 35, Dallas Cowboys 31
January 21, 1979
Orange Bowl, Miami
Attendance: 79,484

Pete Rozelle's travel agent booked the Cowboys into some place along a canal in Fort Lauderdale, and as soon as I hit Florida for Super Bowl XIII, I went off to find linebacker Hollywood Henderson. The Cowboys' hotel was built so as to give the occupants the impression that they were in Hawaii. This was pretty funny, because hotels in the Islands are not built to let you make believe you are in Florida. But then I didn't have much time to dwell on the incongruities we unearth at the Super Bowl.

The lobby was filled with my fellow journalists, and it was still the day before NFL's scheduled media day.

We're suckers for guys who don't have brakes on their mouths. And Thomas "Hollywood" Henderson accurately claimed he had the biggest mouth in Super Bowl history. We gathered around Hollywood, and he told us all we needed to know about Terry Bradshaw.

Super Bowl XIII would be a rematch of X between the Steelers and Cowboys. The bad blood still oozed between these enemy clubs.

Henderson looked us over and informed us: "Bradshaw couldn't spell CAT if you spotted him the C and the T."

America's football writers, some of us not noted for our wizardry in spelling, guffawed. Which was exactly what Hollywood Henderson wanted. He was playing us like the maestro leading the symphony.

152

I had fallen for his spiel two weeks earlier when the Cowboys won another NFC championship game in Los Angeles. Hollywood had zigzagged 68 yards on an interception return for the Cowboys' last touchdown in a 28-0 victory over the poor Rams.

"Choke?" bellowed this bearded, run-off-at-the-mouth Hollywood. "I said they'd choke. Do you think they choked?"

The Rams had just lost the NFC championship game for the fourth time in five years. Four failures, and they'd never been to a Super Bowl.

The Cowboys' Tony Hill and Butch Johnson responded to Hollywood's choke question. They grabbed each other around the throats in the most gross mockery possible of a team in pro sports. I wrote about the entire outrageous scene.

Now Henderson did not predict that the Steelers also would choke, even if he did insist their quarterback had a spelling deficiency. "They're tough, they're mean," Henderson said. "This is going to be one of the greatest Super Bowls of all time. They couldn't put two better teams in the Super Bowl.

"We're a great team, a great team. Pittsburgh's been to the Super Bowl twice. They're a great team. We are too. This is going to be a very classical game because the team that wins on Super Sunday will be the first to win the Super Bowl three times.

"The team that wins will be the greatest of all time."

I discovered that Hollywood not only could spell, but he could count. Perhaps even to III in Roman numerals.

◆ ◆ ◆

The press was again located in the Americana on Miami Beach. Did I say *press?* Even though it was not a difficult word to spell, it had been outlawed officially by Pete Rozelle. We were now all classified under the term *media,* which also had its roots in Roman times. Media meant the entire mob of pushing, clawing, freeloading, freethinking folks who worked for publications, electronic TV stations, films, radio stations. It was an all-inclusive word.

We covered the game from the media box. We were fed snippets of publicity information at media conferences. We newspaper guys—the print medium, the press—were being forced to surrender some of our edge to television and other phenomena of the electronic age. After all, CBS and NBC paid millions to the NFL for the rights to show Terry Bradshaw taking snaps. We rode along to provide the criticism, our newspapers paying for only our hotel bills, meals, transportation, and new underwear if we ran out. Access to the games we covered and the athletes whose brains we picked was free.

So there were certain matters that troubled such clean-living individuals as we print-medium persons at the Americana. It wasn't the $4.10 charged for a bloody mary and a beer at the swimming pool bar. The NFL produced breakfast every morning at the player interviews and drinks of our choice in a media hospitality room, so $4.10 poolside was a reasonable price.

What bothered me greatly was that a glass of pure, plain, tap water had a price of 30 cents on it at the pool.

Try gouging the cream of American journalism, and you get a lousy press. Beg pardon, lousy media!

I was particuarly attuned to the art of Super Bowl gouging because Pontiac, Michigan, of all places, was bidding for a future Super Bowl. The Lions had moved into the Silverdome in Pontiac a few years earlier. It was a marvelous facility for a football game, with more than 80,000 seats, close vantage points, a roof, and controlled temperature.

I had returned to Detroit the Monday after a Super Bowl a few years before, from Rozelle's warm-weather clime, and landed in a blizzard. There were 12 inches of snow on the freeways. Vehicles were stuffed in snowbanks. Nothing could go.

As Pontiac and southeastern Michigan applied pressure to Rozelle for a northern Super Bowl, remembering my mush-mush experiences, I kept writing: "Suppose it snows on Super Sunday?"

I learned in Rozelle's own inner sanctum that nobody really wanted a Super Bowl in Michigan in January. One NFL guy told me that. I wrote: "The NFL was laughing up its sleeve at a Super Bowl in Pontiac."

The Lions complained to the league. The Pontiac Super Bowl Task Force got miffed and became peskier, worked harder.

I knew a Super Bowl in Pontiac would eventually happen, and I feared that an area I cared about would be trashed by the media mob from all over. But at least I knew we could give them a glass of water for less than 30 cents.

◆ ◆ ◆

Dirty, crude, big-mouthed were some of the bons mots the Cowboys had tagged on Jack Lambert in the post-mortems to Super Bowl X. It had been a nasty game. The nasty feelings lingered.

Such were the memories I took with me to the Steelers' encampment out by the Miami airport one morning in the countdown to Super Bowl XIII. Lambert plunked himself down at the round table marked by his name on a card. He glowered at us with eyes that were covered with dark, dark glasses. He yawned. He wasn't bored, just almost comatose. This was Smilin' Jack Lambert, the Yves St. Laurent of middle linebackers.

His theory was that if the NFL did not want its precious quarterbacks damaged, they should be dressed in skirts and high heels and have lipstick and rouge smeared over them. There had been a rash of roughing-the-passer penalties. Lambert had first unloaded his thoughts during a gab session of "Monday Night Football," the show Howard Cosell made famous. "If they don't want the quarterbacks to get hit, they should put them all in dresses," Lambert had said.

The quarterbacks didn't mind his words. They laughed. Terry Bradshaw chuckled while checking his spelling book. What Lambert, the Super Bowl sexist, didn't plan on was the response from some angry folk who sometimes wore skirts.

"I got a lot of trouble," Lambert said, leaning forward over the table so it would keep him up. "A lot of hate mail from women libbers. They called me a male chauvinist. They said my mother should be ashamed of me."

Lambert took a very deep breath. "People think a quarterback shouldn't be touched," he said. "Maybe they should put a flag on them."

To Jack Lambert, the ideal Super Bowl would be played with brass knuckles in a square room. Only one team would be able to come out.

Mean Joe Greene, his teammate in battle, said: "Jack Lambert is so tough that he doesn't like himself."

But on this morning, four days before Super Bowl XIII, this nasty-brawler and semi-fashion expert was calm. Lambert wasn't exactly purring. But he was grumping through his blond whiskers in a voice so quiet it would have soothed a babe. His state could best be described as semi-hangover, his mood semi-serious.

As we flit from camp to camp in our Super Bowl journeys, we automatically become couriers. Somebody says something, we rush to the enemy for a rebuttal. Hollywood Henderson, on the Fort Lauderdale beach, had spoken of Lambert. "He don't have no teeth. He's like Dracula. He's a ghoul."

"I've seen pictures of myself with my teeth out, and I do look kind of ghoulish," Lambert said, softly. Then he leaned closer over the tabletop that was propping him up. He hissed: "If a chimpanzee wanted to get attention down here, he could get attention."

A message for the correspondents to take to Hollywood Henderson.

Again there was this matter of intimidation, the word Cliff Harris once used, the word Lambert used when he thought the Cowboys were knocking the Steelers around in the first half of Super Bowl X.

"The Steelers are supposed to intimidate, I said that then," Lambert said. "Now, I don't say we're supposed to intimidate them in this Super Bowl. I don't see how a 260-pound guy can intimidate a 270-pound guy.

"Mellowed? Well, I'm not as frisky . . . because of nights like last night. But I don't want to talk about the way I feel. The kids . . . the biggest problem with my image is kids. I feel bad about that." As he said this, he lit his third cigarette.

"A lot of people feel I play dirty. I don't, but people feel that way, and kids feel they have to play dirty to play well. They don't. I advocate playing aggressively."

"You really like kids, don't you?" asked some TV guy from Jacksonville.

"I like kids more than adults," he said.

I thought it was strange, that this man who had caused so many yellow flags to be tossed, this part Yves St. Laurent, part Marquis de Sade, really gave a tender damn about his terrifying image.

"When football stops being fun, I'll find out what my true occupation is, other than designing dresses for quarterbacks," Lambert said. "I'm 26 years old and already my fingers ache."

I wondered, in print, what style of outfit he had in mind for Roger Staubach.

While the most dreaded of the Steelers spoke in terms of ridicule about skirts, the Cowboys spoke in terms of endearment. The Dallas Cowboys Cheerleaders, famed around the globe, had been captured on film, for showing at the picture shows. Not even Hollywood Henderson had been so photographed.

Loophole Schramm gloated about the cheerleadin' ladies as much as he did about his team. The cheerleaders were dressed in very short skirts, cleavage-revealing tops, cowboy boots, and cowboy hats. The idea of selling a little bust and bottom with the football was quite Texas chic.

"After all, this is America's Team," Schramm would say. There were parts of America that had the urge to wretch.

◆ ◆ ◆

By now, Tom Landry was a dead act.

"I'm not sure this place is big enough for Thomas Henderson's interview," Landry said as he walked into the sizeable room reserved for his media interrogation.

"I haven't said anything to Henderson. It's not my style. My criterion is when it starts to bother the team, I'll do something about it. It's just out of character to me for a professional coach to sound off. I don't resent very easily. I can tolerate people, what they do pretty well." The translation was that Landry wished Henderson would shut up.

"Did he say that?" Henderson asked, mobbed by half the press corps. "That's better than Duane Thomas not saying anything."

Not that Landry thought so.

"The atmosphere is different," said Landry of the scene. "It's very electric, and everything seems to be happening. It's like a circus. Have you ever been to the circus?"

All XIII of them so far.

There were reflections of Landry agonizing on the sidelines: two yards away once from catching the dynastic Packers, inches from stopping them another time. Through all the hurt, Landry had remained coach of the same team longer than any other man in pro football. And he had this team, once ridiculed as "Next Year's Champions," in its fifth Super Bowl. No other man, no other team, had coached or played in five Super Bowls.

"We know what to expect," Landry said. "We've been through this routine in the same training camp three of the times, going into the Orange Bowl."

We knew what to expect listening to Landry—the same routine statements, never thrilling.

It had been a familiar sort of season in Dallas. The Cowboys Cheerleaders got more attention than the ball players in the early portion of the schedule.

Pete Rozelle had increased the league schedule to 16 games, yielding to the pleas of the TV networks—and their cash. The Cowboys stumbled, and just past midseason they were 6-4. They were in a race with the Redskins and trailing, and their playoff prospects were dimming. Then the old hand, Roger Staubach, rallied them as he had years before, when he was a kid home from the wars.

The Cowboys won their last six games to finish the expanded season at 12-4. They routed the Atlanta Falcons, one of two wild-card clubs now included in the playoffs, a greater reward for mediocrity, and a greater reward from CBS and NBC for producing another weekend of playoff games. But Staubach had to rally the Cowboys in the second half to overhaul and beat the Falcons, 27-20. It was laughingly not nearly as difficult in the NFC championship game as Hollywood Henderson cavorted in Hollywood. The final was 28-0, Cowboys over Rams. Tom Landry and his fedora were headed back to another Super Bowl.

◆ ◆ ◆

Guys flopped around the pressroom at the Americana, sopping up the NFL's gratis juice. They talked football and stuff. Upstairs, maybe, a few writers were slaving over their computers, putting gloss on their prose.

That's when the fire alarms started going ping, ping, ping. It was a minor fire. Some people smelled smoke and heard the alarms and a few even stopped their revelry. Some even panicked.

But not Stu Kirkpatrick, a young official on Rozelle's duty-trained NFL staff. "The first thing I thought of," said Kirkpatrick, amused by his nonchalance, "was going back to my room to get my tickets to the game."

So he did, while folks streamed for the doors and firemen doused the small fire.

◆ ◆ ◆

Our hotel complaints were topped by Terry Bradshaw's. The Steelers' hotel was directly below the approach line to the Miami airport. Planes fly into Miami from all of the banana republics to the south, all the islands of the Antilles, and from every major city in the United States.

"I woke up Tuesday night at three o'clock in the morning," said Terry Bradshaw. "Zooooom. I woke up this morning at five o'clock. Zooooom."

Now Bradshaw sat at the round table in the large room where we questioned the Steelers. We taunted him about Hollywood Henderson spotting him the C and the T, and could he spell C-A-T?

A wise guy asked Bradshaw what he thought about Rhodes Scholars.

"I never did care for hitchhikers," Bradshaw responded. Everybody laughed.

Bradshaw had been the finest pro quarterback of the 1970s, and he had won two Super Bowls—and lost none.

"I'm a good quarterback, not a great one," Bradshaw said. "I don't know what it takes to be a great quarterback. Being great is not one of my goals."

"Well, who's great?" asked a guy.

"Butch Fletcher's great," said Terry.

A bunch of us scratched our noggins. Butch Fletcher? Who?

"He's the backup quarterback with Seattle," said Bradshaw, breaking into a guffaw.

The Steelers were in the Super Bowl for the third time because Bradshaw had gotten them there by sliding 20 yards on his seat on the ice in Pittsburgh's Three River Stadium. The Steelers had gone 14-2 in the season and clubbed Denver, 33-10, in the first game of the AFC playoffs. Then they beat the Houston Oilers, 34-5, for the championship on a slippery field of frozen Astroturf. Terry's seat-skid over the ice helped the Steelers to their victory.

And now he was being brutally mocked, denounced as dumb, by Hollywood Henderson. More than that, Bradshaw was biting his tongue and taking it. He said he couldn't boast back in the manner of Henderson.

"That's the Muhammad Ali approach," Bradshaw said. "I'd worry about backing it up, and I'd be afraid I'd fail. You've got millions of people thinking you're going to do it and what happens if you don't.

"I've just swallowed that image and gone on. I don't think you're ever going to live down an image. It will . . . what's the word? . . . haunt me as long as I play. Even after.

"I don't like talking about it, but it's something I'm forced to live with."

Bradshaw had lugged a huge leather attaché case with him the entire week. All that was lacking was a chain attaching the briefcase to his wrist.

"Inside the case, Terry, the secret plans to the Super Bowl?"

Terry thought for a moment. "Tickets," he said, and there was another guffaw.

At another table, Jon Kolb, the lineman, talked about Bradshaw and a night they had spent at a jamboree in Wheeling, West Virginia. The two Steelers had been trapped by fawning fans and were unable to escape and start the drive back to Pittsburgh. Finally, an official took them to the back of the hall and pushed them out the back door into a dimly lit alley.

"I'm probably doing Terry a disservice by telling this," said Kolb during the C-A-T furor. "My job is to protect him, after all. I don't think he wants it known.

"We came out of the jamboree in Wheeling. We were among all those people, then suddenly we were with nobody. There was this man in the alley. I don't know if he had a weapon and was going to use it on himself. I didn't search him. But he was depressed.

"He told Terry what he was going to do. He said, 'I'm going to kill myself.' Terry talked him out of it. He talked to him for a half hour, one-on-one. I know that. I don't know what he said. I was so cold I went to the car to wait.

"You know, so many people malign Terry. They don't know him."

◆ ◆ ◆

It was absolutely earth-moving getting to listen to Chuck Noll again. He looked us over at the annual Friday media conference as if we were all wearing dunce caps with the NFL crest on the front.

"Somebody said it's a media game," said Noll, pro football's most renowned symphony patron. "I don't disagree at all. I'm not saying that's bad."

Noll had been television-glued during the past two Super Bowls. But he told us what a bunch of jackasses we were for giggling as the Vikings were dismembered for the fourth time and as the Broncos kept slipping on the same banana peel.

"Watching the last two games and then hearing criticism of the games, I know you people are wrong," Noll said. "They were games with great defense. Most people don't understand defense. I'm one of those people who appreciates defense."

♦ ♦ ♦

It was Super Bowl party night, and Pete Rozelle tried to make this one the best of all. The NFL rented the new international arrivals terminal at the Miami airport for the shindig. The party was dubbed Carnival XIII. Rozelle invited 3,000 or so of the NFL's dearest friends to the swinging feed.

What we had was an international gateway, with departures and arrivals to all the points in South America, Central America, and the Caribbean as well as 100 U.S. cities, made into a party site. At seven o'clock. On a Friday night.

The NFL's media bus crossed the causeway over Biscayne Bay from Miami Beach and plugged into the traffic jam. We went the rest of the way an inch at a time. The ramp from the freeway into the airport was gridlock. We just had a party to go to. Regular people, not on Rozelle's number one list, had planes to catch.

At last we reached the airport and rolled onto the tarmac. Outside the window, airplanes were stacked up on the runway while the buses carried Rozelle's guests to the terminal.

The bus disgorged us at the international terminal. We shoved inside. Calypso bands played. A singer tried to imitate Harry Belafonte. We shoved farther inside. The Caribbean theme continued. Young women in Islands dress greeted us with singsong voices. We shoved farther in. With the 3,000 invited guests were an estimated 2,000 gate-crashers. Or passengers off the plane from Curaçao.

All of us were battling to grab a slice of charcoal-burned meat on a stick. Lots of us were straying, getting lost.

Before I made my getaway, I was told about Sonny Jurgensen's escapade. Jurgensen had once snipped at the press in Washington as a quarterback. Now he was working in television, covering the Super Bowl with the rest of us slobs.

Seems Jurgensen strayed from the party. He found himself lost elsewhere in the terminal Rozelle rented. He wanted to go back to the party, but his way was blocked by some people in uniforms.

Jurgensen did get back into the party, I was told. But first he had to pass through customs.

Super Bowl Saturday night in Miami Beach has always been a mess. Sportswriters don't tip maître d's. Sportswriters don't get into restaurants on Saturday night in Miami. But Jack Kemp, the old blond crew-cut quarterback who hadn't make the Detroit Lions ages before, tossed a rather neat party the night before Super Bowl XIII. Kemp was serving in Congress and was noted for handling two kinds of footballs—air-filled and political. I stayed at his party, munching and chatting football, for as long as decorum allowed.

◆ ◆ ◆

The weather had been decent all week. Sunday morning, when Pete Rozelle woke up, the Atlantic Ocean was a cruel sea that churned, gray and ugly. He could hear a staccato pelting sound on the window of his high-rise. It was more than a purring, soothing rain. The torrents came down hurricane-force.

Rozelle went to the traditional pregame brunch. He obviously needed more encouragement than I could offer him when I sidled alongside and murmered: "We ought to move this to Pontiac." Rozelle responded with ironic laughter.

In Fort Lauderdale, Hollywood Henderson woke up in a daze. He was groggy. He had vocalized nonstop all week and was proud. His plan had been productive. His picture graced the cover of *Newsweek*. But even then, Hollywood Henderson did not have enough.

"I'd pampered my nose the night before and had gotten so wired I had to take a couple of Quaaludes to get to sleep," Henderson would admit later in his autobiograpy, *Out of Control*. He had been snorting cocaine all week, he said.

Henderson did not ride the Cowboys' bus to the Orange Bowl. Instead, he took a dreamy ride in a taxicab. In the locker room early, he went into a toilet stall and serviced, as he called it, both nostrils with his inhaler. Then he tucked the inhaler into his football pants to make sure he had it with him.

The rain slackened by the time the press reached the Orange Bowl. I wondered, in my total innocence, what sort of show Hollywood Henderson would put on. Terry Bradshaw had to be seething inside at all the abuse. George Perles had tipped me off about the Steelers' anger. Perles had coached football at schools in Detroit and was on the staff at Michigan State, and now he was Noll's top aide and coordinator of the monstrous Steel Curtain defense. "Dallas talks too much. We're going out to get Henderson," Perles told me.

◆ ◆ ◆

It was the normal start to a Super Bowl. Blimp. Jets flying over. Musical extravaganza. The lilting rendition of the national anthem. Jimmy the Greek's prediction, Pittsburgh by four points. The kickoff.

The Cowboys had the ball first and were in true Super Bowl form. They had a promising drive started and then killed it. They fumbled.

Five minutes and change into the game, Bradshaw struck for the first time. He passed a 28-yard flopping twister to John Stallworth in the end-zone corner.

The next two fumbles were Pittsburgh's. Harvey Martin flipped Bradshaw for a loss and the ball split away. Too Tall Jones recovered for Dallas. Staubach, the old profiteer, quickly struck for the 39-yard touchdown pass to Tony Hill, who danced the last 26 yards along the sideline. It was the first time in their 19 games that the Steelers had surrendered points in the first quarter.

Early in the second period, Hollywood Henderson roared in on Bradshaw and again the ball was stripped away. Mike Hegman, in flight, recovered it and ran 37 yards for another touchdown. The Cowboys were stunning the Steelers, 14-7.

But their lead did not last. Bradshaw quickly called for a pass from the Steelers' 25, identifying Lynn Swann as the primary receiver. Swann was covered. Bradshaw switched and passed to Stallworth again. Stallworth streaked across the field, a stallion, and the play went for a 75-yard touchdown. The score was 14-all.

Mel Blount intercepted a pass by Staubach to get the ball back for the Steelers just before halftime. Bradshaw hit Swann twice and let Franco Harris loose on a run for nine yards. Down at the seven, Bradshaw lofted the ball Olympic shot-put style to Rocky Bleier out of the backfield for another touchdown, his third TD pass of the first half. The Steelers, unlike three years earlier, went in at halftime hugging a lead, 21-14.

It had been a spectacular first half, and who needed more calypso on the halftime show?

The third quarter was a defensive slugfest, building toward a grand climax in the fourth—we hoped. It was 21-17 in favor of Pittsburgh entering the fourth, after Rafael Septien's 27-yard field goal for Dallas.

The Cowboys had just missed tying the score. Jackie Smith, 38 years old, retired after years of heroics with the Cardinals, brought back by the blood-enemy Cowboys, was alone in the end zone on a pass play. He reached for Staubach's soft pass. And Jackie Smith, All-Pro tight end for his receiving skills, dropped the ball.

At the Dallas bench, as Landry paced, Hollywood Henderson reached inside his football breeches before 80,000 in the Orange Bowl and 200 million worldwide watching on TV. As he would later say: "There I was on the sideline taking a couple of major snorts before all of them."

In the fourth quarter, with the ball back on the Pittsburgh 44, Bradshaw passed deep to his right again. Swann and Bennie Barnes matched each other running near the sideline. They bumped, ever so slightly, legs tangled. Barnes fell. Swann fell. The ball went on, not caught. Nearby, with a clear view, back judge Pat Knight signaled incomplete. That's all. The yellow flag flew in from much farther way. Fred Swearington, the field judge, had thrown it. From his distant vantage point, it appeared to him that Barnes had tripped Swann. That was not the case, however, and the Cowboys complained bitterly. But they had no recourse; under the rules, no replay was permitted to change wrong calls.

The penalty advanced the ball to the Cowboys' 23. The Steelers scored another touchdown, Franco Harris rumbling 22 yards in his regal style. It was Pittsburgh 28, Dallas 17 with time dwindling.

The Steelers scored again after the Cowboys' Randy White fumbled the kickoff. Bradshaw threw his fourth touchdown pass, a hard, high one down the pipe, 18 yards to Swann. The Steelers were in command, 35-17.

At their bench, with only a bit more than six minutes left, the Steelers began their celebration. They had their third Super Bowl cinched. Then Staubach marched the Cowboys 89 yards, passing seven to Billy Joe DuPree for the TD. It was 35-24 Steelers, with 2:27 left as they lined up to receive the kickoff. Oops. Septien squibbed an onside kickoff and it rolled, and Dennis Thurman recovered it for the Cowboys.

Now Staubach marched the 52 yards through the cracks of the Steel Curtain defense. The Cowboys reached the four. There, Staubach back-pedaled and passed to Butch Johnson in the end zone. The score was Pittsburgh 35, Dallas 31. And there were 22 seconds left.

The Cowboys tried the onside kickoff gambit again. Septien dribbled the ball. This time Bleier smothered it for Pittsburgh possession. Bradshaw fell on the snapped football twice to run out the clock. The prematurely celebrating Steelers could resume their revelry, their 35-31 victory safe at last. Right on the Greek's button.

Seventy-eight-year-old Art Rooney's Steelers, once the laughingstock of the NFL, had become the first team to win three Super Bowls.

MIAMI—Terry Bradshaw had a chaw of Redman tobacco in his jutjaw and the look of stardreams in his blue eyes.

He would alternately squirt the juice into a Coke cup he'd brought along as a portable spittoon and guffaw with delight.

"I've always been in the back seat," said the 30-year-old quarterback with the sparse blond hair and the traits of L'il Abner.

"I enjoyed it in the back seat. I never wanted to get out of the back seat. I liked it there with Franco Harris and Lynn Swann up front, and it didn't hurt whatever anybody said about me.

"Now everybody is telling me how great I am, how smart I am. And I don't know if I'm ready for that."

Terry Bradshaw has now won three of these Super Bowls. That is one more Super Bowl than Bart Starr, Bob Griese, or Roger Staubach ever won. It is two more than Joe Namath and Kenny Stabler could win. It is three more than Francis Tarkenton ever won.

These are some of the men historians have rated as the smartest quarterbacks ever to tickle a center and take a snap.

". . . I know I said I learned to relax, but I was nervous as a cat," said Terry.

"How do you spell that?" asked a guy. . . .

"C-O-T," said Terry—guffawing and using his paper spittoon.

XIV
The Fourth Ring

Pittsburgh Steelers 31, Los Angeles Rams 19
January 20, 1980
Rose Bowl, Pasadena
Attendance: 103,985

The party stuff started early for Super Bowl XIV, three days before the NFL buglers assembled us in press platoons. The perennially rejected, milquetoast, choker Rams had made it at last to the Super Bowl, certainly a scripted reverie made in Hollywood. They would be playing the ferocious, pig-iron, smelter-cast Neanderthals from Pittsburgh. The occasion called for a celebration on the Saturday night before the usual ceremonies of Super Bowl week could be officially launched by the NFL muckamucks. Strange host; even weirder guest list.

LOS ANGELES—Once you get off the San Diego Freeway, halfway to the Mexican border, you look for Blue Gill Circle. Then a cross street called Suburbia. Then a perpendicular street, Theosis.

"C'mon in," says the host, an enormous grin on his face, an enormous hand reaching out to shake with all those who did not get lost and surrender to the geography.

Raymondo Giuseppi Giovanni Baptiste Malavasi is fitted out in a blue polo shirt and jeans baggy in the seat. It is his celebration soiree, the first event of Super Bowl XIV week. No, not soiree. Any bash Ray Malavasi would toss could not be referred to as a soiree. It was a party, plain and simple, a couple of cases of Coors beer tossed in a cooler, an awning stuck up by the swimming pool, a Los Angeles Rams balloon floating on the surface, a frog swimming in the green water.

The guests are snipers, cynics, critics, and disbelievers. They operate under the collective title of the Los Angeles media.

"I've wanted to have one of these for a long time," says Malavasi. "I should have had it seven, eight weeks ago, but I was . . ." Suddenly, he realizes the occupation of his guests and shuts up.

Seven, eight weeks ago the snipers were shooting, the cynics were frowning, and the critics were criticizing. The disbelievers believed that Malavasi had his thick neck stuck squarely on the executioner's block. He was one defeat from being fired as coach of the Rams, one phone call away from being replaced by the suave George Allen.

Malavasi knows the precarious nature of coaching in the pro football league. So there is great reason for this celebration and for inviting these people to attend his party at his house. In a sporting miracle, with a team busted and demoralized at midseason, Malavasi is coaching in the Super Bowl.

. . . Malavasi looks as much like a Super Bowl coach as Bo Derek does. The Super Bowl is where Tom Landry talks in his soft Texas tones about computerized football. It is where Chuck Noll talks in condescending fashion about the brainless questions he is asked from know-nothing pretenders. It is where Don Shula and George Allen talked about distractions and John Madden about pride and poise.

To be a Super Bowl coach, a man has to be sophisticated. It is as though Pete Rozelle, the urbane supervisor of pro football's growth into a magnificent obsesssion, dictated that requirement.

Sophistication might be a word Malavasi would have to search out in the dictionary. Malavasi, with an old blocking guard's body, a battered face, gray hair, resembles a pipe fitter. He is your prototype hard hat.

"Try some sausage," Malavasi tells his guests. They are ushered inside, where the house is decorated in neo-gridiron. A bashed helmet sits on a table. There are trophies on shelves and football pictures in clusters on the walls. NFL team helmets light the room.

. . . A lot of snipers still can't believe Ray Malavasi is coaching in the Super Bowl with a team that was busted in November. But Pete Rozelle sure would love Malavasi's homemade sausage —if he could find the way.

The NFL had sketched a handy little map for those of us who wanted to hit the camps with our own wheels. It was sort of like the see-the-homes-of-the-stars maps the entrepreneurs sell on Sunset Boulevard. The map had 13 pages of exquisitely etched routes across southern California, the NFL's Super Bowl choice again in the land of nude bowling alleys, Arab property grabs, and sushi restaurants. The NFL thinks of everything. Except this map showed you the way to Mean Joe Greene, not Farrah Fawcett. It was a 42-mile jaunt on picture day to the Steelers' facility at Cal State-Fullerton.

Mean Joe Greene stood towering on the grass, the stereotypical image of the defensive lineman. He was a cruel football player. His business was crunching quarterbacks, young ones, like Vince Ferragamo.

Once upon a time, when he was younger and angrier, Greene snatched the football off the grass between plays and threw it into the stands. He had the image, and he had the sack stats for destruction of quarterbacks, and he had the three rings for three Super Bowl championships in five years.

"We're inching our way further into the history of the NFL," Greene said. "In the seventies, in modern-day football, I never thought that was possible. If we could possibly win this Super Bowl, it could possibly be classified as a dynasty over that period of time. It doesn't mean anything in the future. Just that period of time. Four out of six—it leaves no doubt."

The Steelers had such a powerful grasp on their sport that Madison Avenue violated one of its basic doctrines. The figuring of the guys who run things up the flagpole, and sometimes salute, was that only athletes from the two coasts—New York and California—were marketable in commercials. In between, according to the Eastern insular mentality of the advertising trade, the nation consisted of only Middle American bumpkins. Guys from Pittsburgh lacked the proper sales credentials.

But Mean Joe Greene made this an exception. His image was glorified in two commercials. An airline had him lounging in a cushiony seat, scowling, angry, mean, and understating: "I almost like it." The Middle American bumpkins caught on rather quickly.

Then as Greene mellowed some with the age of a decade in the league, Coca-Cola showed this angry man swapping his football jersey for a can of soft drink with a hero-worshiping lad after a game. The Steelers had become ingrained in the American culture.

Now as the countdown began for Super Bowl XIV, Mean Joe Greene's goal was a fourth ring—a ring that would be symbolic, because he didn't wear the first three.

"I don't want to look back," he said. "I don't want to be thinking about the ring on my finger and let the one I'm pursuing get away."

◆ ◆ ◆

The Steelers were bitching about inequities in the assignment of practice facilities. They were stuck at Fullerton, on borrowed turf. The league had assigned the NFC club the practice facility in Anaheim. It so happened that it was the Rams' own practice field. For the first time a Super Bowl team enjoyed all the niceties of home sweet home.

On photo day, I ran into my old compatriot, Cubby O'Switzer, from the *Daily Steamer.* "Cubby, how you doin'?" I was truly glad to see him again.

"Hi," he said, "good to be back with all the guys."

"Boy, you sure look funny wearing that outfit," I said.

Cubby had shed the tweed cap and vest he'd sported when working Super Bowl IX and was masquerading in a yellow, white, and blue football jersey and gold football pants, what they used to call moleskins.

"You really go to lengths to get the story," I said, looking at the name *Dryer* etched on the back of the jersey.

Fred Dryer grinned back at us. The TV actor in him emerging, Dryer would go along with any story, even now. This time he was in the Super Bowl for real, this time qualifying as a towering defensive end for the Rams. But he relived his Super Bowl week with the sporting press when it seemed that would be the only way he could ever reach one of these roman-numeraled orgies.

"We didn't do an hour's work," Dryer said of himself and fellow poseur Lance Rentzel. "We slept in our suits, came in late, hung around the lobbies, and jingled the change in our pockets. We did everything a great reporter should do."

Like going to Chuck Noll's daily press briefings. Dryer recalled how he had failed to halt Noll's droning monologue.

"It was after somebody asked a three-part question and the guy next to me passed out in his eggs," Dryer said. "I asked Noll what he thought of the zone defense, if it was here to stay, and if not, where was it going. And he gave me a straight answer."

And then Dryer recalled the answer he got when he asked Terry Bradshaw what his hat size was. "Four and an eighth," was the answer.

Mike O'Hara, my colleague for the Detroit *News,* cornered Dryer and wondered if O'Switzer/Dryer could dwell on the popularity of the Super Bowl and why it commands so much attention from sportswriters like us.

"It's the last game of the year," Dryer said. "After that you have basketball and that anesthetizes people for a couple of months. And then you go into baseball and reading about people sleeping in Sarasota."

◆ ◆ ◆

The TV lights burned and the cameramen tried to muscle the press reporters as they clogged around Lynn Swann. It was like that with the Steelers. Swann, Bradshaw, Greene, Jack Lambert, Jack Ham, Franco Harris—they were the glittering stars of the champions, the team with eight straight years in the playoffs, four Super Bowls, and a collective record of 50-and-1 over poor teams that were below .500.

What better location for a Super Bowl than Hollywood? As the CBS network guy said to the rest of humanity about Super Sunday: "This is the second most important day of the entire year. And it would tie Christmas if they gave out gifts."

So it was that the glittering stars of the champions were media mobbed on the field at Cal State-Fullerton. And so it was that John Stallworth was ignored, alone, ostracized, unwanted. Stallworth was the foil to Swann. John, the other wide receiver. Pro football is also a game of images, and Stallworth symbolized the quiet, hard-hat, overshadowed craftsman vis-à-vis the showy, witty, verbose, glamourous, acrobatic Lynn Swann.

"That's the type of person Lynn is," said Stallworth when he was eventually hit on by some journalistic strays. "He's quotable and flamboyant. Who wants to write about a guy who stays at home Friday and Saturday night, whose favorite television show is 'Perry Mason?'"

Swann had been the glamourpuss receiver in Pittsburgh since his rookie year. He had been a first-round draft choice out of Southern California, the Rose Bowl school, in 1974. He played on the Steelers' first championship team as a rookie and played in the Super Bowl. He had been the game breaker in a couple of Super Bowls.

On the other side stood John Stallworth, Pittsburgh personified. He, too, had been drafted in 1974, on the fourth round out of Alabama A & M, which had never been invited to play in a Rose Bowl. He, too, had played on the Steelers' first championship team and was a rookie in the Super Bowl. He, too, had caught some vital passes in three Super Bowls. But mostly he was Everyman, representing all of us, and the spotlight seldom searched him out.

Now, John Stallworth had escaped the shadow of Lynn Swann. As the Steelers crunched the opposition on their voyage to their fourth Super Bowl, Stallworth became Bradshaw's top receiver. It was not by choice, but necessity.

Swann was damaged by injury in the early season. Bradshaw turned to Stallworth. But, then, so did the double-coverage attention that had previously been devoted to Swann.

Nonetheless, Stallworth caught 70 passes, the most ever on the Steelers, as the club went through an erratic 12-4 season. First place in the AFC Central was contested by the Houston Oilers and the Steelers until the final weekend. Only then did Pittsburgh latch onto the title in their own division. It was then that the Steelers hit playoff peak, beating the Dolphins, 34-14, with Stallworth and later the healed Swann catching scoring passes. Then in a bloodbath, full of controversy, the Steelers beat the wild-card Oilers, 27-13, for the AFC championship. Stallworth caught a 20-yard TD pass from Bradshaw, the key scoring play.

But now as the hoopla started for Super Bowl XIV, John Stallworth was again treated like the second fiddler. The role was familiar and did not upset him.

"In past years, except for last year, when we'd gone to the Super Bowl, I'd felt I hadn't contributed anything," Stallworth told those few curious enough to interview him. "I didn't do anything to help us get there.

"That means I was part of it. And now, I feel like I contributed something."

◆ ◆ ◆

The agonies ripped through Carroll Rosenbloom. For years he had watched the Rams nudge their way to the brink. He cajoled his coach, he wet-nursed his players, he saw them win—and then in the terrifying weeks of late December or early January, he saw them turn over, flop, and die.

The wounds incurred in the loss to Joe Namath in Super Bowl III had healed in the sweet revenge, vindication of the Colts' victory in Super Bowl V. Rosenbloom then yearned to escape the crabcaked Chesapeake shores of Baltimore for the sunshine in California. In 1972, Robert Irsay, a florid-faced Midwest air-conditioner magnate, purchased the Rams for 20 million. Somehow, Rosenbloom sweet-talked Irsay into swapping franchises, the Colts for the Rams. It was a ripoff, in Carroll's favor.

But this was an owner of a great ego moving into an ambience of greater egos, Los Angeles. Each year, Rosenbloom's coach, Chuck Knox, managed to get the Rams into the playoffs. And each year there was some disaster, death, missed field goals, mud, dumb decisions, choke-ups. The record was cruel:

1973—Rams lose first round to Cowboys, 27-16.
1974—Rams lose NFC championship game to Vikings, 14-10.
1975—Rams lose NFC championship game to Cowboys, 37-7.
1976—Rams lose NFC championship game to Vikings, 24-13.
1977—Rams lose first round to Vikings, 14-7.
1978—Rams lose NFC championship game to Cowboys, 28-0.

Coaching changes did not change the agonies. Quarterback changes did not change them. Rosenbloom, at last, dumped Chuck Knox after

1977, trying to steer him toward Detroit and watching him alight in Buffalo instead. He picked George Allen as Knox's successor, but quickly had enough. He fired Allen before the '78 season started. Leather-helmeted Ray Malavasi, the old soldier and career assistant coach, was the new head coach. The pain continued for Rosenbloom. The Rams shuffled quarterbacks—James Harris, Ron Jaworski, Pat Haden, Jeff Rutledge, even the aching, aging Joe Willie Namath. But still, the final result did not change.

In April 1979, following the Rams' fourth failure in five years in NFC championship games, Carroll Rosenbloom plunged into the Atlantic Ocean at his home on Golden Beach, near Miami. He swam out briskly through the waves, with a strong stroke. He never returned. Supposedly he got caught in a riptide and drowned, although rumors of foul play circulated.

The Rams played the 1979 season with the initials CR on their uniforms, in Rosenbloom's honor. They would wear those initials on their shirts in Super Bowl XIV.

◆ ◆ ◆

Georgia Rosenbloom was the widow of pro football's godfather. She was blond and pretty in a show-business kind of way. She dressed to the nines and was of an age that was difficult to determine. She was also as tough as her late husband. In his will, she inherited 70 percent of the Los Angeles Rams football club.

A month after Carroll Rosenbloom's drowning, the dowager new owner appointed herself club president. The day the Rams opened training camp, Georgia Rosenbloom regaled the photographers by attempting to kick field goals—in her skirts.

Her official biography was prepared by a specially hired public relations agency for use by those interested in furthering their knowledge. Portions of the biography, as released by the Rams, are hereby reprinted:

> Having shared with her late husband, Carroll, the step-by-step building of a championship football team through six consecutive division titles and having experienced a record of winning seasons in Baltimore, including two Super Bowl appearances, Georgia Rosenbloom has the confidence of a well-trained, knowledgeable heir to one of the NFL's most powerful franchises which has been left in her capable hands to continue the winning ways that are the legacy that Carroll left and Georgia helped build.
>
> Georgia Rosenbloom, a direct descendent of poet Ella Wheeler Wilcox, and a poet of note herself, was born in St. Louis, Missouri. Blessed with a natural soprano voice and early formal training. . .

The biography continued to inform the enrapt Super Bowl press that the owner of the Rams starred in light opera, including *The Magic Flute,* and that she had once co-hosted "The Today Show" with Dave Garroway.

One year earlier, the Rams' press guide had managed to condense the biography into a single sentence: "Carroll is married to Georgia."

The L.A. *Times* investigated Georgia Rosenbloom and discovered her age to be 51, not the 42 announced by her special PR firm. The *Times* also discovered that her professional show-biz career included time as a chorine at the Silver Slipper in Las Vegas. And the *Times* told the world that Carroll Rosenbloom was her sixth husband.

Georgia was also described as habitually tardy. For example, she was reported as being an hour late for Carroll's funeral. She was reported as being 55 minutes late for his wake, attended by 600 people, many of them Hollywood boppers.

None of this seemed to bother the motion picture or professional football establishments. But what people could not forgive Georgia for was that she promptly fired Steve Rosenbloom, Carroll's son, who had been trained from boyhood in the intriguing methods of operating an NFL franchise. Steve had started in football picking up dirty towels in the locker room. He grew up and chugged beers with the players, drove the team bus, and learned the business. With 23 years in the game, Steve had become his father's closest advisor. And he was a great news source. He was a good guy to know when you needed guidance about his father's moods, about his reactions to coaches' behind-the-scenes manipulations, about which way a Chuck Knox might go on the road out of Los Angeles.

Georgia slipped her wise, knowledgeable stepson the ziggy before the '79 season started. The town was in an uproar about the firing.

But then sports continues through the oddest of ironies.

♦ ♦ ♦

Rejected so often, pained, frustrated, the Rams got to the Super Bowl, at last, and should have grinned, laughed, giggled with delight. We had reached the eighties, and it was not difficult for athletes to find reasons to get pissed off. So the Rams groused.

Although being at home was a geographical coincidence, the league insisted that the Rams be put up at a hotel so they could meet the obligation of the daily media briefings. The routine must never change—SB Decree XXXXV. So the Rams moved from their own bedrooms into the South Coast Plaza in Costa Mesa, down the freeway from Anaheim.

The papers were delivered there daily, and the Rams could read. They saw that they were 11-point underdogs to the Steelers. They saw the Steelers portrayed as worthy champions, laden with heroic performers who spoke glib sentences and were worthy of attention. They saw themselves described as an unworthy team with funny horns on their helmets. They saw themselves depicted as a team that finished the season at only 9-7, just a shade over .500, the milestone of mediocrity.

Besides, the veteran survivors of the Super Bowl media knew a story when it slapped them in the face. The athletes who played for the Rams were upstaged by the bombshell who owned the club.

Indeed, Ray Malavasi did have a good reason for discomfort during the middle of the season. In November, the Rams were stumbling at 5-6. They had gone through a three-game losing skid.

Georgia Rosenbloom was measuring Malavasi for a noose and was considering hiring the always-available George Allen for a quick fix. Given a reprieve, Malavasi provided the quick fix himself.

He went through a bunch of quarterbacks. Haden. Rutledge. Bob Lee, the ancient Viking who had once replaced Fran Tarkenton in a lost Super Bowl. Then Malavasi gave the job to Vince Ferragamo. Ferragamo, with meager experience, was a medical student who looked more suited for the role of Dr. Ben Casey on the TV series than that of a Super Bowl quarterback.

But the Rams started to win. The 9-7 record was enough to win the NFC West, where their most despised rival up in San Francisco had finished 2-14 in a rebuilding scheme of a new coach named Bill Walsh.

In the playoffs again after winning their seventh successive division title, the Rams beat the Cowboys, 21-19. They won it on Ferragamo's 50-yard pass to Billy Waddy. They were back in the NFC championship game for the fifth time in six years. And this time they did not take their annual pratfall on the edge of the Super Bowl. They managed to prevail over the Tampa Bay Buccaneers, 9-0, winning it with three field goals by Frank Corral. That was good enough, and the Rams were in the Super Bowl at last, with Ferragamo, a quarterback whose experience consisted of seven professional starting assignments.

The Rams were grousing and blaming the world's most accessible scapegoats, the media. They hated the press they were getting and the publicity Georgia Rosenbloom was getting. They complained that the press kept reminding them of their penchant for losing the important games, and that it would happen again in Pasadena. The Rams threatened boycotting the NFL's most carefully planned press sessions. They just weren't going to show up.

"If we don't get some positive stuff written about us soon, we're going to freak out," said Dennis Harrah.

It was tough to find something positive to write about the Rams. This looked like the all-time Super Bowl mismatch. Rozelle's flacks couldn't feel relief until the prelude ended, and the Rams had showed up for all the press sessions, as scheduled.

◆ ◆ ◆

I just wished we'd recruited Jack Reynolds to perform his specialty on the NFL's Super Bowl buses. Reynolds was one of the discontented Rams, their middle linebacker. He was called Hacksaw. He got his nickname the old-fashioned way. He earned it.

Back in his college years at Tennessee, Hacksaw was particularly miffed after a bitter loss to Ole Miss that cost a trip to the Sugar Bowl. "I was very upset," Hacksaw told us. "And I guess I had a lot of nervous energy. So when I got home I sawed this car in half.

"Well, there are stories it was a Chevy, and there are stories it was a Jeep. Let's put it like this: It had four wheels on it, and when I got done with it, it was in half. It was a car we'd pushed around a lot. The interior was sort of dumpy. It looked like somebody's pet pig had slept in it.

"I don't remember how long it took. I guess about eight hours. It took me 13 blades. The hardest part was getting through the drive shaft."

I immortalized Hacksaw Reynolds with some of my finest prose. Feeling giddy, I headed out for NFL Properties' pre-party party at Marina del Rey, then to Pete Rozelle's annual superduper party in Pasadena. Now I was aboard the bus stuck in traffic on the Pasadena Freeway, en route to a party at which 5,000 people with 10,000 sharp elbows would contest me for a taste of taco. I wondered where Hacksaw Reynolds was when he was really needed.

The next night, Super Bowl eve, I drove off in a daze for the NFL Players Association Party washed down by Jack Kemp's annual Super Bowl soiree at the Century Plaza. Somehow Pete Rozelle hit them both, before hitting the CBS bash—no sportswriters wanted.

L.A. was lucky for Pete Rozelle. He had grown up in the neighborhood, gone off, and become a PR man in San Francisco. Then he returned and went to work for the Rams, first as their press agent and then as their general manager. He was the GM at age 33 when Bert Bell died and the NFL was voting in a new commissioner in 1960 at the Kenilworth Hotel on Miami Beach. The league consisted of a dozen clubs. And they were deadlocked in the voting for commissioner, between Marshall Leahy of Cleveland and Austin Guntsel from the league office. The owners went politicking and spent two days dickering, but they were still stalemated after 22 ballots.

At last, before the owners took their 23rd ballot, Carroll Rosenbloom, the Baltimore owner, suggested Pete Rozelle as a compromise candidate. Pete was asked to leave the room, so he went into the washroom in the basement to wait out the voting, and he just waited. Every time the men's room door opened, he jumped to the sink and rinsed off his hands, casual-like, as though he had just completed some business. Usually, it was a reporter coming in to go to the john. Nobody thought Pete was a candidate. They'd nod, the reporter would leave, and Rozelle would resume his waiting. This happened several times. At last Rozelle was summoned, and the owners told him he had been elected as the new commissioner of the NFL.

"At least I'm going into the job with clean hands," Rozelle said.

So now, 20 years later on the morning of the 14th Super Bowl, during southern California's rainy season, Rozelle woke up to glorious sunshine. It was as though he could command the weather in his native territory.

◆ ◆ ◆

Only a few diehards gave the Rams, with their unproven quarterback and mediocre record, any chance versus the battle-scarred Steelers with Terry Bradshaw.

"They're a team with nothing to lose," Joe Greene had warned. "Nothing to lose. The 12-4 we had this year, the 9-7 they had. That doesn't matter any more. The only tangible thing is winning the damn football game."

The mountains were sharp and beautiful looking north from the press box. The pregame ritual, with Cheryl Ladd singing "The Star-Spangled Banner," was the same stuff. We figured the game would be the same stuff, too—dull, boring, lopsided, an anticlimax. The hard-hat fans from Pittsburgh clutched their cans of imported Iron City beer and relished their thoughts of the upcoming rout.

It started that way. Ferragamo, in his eighth pro start, could not get the Rams' offense moving. But Bradshaw moved his. The Steelers scored first on Matt Bahr's 41-yard field goal.

Now the Rams moved on the ground. Wendell Tyler swept end and gained 39 yards. Cullen Bryant scored from the one. The Rams were ahead, 7-3. Back came the Steelers with Bradshaw in control, mixing his plays. He passed. Franco Harris ran. Bradshaw passed again. Then Harris went around the end to score from the one. The Steelers were in front again, 10-7, early in the second quarter.

But the Steelers' offense fizzled through the rest of the first half. Ferragamo did well enough to mount two productive drives, and Frank Corral kicked field goals of 31 and 45 yards.

Something very funny was happening at Super Bowl XIV. The Rams were in front again, 13-10, at halftime. The Pittsburgh fans anxiously squeezed their cans of Iron City. And in the Steelers' locker room Jack Lambert raised hell.

"I'm scared," he yelled at his teammates in full tirade. "They have the momentum. We don't have any intensity. We're not flying around. We're not gang tackling." He was vintage Lambert. He scared the stuffings out of the rest of the Steelers.

Early in the third quarter, Bradshaw dropped back and passed deep, and his old pet receiver, Lynn Swann, caught it for a 47-yard touchdown. The Steelers were in front again, 17-13.

Boom. Ferragamo dropped back, and he connected with Billy Waddy for a 50-yard gain to the Steelers' 24. Malavasi called the next play. It was the halfback option pass with Lawrence McCutcheon sweeping toward the end. He froze the Steelers, halted, and passed the 24 yards to Ron Smith. Corral missed the extra point, but the Rams were in front again, 19-17.

The Steelers stalled again. Bradshaw threw two interceptions. Ferragamo was outplaying the best quarterback in football. The Rams were outplaying the best team.

It was now that Chuck Noll sent in the play designed especially for this Super Bowl. They had tried the play in practice eight times, and it had never worked. When Noll sent it in earlier, Bradshaw vetoed the play call in the huddle. This time John Stallworth, the underpublicized foil to Lynn Swann, talked his quarterback out of another veto. The Steelers were back on their 27. It was third-and-eight. It was the fourth quarter, early. If the play failed, the Steelers would have to punt.

Stallworth came out of the slot, dragged two defenders with him for 15 yards, hooked, pirouetted, and raced deep. Bradshaw hit him perfectly in the hands, 39 yards downfield. Stallworth caught the ball in flight and ran with it the remaining 34 yards. It was a 73-yard touchdown, and the Steelers were in front again, 24-19.

Back came Ferragamo. By now Lambert was frothing and screaming. The Rams were threatening at the Pittsburgh 32. Ferragamo tried to gain half the distance with his next pass. Lambert bumped in and intercepted the ball. His play might have saved the game, this fourth Super Bowl for the Steelers.

With some four minutes left, Bradshaw spotted the Rams in the same coverage as they were in the turnabout bomb to Stallworth. Terry called it again. It worked for 45 yards to the 22. Then Harris scored from the one with less than two minutes to play. Only then were the Steelers safe, 31-19 victors.

◆ ◆ ◆

Pete Rozelle had come up with spectacular Super Bowls back-to-back. There had been six lead changes in this one, a deep underdog losing after a valiant battle, and a true champion winning for the fourth time in a true dynasty.

It was a fourth Super Bowl for Chuck Noll, which was twice as many as Lombardi and Shula and Landry had. It was a fourth for Bradshaw, twice as many as Bart Starr and Staubach and Griese had. And it was a fourth for the wonderful Art Rooney, nearing 80 years of age.

And it was a fourth ring for Mean Joe Greene. Greene thought about the accomplishments of his Super Bowl champions, and said: "Now, one for the thumb."

XV
The Yellow Ribbon

Oakland Raiders 27, Philadelphia Eagles 10
January 25, 1981
Louisiana Superdome, New Orleans
Attendance: 76,135

We took a cab out St. Charles Street, parallel to the streetcar tracks, to Pascal Manales and ordered a batch of fried shrimp and Gulf oysters and beer. Francis Tarkenton was there at the next table. He was a winner now, in TV, and he was laughing and making cracks about Detroit and the Super Bowl to be played there next year. But this year, 1981, we were back in New Orleans, and we tried to analyze what had gone haywire and how Pete Rozelle had come up with this match-up for Super Bowl XV—the Raiders versus the Eagles. Joe Greene's thumb would remain naked. Rozelle's invitation to the Super Bowl XV club party was stuffed in my pocket, another fete for the diminishing group of elite masochists who'd been privileged to cover them all. In Pete's pocket was the lawsuit he'd been slammed with by Al Davis.

My friends L.A. and Newark listened mostly as I talked mostly. I said, "This Super Bowl is going to turn into a whopping bonanza for America's breweries. Oakland versus Philly and take your choice. Tough Town East versus Tough Town West. There aren't going to be any martini drinkers at this Super Bowl, and nobody will be ordering a grasshopper. It's going to be Schmidt's beer imported from Philly versus Coors for the Oakland fans, and they'll switch to Dixie, the New Orleans brew, when the stuff from home runs out.

"Every time Philly wins anything, the mayor has to send out the police dogs and the cops on horseback," I said. "Otherwise the fans will rape the stadium. The attack dogs straining on their leashes, trying to bite the seat off some nut's pants, that's America's view of Philadelphia. It used to be Betsy Ross sewing stripes on the American flag. But no more.

"The Liberty Bell has been busted for two centuries. If Ben Franklin flew his kite today in the air over Philadelphia, the thing would come down black with soot."

"You're crude," said L.A.

"Me? The Philadelphia fans are noted for their booing. A few years ago they brought Santa Claus in at halftime of an Eagles game. They booed Santa Claus in Philly.

"W.C. Fields preferred to be dead rather than be in Philadelphia, but he probably never played Oakland." They couldn't shut me up.

"Nobody ever bothered to fly a kite in Oakland," I said. "Downtown is deserted at high noon. Look at Al Davis and his head coach, Tom Flores. The highly banked pompadour is still the height of fashion in Oakland. When the crowds get unruly in Oakland, the cops don't have dogs to keep the mobs in control. They use their billy clubs. A broken skull should be the symbol of the Raiders, not that pirate with the eye patch.

"The visiting players in Oakland have learned to keep their helmets on at all times. Remember the San Diego player? He took off the headguard and got bopped in the skull with a beer can. It was full of beer. Nobody ever went to Oakland voluntarily. And now even Al Davis is trying to leave."

"Nice speech for a guy from Detroit," somebody said from a nearby table.

I don't think it was Fran Tarkenton, but . . .

◆ ◆ ◆

The next morning we trooped across the bridge connecting the Hyatt, where we'd been put again, to the Superdome. It was photo day, and the NFL brought out the Eagles and the Raiders separately. We gathered around them in our journalistic packs and asked the same sorry questions as before.

"Excited about being in the Super Bowl?"

No, stupid, it's boring as hell.

"I'm excited about it," said Ron Jaworski. "It's the kind of game you dream about when you're a little kid. I'm as excited as I've ever been."

Jaworski was the Eagles' quarterback. He'd been with the Rams in their frustration years and had been shunted to the bench and tried to escape.

Finally the Rams dumped him to the Eagles. He was nicknamed Jaws, because, I assumed, he had a big mouth.

Somebody asked, grinning, if Jaws had gotten a telegram from Don Klosterman, the GM of the Rams.

"No, I wouldn't expect a nickel from him," Jaworski said.

"Happy he traded you to Philly?"

"When they sent me here," Jaws said, "they felt they were exiling me to Siberia. This was a team that had never gotten up off the floor."

Jaws thrived in Philly. He had his finest season as the Eagles won the NFC championship, throwing 27 touchdown passes and with only 12 interceptions in the 16 games.

I saw Jimmy Murray on the field, among the Eagles. This wasn't the L.A. wordsmith who used the byline Jim Murray. This was the Jimmy Murray who was GM of the Eagles. It said a lot about the Eagles that their GM wasn't as famous as a sportswriter with the same name.

Jimmy Murray was the little potbellied guy with the moon face you might have seen on TV. He was the one hugging first the owner, then the coach. He was the only GM in the NFL who got there by lugging water buckets and squirting drinks down the gullets of the players. He was a reformed water boy from Villanova.

At Villanova he'd been student manager of the baseball team. He went looking for a job in sports. He borrowed $600, hitched a bus to Tampa, and enrolled in the Florida Baseball Placement Bureau. He found himself in a class with two other students, learning the sports business. Once graduated, Murray latched onto a job as general manager with the Leesburg Phillies of the Class D Florida State League. When he got there to assume his executive role, the boss said: "Hey, kid, we've got to integrate the ballpark."

It was 1961. Murray's first job in pro sports was to spread whitewash over a sign that said *Colored Only* at the Leesburg baseball park.

"But," said Murray, "everything I did was at 78 RPMs, while everybody else was going at 45."

He worked his way back to Philly through Atlanta and Malibu. He went to work with a guy whose job was selling plastic worms to fishermen. The guy also owned a restaurant called The Raft, which was going bankrupt. The boss put Murray in charge. Murray turned it into a Hollywood hangout.

"But it was starting to get to me," he said. "Listening to characters like Lee Marvin until five in the morning was not my idea of fun."

Murray learned that the Eagles were looking for an assistant PR guy, so he wrote the club: "I would be remiss if I didn't throw my hat in the ring." He was hired. On his first day, he was told to check out the publicity files, and he found 104 applications for the job he'd just been hired to do.

"I sat down and listed the guys in the order I would have hired them," Murray said. "I finished 88th."

From there it was just a crapshoot to the general manager's job. That was five years before Super Bowl XV.

New GM Jimmy Murray said: "The only thing I know about football is I look like one."

But he could also spot a head coach when he saw one.

The five-year plan to the Super Bowl started the day Murray was tapped out of the gofer department. Murray had plenty to do. Unwise trades had left the Eagles stripped of number one draft choices. A year after being named GM, with the franchise in chaos, the Eagles fired Mike McCormack as coach.

"Find us a coach," Leonard Tose, the Philly owner, commanded Murray.

Tose and Murray talked to all the applicants. Hank Stram, Norm Van Brocklin, Allie Sherman—ex-head coaches in the pros—came by. Some college candidates were interrogated. Joe Paterno turned down the job. Joe Restic and Frank Kush were candidates.

The two Eagles broke off their interviewing to watch the Rose Bowl on TV, UCLA versus Ohio State.

"There's a coach right out of central casting," said Murray, looking at the screen.

Not Woody Hayes. The old man was out-slickered that New Year's Day by Dick Vermeil, the UCLA coach.

A week later in California, Tose and Murray met with Vermeil. Vermeil turned them down flat.

"Why would I give this up for Philadelphia?" Vermeil said. "Why leave California? I love UCLA. I'd be crazy."

Murray made a stronger pitch.

"We got a great town, great fans, we sell out the stadium win or lose, they even go nuts when we win a coin toss," Murray said. "There's no place to go but up."

Vermeil again said no. He drove off, down Sunset Boulevard toward the UCLA campus in Westwood. "Nuts," said Vermeil. He pulled over, found a pay phone, and called Murray to request a second interview.

"Hey," said Murray, "you didn't need gray hair and a whistle around your neck to know this was a real football man."

♦ ♦ ♦

As we wandered from pack to pack, news-gathering on NFL photo day, I happened to check the date on the paper. It was January 20. In a few hours Ronald Reagan would be inaugurated as 40th president of the United States, with all the privileges of the job, including phoning the winning coach in the locker room after Super Bowl XV. And on this day the hostages had been released from their long captivity by the Ayatollah in Iran. Tie a yellow ribbon 'round an old oak tree!

About 2,000 of us journalists scrambled from player to player, from GM to coach, jabbing elbows at each other, getting slugged by eager TV cameramen in the annual Super Bowl war for better positions so we could better ask questions to a game-player called Jaws. Priorities.

We skipped Bourbon Street and the Old Absinthe House for a night. Instead, we went downstairs to Georgie Porgie's in the Hyatt, our press headquarters. The place was jammed. With members of the Oakland Raiders.

Pete Rozelle's idea was to keep the athletes from mingling with the journalists this week of propaganda hype. Separation was not a bad plan because funny things happen in bars. So here were the Raiders invading the hotel delegated to the writers. At least half the AFC champions were there.

Jim Plunkett had a cool one in his hands. He was causing some cooing among the ladies. And vice versa.

Plunkett intrigued me. Son of a blind mother and a blind father, Mexican-American, he had been the most prized quarterback in college football a decade before at think-tank Stanford. In the NFL, he had been kicked from club to club, a failure, a flop, a lost soul. He hurt, he despaired. He was ready to give up football. Now he was 32, graying, and in this crazy Super Bowl media spotlight. He was a hero, reborn.

I made up my mind to hit Plunkett at the Raiders' interview session and write his story. I felt he typified half the American population.

NEW ORLEANS—The characteristics of the Oakland Raiders don't change through the years. They are a collection of rogues and pirates, mostly dropouts from teams that dumped them for social reasons having nothing to do with football—plus a fullback from Colgate.

Al Davis is the sinister agent who puts this dirty dozen kind of team together. He has gotten players out of jails as well as off the college campus. . . . His team is more qualified to sabotage the rail tracks behind the enemy lines than play in the Super Bowl.

But the Super Bowl is where the Raiders are going to play again.

That's largely because of another guy Davis picked out of pro football's skid row and rehabilitated.

There had never been a more dismal failure in pro football than Jim Plunkett. In 1970, he was the Heisman Trophy winner out of Stanford. He won the Rose Bowl. He was the first player picked off the board at the pro draft. He was a guaranteed future star in the NFL.

The New England Patriots were the team that drafted Plunkett and made him their starting quarterback as a rookie. It wasn't long before Plunkett's Stanford-educated head was confused with all the intricacies of pro footall. He was traded to the San Francisco 49ers, back home for him.

Monte Clark, the coach then, had to bench him. Plunkett couldn't throw the ball to the right guy. He was all confused. A year later the 49ers had to ditch him. Jim Plunkett thought about a steady job in a bank. Pro football's establishment teams considered him a lost cause. Nobody wanted to give him another chance.

Then Al Davis found him and brought him over to Oakland. It was 1978 and Davis talked Plunkett into signing as a free agent. He could sit on the bench and watch Kenny Stabler.

. . . Davis's reclamation project is complete. Plunkett has turned brigand. In the AFC championship game, he dropped some bombs on the San Diego Chargers. He snipped their wires and put out their lights. Then he outslugged them in hand-to-hand fighting.

Ten seasons after he came into pro football as a glory boy, Jim Plunkett vindicated himself. He dragged his team to the Super Bowl.

Davis said: ". . . I liked Plunkett even when he had a bad game against us in '78. He went 0-for-11 in a preseason game with the 49ers. John Madden, my coach then, wasn't particularly enthused, but we signed him shortly thereafter. I told him he'd be best to lay out a year.

"I thought he had his mind shot.

"People talk about players who reach a pinnacle, then reach a downgrade. I had to sell it to Jim.

"He was mixed up. Disappointed. I told him I believed in him. He didn't want to do it. I told him we'd make it work, make it happen."

Plunkett didn't play a single down for Oakland in 1978. In 1979, he appeared in four games in relief of Stabler. Davis had quarreled with Stabler and after the season traded him for Dan Pastorini.

Pastorini came to camp number one this year. . . . He tore up a knee in the fifth game of the schedule. Plunkett rushed off the bench. He hasn't sat down since.

. . . "I was a little skeptical I'd ever be here," he said. "I wasn't playing. I doubted if I could perform, if I could play, and if not, get out and do something else.

"When I was released by San Francisco, it had to be a downer. The way it all crumbled around me. Then in '78 I didn't play a down. I felt a lot of times I'd try to do something else. Even in '79 I felt that way.

"Even this year in training camp I asked to leave. I asked Tom Flores, the coach, to trade me. He said he had to keep me, that we needed an experienced backup quarterback.

"You know, when I was drafted by New England, it wasn't easy.

"I thought my career was going to be set in the NFL, and I was going right to the top. It didn't work that way.

"And now, I've proved something to myself. I proved that I could play in the NFL."

The Raiders were not a football team reckoned to be a Super Bowl contender when they assembled in the summer of 1980 at Santa Rosa and paraded for the townspeople. The character was not any different, but the characters were. Pastorini, drafted behind Plunkett nearly a decade earlier, had come over from Houston to quarterback the club.

John Madden, unfloatable in the arms of his victorious players after Super Bowl XI, had chucked his job. Burned out, perhaps by his own engery, Madden decided he'd be happier crisscrossing America by bus and turned into a Sunday-afternoon TV pundit. He did it with bluster and brains, and the admen of Madison Avenue quickly learned that when Madden yelled, America could not help but listen. They turned him into a tack-hammer salesmen between tricks.

So Tom Flores, the quiet, former quarterback, became head coach under Davis. And a bundle of the other Raiders' renegades retired, making places for the newly recruited juvenile delinquents.

Thus, in 1980, Davis hoped the Raiders would be presentable as he fought Rozelle in the courts, trying to evacuate Oakland for the glamour of Los Angeles and its vacant Coliseum.

The Raiders were decent enough through the season. Plunkett was exactly what the Raiders had to have after Pastorini went down in game five. Lester Hayes, preening, prancing, led a thieving defense with 13 interceptions. John Matuszak broke up some ball carriers and menaced some quarterbacks. Rookie Matt Millen blended in perfectly at linebacker with the scheme of the club. Rod Martin played decently on the outside. Gene Upshaw, at a dignified 38, led the team from the offensive line and provided the linkage between the old Raiders and the new.

It all resulted in an 11-5 season. Not good enough to beat San Diego for the title in the AFC West. But good enough to make it to the playoffs in Pete Rozelle's expanded wild-card setup.

So for the first time, Plunkett entered the playoffs as a participant. The Raiders beat Houston, 27-7, in the wild-card match-up. Plunkett passed for two touchdowns. Hayes returned an interception for one touchdown.

Then at Cleveland, in the cruel cold, the Raiders beat the Browns, 14-12, in a cruel game.

The Raiders were in the AFC championship versus the Chargers, their hated rivals. Plunkett started it off with two touchdown passes in the first quarter, and another he scored himself on a battering run. It turned into a slugfest. By the fourth quarter, the Raiders were struggling with a seven-point lead. They got the ball with six minutes, 43 seconds left. Plunkett shoved the ball at the Chargers and ran out the clock in a marvelous display of time-wasting ball control. Mostly Plunkett handed off to Mark van Eeghen, the fullback developed at Colgate, or jolted it ahead himself. It was an inching process guided by a master. The Chargers never got the ball back, and the Raiders won, 34-27.

Ten years after it all started in a tub of publicity, Jim Plunkett, turned brigand, had coaxed a band of renegades and a swell from Colgate to the Super Bowl. They were the first wild-card team to get there—since the merger had made them all one league, sort of.

◆ ◆ ◆

Another photo session. The photographer jumped around and hovered, and 23 grim guys hoped he'd get the crap over with fast.

"Smile, smile," begged the photographer, dancing a two-step. "Nobody's smiling."

"Think of Detroit," said Pete Rozelle, from his seat in the corner. A few guys giggled.

Here we were, the 23 battled-scarred, intrepid survivors with chevrons on the sleeves of our tweed jackets. We were the last who had covered all the Super Bowls. Rozelle was tossing the special bash he had every five years for those of us who kept coming back for more.

Who would drop out for Super Bowl XVI? That would be next year's, with the Super Bowl swinging off its New Orleans-Los Angeles-Miami axis to play Detroit. In the dead of winter.

"What's going to happen to our Super Bowl golf tournament?" one of the Super Bowl 23 asked Rozelle.

"Bring your skis, bring your skates, bring your fur-lined jocks," I responded, taking the heat off Pete.

The Michigan Super Bowl Committee, doing the groundwork for the next game, had come to New Orleans to provide seductive literature to the media hordes. Pamphlets extolling the virtues of Detroit and Pontiac, the next Super Bowl neighborhood, were stacked on tables in the Hyatt media room. My colleagues, my friends, were informed that the Detroit Zoo was open year-round. The press was told that vintage kitchen appliances would be on view at Greenfield Village, near where the press would be head-quartered.

That was nice, but in traveling to 15 Super Bowls, I had yet to find one guy who wanted to go to the zoo.

◆ ◆ ◆

But first, we were concerned with Evil versus Philadelphia. Five hundred of us were packed into a hallway at the Airport Hyatt waiting to be fed with instant cholesterol. Then we could listen to Dick Vermeil and his jolly comments. As we lined up, shoving, pushing, parading through the chow line, fellow marchers were John Madden and Rocky Bleier, once regaled participants at triumphant Super Bowls, now having joined us as media stars.

"We normally practice three hours and 15 minutes," Vermeil told us, as though he were revealing a dark secret. "We're down to two hours now. It's like a vacation. We don't have any bedchecks, but I recommend they stay out of Bourbon Street. I hope they'll be in bed by 11.

"They've all come down here for one thing. To win a football game. We might never get down here again. We might get only one chance."

On this morning, we learned the terrible shocking news that John Matuszak had been snared as a curfew-breaker. Horrors.

He had been out on his stomping grounds on Bourbon Street. The reason none of us saw him was that Tooz was out after every respectable sportswriter had vacated the Old Absinthe House and returned to drink free in the media hospitality room at the hotel. It was about three or four when Tooz rolled into the Raiders' quarters at the Gateway.

Matuszak had been at war with society for years. He admitted slugging a guy while in college at Missouri because the guy tried to take the clothes off Tooz's girlfriend. He switched colleges to U. of Tampa: "An outlaw school," he said. He battled the NFL and its draft, the cops, George Allen at Washington. He was subpoenaed on the field of a WFL game after he defected from the Oilers. "Twenty cops and a hundred reporters were there," Matuszak said. "I got the subpoena after seven plays in the game."

Landing in Oakland, he said: "The Raiders aren't a team where you always have to straighten up your tie and wear your hair a certain length. As long as you put out at practice and on Sundays, they don't care. As long as you stay out of jail." He got a part in the film adaption of Pete Gent's true novel, *Dallas North Forty,* stole it, and went on to a second film, *Caveman.* "I have a 16-word vocabulary and 1,000 different grunts."

Tooz had sworn he was going to be on his good behavior this week, shepherding his teammates out of the trouble spots. Now he had been caught. And we had fun writing about it. Flores hit him with a $1,000 fine for busting curfew.

Such uncivilized behavior shocked Vermeil. "If I had a player who broke curfew, he'd be home now," Vermeil told us.

Most of us had never listened to Vermeil before. He had not become a cult figure. He seemed a cross between George Allen and Chuck Noll, all X's and O's and concerns about distractions. The perfectly molded coach out of central casting seemed uptight, a prime candidate for burnout.

It was his fifth season in Philadelphia, and he'd taken a sad-sack franchise in 1976 and worked it and molded it. The Eagles hadn't had a winning season since 1968. They hadn't had a first-round draft choice in three years. It would be another three before they'd get one. Spendthrifts, they'd traded away all their number ones and still lost. It was a painstaking process from 4-10 the first season to 12-4 in 1980. Having reached the Super Bowl, Vermeil, with a powerful work ethic, was regarded as some sort of mastermind.

"The team's morale was low and it had very little physical talent," Vermeil said of the club he forced to climb. He was logical and possessed, but never exciting. He said, "If the team had had some talent, it probably would have won some games and the job wouldn't have been open."

It won the dozen games in '80 via the efficiency of Jaws, the power running of Wilbert Montgomery, and the stretching receptions of Harold Carmichael, a graceful gazelle at six-feet-eight. They were awarded their NFC East title by Rozelle's formula as Dallas, too, had a 12-4 record. It was Carmichael, Jaworski, and Montgomery who carried the Eagles through the playoffs.

In their first playoff game since the club beat Vince Lombardi's Packers for the NFL championship in 1960, the Eagles knocked off the aging Vikings, still dominating the NFC Central. Montgomery scored two touchdowns in the 31-16 victory.

Next it was the Cowboys, relegated to wild-card status. Dallas and Philly had split during the season. The Eagles dominated the third meeting for the NFC championship with a second-half rush, 20-7.

Rozelle was semi-pleased—an all-wild-card Super Bowl was avoided, despite the presence of Al Davis.

◆ ◆ ◆

The interview sessions were over on Thursday. That night I celebrated by attacking a mile-high pie, a delicacy. Joe Browne, from the NFL office, invited me to dinner at the swank Caribbean Room at the Ponchartrain Hotel far enough away from the hustle of Bourbon Street. It was a good night of camaraderie with Joe's family and a few of the guys who'd spent much of their lives covering Super Bowls.

The mile-high pie is a tummy-aching mountain of cake and various ice creams and sauces piled onto a plate. It is actually only a foot and a half tall, but it defies any normal human being to turn pig enough to shove it all down the gullet. I was proud of my work, but I lost, soundly defeated, as the waiter took away the still ample remnants.

Friday morning, Pete Rozelle had his annual duel in the ballroom with America's select media. The questions and Rozelle's skilled escape responses were usually tame and tepid. But this time, Pete was assaulted by a bunch of slugging questions about Al Davis and their relationship. Davis had sued the NFL for $160 million because of the league's refusal to sanction his planned move from Oakland to L.A. Rozelle, always slick and cautious, responded with descriptive words such as *divisive* and *outlaw* about Davis.

But you root for stories when you're a columnist. A lot of us could picture Rozelle squirming if the Raiders won. And Pete would have to award the trophy to Al Davis in the locker room.

◆ ◆ ◆

The party scene intensified. There were more of them. I hit the *Sporting News* party and the annual hot-ticket original Super Bowl party tossed by Rozelle with the Mississippi Mud motif and the freeloaders by the thousands.

Yogi Berra once described a chic New York restaurant with this logic: "It's always too crowded. Nobody goes there any more." That was New Orleans on the Saturday night before the Super Bowl. You couldn't get into Commander's Palace. You couldn't get into Antoine's. The booers from Philly and the bikers from Oakland, biceps thick, had taken over the town.

But Jack Kemp had invited a few of us back for his dignified bash, this year at the Fairmont. And Dick Schaap, the New York TV guru and sports author, invited us to the party he and his wife, Trish, were tossing at the Hilton Tennis Club. Guests included a couple of athletes, a couple of intellectuals, and friendship. Nibblers did not need to go hungry on Saturday nights before Super Bowls any more.

◆ ◆ ◆

I straggled across the footbridge linking the bustling Hyatt and the Superdome to cover my 15th Super Bowl. I slipped around the drunks, raving about their football teams already, on mid-Sunday afternoon. We work in the "toy departments" of our newspapers. We take ourselves seriously and treat our subject matter with grave regard.

Then I saw the yellow ribbon wrapped all the way around the Superdome, and the bitter ends of it knotted into a bow. The ribbon was 369,984 feet in length and cost $4,500. The impact of the view forced me to stop. The 52 American hostages were free from the claws of the Ayatollah after 444 days of captivity. Rozelle had sent them 52 copies of the Super Bowl XV program so they could refer to them as they watched the game on television in Germany.

"Shit," I said aloud. "The hostages probably don't even know who won last year's game."

I shrugged and trudged onward to cover Super Bowl XV. There was a job to do, I rationalized.

Marie Lombardi, widow of the great coach, flipped the coin amid high ceremony at midfield. The Eagles called the toss and guessed right. Helen O'Connell sang a subdued version of "The Star-Spangled Banner." No Air Force jets in the closed stadium, only stray pigeons. But the Superdome swelled with patriotism as the crowd was asked to think about the released hostages.

Later Mrs. Lombardi was asked what Vince might have said if he had viewed her coinflip. She replied: "He probably would have said, 'what the hell's a woman doing on the field?' "

♦ ♦ ♦

"If he wants to catch any passes he shouldn't stay on my side of the field," Lester Hayes, the Raiders' pass defender, had said about Harold Carmichael, the Eagles' towering receiver. Hayes had actually said it in a stutter. During the week, I'd sought to sit in on an interview with Hayes. So did Mike O'Hara, my colleague from the Detroit *News*. He was the beat man, so I yielded to find a different subject. Later I walked by Hayes's interview table. I could overhear Lester stuttering. I looked at O'Hara, the victor in our coverage scheme. He looked at me. He rolled his eyes as Lester tried desperately to communicate another sentence.

But how beautifully Lester tried to speak without his stutter, eventually conquering it, and how ugly he could be when playing pass defense.

♦ ♦ ♦

The Eagles were three-point favorites in the mind of Jimmy the Greek. They received the opening kickoff. Jaworski threw his first pass on the third play. Jaws had been as close to being interception-proof as any quarterback this season. Now, his throw, aimed to the left, was intended for John Spagnola, the tight end out of Yale. Rodney Martin, Oakland's right linebacker, a reject from the 49ers, picked off the ball.

Jim Plunkett, craggy and reborn from the scrap heap, went out on offense. A couple of runs moved the ball a bit. Then Plunkett dropped back, in the classic form, and fired to Cliff Branch. Branch caught the ball for a 14-yard gain. The Raiders were at the Eagles' five. Moments later, Plunkett passed to Branch again from the two. It was good for a touchdown. Quickly the underdog, wild-card Raiders were ahead, 7-0.

Late in the first quarter, the Raiders had the ball at their 20. The Eagles' rush chased Plunkett out of the pocket this time. He dodged toward his left. Kenny King, out of the backfield, was streaking along the sideline. Plunkett hit him with a floater. King ran away, the last 60 yards on foot, for an 80-yard touchdown, the longest TD pass in a Super Bowl. The Raiders were up, 14-zip.

The Eagles managed a field goal by Tony Franklin, a barefooted 30-yarder. It was 14-3 Raiders as the performers hit the field for the halftime pomp.

In the third period, Plunkett brought the Raiders along on the running of the fullback from Colgate, Mark van Eeghen, and his passing to King and Bob Chandler. Then at the 29, he lofted the ball toward the end zone again. Branch grabbed it at the one and grappled himself into the end zone. Now it was 21-3, Raiders. Plunkett had three TD passes. Dick Vermeil was hung up with nervous energy at the bench.

Again, Jaworski attempted to pass to his left. He was, indeed, staying away from Lester Hayes's coverage. Rodney Martin again intercepted the ball. The Raiders advanced onward, and Matt Bahr kicked a 46-yard field goal for a 24-3 lead.

This time, Jaworski brought the Eagles back. He hit Charles Smith with a 43-yard pass. Then, early in the fourth quarter, he passed eight yards to Keith Krepfle for Philadelphia's touchdown.

Plunkett switched to ball control, the time-consuming practice he had worked so destructively at San Diego. The Eagles stopped the movement, but Bahr kicked another field goal, a 35-yarder, for a 27-10 lead.

The Eagles tried once more. Upstairs in the press box, Al Davis was munching on his fingernails and bellowing curses. He alone believed the game wasn't over. But he thrust his fist upward when Jaworski threw once again to his left, and for the third time linebacker Rodney Martin intercepted the pass.

Downstairs in the locker room, Davis said, "Dammit, they did it. This is a funny bunch. They did it no matter where Philly had the ball. They attacked all day. On both sides."

Rozelle went in to present the silver Vince Lombardi Trophy. The men, these enemies locked in the courtroom in a bitter suit regarding franchise sovereignty and the establishment power of the NFL, looked at each other.

The hatred was put aside as the TV camera beamed in and the ink-stained wretches pressed closer. Pete made it sweet.

"As the first wild-card team to win the Super Bowl," Rozelle said, in his tone reserved for platitudes, "it's a tremendous compliment to your organization because you had to win four postseason games."

"Thank you, commissioner," said Davis, biting his tongue. "When you look back on the glory of the Oakland Raiders, this was our finest hour."

It was not lost that this would-be vagabond, Al Davis, had referred to them as *Oakland* Raiders.

Rozelle went over to Jim Plunkett, reclaimed at age 32 after his decade of failure and despair. "I know of no athlete in the history of sport who has made a greater comeback than Jim Plunkett," said Rozelle, with deep sincerity.

"We're the halfway house of the NFL," said Gene Upshaw, the old guard who had played the longest for Davis.

"No one still believes we're here. We felt all season we were against the league and against the world. I really had that feeling. I wanted it for Davis because he was up against the world."

XVI
The Z Factor

San Francisco 49ers 26, Cincinnati Bengals 21
January 24, 1982
Pontiac Silverdome
Attendance: 81,270

The two buses chugged up to the Sheraton in Southfield, Michigan, their exhaust fumes turned into plumes of gaseous smoke in the eight-degree cold. The young giants stepped off the buses and went for their luggage. They could see their breath in snorts in the atmosphere. Just then the man in the porter's cap, his greatcoat turned up around his neck, popped through the revolving door onto the driveway.

"Help you with your bag? Help you with your bag?"

The young giants ignored the codger. "Carry my own. Carry my own." They paraded into the lobby and found their room keys.

"It's me, it's me," yelled the man in the porter's cap. He yanked off the cap. "See, it's me."

They didn't bother to look. These San Francisco 49ers were so young and so new to the Super Bowl magnifying glass that they didn't want to tip quarters. They'd rather stiff the bag man.

The porter would laugh all through the week before Super Bowl XVI as he repeated the story. His name was Bill Walsh, and he was a football coach by profession. He had borrowed the hotel porter's uniform as a disguise. The players had been fooled.

Or so Walsh insisted. "They couldn't believe I was dressed as the bellman," he said. "Even when I took my hat off they still didn't believe it."

Bill Walsh had flown into Michigan alone earlier that Sunday before Super Bowl XVI in January 1982 with an obligation to meet the media. His team followed. It was eight below zero when Walsh's flight from San Francisco landed in Detroit.

So it was that the prelude to the Super Bowl that I had dreaded, the Super Bowl up North, the Super Bowl in my hometown, began with a masquerade. The moveable feast had come home!

♦ ♦ ♦

I backed out of my driveway and steered cross-town through Detroit, in the direction of the Detroit Metro Airport. Fifteen times before at this time in January, I had headed this way. To the airport. Aboard a plane. Off to cover the Super Bowl. No matter the gripes, the repetitiousness, I had always looked forward to covering this event, hoping I could do something different.

This time, I veered off the freeway miles before the airport, at the Rotunda Drive exit in Dearborn. I drove up to the Hyatt Regency. This would be the press headquarters for Super Bowl XVI, the meeting between the San Francisco 49ers and the Cincinnati Bengals.

The *News* had agreed to let me cover this hometown Super Bowl the same way I had covered all the others—to live in the headquarters hotel in my own town, eat in the restaurants where the other Super Bowl writers would eat, go through the entire rigmarole as though it were New Orleans.

With one exception. I—all the guys covering for the *News*—would be on display. Every day we'd be vulnerable. Two thousand other writers, from Missoula to Miami, would be scrutinizing my words. Sportswriters happen to be highly critical of prose contained in other newspapers. It's in the blood. There would be snipers and gigglers. It had happened in all the other towns, as the writers swapped gossip in the hospitality rooms, quaffing the NFL's offerings.

I took vows to try to cover the event as I would an ordinary Super Bowl. I wanted to dwell on football, game personalities, including some analysis, some anecdotes, and weaving in some images of the crazy scene. I wasn't going to do any dancing bear stuff.

"Welcome to Detroit." I had called upstairs to the NFL suites to contact Joe Browne. It was my town, and I was going to be a sport. I was taking Pete Rozelle's top public relations expert to dinner. A rarity there, a writer grabbing the bill for the PR guy.

"Well," said Joe, "it's here at last."

"Yeah," I said, "I hope it doesn't snow on Super Sunday."

We went outside to get the car. It was 12 above. We drove downtown to the Ponchartrain Wine Cellars to talk football and Super Bowls and about what sort of hell might occur during the next week in Detroit.

The NFL doesn't merely visit a place and play a Super Bowl. It occupies a city. It comes with its own highly trained regiment of security guards to protect its headquarters. They are uniformed in yellow jackets.

In Dearborn, the security guards were protected by security guards. You couldn't get to a yellow jacket until you were cleared by a blue-shirted sentry.

On the approach way to the Hyatt, the roman numerals XVI stood high and mighty. They resembled a massive enlargement of those dripping ice statues at Super Bowls gone by. But this XVI had been sculpted neatly out of straw. The straw turned to ice.

The NFL flag waved proudly atop a flagpole near the entrance to the Hyatt. You felt like snapping to a salute.

Alas, even before the beginning of the pageantry, some citizen member of the resistance had inflicted sabotage on the elite occupation force. This daredevil ripped off the NFL's most enormous flag, the one reserved for major campaigns such as Super Bowls. The souvenir collector escaped, despite the yellow jackets and blue shirts. But the NFL was eternally prepared for emergencies. It invaded Detroit with a backup flag. The shrunken second-stringer—the same size as the American flag raised at Iwo Jima—was immediately run up the flagpole.

◆ ◆ ◆

The bus rolled along the familiar roadways laden with the familiar writers, all expectant. We were off to the photo day, the ritual formalities that made this Super Bowl like its 15 predecessors. The sun was out, and it was crystal clear, but very cold. Brrrr! The bus dropped us on the tarmac of the familiar parking lot outside the Silverdome. The 49ers were inside, prepared to pose, new characters to be asked the same questions.

"What about curfews, and where will you guys hang out this week, and if you were a tree what kind of tree would you be?"

"Who the hell could find any trees around here?"

The 49ers kept us waiting. Bill Walsh was conducting practice, and it was running long. He was damned if he'd cut his practice just because the NFL's official timetable said the 49ers must be interviewed at 10:30 and he wanted to practice until 11:30. So the rent-a-cops kept the media elite waiting in a wide rampway outside the Silverdome in the bitter cold. A thousand of us stood there for most of the hour, shifting from one foot to the other, griping about the bleeping NFL and bleeping Detroit and cursing the weather. Why wasn't there some room inside where we could all wait in some sort of warmth?

There was. But the bleeping guards had their orders from some muck-amuck who'd never been to a Super Bowl before. And they had no far-fetched idea what common sense was.

I wished I were in Miami. It was that bad. I could see papers from Yakima to Yeehaw Junction, Florida, ripping Detroit because it was such a dumb place to hold a Super Bowl. There were a lot of surly guys.

Finally, they opened the doors. We charged inside, into the home dome that for years had made me writhe with claustrophobia. Every ink-stained wretch, every electronic media marvel skittering around the field doing his job, would be reading my stuff tomorrow. No exotic datelines this Super Bowl, just turn on the juice, punch the keys, and wing it.

A column, Detroit *News,* January 1982:

Now any team can win and go to the Super Bowl.

That's the way with the miracle of parity.

This year the 49ers and Bengals. Next year the Saints and the Patriots? The year after the Giants and the Colts? Some day—maybe—the Detroit Lions?

The time is over when the Pittsburgh Steelers can go to four Super Bowls in six years and win them all. It is no longer possible for the Minnesota Vikings to go to four Super Bowls in eight years—and lose them all.

The Cowboys are out—in need of rebuilding. The Dolphins have risen again. The Raiders have fallen. The Rams have come up and dropped back. . . . The trend is for the new teams to come up from the dungeon.

The Super Bowl was originated for the swells of two warring leagues. They shook up all the teams and out came the Packers and the Chiefs to play in the first one. They were teams with the expected traits of winners. They had All-Pros at the skill positions. . . . They were coached by men who became legends. And they had some tradition for winning.

Now we have ragamuffins going to the Super Bowl.

The 49ers are there riding the crest of four losing seasons. They were below .500 in seven of the last eight years. They employed six different head coaches in the last seven years. In 1978 and 1979, they went 2-and-14.

They were the pits of the league. And finishing down there didn't help them much in the draft. It helped Buffalo. The 49ers had traded an oodle of high draft choices for O.J. Simpson.

O.J. was a home son who had grown up rooting for the 49ers when they frustrated the city playing under the seagulls at Kezar Stadium. . . . It was a sweet, sentimental gesture mortgaging the future to bring back O.J. Simpson. But by the time he got home, he was beat up and slowed and had gone Hollywood. And the rest of the team was so pitiful it hurt watching O.J. try to struggle forward.

The Bengals advanced to the Super Bowl after three losing seasons in a row. They weren't just little losing seasons. The Bengals went 4-and-12 a couple of times. In the last seven years, they had four coaches. . . . These two clubs never mastered the pro mystique with the ease Chuck Noll and Pittsburgh did. They never showed the spit and polish of Don Shula's organization in Miami. Nobody ever mistook the 49ers and the Bengals for America's team.

Cincy was a baseball town all the years the Reds were winning. . . when the World Series ended, Cincinnati took the winter off. Pro football was an imposter.

They were more fervent in San Francisco—at least for a while. The 49ers never won a championship until two weeks ago. They'd been in business 36 years. No other franchise in pro football had suffered longer without a conference or league championship. . . . Three years ago the two teams between them won a grand total of six games for the season.

Now it's different. Schedule formulas, the draft, and relaxation of the blocking rules plus restrictions in pass defense have created a league of equals. And a bright coach can build a team faster than ever before.

A brain such as Bill Walsh put the 49ers together in three years. Sixteen of his players were culled from the rejects of other clubs. Eleven more are raw rookies.

The difference between a ragamuffin and a champion isn't so much anymore. Now any team can go to the Super Bowl.

It was fashionable for out-of-towners to use Detroit as a punching bag. The worst thing was the town had a glass jaw. On the morning after the cream of American journalism was kept outside in the cold at the Silverdome, the "Good Morning America" show originated from ABC's Detroit studio.

Paul Zimmerman, founder of the pressroom pick-'em pool tradition, was a media guest. Paul had switched from his New York paper to *Sports Illustrated*. He was being venerated as Dr. Z. He was asked how he liked Detroit as a Super Bowl city.

SUPER BOWL I – Chiefs running back Bert Coan tries to elude the grip of Green Bay's Lee Roy Caffey. (Vernon Biever)

◆ ◆ ◆

SUPER BOWL II – Legendary Packers coach Vince Lombardi shares a light moment with reporters before the showdown with the Raiders. (Vernon Biever)

SUPER BOWL III – Joe Namath's famous poolside interview in Fort Lauderdale before Super Bowl III. Author Jerry Green, sporting a Princeton crew cut, is seated behind Brent Musburger, then a Chicago sportswriter (left), and Ray Sons, then of the Chicago *Daily News*. Seated in the foreground, his head covered by a newspaper, is the now-deceased Dayton sports editor Si Burick. Next to him is Chuck Heaton of the Cleveland *Plain Dealer*, the man responsible for arranging this meeting with Namath. (Walter Iooss, Jr. / Sports Illustrated / © Time Inc.)

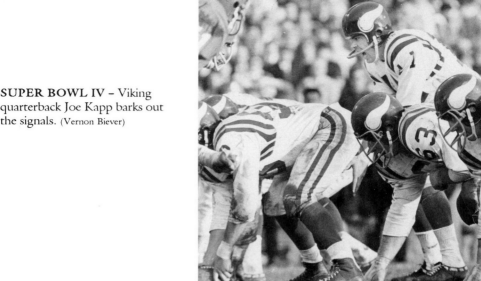

SUPER BOWL IV – Viking quarterback Joe Kapp barks out the signals. (Vernon Biever)

SUPER BOWL V – Although Tom Nowatzke was the Colts' leading rusher with only **33** yards, their passing attack contributed 260 yards and helped Baltimore prevail over Dallas. (Vernon Biever)

SUPER BOWL VI – It probably looks more painful than it was, and it didn't prevent Roger Staubach from tossing two touchdown passes to lead Dallas to its first Super Bowl championship, erasing the memory of the frustrating loss to the Colts a year earlier. (Vernon Biever)

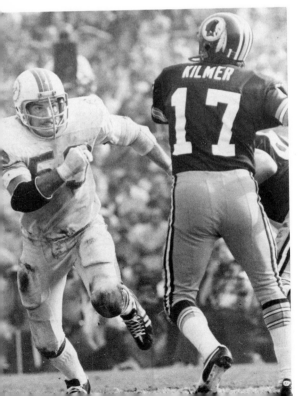

SUPER BOWL VII – Billy Kilmer about to unload before being rushed by Doug Swift. Miami's "no-name" defense frustrated Kilmer all afternoon, forcing three interceptions. (Vernon Biever)

SUPER BOWL VIII – Oscar Reed (32) rushes for several of his 32 yards after taking the hand-off from Fran Tarkenton. Miami's Larry Csonka, who rushed for 145 yards, more than doubled the rushing yardage for the entire Minnesota team. (Vernon Biever)

SUPER BOWL IX – Pittsburgh's Terry Bradshaw led the Steelers to the first of an unprecedented four Super Bowl championships, this time against the hapless Vikings, who suffered their third Super Bowl defeat. (Vernon Biever)

Overleaf

SUPER BOWL X – Steeler running back Franco Harris again led in rushing, but his 82 yards paled beside his 158 of the year before. (Vernon Biever)

SUPER BOWL XI – In 1976, Raider quarterback Kenny "Snake" Stabler led the NFL in passing. He passed for 180 yards and one touchdown in Super Bowl XI, while Clarence Davis (28) rushed for 137 more as Oakland totally dominated Minnesota, which lost its fourth Super Bowl. (Vernon Biever)

◆ ◆ ◆

Overleaf

(Top) **SUPER BOWL XII** – Although he led the Broncos to Super Bowl XII with steady performances through the regular season and playoffs, quarterback Craig Morton threw four first-half interceptions against the Cowboys and had to be replaced by backup QB Norris Weese, who was unable to stop the Dallas juggernaut. Here Weese feels the wrath of Ed "Too Tall" Jones. (Vernon Biever)

(Bottom) **SUPER BOWL XIII** – Tony Dorsett is crushed under the Steel Curtain defense in what was one of the highest scoring Super Bowls ever, and one of the best. (Vernon Biever)

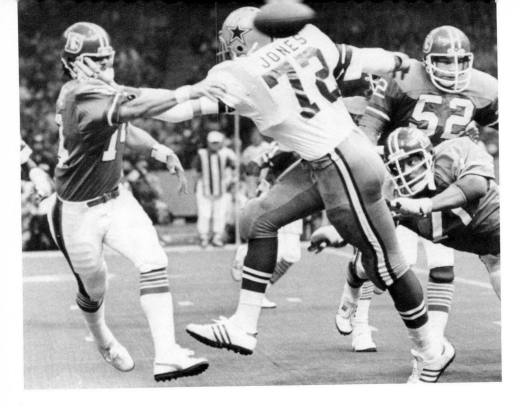

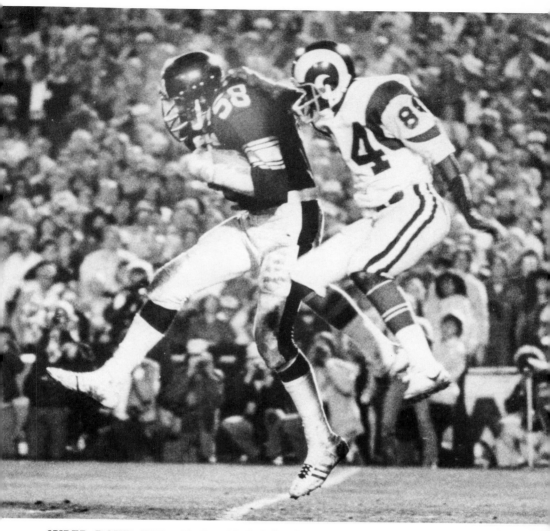

SUPER BOWL XIV – Pittsburgh's Jack Lambert picked off an errant Vince Ferragamo pass late in the game to set up the decisive touchdown and put Pittsburgh in the lead, 31–19. (Vernon Biever)

◆ ◆ ◆

SUPER BOWL XV – The Louisiana Superdome, decked out in formal attire, on January 25, 1981. (Vernon Biever)

SUPER BOWL XVI – Forty-niner receiver Charle Young catches his only pass of the day, good for 14 yards. (Vernon Biever)

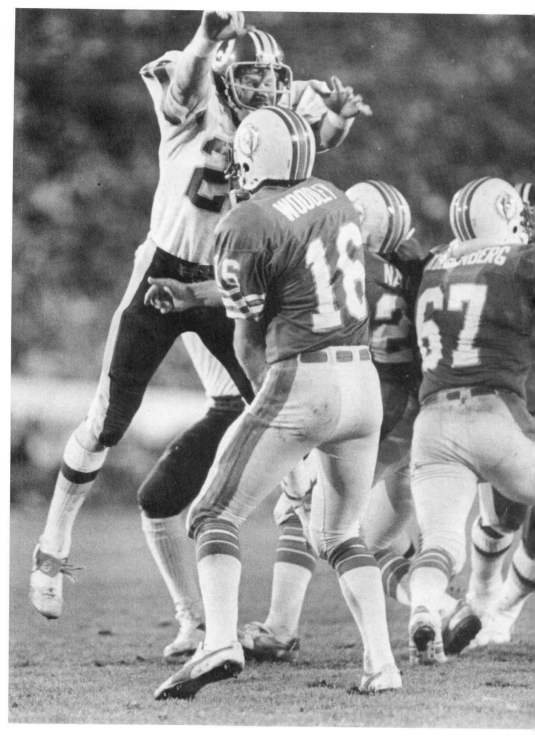

SUPER BOWL XVII – Part of the reason Miami quarterback David Woodley completed only 4 of 14 passes was the fearsome Washington pass rush.
(Vernon Biever)

SUPER BOWL XVIII – That's the kind of day it was for Joe Theismann and the Washington Redskins, who were humbled by the Los Angeles Raiders, 38–9. (Vernon Biever)

SUPER BOWL XIX – Perennial All-Pro cornerback Ronnie Lott tips the ball—and a touchdown—away from Miami receiver Mark Clayton.
(Vernon Biever)

SUPER BOWL XX – Chicago coach Mike Ditka with the Vince Lombardi Trophy.
(Vernon Biever)

(Left) **SUPER BOWL XXI** – Giants Mark Bavaro holds teammate Phil McConkey high aloft in celebration. (Vernon Biever)

(Below) **SUPER BOWL XXII** – Redskins QB Doug Williams passed for a Super Bowl record 340 yards, reason enough for Anthony Jones's jubilation. (Vernon Biever)

(Above) **SUPER BOWL XXIII –**
Boomer Esiason suffered through a long
afternoon, as did the rest of the Bengals,
who lost their second Super Bowl to the
San Francisco 49ers. (Vernon Biever)

(Right) **SUPER BOWL XXIV –** NFL
Commissioner Paul Tagliabue addresses
the media. (Vernon Biever)

Overleaf

SUPER BOWL XXV – A dejected
Scott Norwood leaves the field after
missing the 47-yard field goal that
could have won the game for Buffalo.
(Vernon Biever)

• • •

"Who sees Detroit?" Zimmerman told the audience across the U.S. "We're 15 miles from Detroit. We're holed up in a hotel overlooking frozen tundra. The whole atmosphere is depressing. . . . They got Cossacks guarding the stadium. . . . It was like being trapped in Russia for the Moscow Olympics, but the security guards were nicer in Moscow."

Detroit's glass jaw shattered into a million fragments.

◆ ◆ ◆

At 73, Paul Brown had built himself another championship team. He had started the Cleveland Browns from scratch in 1946, the year after World War II ended and some rich men founded the All America Football Conference. He was the owner, the coach, the brains. The Browns—Paul named his team for himself—won the AAFC championship for four years, with Otto Graham winning games as quarterback. This new league challenged the old NFL, picking off some of the finest players of the late forties. After the fourth season, the NFL sought peace. The Browns and a few of the other AAFC clubs—including the San Francisco 49ers—were merged into the NFL. Paul Brown's football team proceeded to dominate the NFL, winning a fifth successive championship.

But Brown was ultimately forced out of the franchise in Cleveland. When the American Football League expanded in 1968, Brown set about starting another team from scratch, the Cincinnati Bengals. Three years later Brown returned to the NFL with the Bengals in another merger.

A championship was tougher to attain this time. Brown kept building and rebuilding, changing and tinkering. No longer active as a coach, he went to work every day in the front office, lugging his lunch with him in a brown paper bag. The struggle went on. Brown was a difficult man to satisfy. He fired coaches in a machine-gun series.

The Bengals could not win without a bona fide quarterback. Brown knew that. He sent his offensive coordinator to check the quarterback from little Augustana College in rural Illinois. The kid's name was Kenny Anderson. The assistant coach urged the Bengals to draft Anderson. And so they did, and the assistant coach took on the task of training Anderson so he could become a competent pro quarterback. The assistant patiently molded Anderson into the most effective passer in the AFC.

That assistant's name was Bill Walsh. Walsh was a graying man in his forties, and he was regarded as something of a wizard of offensive strategy. He had worked for Paul Brown for eight years.

And through trying seasons, dipping to 4-12 on occasion, Brown kept looking for the proper coach for his team. He tried craggy Bill Johnson, fired him, and tried Homer Rice. He fired him and hired Forrest Gregg.

Bill Walsh, the assistant, had left when Paul Brown gave up active coaching and appointed Johnson as his successor. But the lessons Walsh taught Anderson remained, and the quarterback was now a veteran, about to play in Super Bowl XVI.

◆ ◆ ◆

The Michigan Host Committee busted its butt to transform Detroit into a Super Bowl city. Frank Sinatra and Rod Stewart were imported to perform concerts; Diana Ross returned to her hometown to sing her Motown songs. Henry Mancini conducted the Detroit Symphony Orchestra in a pops concert.

For those interested, there would be some dogsled races. Ignore the cold and party. There were parties all over town, every night.

A Supercrawl was organized, involving 70 local bars, taverns, and pubs. For five bucks, the partygoers could loop around town via bus from one saloon to the next.

In Pontiac, Saginaw Street—the main drag, a row of mostly boarded-up shops and failed businesses—was converted into a party place. They called it Bourbon Street North.

The Michigan Host Committee tossed a midweek party for the media in the museum at Greenfield Village, amid the ancient Model T Fords and with Thomas Edison's original electric light on display. They introduced all the writers who had covered every Super Bowl. When the announcement was made introducing the only hometown writer among those who'd been to all the Super Bowls, there weren't the usual boos and barbs, but rather cheers and a standing ovation.

Detroit's heart burst with pride at this Super Bowl. Anybody using Detroit for a punching bag this week would get his block knocked off.

◆ ◆ ◆

Pete Rozelle was ill back in New York. He'd had a strep throat and was still afflicted with laryngitis, and was not due to come to his Super Bowl city until late in the week. Joe Browne arranged a telephone interview, so I could ask Pete his favorite Super Bowl memories.

Rasping into the phone, Pete listed them roman numeral by roman numeral. Among the best were:

I: That was frantic. Both networks were doing it. I remember we were going to try to control the clock, run the clock with a remote radio control. The day before we tested the clock for several hours—backward and forward, backward and forward, backward and forward. Then on the first play, on the kickoff, the clock fell off. It was metal fatigue from all the testing the day before.

VIII: Sparrows got into the Vikings' shower. Bud Grant admitted later he trumped it up to take pressure off the Vikings. And we held our party in the Astrodome. It was the only time we had room.

IX: Mr. Rooney won it. He'd been trying since '33.

XIII: That was the last time we were in Miami. I remember we had a map of the Caribbean on the field at halftime. It took 32½ minutes to do it instead of the 11 we'd expected. I nearly died.

XV: . . . the trophy. I was curious about how it was going to be received, the trophy presentation to the winning owner. It went fine. There was no problem with Al Davis. When I got off the stand after giving Al the trophy, one of the Raider players took my hand. He really jammed it. Then he whispered in my ear, "Mr. Rozelle, I want you to know we all don't think this way about it."

XVI: With the press complaining about the weather in Detroit, they'll have to give up the column they write each year about fat-cat owners in their cabanas on the beach at the Super Bowl.

◆ ◆ ◆

Some of the most memorable moments in the 36-year history of the 49ers occurred late on Sunday afternoons. The seagulls would swing around above the flat grandstands of Kezar. It was as though they were waiting, anticipating, hungry, with full knowledge that it was nearly dinner time. Then the football game would end. The 49ers were losers once again. John Brodie, the bedeviled quarterback, would dash for the tunnel. And this was the highlight for the pained San Francisco partisans. The fans would stand over the runway and heap garbage on their quarterback.

Those were well-fed seagulls they had in San Francisco.

Now the 49ers, in a quick swoop, had grown into champions and contestants in the Super Bowl. Walsh was quite willing to take credit for the turnabout. He had been hired in 1979 as the head coach of a barren franchise. The club was strapped for quality players. In 1976, it had traded for Jim Plunkett at the price of three number one draft choices and a number two, yielded over two years. Plunkett was a bust, an abject flop, and it was then that he considered quitting football.

The 49ers followed that failed trade by giving up four more high draft picks for the battered O.J. Simpson in 1978. Again it was a rotten trade. Beyond that the 49ers wasted an additional first-round draft choice.

San Francisco was Russian roulette for coaches. Three of them were blasted away in '77 and '78. Eddie DeBartolo, Jr. became the new owner, a gift from his father for the kid who had everything else. The negotiations to purchase the 49ers were engineered by Al Davis, who had a vested interest in the other pro franchise across the Bay.

"They traded away 23 draft choices from 1976 to 1979, and we don't have one player to show for it," Walsh told the hungered media as the NFL started thumping its Super Bowl tub. "We haven't had draft choices. We sort of had to make do. They had a tremendous turnover of personnel. Consequently, it wasn't that difficult to get things organized. People were looking forward to being part of a reasonably orchestrated organization."

Gobbling the NFL's gratis nourishment, we translated those words by peeking between the lines. Bill Walsh was thumping his own tub. He was known to do that. By Super Bowl XVI, as he spoke at the morning sessions at the Sheraton Southfield, Walsh was being called a genius. He didn't deny it.

He was, to me, a man with a bunch of hurt inside of him. He was 47 and grizzled before he became a head coach in the NFL. Yet his brilliance in tutoring quarterbacks was common knowledge in the league.

Paul Brown's snub when he was the assistant in Cincinnati, handy and ambitious, chased Walsh away. Hurt, Walsh became a staff member in San Diego. There he tutored Dan Fouts, who developed into the league's most artistic passer.

From San Diego, Walsh moved back into the colleges, when Stanford made him a head coach. The brilliance continued. And, finally, in 1979, the 49ers brought him in to fix their chaotic situation.

"Basically, I'm scared to death," Walsh said during the Super Bowl hoopla. "I was an assistant coach for so long that when I became a head coach I wasn't awed by the job. The thrill of being a head coach had passed me by. I just didn't have the hype thing.

"Senility, I guess it is. I'd be more wrapped up with myself if it had happened earlier."

Walsh went into the '79 draft lacking a first pick. He drafted a wide receiver, James Owens, on the second round.

Next Walsh decided he wanted a quarterback. The 28 teams had gone around twice. The Cowboys, with their scouting wizardry, did have a quarterback logged into their computer. But the quarterback's grades were wanting, and the Cowboys' computer spit him out.

The quarterback wasn't perfect, but Walsh felt he could be taught some things. So Walsh drafted him on the third round, after 81 other players had been selected. The quarterback's name was Joe Montana.

◆ ◆ ◆

Forrest Gregg knew all about the strain of the Super Bowl. He had played in the first two of them. He was a giant offensive tackle for the Packers, guarding Bart Starr. He played for Vince Lombardi. He learned from Lombardi's theories of discipline. When Gregg retired from the Packers, he was talked into playing one additional season. It was Tom Landry who convinced Gregg he was needed. And so Gregg played in a third Super Bowl when the Cowboys beat the Dolphins in Super Bowl VI.

Now he was the first Super Bowl player to become a Super Bowl head coach. He was the recipient of a talent pool after the Bengals went through the switches, from one coach to another. The Bengals had successive 4-12 seasons in '78 and '79 with rosters that should have done better.

"One thing in my mind when I came here was how tough they were," said Gregg in one of his interview sessions. "They had good talent. Something had to be wrong. We lost the first two games in 1980. I thought it was an indication of the attitude."

There was a collective yawn among the media as Gregg spoke at the Bengals' headquarters, the Troy Hilton. This was Lombardi, Landry, and Noll rolled into one massive frame. Vintage Super Bowl poop.

"A coach puts down X's and O's and gets the right people into the game and is responsible for the mental approach," Gregg said. "You've got to be physically and mentally ready. I can try to get them to give everything they can, work as hard as they can for 60 minutes." I started to miss Bud Grant.

Gregg said he was neither Lombardi reincarnate nor Landry's clone. But he did confess stealing some style from them.

"I paid attention to the techniques of Lombardi and Landry because I knew I wanted to go into coaching," he said.

And in 1981, the Bengals jumped to 12-4.

It was Walsh's protégé, Ken Anderson, who was most responsible for the quick coaching success of Gregg.

"I don't know any player who has done more for this team than Ken," Gregg said.

Anderson, out of the collegiate boondocks of Augustana, had unexpectedly become what Bradshaw and Starr and Staubach had been. His statistics were in the range compiled by Tarkenton. All this at age 32 after 11 seasons in the league, after the football fans of Cincinnati jeered and hooted his passes and cheered his injuries.

Quarterbacks get too much credit when they win and too much blame when they lose, my old tutor, Russ Thomas, told me when I was in my journalistic youth, and he was GM of the Lions.

This was the case with Anderson. He was hurt in '80, booed, then cheered off the field. As the '81 season started, Anderson was booed again after throwing two interceptions versus the Seattle Seahawks. Gregg benched him. The Seahawks were up 21-0. The relief quarterbacks rallied the Bengals to a 27-21 victory. Then, after one game, Gregg had to agonize over the decision that coaches hate the most: what to do for the next Sunday after the top quarterback has stunk and his replacement has come along, dashing and daring, and yanked the victory out of those proverbial flames of disaster.

"I didn't think he was washed up," Gregg said. He decided to start Kenny Anderson.

"All of us have bad days," Gregg reasoned. "I'd have hated to have my career as a starter ended by one bad day."

Anderson pitched Paul Brown's second team to first place, for the first time.

In the playoffs, the Bengals beat the Bills, 28-21, in the first round. The Bengals were the home team for the AFC championship game. On Sunday morning, January 10, 1982, shoots of ice formed on the blue bridge spanning the Ohio River outside Riverfront Stadium. The Astroturf was frozen. The wind whipped in knifing gusts. Gregg remembered a day such as this years before in Green Bay. But then he could play. On this day, he was forced to stand at the bench and coach. It was 11 degrees below zero. And gauged by that new stat developed by TV's weather guessers, the wind-chill factor was 59 below.

Pete Rozelle considered postponing the game until the cold broke. But they decided to play. Battling frostbite, the players turned in a classic. Anderson flipped two touchdown passes. The Bengals won, 27-7, over the Chargers. Cincinnati, the baseball town, had a team in the Super Bowl.

◆ ◆ ◆

The media practices were getting worse, gradually, painfully. Now in Detroit, my town, we experienced the breakthrough. The Super Bowl had become an event at which the media covered the media more than they did the football game, the football players, the football coaches. The out-of-town sportswriters became celebrities. The locals were, well . . . I was on Channel 2, 4, 7. I was on radio talk shows. I was wandering through the lobby at the Hyatt one afternoon when a reporter stopped me.

"You with the media?" she asked, identifying herself as an employee of the Detroit *Free Press,* our sworn enemy.

"Yep," I said.

"Whatcha think of Detroit?"

"It's ugly, the only thing I liked so far was the smokestack judging contest," I said.

"Oh, yeah," she said. "What paper you work for?"

"Detroit *News,*" I said.

She looked at me—and it was great, she had a sense of humor. She knew her editor had sent her out on a dippy assignment. She laughed. The rest of it was dippy, but not funny.

Paul Zimmerman was under assault for his comments on "Good Morning America." Every disk jockey in town started a crusade to tar and feather Dr. Z, then stick him starkers, tied to a post, on the frozen tundra of Dearborn. But you expected that from them. When the movie critics and the gossip columnists of the newspapers went after Paul, it became embarrassing. Minor-leaguesville journalism, baby.

It was time to borrow a disguise from Bill Walsh. Not for Zimmerman. For me.

◆ ◆ ◆

No matter what the computer printouts say; no matter how much the scouts drool over college prospects; no matter what the size and strength and speed tests show in the pre-draft evaluation drafts, the annual NFL draft remains a game of pin the tail on the donkey. You've got to be lucky.

In his second season at San Francisco, with Montana as his part-time quarterback, Walsh went 6-10. The offense was improved. The pass defense was porous, fragile.

So it was that Walsh went into the draft of 1981 with a radical plan. On the first round he drafted a defensive back, Ronnie Lott out of Southern Cal. On the second round, he drafted a defensive back, Eric Wright from Missouri. On the third round, he drafted a defensive back, Carlton Williamson from Pitt. Without a pick on the fourth round, on the fifth round, with the second of two choices, Walsh picked a defensive back, Lynn Thomas from Pitt. Walsh had played pin the tail on the donkey. He had aimed for four defensive backs among the first five players he drafted. And he was very lucky.

Lott and Wright made it as starting cornerbacks and Williamson as a safety as rookies in '81. And Walsh was lucky on the fourth defensive back, Dwight Hicks. Hicks had flunked trials with the Lions and Eagles and then had gotten a job. Hicks went to the 49ers straight from serving up carrot juice cocktails at a Healthy Jones restaurant in suburban Detroit.

Mixed new into Walsh's defense with these rookies and converted health-food server were two grizzled veterans. To boost the pass rush, Walsh traded for Fred Dean, who was involved in a bitter contract struggle in San Diego. To improve the linebacking, he picked up an ancient legend dropped by the Rams: Hacksaw Reynolds. The 49ers' defense knotted into something stingy.

And so it was that this ragamuffin club with losing records for four consecutive years went through the '81 NFL season at 13-and-3. In the playoffs for the first time in 10 seasons, the 49ers beat the Giants, 38-24. Montana threw two touchdown passes, and Lott made matters safe with an interception.

The next week, as the Bengals and Chargers played in weather that felt like 59 degrees below, the 49ers and Cowboys played in the San Francisco mud. It was a monumental battle. Trailing by six, the 49ers were whipped 89 yards in the last five minutes by Montana. Then in the final minute, Montana scrambled. He spotted Dwight Clark in the end zone and launched a jump pass for a spot behind the end zone. Clark rose into the air and caught the ball before it went out of bounds. The 49ers were NFC champions for the first time, 28-27.

◆　◆　◆

I had picked the Bengals to win in the pool in the pressroom, so I went to find Paul Zimmerman to pay my buck. I found him playing one of the PacMan games the Host Committee had set up in the press area. It was the only place he was safe from the disk jockeys, amateur journalists, and just plain crank callers who phoned death threats to his room.

The week went on, a nonstop party. A headline said: *Get Looped on Supercrawl,* referring to the bus that looped around town transporting folks to spots where they could get drunk. One of the buses had a defective door and two of the revelers fell through, flopped to the icy street, and were killed. But the partying did not stop to recognize tragedy.

A ticket to Pete Rozelle's party was the hottest piece of cardboard in the cold town. Tickets to the Super Bowl were available for a reasonable price. But not tickets to Pete's party. The papers wrote about it until you wanted to barf.

Detroit lacked a reasonable party site, really. No dowdy ocean liner was available, and the airport had to be used to bring in visitors. "We thought about the Lindell A.C.," Rozelle said. Joke. The Lindell was the place Alex Karras had a piece of when Pete suspended him for betting.

In the end, the party—music by Peter Duchin—was held at the Fairlane Center in Dearborn on a bitter cold night. And it was a nice party, once you scraped the ice off the windshield and were able to get to it.

◆　◆　◆

It did not snow on Super Sunday. It was just cold, windy, raw, freezing, gray, ugly.

The Silverdome is a hellish place to reach on an ordinary football Sunday. The traffic clogs on the thin access roads and spills back onto the freeway. From experience, I've always given myself three hours to drive to the dome and to wind down inside, reading, chatting, nibbling.

This football Sunday, I stuffed myself fast at the pregame brunch and headed for the front door of the Hyatt. I wanted to be aboard the first bus, four hours before kickoff. I would leave the driving to the NFL-provided expert. He took off and started following the circuitous route sketched out on the offical NFL map. We went round about, past central Detroit, ignoring the straight-line theory. When we got off the freeway, the access road was gridlocked already. At last we inched into the parking lot, in which cars were being turned about helter skelter.

The bus door opened finally, and we trooped out onto the vast asphalt, strewn with jagged chunks of ice. Guys skidded and slipped, lugging their portable computers. I got inside, plopped down into my seat, and pounded happily on the box lunch the NFL had thoughtfully provided. Other groups of writers straggled in with horror stories. The traffic outside was impenetrable. Guys had to walk a mile over the ice to get there. They told tales of bus drivers getting lost and having to stop to ask directions to the Silverdome. All the rookies were not employed in the 49ers' defensive backfield. The next groups reported conditions worsening.

Kickoff approached. Mike O'Hara, my colleague from the *News,* wasn't there. His seat was empty. He was supposed to write the game lead. Now it was almost kickoff. O'Hara showed up, panting, his face flushed. He had gone to the Silverdome for all the Lions' games. He had his own routine, and he didn't change it for the Super Bowl. It was a good thing he was a marathon runner. He got to a spot a mile and a half from the Silverdome, got trapped in the traffic, and ran to the game.

Outside, all flow of automobiles for miles around had been stopped. George Bush, the vice president, had decided to attend the Super Bowl. The police shut the freeway accesses near the Silverdome for 15 minutes to allow the vice president's cavalcade to drive through.

Thousands of fans, hundreds of writers were stuck, waiting. A hundred or more cars were abandoned alongside the roadways. Their occupants continued on foot. It was a mess.

Bobby Layne flipped the commemorative Super Bowl XVI coin. The 49ers won the toss. Amos Lawrence fielded the kickoff and ran it back 17 yards. Then he was hit and coughed up the football at the 26. John Simmons recovered for the Bengals. Anderson took them to the five. He was sacked back to the 11. Next play he passed. The ball was in the air and Dwight Hicks intercepted it.

Nothing outside mattered now. The football game was being played. At last. And it was a traditional Super Bowl right in the opening moments. A fumble lost, an interception. Ragamuffin football. Joe Montana guided the 49ers the 68 yards for the first touchdown. He scored himself from the one after a couple of passes to Freddie Solomon.

Kenny Anderson was as sharp as Joe as the Bengals marched in the other direction. He got them to the 49ers' 27 and then launched a pass to his prize rookie receiver, Cris Collinsworth, for 19 yards. But then Cris fumbled. For the second time the Bengals were thwarted, inside the 10, when they should have scored.

It was Montana's turn again. This time he took the 49ers the 92 yards to score in a display of ball control. He passed the last 11 yards to Earl Cooper for the second touchdown. It was early in the second period. The 49ers were ahead, 14-0. Stuck deep by a poor kickoff return, the Bengals had to punt. Montana charged the 49ers to the five. Then Ray Wersching booted a 22-yard field goal 18 seconds before halftime. The 49ers were up, 17 to zip, and they managed to score once more before the halftime interval. Archie Griffin fumbled away Wersching's squib kickoff, and Milt McColl recovered for the 49ers. Wersching kicked another field goal, from 26 yards. The 49ers had scored on field goals 13 seconds apart. They were in command 20-0 at the half—and Walsh was worried.

Perhaps more worried than Gregg, who reminded the Bengals that they had trailed the Seahawks 21-0 once and had won.

After the halftime show, the Bengals moved downfield to the San Francisco five. There, Anderson, planning to throw, suddenly dashed off and scored the touchdown. No more zip, the Bengals were aroused. Soon they were moving down the field again. Anderson passed to Collinsworth on a third-and-23. It was good for 49 yards. The Bengals were at the 14. They got one more first down at the 49ers' three.

And then, Pete Johnson, 249 pounds, hit center to the one. Johnson hit guard and was halted for no gain. Anderson passed to Charles Alexander, and before the receiver could advance the one yard over the goal line, Dan Bunz felled him for no gain, again. It was fourth down. Gregg disdained the field goal. With Hacksaw Reynolds bellowing enouragement, the 49ers' line swarmed on Pete Johnson again as he tried to barge over. They stopped him—a magnificent goal-line stand—and the 49ers had the ball back.

The 49ers, beginning from their one, had to punt. This time the Bengals made it to the touchdown. Anderson passed four yards to Dan Ross, his tight end. With ample time in the fourth quarter—more than 10 minutes—the Bengals had pared the 49ers' lead to six points. The score was 20-14, San Francisco.

Now Montana wanted to squeeze time off the clock. He ran off 10 plays, seven of them on the ground, before the drive faltered. Then Wersching kicked his third field from 40 yards. With nearly five and one-half minutes left, the 49ers led 23-14.

Now Anderson tried to score quickly. His pass for Collinsworth was picked off, intercepted by Eric Wright. Montana used up three more minutes. Then Wersching kicked his fourth field goal, a 23-yarder. It was 26-14, in favor of San Francsico, time to celebrate, with less than two minutes left.

But wait. Anderson had one more strike left. He completed six successive passes, none out of bounds. So the clock continued to run. The last was three yards to Dan Ross for the TD. It was 26-21, 49ers, and if the onside kickoff succeeded, Anderson would have one more shot. But the bouncing ball was trapped and gathered in by Dwight Clark. Montana retreated and knelt with the ball on the next play. And then he raised both arms in triumph. The 49ers had risen from the depths, from decades of frustration, from garbage-heaped abuse by their own fans. They had won a Super Bowl, 26-21.

Outside it was a mess again as cars and fans skidded across the iced parking lots. Another traffic jam as George Bush left.

Downstairs, standing on a pedestal, Joe Montana's face was full of starlight as he spoke to us in the press.

A column, the Detroit *News,* January 1982:

Joe Montana can't handle it. The bright lights make him blink. He can't stand the fuss. He sips Pepsi from a can; never mind the Johnny Walker Red.

When he left the Silverdome after winning the Super Bowl, he didn't walk out with a blond on one arm and a brunette on the other. His entourage wasn't accompanied by a cop with a dog on a leash.

But . . . he has done exactly what his hero, Broadway Joe Namath, did 13 years ago. Indeed, Joe Montana won his Super Bowl on the same day of his life that Joe Willie did. They are even up as the youngest quarterbacks to win the Super Bowl—25 years, six months, 13 days old.

They came to the Super Bowl doubted and disbelieved. Their teams were scoffed at and ridiculed. But they won.

"People didn't believe we'd make the playoffs," Joe Montana said. . . . "We started winning big games, and people still didn't believe us. I mean people around the country.

"We beat Dallas, and nobody believed in us. We beat Pittsburgh. We beat Cincinnati in Cincinnati. And they still didn't believe in us. Dallas a second time in the championship game, and people still didn't believe.

"Even the coaches around the league. Most of them picked against us in the Super Bowl.

"People didn't start to believe in us until—oh, about two minutes ago."

———

Jim Steeg, Pete Rozelle's deputized Super Bowl planner, surveyed the chaos, heard the gripes from owners and writers about the mess made of the Super Bowl in Detroit, about the ice and traffic clogs. Steeg memoed Rozelle about how to prevent such problems at future Super Bowls: "Most importantly, we should totally discourage a presidential or vice presidential visit unless they abide by our recommendations."

XVII
The Mickey Mouse Playoffs

Washington Redskins 27, Miami Dolphins 17
January 30, 1983
Rose Bowl, Pasadena
Attendance: 103,667

Just like England, there'll always be a Super Bowl. There'll be a Super Bowl when its numerals reach CMXVI. If there was a Super Bowl in 1983 as usual in January, there could be one any year.

Nuclear wars and atomic blasts and holocausts and wrecks and typhoons and crippling scandals could not ever stop the Super Bowl from going on. No matter—America would always have its finest week of football debauchery.

I arrived in Los Angeles cynical, with the super blahs, for Super Bowl XVII. It would be the Redskins—John Riggins, Joe Theismann—and the Dolphins, Don Shula again. But in my mind it was an awful charade.

Pro football—the sport, the business—was in a horrible mess. No other sport had been pounded and bloodied the way pro football had been during the previous six months.

1. It was the season of the game's first strike, a 57-day lull without games. People grabbed at the false notion that they didn't care. The NFL kept saying there would be no Super Bowl if there was no agreement this week; no settlement now, and the Super Bowl's a goner.
2. It was the season of renewed charges of payoffs to players and fixing of pro games by gamblers wanting an edge. Public

Broadcasting Service voiced these allegations on television, accusing without much substantiation. It was a season of charges that Pete Rozelle had been negligent in safeguarding the integrity of the game. It was a season of a public charge that one owner had been murdered by angered underworld gamblers. Carroll Rosenbloom's agonizing drowning returned to the news with broadcasted suspicions that it was not a mere swimming accident.

3. It was the season of one cocaine scandal after another, from revelations by *Sports Illustrated* to blanket accusations by Bill Walsh. Nobody knew when his favorite fullback dropped the football whether it was due to a noseful or butterfingers. Three former NFL players were tried, convicted, imprisoned.

4. It was the year Pete Rozelle was beaten to a pulp in the courtroom by Al Davis, who carpetbagged his franchise from Oakland to Los Angeles against the wishes of his 27 fellow owners.

5. The United States Football League was horning in on the NFL's turf, starting up with a supposed springtime league. But it was picking off some prize players. Rozelle did not disdainfully refer to this upstart league as the Other League this time. He was respectful. The USFL had challenged his establishment by plucking Herschel Walker right out of Georgia with college eligibility remaining. More danger loomed for the NFL.

But the NFL is a tough codger. The mighty old Super Bowl persevered when a lesser event would have collapsed. Anywhere else, they'd call off the Coronation Ball if the queen were sneaking out to meet the gardener, or if somebody stole the family jewels.

But here we were again, a media army of 2,000, about to go through the same rigmarole. The drums would beat, and the media marvels would beat a path to the athletes to discover whether their preference was Wheaties or Corn Flakes. I kept wondering. Why? How?

Rozelle employed the finest pitchmen in the business. The countdown to Super Bowl XVII would move swiftly and precisely. It would go on with the normal glitter and polish. And whitewash. The Goodyear blimp and the footballs would be pumped up in a year when pro football should have burst with its internal agonies.

A week earlier as Riggins pounded forward with the lugged football, senators and congressmen, Republicans and Democrats, stopped what they were doing in Washington to root the Redskins on to the Super Bowl. Ronald Reagan, president of the United States, phoned his congratulations to the locker room.

I thought: We are either the most gullible nation on earth—or the most passionately devoted.

So, we the press checked into the L.A. Marriott to repeat the annual rites of January. Cynics. Skeptics.

The labor strike had compacted the end of the season, extended it, fouled the playoffs, wiped out the customary two-week interval between the conference championship games and the Super Bowl. The clubs played nine games in the reduced regular season. Division titles were rendered meaningless. Then, 16 of the 28 clubs were bunched into the playoffs. My wondrous Detroit Lions even qualified, with a 4-5 record for the season.

"Pete Rozelle's Mickey Mouse playoffs," said William Clay Ford, owner of this sub-.500, playoff-bound club.

But then the people danced in celebration the day their club made it.

So, I was a sourpuss as I allowed myself to be prodded onto the bus for the traditional opener of Super Bowl week. We were off to see the athletes who had spent nearly two months of their season as laborers on strike.

We stopped at Anaheim, a few blocks from Disneyland, home turf of Mickey Mouse, and training quarters for the Redskins.

John Riggins was doing his impersonation of Duane Thomas. He refused to speak. He didn't even care what time it was. Joe Theismann rejected silence. This was the Mickey Mouse of the playoffs himself.

ANAHEIM—The arm and the mouth are in sync.

This is the Super Bowl, the number one gala in professional sports. It is time to get up and shout and show.

Underneath the goalposts of the football field, John Riggins is mum. . . . Joe Theismann stands 20 yards away. You can't shut him up. His arm got the Redskins to the Super Bowl. And now his mouth is the one which roars.

Rat-ta-ta-tat. Washington Joe Theismann is holding court. Twelve years of silent frustration are gushing out.

He is angry. He is glad. He is sad. He is melancholy.

"This is wonderful here," says Washington Joe. "We're not a great team, but we're proud. You know our Al Garrett. Al's a street fighter. Put him in a gutter and Al will come out. That's the makeup of our team.

"We're a bunch of street fighters."

Theismann . . . is not the best quarterback who ever came to the Super Bowl. But he is the hottest talker.

"Johnny Unitas was an idol," says Joe. "Joe Namath was an idol. Bart Starr, too. I used to do my face mask like Kenny Stabler. I used to walk with a hunchback like Unitas. With a limp like Namath."

"This is a 12-year-old wrapped in a 33-year-old body."

There is slight intrigue to this Super Bowl. It is a simple game. Washington versus Miami. There is no Terry Bradshaw to prove his smarts by spelling C-A-T. There is no audacious Namath to guarantee upset victory while inhaling Johnny Walker Red and walking his lady.

All the undercover stuff is wrapped up in Joe Theismann's Miami Connection.

Washington Joe was a draft choice of the Dolphins back in 1970 when he left Notre Dame. He agreed to terms with the Dolphins.... He jumped out of his agreement to sign for 50 grand with the Toronto Argonauts. He says there was a problem with the Dolphins' signing bonus.

"Ticked me off is a good description of the way I felt," Don Shula said of Theismann's defection. "He went on TV in Miami to say he was glad he was a Dolphin. Then the contract never came back. I went to South Bend to find him, and he said it was all set. Then two days later he announced he had signed with Canada.

"I was ticked off at the time. He didn't honor his commitment."

"Ah," says Motormouth Joe. "I remember my infamous statement: 'Come hell or high water, I'll be a Miami Dolphin.'" He squinted into the sun and spoke on.

"I made a mistake. I made a mess. I did it to myself. It was a very regretful experience. I embarrassed them, and I embarrassed myself."

Three years later Theismann wanted to come back to the States. But not to Miami. Shula traded Theismann to George Allen's Over-the-Hill Gang in Washington for a number one draft choice. Theismann thought he was going to be a number one QB in Washington. He found Bill Kilmer and Sonny Jurgensen playing ahead of him.

"I got there and made up a ring for myself," Theismann says, never shutting up. "It had a Redskin on it and three small diamonds for the three Super Bowls I missed with Miami.

"The Dolphins played in three Super Bowls while I was under contract in theory.

"And when I came back from Canada, Bob Griese had played in three Super Bowls and I'd have been in the same position as Earl Morrall.

"I didn't realize I'd be behind Bill Kilmer and Sonny Jurgensen in Washington.

"I remember once I woke up in the middle of the night and knocked on Coach Allen's door. Trade me, I asked. I must have asked him a hundred times to trade me."

Theismann had been sent into one game, and Kilmer, looking up from the huddle, saw him. Kilmer waved Joe back to the bench. Theismann slinked off the field, humiliated.

"I knew I didn't have a chance as long as Bill was there," says Washington Joe. "Trade me. I'll come back when I'm 30."

Theismann says his total outlook changed in 1976, when he wasn't playing. His daughter Amy, then three, took ill with a heart disorder.

"It was the low point of my life," he says. "I did have a job. I didn't have a job. I thought I'm Joe Theismann, the football player, and the world owes me a living.

"I was wrong. And then Amy had to have an operation—she's fine now—I said, 'Who me? I'm Joe Theismann, my name is in the paper. This can't happen to me.'

"I went to the hospital and tubes were running out of her little body. She looked up with her oxygen mask on her face and said: 'Daddy.'

"I was 26 years old and didn't know right from wrong. That one word changed my life."

I had known Don Shula when he was a studious assistant coach, more than 20 years ago. He impressed me then. He impressed me more now at Super Bowl XVII. I always saw the solid jaw, the pure emotion, the pain in defeat, the professionalism in victory. But now I realized what a rock this man was, the consummate NFL coach because of his durability.

Dick Vermeil had gone down in flames the day he quit, a couple of weeks earlier.

"I'm burned out," Vermeil had said, quitting in Philly as other clubs played in the Super Bowl playoffs. "I'm physically and mentally drained. I just have to get out for a while."

Two years earlier he had coached in the Super Bowl himself. He torched himself with his own intensity.

Bill Walsh almost went down in flames, too. He was set to quit in San Francisco and was hunting for his own successor. "Bill Walsh is a basket case," people said around the NFL. Walsh finally decided to keep working, persuaded by Eddie DeBartolo, his owner.

Only a year earlier Bill Walsh had coached in the Super Bowl. The head coaching job is a killer.

A few years before Super Bowl XVII, John Madden put the torch to himself with his expressive hands. "I'm through," he said at the height of his career with Oakland, winner of a Super Bowl. "Too much pressure for me and my family. The day I had to sign a driver's learner permit for my son and asked my wife how a kid of 11 qualifies and she said, 'John, he's 16'. . . that was it."

And that is why I watched Don Shula on the Dolphins' field on photo day before Super Bowl XVII and admired the man so much. He was fireproof. He had been a successful NFL coach, a coach in the Super Bowl, before Madden, before Vermeil, before Walsh went to work as head coaches.

"Each of us has his own style," Shula said. "Vermeil put a lot of himself into it. He had early morning meetings. He'd stay overnight in the office.

"I just enjoy what I'm doing. When the time comes to sign a new contract, I step back and become more objective about my job. The coaches who did it this year did it in an asterisk situation. It was a different kind of year.

"I'd prefer for coaches to stand back and give it some breathing room, and then evaluate it . . . not like Vermeil did, jumping right out."

Shula had developed, mellowed through the decades.

He was a dour man without other interests the first time he went to a Super Bowl with the Colts in 1969. The loss to Joe Namath still was etched on his skin, like a scar across his nose. "That was one of the darkest moments of my career," he said this morning at the asterisk Super Bowl as the Dolphins pranced for the photographers at Cal State-Fullerton.

He had started loosening up on his third trip to the Super Bowl, with the team of perfection at Super Bowl VII. And now on this, his fifth trip to the Super Bowl, he had become a gregarious man undisturbed by the routine distractions.

"I always had a sense of humor," he said. A joke.

"We had a players' meeting after we won last week," Shula said. "They wanted to know about their wives coming to the Super Bowl. Then the guys without wives wanted to know about bringing their girlfriends. Then the guys without wives or girlfriends wanted to know about bringing their mothers.

"The guy I was worrried about was the one who wanted to bring his wife, girlfriend, and mother." We all grinned.

"I learned a lot in the last 10 years," Shula said.

◆ ◆ ◆

John Riggins promised a single press conference for Wednesday morning of Super Bowl week. He would break his 18 months of silence for this one appearance and then return to the mum status. Perhaps forever, perhaps only until after the game. So every reporter in the western world descended upon the Redskins' hotel headquarters in Costa Mesa, prepared to discover what made John Riggins tick, tick, tick.

This man of many costumes and multiple disguises, including the Mohawk arrow hairdo and the shaved-skull look, showed up with a bushy mess of curled hair. He appeared in camouflage pants and a T-shirt proclaiming the Five O'Clock Club. This would be a switch from the night Jack Kent Cooke, his team owner, tossed a Super Bowl party. That night, Riggins attended in a top hat and tails.

Delighted to be in our presence at last, Riggins sported a large shit-eating grin. "John," a reporter asked, "to what do you attribute your longevity?"

"Formaldehyde," responded Riggins.

He was then asked his opinions of the famed Hogs, those slimy creatures up front who block for him.

"Those Hogs are a real bunch of slobs," said Riggins, "but they're my kind of guys."

"How do you describe yourself?"

"I've been described by other people as somewhat boring, which is probably true," said Riggins.

"You stayed out of football for a year in 1980. What did you do with your time?

"I painted my house," said Riggins. "That's about it. I'm not a particularly fast worker."

"Did you get a new perspective on football by not playing?"

"Yeah," said Riggins, "through the eyes of my banker."

"Your coach, Joe Gibbs, visited you in Kansas before you decided to come back to the Redskins. What did he say?"

"I can't remember that well," Riggins said. "I'd been out a little late the night before. I was drinking a can of beer when he came to the door at nine that morning."

We're real nosy SOBs, and we had Riggins standing at the lectern in front of us in the hotel ballroom, and he was making our week.

"What do you do with your time off from football?" asked another interrogator. "Are you one of those people who goes up in the mountains?"

"Not in Kansas," said John Riggins.

"But what do you do?"

"I spend a lot of time outdoors," said Riggins. "I hunt and fish a lot."

"What do you hunt?"

"I'd just as soon not get into it," Riggins said. "There are a lot of animal lovers out there. I don't want to start a save-the-quails campaign."

"How do you fit in with the Washington crowd?"

"Life in Washington is like being on a roll of toilet paper. You know you're going to get smeared, but you try not to get flushed down."

ready to steam. Then the phone rang. It was the office calling. Bear Bryant had died. They wanted a column on the Bear. Mike O'Hara had himself a party doing Riggins for our paper.

◆ ◆ ◆

I was sound asleep in my room in the L.A. Marriott when a sharp ring jolted me to semi-wakefulness.

"Hulloooo," I muttered into the phone.

"Jerry," said a female voice.

"Yeah, that's me."

"Jerry Greene?" said the voice.

"Yeah, who is this?" I said. The female voice sounded annoyed.

"If this were really Jerry Greene," said the voice, "you'd know it was your wife Judy in Florida."

"Oh," said the drowsy one, "you want the other Jerry Greene. What time is it?"

"Seven o'clock and I'm going to work," she said.

"Four o'clock in the morning out here."

"Did you speak to your wife?" I asked Jerry Greene, South, the football writer from Orlando, when we happened on the same bus to the Dolphins four hours later.

"No," he said.

"She sounded fine," said Jerry Green, North.

◆ ◆ ◆

The kid who played quarterback for the Dolphins this championship season was barely a year older than Shula's newest assistant coach, his own 23-year-old son David. David Woodley had been an eighth-round draftee, an unlikely follower in the lineage of Bob Griese. Woodley was a third-year pro. During the players' strike in midseason, he drove a truck. His image was far from the flamboyant, crazy, boisterous image of so many Super Bowl quarterbacks.

"Obviously, this is the biggest game of my life," Woodley said in one of his few Super Bowl comments. "It's the biggest game of any player's life."

Obviously.

Don Shula used a quick hook with Woodley, sitting him down when he was in trouble, starting him the following Sunday. With this arrangement, the Dolphins went 7-2 in the shortened regular season.

They entered the Mickey Mouse playoffs with the mob. Then they beat the Patriots, 28-13, on two TD passes by Woodley. The next week, he threw two more and and ran for another touchdown. The Dolphins beat the Chargers, 34-13. They were, quite unexpectedly, in the AFC championship game.

The Orange Bowl's field was a mess of mud for the championship game against the Jets, the natural habitat for the Dolphins' gimmick-nicknamed defense, called the Killer Bees. After a 0-0 half, the Killer Bees' A.J. Duhe intercepted a pass. Woodley moved the Dolphins 48 yards to a touchdown scored by Woody Bennett. In the fourth quarter, Duhe made his third interception and returned the ball 35 yards for another TD. The Dolphins beat the Jets, 14-0. Don Shula was in his fifth Super Bowl.

◆ ◆ ◆

The jurists of the Supreme Court adored their Redskins. The members of Congress scrambled for tickets to the 'Skins games. Ronald Reagan himself believed the Redskins were pretty neat.

So, for the climax of a season that was somewhat imperfect for Pete Rozelle and pro football, it was entirely fitting that the Super Bowl would be played with a cast of oddballs and miscasts. Favorites of our governmental muckamucks, a team of weirdos. The Redskins would line up with a disk jockey at quarterback. The star running back might appear dressed in his camouflage suit, his ties and tails with the top hat, his head skinned bald by a razor. When the game ended, he was apt to vanish in silence and not reappear until discovered, passed out beneath a banquet table occupied by several Supreme Court justices.

When upright, this star might be accompanied by a group of bawdy ruffians who call themselves the Hogs.

Field position being elementary to victorious football, the kick returner so vital to such geographical placement was a guy who did birdcalls on the side.

And when this team did manage to score a touchdown, five or six of these Redskins would gather in a circle in the end zone and sing and dance and jump up in a communal High Five. They called themselves the Smurfs.

Championship football teams must be coached. The coach of this team was one of those intensity men who avoided going home during the season. Instead, he believed he'd get an edge by sleeping with his head on his desk in his office.

And such teams must always have somebody who collects these individuals and assembles them into a unit. Procurement is the game, and the guy who did this for the favorite team of America's politicos was an executive who wore jogging shoes and ran in marathons.

The last time the Redskins had made it to the Super Bowl, the only time they managed to score was when the other team's placekicker decided to try to throw a forward pass. But now the 'Skins were known as a team of destiny. They were one-year wonders. And this was that one year.

Jabbering Joe Theismann was the quarterback with the hottest hand. He was never a remarkable pro quarterback. But at 33, he had struck the right tune. He began each day by going to a radio station, where he spinned some platters and added a dose of talk.

From there, he turned to football and used his hot hand to stick the ball in John Riggins's tummy. Except for occasional grunts, and the day he attributed his longevity to formaldehyde, Riggins's silence had made as much impact as Theismann's nonstop mouthings. On the field, Theismann would hand the ball off 25 times to Riggins. Riggins would plow down the field at five yards a pop. At the end of the game, he would bow to the crowd and escape in a helicopter.

"You never saw a Hog stung by a Killer Bee," Riggins said in his one day of public conversation.

The Hogs were the first blocking unit ever to be romanticized with a nickname. They were proud and exclusive. Once Theismann flipped a block on a reverse. He applied for membership in the Hogs. They rejected him.

"They only let me become a piglet," said Joe.

Joe Gibbs had become coach of the team once coached by Vince Lombardi and then George Allen. But even they went home at night, Vince to Marie, Allen to his vanilla ice cream. Gibbs believed he could improve his game plans by sleeping in the office, improvement by osmosis.

But while he slept, Gibbs urged his players to have fun during Super Bowl week. He did this unlike any Super Bowl coach before him. So the Hogs were out and around. One night, we spotted lineman George Starke with a Hogs' jacket on his immense body at The Ginger Man, the chic Beverly Hills spot.

One reason the 'Skins reached the Super Bowl was Mike Nelms. He had made some vital kick returns during the season. During the days before the Super Bowl, he was in evidence on local TV screens, trilling his birdcalls with a sweet pitch.

The Redskins were not a football team assembled out of a computer. That's the way the Steelers always did it, the Cowboys always did it, the old Dolphins did it. But the Redskins became champions off the waiver lists, out of the lower draft rounds. They were in Super Bowl XVII with 26 players who were once free agents. Fourteen of those had never been drafted. The man who discovered all these individuals, assembled them, blended them, was Bobby Beathard—the GM in jogging shoes, a four-time Boston Marathoner.

This group of oddballs and curios played through the disrupted season with an 8-1 record. The Redskins wound up with a gimme in the first round of the playoffs, the sub-.500 Lions. Mickey Mouse roared at the joke. The Redskins beat the Lions, 31-7, as Theismann exploited a cornerback deficiency with three TD passes to Smurf Alvin Garrett. Next the Redskins took care of the Vikings, 21-7.

So it was that the Cowboys and Redskins resumed their bitter rivalry in the NFC championship game. Riggins was the crunching hero as the Redskins won it, 31-16.

Hogs versus Killer Bees in the Super Bowl.

◆ ◆ ◆

To commemorate this spectacular season of pro football, Pete Rozelle canceled the traditional Super Bowl party. The moochers could go out and buy themselves their own booze, pay for their own food. Or in the case of the hardened press people, who are iron-bound in the belief they should never use their own money, they could use their expense accounts.

A number of us celebrated what would have been party night, under normal conditions, by going to Chasen's. We supped with Frank Sinatra dining several tables distant, with Gregory Peck ensconced in the next room. Otherwise, those of us at this large media table were the special stars of the night at Chasen's. We were lucky they didn't throw the whole mob of us out into the street. But green money is green money, no matter who spends it.

It had been a rainy week with mud slides along the California coast. It meant Saturday night without a party, too. I couldn't drive up the coast to Dick Schapp's party in Malibu. Shucks.

◆ ◆ ◆

Something funny had happened at Super Bowl XVII. Not everybody succumbed to the narcotic effect the NFL presumed it held over the American public. You could buy a ticket for a seat in the Rose Bowl.

"Ticket pressure isn't as high as it has been for other Super Bowls," Pete Rozelle said at his annual press conference.

The Mickey Mouse season.

Jimmy the Greek figured the Dolphins to be three-point favorites, a neat, conservative spot. And once the pregame festivities were out of the way, the Greek looked good. The Dolphins struck first. Woodley, the youngest quarterback to start in a Super Bowl, clicked on his second series. He hit Jimmy Cefalo with a 76-yard scoring pass. Cefalo won a footrace over the last 45 yards to put the Dolphins up, 7-0.

The Redskins got three back after Dexter Manley, crashing in from end, batted Woodley and caused a fumble. From Miami's 46, Riggins plowed forward. He carried four times. The Killer Bees halted the advance at the 14. Mark Moseley kicked a 31-yard field goal.

The Dolphins replied with their own field goal, following Fulton Walker's 42-yard kickoff return. Woodley got the Dolphins to the three. Then Uwe von Schamann kicked a 20-yarder, and the Dolphins led, 10-3. Washington's return drive was featured by the running of Riggins and the scrambling Theismann. They got it to the Miami four. Then Theismann went to the Smurfs. He passed to Alvin Garrett, who first caught the touchdown pass, then led the jumping celebration circle in the end zone. It was square at 10-10.

Less than two minutes remained before the halftime show. Jeff Hayes kicked off for Washington. Fulton Walker caught the kick at the two and veered to his left. He found a gap and streaked through it, beating the futile grab by the kicker, going the 98 yards for the touchdown. The Dolphins were again up by seven, 17-10.

In the third quarter, the Redskins picked a reverse out of the plays Gibbs had dreamed up at night in his office. Riggins reversed the ball to Garrett, and the end-around was worth 44 yards. But this time Theismann's end-zone pass misfired. Moseley kicked a 20-yard field goal to cut Miami's advantage to 17-13.

We had some Super Bowl melodrama again—after the cartoon-character season.

The two clubs battled, their defenses now dominant. Duhe, the interception specialist, picked off one by Theismann. The Redskins got it back when Mark Murphy made a juggling interception. Theismann threw another right into the hands of Killer Bee Kim Bokamper. He had the ball on his fingertips. Theismann ran over and swatted at the ball, and it fell loose. It was a gigantic play.

Rescued by that, the Redskins advanced to the Dolphins' 43. Here Theismann pulled something deep out of Earl Morrall's ancient Super Bowl playbook. Joe flipped to Riggins. Riggins flipped back. Off the flea flicker, Theismann passed deep for Smurf Charlie Brown. But Lyle Blackwood intercepted the ball at the one. Woodley was unable to do much with the possession. The Redskins got the ball again at their 48. They picked up nine yards in three thrusts.

It was fourth-down-and-one at the Miami 43. In conservative Super Bowl style, a punt situation. Gibbs called a special run. Tight end Clint Didier went in motion. Don McNeal, the Miami cornerback, tracked him. Then Theismann handed the ball off to Riggins, who hit the left side and broke free and open into the region McNeal had vacated moments earlier. McNeal's one-handed reach was futile against Riggins's power. John was clear and rumbling—43 yards for the touchdown. It was the fourth quarter, and the Redskins were ahead, 20-17, for the first time.

There were 10 minutes for Miami. But Woodley had been blanked as a passer in the second half. He would not complete a pass. He would ultimately be yanked for Don Strock, who also would fail to connect.

Theismann, meanwhile, engineered another touchdown drive. He consumed time off the clock. Twice he hit Charlie Brown on passes. The second produced another touchdown, six yards. And the Smurfs again put on their end-zone jamboree.

It ended Redskins 27, Miami 17. Riggins had grounded out 166 yards, a Super Bowl rushing mark.

The NFL's messiest season ended with an honorable Super Bowl.

PASADENA—John Riggins did not come dressed up for the ball. This was not Bart Starr in a buttoned-down shirt and striped necktie. It wasn't Joe Willie Namath in a llama fur coat, a doll on each arm, leaving the Super Bowl in the darkness with an escort of cops and police dogs.

This was John Riggins, the ultimate free spirit in the ultimate game.

It was John Riggins out of Kansas running behind a prideful group called the Hogs.

All of it means wallowing in slime, burrowing in the dirt.

John Riggins arrived at the Super Bowl dressed in a gray workman's shirt and camouflage hunting pants with big pockets. On his head, he wore a camouflage hat with the inscription "Ducks Unlmited."

And this day's work was the same as shooting ducks for John Riggins.

When he bolted 43 yards with 10 minutes left, he won the Super Bowl for the Washington Redskins. . . . His body was racked. Bruises and splotches of blood covered the hands that had held the football. . . . President Reagan had called the Redskins' locker room with his felicitations. The president made some plays on the similarity between their names.

"Ron's the president, but I'm the king," said Riggins.

XVIII
The Devil's Laugh

Los Angeles Raiders 38, Washington Redskins 9
January 22, 1984
Tampa Stadium
Attendance: 72,920

Even Al Davis, although he would dispute the notion, had missed attaining devilish perfection. He had never had the perfect Raider, never before. He had knifers and muggers and real-life crooks who had spent time in stir before roaming through enemy secondaries. But the absolute, 100 percent, totally uncouth, perfect Raider did not exist—not until Lyle Alzado joined up with Davis in a match formed in hell.

Late in his career, Alzado threatened to strangle a coach in Cleveland, an urge similar to one he once felt in Denver. The Browns told him to go away, he was too uncivilized for their style of football.

Naturally, Alzado emigrated to the Raiders, wherever they could be found. He was home, for the price of Al Davis's eighth-round draft choice. Gigantic, with a broken face, Alzado played the '83 season with clenched fists and returned to the Super Bowl with his new associates.

During the playoffs, Alzado had been requested to do a TV interview. The Raiders would be playing their old playmates from Pittsburgh.

"What about this game with the Steelers?" the TV guy asked, figuring a meek first question might be smart.

"Bleep, bleep, bleep, you go bleep yourself," Alzado responded.

"But what do you really think of the Steelers?" The TV guy was persistent.

222

Alzado spotted a Steelers' helmet that was being used as a TV prop. He spit into it.

Now Alzado and the Raiders had descended on Tampa, where Pete Rozelle's chummy league had opted to place Super Bowl XVIII. The Raiders were pitted against the Redskins.

"It's God's game," said Howie Long, another of Al Davis's hired busters. "The Raiders and Redskins. It's the game He wants to see. And not only God. Dick Butkus is going to be glued to his set."

"It's the greatest spectacle created by man," said Joe Theismann, opting for the secular.

"Theismann," grunted Alzado. "I'm gonna tear his head off. I'm going to tell you something about Joe Theismann. Nobody knows this. We were in 'Superstars' together. You remember 'Superstars' on television? We were filming it in the Bahamas, and Joe Theismann and I rented some mopeds and took off. We passed a candy store and Joe Theismann said, 'Let's get some candy for the kids.'

"So we filled our baskets with candy and took off into the ghetto down there. We had 50, 75 kids following us, and we were pitching candy to them."

Alzado rolled his satanic eyes. "Joe Theismann is a magnificent guy," he said. "And if I can tear his head off in the game, I will."

Alzado told us how he wound up playing college football for Langston, somewhere in South Dakota. He couldn't get into New Mexico State because of his reputation as a gang warrior in New York.

"They didn't want my kind in school," he said.

"Why?" we asked him.

"I'm half-Jewish and half-Italian," Alzado answered. "I guess they didn't know how to cook for me."

Super Bowl XVIII loomed as the best mix of all since Pete Rozelle had concocted this postseason slice of glitz in the quest for high profit. The Redskins and Raiders together produced a chemistry that generated touchdowns. They had played each other the previous October in a regular-season game, which Washington won, 37-35. Joe Theismann passed for the winning touchdown with 33 seconds to play. The guy he eluded to get off his desperation pass was Lyle Alzado.

All this for the rematch in the Super Bowl—and John Riggins, too.

◆ ◆ ◆

Here we were in Tampa. Pete Rozelle was punishing Miami. It had been placed on the no-longer-wanted category as too inhospitable. Moreover, the Orange Bowl had become a relic, and it is an unwritten law that the Super Bowl must be played in a nifty, gleaming place with lots and lots of seats. Even if it was in Pontiac, Michigan.

So Rozelle's moveable feast played Tampa, where there were dog tracks and jai alai matches, and Busch Gardens for all those who had not made it to the Detroit Zoo two years earlier. We media citizens were put up in the Tampa Hyatt. My room overlooked a ditch that was being dug as I wrote. On the whole, a lot of us would rather have been in Dearborn.

Al Davis's floating franchise was playing Los Angeles. These were the Los Angeles Raiders in Super Bowl XVIII. They had successfully evacuated Oakland, against the might of Pete Rozelle, against the wishes of the NFL's franchise owners. Davis had been the victor in a bitter courtroom war with Rozelle and the NFL's attorneys. On top of invalidating Rozelle's franchise-transfer strictures, Davis was awarded millions and millions of the NFL owners' dough for his pains. "Nobody ever left his heart in Oakland," said Al Davis.

◆ ◆ ◆

Ron was president, but John was still king.

John Riggins was silent again as the hordes descended on Tampa Stadium, bundled together for the NFL's traditional photo day. While writers did pitched battle with TV men lugging their bulky cameras in the area around Theismann, Riggins stood stolidly in the end zone in his Redskins' uniform and cowboy boots.

He would condescend to speak to us, again at his private press conference the next day. This time the regal Riggins mounted the backstairs, marched through a kitchen, entered through a stage, and popped out through the splits in a drawn curtain.

"What, no applause?" he said, completing his Groucho Marx entrance.

He was adorned as an aviator—a bombardier, one of Uncle Sam's heroes fit to fly off into the wild blue yonder. He wore an olive flight suit with shoulder patches. He had a white scarf tucked flutter style around his thick neck, a la the Red Baron.

"Last year the Redskins marched through Miami," said Riggins. "This year we fly over L.A. Bombs will be hot and heavy in the first half allowing our troops to position themselves and carry us to victory."

Riggins stuck two fingers above him in the shape of the V, made famous by Winston Churchill. "Ask me something I can get my teeth into."

So somebody asked him what he had been thinking about the day before, when, in silence, he had stood in the end zone in his uniform and boots during the media madness.

"I was standing there looking for a soft place to land," he said. "If Lyle Alzado is going to knock my block off, I hope he's a gentleman and hands it back.

"Those Raiders. They're such bruisers."

Riggins had switched his voice to a falsetto. He dangled his hand off his wrist. "It'll be so much fun in the pileups."

The voice deepened to a normal base. "Now, that's intimidation," said Riggins.

Another question that would test his bite . . .

"I read all those articles that said we were lucky last year," John said. "Those that said we were lucky because of the strike. I worked harder in the off-season because I didn't want to fall into that trap. So that all the experts won't be experts. Such as Jimmy the Creep. I mean Jimmy the Greek."

Some of the Raiders managed to get themselves into trouble again. Not for busting curfew, not for staying out and kicking the gong around. After all, this was Tampa. Tom Flores, the coach, fined seven of his players—for sleeping in. The unholy seven, Jim Plunkett among them, slept through an 8 a.m. meeting, their body clocks ticking on West Coast time. They donated 1,000 bucks apiece to Flores's fine fund.

Flores remained pro football's best-kept secret. But this was the Raiders' scheme. If they could get away with it, they'd never tell a soul the name of their coach. Every once in a while, the TV camera peeped in on the Raiders' bench. Flores was the guy with the black pompadour and the black sweater with the game plan rolled up in his fist. His record as a pro coach was 54-27. Three years earlier, he won his first Super Bowl with the Raiders and escaped without being identified.

"We are a very private organization," Flores told us. He fit perfectly into Al Davis's scheme. "I'm not a genius," Flores said. "I'm just a coach who works hard."

Flores admitted he lagged behind the image of Al Davis. "I think so," Flores said. "I don't try to do anything to disprove it." He was an old quarterback in the old AFL, mostly for the Raiders. He had become successor to John Madden. Flores got into coaching out of the plastics business.

It sort of figured.

◆ ◆ ◆

Over at the Hilton, I pigged out on the standard NFL breakfast before I encountered Matt Millen. Millen had developed into the typecast Raider in his young pro seasons. He was born in a town called Hokendauqua, which is located in eastern Pennsylvania near Allentown. Millen managed to get rid of the soot from the mines at an early age. Joe Paterno discovered him and took him to Penn State. Then destiny placed him in the black and silver of the Raiders, with the picture of the one-eyed pirate on the helmet.

Millen was a destroyer linebacker with a fierce mustache by the time Al Davis left Oakland and took the team on the lam for Los Angeles. Millen left his heart in Oakland.

"I don't say I don't like Los Angeles," Millen said to the circle of writers at his interview table. "I just couldn't live there. It's too crowded. I have no family there, the houses are all 10 feet away, you can't sit down and talk to somebody. And the women; who knows where their minds are?

"Somebody wrote and said if you don't like Los Angeles, leave. If I didn't have to work there, I wouldn't be there. But I love the Los Angeles Raiders. My veins bleed silver and black.

"But at my house in Hokendauqua I can walk naked into the backyard— and have."

We scribbled furiously in our notebooks.

"Hokendauqua—that's an Indian name from the Len-e-pa tribe— means 'in search of water.' It's in the township of Whitehall, and a couple of years ago in *Time* or *Newsweek,* they said it had the highest per capita ratio of hired killers in the country. They serve both the New York and Philadelphia markets."

Somebody happened to mention the Redskins, which was a strange topic to bring up. We snickered at the cute Washington nicknames—the Hogs, the Smurfs, the Fun Bunch.

"A nickname never won a football game," said Millen. "Those nicknames are not very professional. But a lot of things are not very professional in the NFL. You see a guy doing an earthquake dance if they get the quarterback, jumping in the end zone when they score a touchdown. You see the quarterback dancing when he throws a touchdown pass. If you want to pick your nose, it's OK."

So, somebody asked Millen how he might demonstrate if he intercepted a pass in the Super Bowl and ran for a touchdown. "Me," Millen said, "I'm a nose-picker."

We had been with Millen for a half hour now. My fingers cramped from scribbling. But somebody asked him about John Riggins. "I'm one of Riggins's fans," said Millen. "He'd make a tremendous Raider. Last game I thought I had a real good hit on him. I had him lined up, and he got a real good hit on me. He broke my face mask.

"This game is X's and O's, but as far as defending your turf, yeah, you got to knock Riggins over. You hit him and nothing happens. We hit him five yards ago. Why is this guy still running? Times I'm going to kill this guy and 50 yards later he is still running and I'm wondering what I did wrong. I know when I've made a good hit I black out or get white spots."

Somebody else asked if Riggins grunts when he runs.

"John Riggins makes no sound," Millen told us. "He justs breathes hard. I hope he brushes his teeth for this game."

I hoped my fingers would stop aching so I could type.

◆ ◆ ◆

Tampa imported the celebrities to make the Super Bowl a genuine scene. Frank Sinatra was crooning in town. John McEnroe was crying. It was reported, with confirmation, that Jane Fonda would arrive late in the week.

It had turned into a feast week, even in Tampa. I had gotten to know the restaurants covering the baseball camps in spring training. The Columbia was supurb, as usual, for paella and that heavy yellow Spanish rice. A bunch of us had gone there the first night. Malio's was fine again, as recommended first by Johnny Bench.

Then for the highlight of the week, we went to Bern's, where we got another tour of the massive wine cellar, perhaps America's best. And pigged out on one of the best steaks in America.

I had just sliced my medium rare when in walked Paul Zimmerman, the fine wine expert. Paul hadn't voiced any complaints about Tampa, so he was safe. But just in case, he had Lyle Alzado and Matt Millen in tow. Sportswriters are incorrigible slobs. But all the writers at our table had outdressed the two Raiders for our appearances at this restaurant for the swells.

The two Raiders said hello, and Paul took them faraway into another room. We gossiped about them.

Then we started talking about Jane Fonda. We wondered what her function would be at Super Bowl XVIII. I said: "I think Jane's either going to lead the Raiders and Redskins in pregame pushups or preach the cause of pacifism between Alzado and Riggins." Newark gave me a dirty look.

◆ ◆ ◆

All Joe Theismann lacked at the Super Bowl was a jar of mustard. There wasn't a spicier hot dog in the NFL realm than Washington Joe. A multicorporate businessman/quarterback, Theismann knew the value of ballyhoo. Lyle Alzado said he was going to knock Joe's head off. Joe responded.

"Most teams don't challenge us one-on-one," Theismann told us as Alzado's claims were turned into thick headlines. "But the Los Angeles Raiders do. That's the difference between them and the rest of the National Football League. They're tough guys. Lyle Alzado's got a nasty image. I expect them to be tough.

"I'm going to find an alley here in Tampa and get beat up every night . . . because Sunday I'd be surprised if I don't get my head handed to me."

We scribbled his quotes down as fast as we could. We were the messengers. Super Sunday America's ghouls would expect to see blood spilled on the TV-painted green grass of Tampa Stadium. Ratings would jump. Players could demand higher salaries. The Super Bowl was more than a game.

"Football's my relaxation," Theismann said, motor mouthing. "I have my restaurants. I have my newspaper. I have my real estate. That's my work.

"On Sunday, I get between the white lines and play football. Football's my hobby.

"What'd I do last week? On Tuesday, I had dinner at the White House with the president and first lady for the premier of China. Wednesday, I had to go up to New York for the player of the year award. Thursday, I went to see *Hasty Heart* with Burt Reynolds and the president.

"If I weren't in the football profession, I don't know what I'd do. Eventually, I'd like to be an actor. I'd like to do football analysis on television.

"I'm not marketable at all. I'm not opinionated. I'm not a sex symbol. I honestly don't know what I'd do if I weren't in football."

We actually quoted him. He was feeding us nonsense, and we knew he knew he was feeding it to us, and he knew we'd write it, and we knew he knew we'd write it

Joe then said: "I used to live life in the fast lane. But now I drive on the median."

Theismann's BS aside, the Redskins' cutsy nicknames, Riggins's staged silences, Joe Gibbs's penchant for catnapping through the night in his office—none of it would mean a thing, none of it would be recorded by 2,000 journalists if the Washington team could not play a helluva game of football.

The Redskins had rolled through the season, crushing 14 of their 16 opponents. In 12 of their games, they scored at a rate of four touchdowns or better. Each of their two losses was by one point. And they were merely getting tuned for the playoffs. In the first playoff game, they eliminated the Rams, 51-7. It was a monstrous laugher.

They played the 49ers for the NFC championship. The Redskins managed to win, 24-21, on Mark Moseley's 25-yard field goal with 40 seconds left. Bill Walsh went away screaming that the 49ers had been robbed by the officials on two defensive penalty calls on the Redskins' game-winning march.

Marcus Allen versus John Riggins?

"Nah," said Marcus Allen. "It's going to be built up, but I'm not thinking about it."

In collecting his rogues and renegades, and molding them into a team, Al Davis also was a collector of running-back gems. Marcus Allen failed to fit the image of the hellish Raiders. He was soft-spoken, clean-cut, friendly—sort of a Mercedes among junkers. He was too tall to fill the NFL's requirements for a tough runner and too thin. But he had the talent to slide and slip and accelerate vis-à-vis Riggins's plodding, plowing, churning methods.

"I've said every time," Allen said, "it might sound vain, self-centered, conceited: If I do things, have a good day, it opens the way for others."

◆ ◆ ◆

Flores had kept the team winning although he had a quarterback problem. Jim Plunkett, the quarterback once picked off the scrap heap, was tossed back onto it after seven games. Plunkett was 35 now. When Flores benched him just before the midpoint of the '83 season, it seemed that Plunkett's career again was finished. The Raiders were 5-2, winning. But Flores switched to the acclaimed Marc Wilson.

"Here we go again," said Plunkett.

Marc Wilson was the pass master drafted by Davis. He had been groomed as the Raiders' quarterback of the future, and now he was to play. But in his third game, Wilson's shoulder was broken.

It was time to bring back Jim Plunkett. Again. Plunkett took the Raiders through the rest of the season—and to the Super Bowl. Again.

"I've had my ups and downs, like a lot of other people," Plunkett said, and there was no Super Bowl hype, no ballyhoo to this man, just truth. "People see it in other professions. This is just one of them. I've learned to live with a lot of things. I know what happens today may change tomorrow.

"I was benched unfairly. They wouldn't have benched Ken Stabler. But they did bench me. I was down. It hurt.

"Then after a week, I decided to go back to basics. You never know what happens.

"I always had a work ethic. Maybe it's because of my parents." This son of two blind parents, who worked hard to live with their handicap, quarterbacked the Raiders to a 12-4 record at the season's end.

In the playoffs, the Raiders routed the Steelers, their arch-rivals, in the opening game, 38-10. Meanwhile the young Seattle Seahawks upset the Broncos, 31-7.

The Raiders and Seahawks met in the AFC championship game. Alzado and his accomplices started two fights on the first four plays. Allen slithered for 154 yards, caught seven passes for an additional 62 yards, and while he was doing all of that, he blocked. The Raiders won, 30-14.

Al Davis was in the Super Bowl for the fourth time, this time with the Raiders from Los Angeles. "The only thing more important than winning is living," said Davis.

Davis had festooned Tampa with the Raiders' motto. He bought space on billboards that were colored silver and black and proclaimed *Pride and Poise*. They showed the picture of the Raiders' helmet—and had Al Davis's signature. The silver and gray blended into the Florida gloom. The entire week was cold and gray. Floridians talked all week about the Siberian air flow, and how could this happen in the Sunshine State? A lot of guys who'd made funny remarks about Michigan's frozen tundra two years earlier started apologizing after they received wake-up calls telling them the temperature was 41 degrees.

But the town was not socked in. Aircraft were flying. A chopper buzzed over the Redskins' camp. It fluttered a trailer: *Lyle Alzado wears panty hose*. Joe Gibbs had to halt practice while his Redskins rolled on the ground in uproarious laughter.

♦ ♦ ♦

The NFL felt the Super Bowl might be endangered by stray aircraft. Tampa Stadium was located within three miles of Tampa International Airport. With typical chutzpah, the NFL went to the Federal Aviation Administration to request that the airspace over the stadium be blocked out during the Super Bowl. The way the NFL phrased it: ". . . prevent any aircraft not necessary to Super Bowl production from flying over."

The FAA told the NFL to swallow its alphabet soup, translated go take a hike. Maybe the FAA recalled the grounding of international air traffic during one of Pete Rozelle's Super Bowl parties at the Miami Airport. Or maybe Vice President George Bush, grounded by the NFL from future Super Bowl attendance, told the FAA to read his lips.

Al Davis had more control over dangerous situations. All suspected spies are to be captured and interrogated. One such suspect was caught right next door to the Raiders' practice field, the Tampa Bay Buccaneers' complex. Next door was the Hall of Fame Inn, a hotel. And it so happened that a registered guest at the hotel attempted to enter his room on the fifth floor. A Tampa cop on special watchdog duty stopped the hotel guest as he shoved his key into the door lock.

"Either you have to leave or go to jail," the dutiful cop told the hotel guest.

The man argued that he believed in this country he had the right to enter his hotel room, which he had paid for.

The case was ultimately resolved. The suspected spy was given a security check and passed. He was told he could use his own hotel room—if he kept the shades drawn.

◆ ◆ ◆

After the one-year lapse, Pete Rozelle tossed a Super Bowl party again two nights before Super Bowl XVIII. His 3,000 well-selected guests were transported by bus, through the Tampa mist, to the Florida State Fairgrounds. The theme of the party was "A Night at the Circus."

Quite appropriate. At this circus there were trapeze acts and animals and long lines to get the free food and drink. It was good to see that Pete was back on the party circuit.

Among the guests was Todd Christensen. Christensen kept cuddling his newborn infant like a football he'd just caught. Matter of fact, Christensen, the Raiders' tight end, was the first active Super Bowl participant ever spotted at one of Rozelle's parties by habitual partygoers.

It had been an odd week. The Super Bowl match-up had been made in hell; Tampa should have been clogged with tourists and football fans. Instead, the downtown streets were deserted. Joe Theismann couldn't get himself beat up. No revelers, no fans, no people, no cheer.

Still, there was plenty of action. Jimmy the Greek had made the Redskins three-point favorites, no matter what Riggins said about him. And the action was going clear across the Atlantic. The Super Bowl had started to captivate the British. The London bookmakers developed a brisk trade on that game they play over in the Colonies.

So it was that we reached another Super Sunday with great expectations. The Redskins, the most powerful club in all of pro football, versus the team Al Davis had taken into exile to the anguish of Pete Rozelle and his NFL establishment.

Once the pregame ceremonies ended, the same old stuff, the flyover began. It was not exactly what Rozelle wanted. These were old putt-putt jobs, trailing advertising streamers behind them, beckoning to the captive stadium audience. The FAA had prevailed.

And then the Raiders scored on the Redskins' first possession. Alzado, Millen, Long, and their bunch stopped Theismann deep in his own end. Punt formation, Washington. As Jeff Hayes caught the center snap, Derrick Jensen was rushing forward, through the Redskins' middle. Hog poop. Jensen blocked the punt, and the ball bounced over the green-painted Florida landscape back into the end zone. Jensen plopped on the ball in the end zone. The Raiders had themselves a touchdown.

Theismann moved the 'Skins 50 yards forward. For nothing. Mark Moseley, the NFL's field goal record-setter in the '83 season, misfired on a 44-yard attempt. The Raiders promptly moved the ball the other way. Plunkett, the reclaimed quarterback, fired sidearm to Cliff Branch for a

50-yard gain. Then from the 12, the two ancients, Plunkett and Branch, clicked again for the touchdown. The Raiders were in the lead, 14-zip.

It had only started. The Redskins' weak retaliation was a field goal, 24 yards by Moseley. It remained 14-3, Raiders, until 12 seconds before Rozelle's halftime festivities. The Redskins were back on their 12. Here Gibbs, the conservative who stayed up nights figuring out the safe way to play, decided on a screen pass, with three receivers lined up right and runner Joe Washington lined up left. For some reason, Gibbs figured it would work for 88 yards. But then in the 37-35 regular-season game, won by the Redskins, it had worked for 67 yards against the Raiders.

The Raiders recognized the formation. They were ready. Jack Squirek, a reserve linebacker who seldom had his name in the papers, was inserted into the game. Theismann went through his legerdemain and let go the screen pass over the charging Alzado in the general direction of Washington. Squirek picked it off and stormed the five yards back to the end zone for one more touchdown. The Raiders had stopped Theismann, they had neutralized Riggins. They had the Redskins whipped, 21-3, at the half.

The Redskins counterattacked at the outset of the second half. Theismann now completed three passes. Riggins was able to plow for some yardage and finally scored a touchdown from a yard out. The Redskins had a shot, but then Moseley missed the extra point, too. It was 21-9, Raiders. And the Raiders quickly scored another touchdown. Marcus Allen slipped across from the five. It was 28-9, Raiders, and the outcome seemed settled.

Twice the Redskins sputtered. Alzado was knocking heads off. Next time they got the ball to the Raiders' 26, where it was fourth-and-one. Riggins had broken for 43 yards and the vital touchdown in the Redskins' victory in the Super Bowl the year before. This time, Rod Martin hit Riggins and stopped him for no gain.

The Raiders got the ball back. It was time for Plunkett to waste time on the clock. He handed off to Allen, and Allen hit the left side. It was stacked. He stopped, pirouetted, and cut back right and found a gap. He had escaped, he was free, and he was going—74 yards, the longest touchdown ever run in the Super Bowl. It was 35-9 and later on Chris Bahr kicked a 21-yard field goal. The final score was 38-9.

Al Davis was a winner for the third time in the Super Bowl.

Pete Rozelle went gingerly into the locker room to present the Vince Lombardi Trophy to Al Davis. There was more warmth on the USS Missouri when the Japanese surrendered to Douglas MacArthur.

"Two years ago, when we came to Los Angeles, I believed in the future of the Raiders," said Davis, taunting Rozelle. "In my opinion, this is not only the greatest Raider team, but one of the greatest teams in all professional sports of all time. . . .Our organization has taken a lot of harassment from the National Football League, all the harassment and all the outrageous things the league has done to this team.

"We can't move. Our people had to live in two places. They had to have homes in Oakland and Los Angeles. A lot of the coaches don't know where they'll live next year, and I kind of feel guilty because of this—though the league is responsible for it." This was his moment of vindication, the sweetest taste of all. But he remained typical Al Davis, suspicious of the enemy, ready to attack on the defensive.

"Secrets?" he said. "I'm not going to answer such a question. Irony? What's irony?

"Vindicate? I don't believe in vindication.

"Rout. I don't think in terms of rout. I think in terms of domination."

His football team dominated as no other team had been able to damage and destroy an opponent in any of the prior Super Bowls. His team was more dominant than the Packers of Lombardi. It was more powerful than the Dolphins of Shula. It was more awesome than the Steelers of Noll.

Al Davis beat history with his football team. And the Raiders did it alone, setting their own tone, in their own particular fashion.

And when the horror his football team inflicted on the whole of the NFL was fully realized, Al Davis rode off still gloating, still alone. He could be heard laughing and snarling. From him, they sounded the same.

XIX
The Golden Gate

San Francisco 49ers 38, Miami Dolphins 16
January 20, 1985
Stanford Stadium, Palo Alto, CA
Attendance: 84,059

I hoisted the venetian blinds and looked at the view. Out there was The Rock. Alcatraz.

It was Super Bowl XIX. That meant, by week's end, 19 weeks of captivity for me. Even so, I had been lured out to this Super Bowl early, two days before I had to be there. It was going to be the 49ers versus the Dolphins—San Francisco's champions at 17-1 versus Miami's champions at 16-2. It was going to be Bill Walsh versus Don Shula, and Joe Montana versus Dan Marino.

All the elements pointed to a classic. But I knew after 19 years of Super Bowls that what was shaped in epic proportions when the match was arranged in Pete Rozelle's heaven usually turned out to be a resounding dud when the players performed on the football field.

I went out early because after all these years Rozelle had arranged for a Super Bowl in San Francisco. I went out early because I could drive south to Carmel and Monterey and soak in the atmosphere of northern California. I went out early so I could gaze out the window and fantasize.

I had stayed in 19 Super Bowl hotel rooms, each with a view. Now I was high up in the Hyatt Regency on the Embarcadero. The view belonged on a picture postcard. The Rock was out there, and by craning my neck, I could watch the freighters chugging slowly toward the Golden Gate on their way into the Pacific.

234

Things had changed since I'd covered my first Super Bowl. At Super Bowl I, I'd used an obsolete device known as a portable typewriter to write. Now I had with me my Computer IV, having advanced through the first three, which themselves had become antiques.

Modern technology being what it was, I now dispatched my imperishable prose back home via telephone lines. The phone in my hotel cell . . . er . . . room, was so pretty, so fancy, so advanced that it was incompatible with Computer IV.

To file copy, it was necessary for me to ride down one of the glass capsule rocketship elevators overlooking jungle gardens and futuristic circular artwork to use a 1967-style pay telephone in the lobby. But such is progress.

Pete Rozelle kept pace.

Tickets for Super Bowl I way back in history sold for 15 bucks and Pete couldn't give them away. The first Super Bowl was played before clusters of unoccupied seats.

Tickets for Super Bowl XIX were priced at $60 and the good citizens of San Francisco were demonstrating because they couldn't get them. Scalpers were charging $600 for one ticket, and the buyer had to be wary. His purchase might have been printed in some entrepreneur's basement shop.

It was another Super Bowl at which it helped to have been a Boy Scout. We needed maps, compasses, pith helmets, and enlarged bladders. As noted, the press stayed in San Francisco at the Hyatt. The owners stayed a cable car ride up Nob Hill at the Stanford Court. Super Bowl XIX itself would be contested down the peninsula at Stanford Stadium in Palo Alto. The 49ers used their own training facility south of The City in Redwood City. They would be required to meet the press at a hotel in Burlingame, which was someplace off in the direction of Redwood City. The Dolphins, meanwhile, were billeted across the Bay Bridge in a hotel in Oakland and would be interviewed over there. It was all quite dizzying.

On picture day, we would be permitted to invade the Dolphins' practice facility at Oakland Stadium, and the 49ers would show up at Candlestick Park, where they played their home games. As a service to out-of-town press, the NFL arranged for a missing persons bureau that sent out rescue missions to find lost media.

So, under the prevailing conditions, 2,000 of us were herded to the 49ers' photo day session at Candlestick. TV guys interviewed writers. TV cameramen stuffed TV cameras into the backs of writers who were trying to hang onto the wise words of Bill Walsh and the mumbles of Joe Montana.

Me, I settled for listening to Russ Francis, who was part nuts, part tight end.

"The game terrifies me," Francis told his tiny but select audience. "There are a lot of crazy people out there."

He did not include himself in this category, just the crazies who were out to maim fellow athletes in games such as the Super Bowl.

"Jack Lambert and I were sitting by the pool in Tampa at the Pro Bowl," said Francis. "We started talking about Hawaii . . . how you jump off the rocks into the water. I'm drinking iced tea. Jack is drinking beer. You know how it is. Jack says, 'Why don't you jump into the pool?' Jack has some more beers. I have some more iced tea. I get on the elevator and somehow push six. So I jumped from the sixth floor of the motel into the pool."

But the football game on Sunday terrified him.

"I didn't get hurt," he said. "I missed the edge pretty good. But I didn't miss the bottom by too much. I scraped my knees.

". . . You know the year I was sitting out, when I retired with the Patriots? Everybody should try it. Take a year off. If you spend a lot of time in sports, you get the wrong idea. You should spend a year off to see how it is out there on the other side. Prepare yourself for when you're through playing.

"I learned to keep my left up. It's a jungle out there.

"I got a job with ABC.

"I flew around the country in my open cockpit biplane, a 1941 World War II trainer. It was much needed and very refreshing. It was windy and frightening, totally because you're out there in the open. Once you get used to flying upside down, it's not bad.

"What I like to do is take my motorcycle or my plane and disappear for a couple of weeks. Skydive. You roll over and fall out of the biplane. It's not that bad. You just kinda fall out. It's great.

"I don't do things recklessly or carelessly because I realize the finality of it. People say you have some kind of death wish, going so fast on your motorcycle and skydiving. I say, no, that's not terrifying.

"My first parachute jump was a little exciting. The chute took a little while opening. . . . I want to go for a world speed record in the plane. Walsh didn't say I couldn't do it. He just said he wanted me to know the dangers of it. For the team. For the expense of rehabilitation.

"I said, 'Bill, this plane is going to go 300 miles an hour, 50 feet over the ground. If something goes wrong, there aren't going to be any injuries.'"

But Russ Francis told us he was scared stiff about playing in the Super Bowl because there were crazy people on the other side.

The cavalcade of NFL-chartered buses crossed the Bay Bridge to Oakland. Back to Don Shula, who would be coaching his sixth Super Bowl. It was his 22nd season as a head coach. Some statistician with a calculator had figured out that Shula had a .732 win-loss percentage in his years at

Baltimore and Miami—and that he was the most successful NFL coach in history. He had three championship eras in his career: one with the Colts in the sixties, and two with the Dolphins in the seventies and eighties.

There were many reasons for Shula's longevity in a business of turnovers and firings and burnouts and defeats. But his willingness to adapt, to roll with his talent, was the basic reason for his durability. When his Dolphins won their two Super Bowls in the seventies, they were a team that lived by running the football. The attack was built around Larry Csonka, Jim Kiick, and Mercury Morris.

Shula junked all his concepts in the mid-eighties and started fresh. The Dolphins got to Super Bowl XIX by throwing the football. Only Shula had been smart enough to realize the potential of Dan Marino after 26 teams had ignored him in the draft two years earlier.

In 1984, Marino had shattered the season records for passing the football. He came to the Super Bowl with 48 touchdown passes notched during the 16 games of the regular season, plus seven more in the two AFC playoff games. These were monumental statistics. And he did it all because his release of the forward pass was so quick, so rapid he was seldom sacked by the enemy pass rushers.

Five other college passers had been selected as Shula sat with patience through the first round of the 1983 draft. John Elway from Stanford was the first off the board. Then Tony Eason was picked, Jim Kelly, Todd Blackledge, Ken O'Brien. Marino was untaken.

There were rumors. Marino had a bum season his senior year at Pitt. Stories that he was on drugs popped up, and, true or false, the pro clubs became concerned. Shula heard the rumors, too.

"Everybody had Elway number one," Shula told the Super Bowl press. "Then everybody else would call around lying to each other about who they liked and didn't like. We had Marino right after Elway.

". . . I brought him into the office and told him what I'd heard. I told him he'd be judged by what he did for me. He said, 'That's good enough for me.' In my mind, it was worth a shot. The people I had talked to said he was a helluva young guy who wanted to be a great quarterback."

Shula's risk in taking Marino was similar to Bill Walsh's drafting of Joe Montana several years earlier. Montana had gone ignored by all 28 clubs through the first two rounds of the draft. At last, Walsh decided to take the young quarterback out of Notre Dame on the third round, as a gamble. Now it was Marino versus Montana, Shula versus Walsh providing the romance in Super Bowl XIX.

◆ ◆ ◆

The Genius in San Francisco demurred when one of us used that word in a question to him. Walsh was in his sixth season. He had won one Super Bowl. Then the season following, his team collapsed, and Walsh spoke of all sorts of problems that afflicted the 49ers—including that terrible peril, drugs. He had tried to quit coaching to concentrate on his functions as general manager. He had stewed about it for three weeks of what he called doubt and difficulty. Finally, he was ego-massaged and talked out of it by his owner, Eddie DeBartolo, Jr.

And now the 49ers were back in the Super Bowl in their home territory. There were no bags for a gray-haired man, masquerading as a porter, to carry when the 49ers checked into a Super Bowl hotel, because Bill Walsh permitted his Super Bowl players to live at their homes with their families.

It was part of Walsh's character to deliver a sermon when most coaches would respond with a straight answer. So he spoke softly to us when that word *genius* was mentioned during a morning press session at Burlingame.

"I don't associate myself with that description," Walsh said. "It's the product of some highly emotional newspaper people.

"I'm supposed to be egocentric. I can't figure that. When I compare myself to some personalities in sport, Good God."

Two years earlier, DeBartolo had convinced Walsh to remain coaching with the 49ers by promoting him to club president, in addition to his other titles. And that to him was better than genius.

Back in Oakland, Don Shula was at the microphone when he heard somebody ask him at this, his *sixth* Super Bowl, if he had learned anything from Walsh's style.

"Bill Walsh's impact on my coaching career?" said Shula. "I want to make sure I heard that right."

◆ ◆ ◆

I preferred San Francisco as a restaurant town to New Orleans. Always had. This was the true moveable feast.

So it was that early in the week I hit the Washington Square Bar & Grill, which was a watering and dining spot for local journalists and sports freaks. Visiting writers and network TV folks from out of town always seemed to congregate at the Washington Square. For those who travel a lot to cover games and athletes, there is always the homesickness. The first time I'd stopped at the Washington Square Bar & Grill, I was overcome by a touch of home. Just inside the door were some green stadium seats. I was comforted immediately by old friends. The green seats had once been situated in Tiger Stadium, Detroit, before the ancient ballpark underwent a half-hearted renovation. I plopped down and was happy.

There were other nights this Super Bowl week. San Francisco was not a Super Bowl town, not in the tradition that had been established at New Orleans and Miami. We hit Fournou's Ovens with my *Football News* friends Roger and Pam Stanton, and Ernie's with a mob from *Sports Illustrated*.

San Francisco just let us go on our own at night, and we could gorge ourselves and fill ourselves with camaraderie. But dear Oakland did interrupt our nocturnal meanderings one night with a party to tout itself. The nice people of Oakland sent party boats across to San Francisco for us and ferried us across the Bay, accompanied by music and the usual drink. Pete Rozelle had picked a winner. Nobody longed for Bourbon Street.

◆ ◆ ◆

Quarterbacks can't be God Almighty, Bud Grant had told us once. But they sure are good copy. And through these 19 Super Bowl years, I had been eyeball to eyeball with Starr and Namath and Dawson and Staubach and Unitas and Bradshaw and Tarkenton and Griese and Morrall and Kapp and Kilmer and Stabler and Plunkett and Theismann and Montana. I remained fascinated by the Quarterback Mystique through all the years. And now there was young Danny Marino.

OAKLAND—He comes along as the plump Namath. He is a mama's boy, and she makes great lasagna, and it looks as if Dan Marino is full of second helpings.

There is a handsomeness to the face, as there was to Joe Namath's at another Super Bowl in another era. Dan Marino has the sharp, sculpted nose and the bright blue eyes, and the curly locks down close to his shoulder pad.

But the face is dominated by pudgy cheeks. Dan Marino has a double chin.

But it is his arm and his brain that count. And people are saying that it is his arm, which propelled the Dolphins into this Super Bowl, that is the sweetest since Joe Namath was a brash lad with his audacious guarantee.

Joe Namath came to the Super Bowl 16 years ago drinking Johnnie Walker Red and drawling in his falsetto Alabaman. He sat poolside in Fort Lauderdale, the king with a court. His club, the New York Jets, was the 18-point underdog. Then there was the night Namath guaranteed that the Jets would defeat the mighty Baltimore Colts. And he delivered. The Jets won.

Dan Marino came drinking coffee out of a styrofoam cup.

"When I was in college, I used to be a shot-and-a-beer guy," Marino said in fun, responding to a remark that Pittsburgh is a boilermaker town. "Now I just drink beer."

Marino came speaking Western Pennsylvanian, which was Namath's native tongue also. He sat on a pedestal, not at a swimming pool. He tried to keep up with the Super Bowl hype. But he was caught in the blitz. . . .

But he's just a fat kid in his second year as a pro.

"What do you remember about Namath?" a Super Bowl guy asked Marino.

"Nothing," said Marino. "I was too young. I watched him once on NFL highlights."

"Are you going to make a guarantee like Namath did?"

"What guarantee?" said Marino. He was very uncomfortable. He swung his foot and kicked it against a post. He wiggled a little in his seat.

"You know, when Namath guaranteed he'd win the Super Bowl. Are you going to guarantee that you'll beat the 49ers?"

"No," said Dan Marino.

He has plenty to learn. Marino shredded the record book with 48 touchdown passes and seven more in two playoff games. It is hard to believe that he is an immature 23. It is harder to believe that he was seven at the time Namath was full of romance and building targets for future quarterbacking generations long ago in 1969.

Dan Marino is bashful and awed. It is unfair to expect him to react in the Super Bowl atmosphere with the poise and the charm of a Joe Namath.

. . . It could be, as the 49ers rush him, he must fight back panic. Kid quarterbacks tend to get panicky.

"Everything Dan Marino does seems natural," said Don Shula. . . .

"He does this. He does that. Nothing overwhelms him. He handles it. Everything he meets face to face he handles."

What Marino has done this past week of heavy hype has been to handle himself with a measure of poise. He has not lost his temper. He has been polite and courteous. He could fulfill the Boy Scout oath.

But he has not been exciting.

". . . No, I'm not a man of a few words," he said. "I talk a lot. I talk so much people tell me to shut up. I'm extremely tough on the field. I guess I get a little more excited than I should."

"Italian moods?"

"Do I use my hands when I talk?"

This is the most hyped Super Bowl of them all. Marino is the glamour star of the glamour show. It is more than Bill Walsh trying to outsmart Shula. It is more than Marino in a pitchers' battle against Joe Montana. It is Marino against the San Francisco pass rushers. And most vital, it is Marino against Marino.

He is a kid with baby fat, the plump Namath. And there are doubters who still must be shown.

"This week we are playing against the greatest passer of all time, as I understand it," said Bill Walsh. His voice was full of sarcasm and mockery.

Walsh's voice was full of belief and conviction when the discussion of the Quarterback Mystique switched to Joe Montana.

"He's the most resourceful man on the field," said Walsh. "He can move men better than anybody who's played the game, except Fran Tarkenton."

Belief? Conviction? Walsh spoke those words with a straight face.

Montana had already won a Super Bowl game, quite young in his career, long before age 30, which Tarkenton had once said was the barrier dividing the flighty, hopeful quarterbacks and those such as himself with proper savvy.

But there had been changes in the Quarterback Mystique. Guys were becoming savvy younger now. Montana was 27, four years senior to Marino.

The comparisons popped up all week. Every time it happened, Montana responded, without flair, unwilling to be trapped despite the media's repetitious insistence: "I'm not playing against him. I'm playing against their defense. He's playing against our defense."

Montana had quarterbacked the 49ers to 17 victories in this season. The club had the best record in pro football since the Dolphins of the unbeaten '73 Super Bowl VII. They traveled through the regular season with a 15-1 record. Walsh had spread talent throughout his team. Beyond an excellent quarterback, the 49ers had a brilliant runner in Roger Craig and an acrobatic receiver in Dwight Clark. They had the most feared pass rush in the game, made better still by the addition of Fred Dean from the Chargers. The secondary, with Ronnie Lott the leader, remained spectacular. The only loss during the season was to the Steelers by three points.

The 49ers whipped the Giants in the first round of the NFC playoffs, 21-10. Montana threw passes for the three touchdowns. The following week, in the NFC championship game, the 49ers beat the Bears, 23-0, in a powerful mix of defense and offense. In two years, Walsh had revived a fine team that had destroyed itself in the aftermath of a Super Bowl season.

Now, if Montana and the 49ers could beat the Dolphins in Super Bowl XIX, they would have the most victories ever recorded in NFL history.

There was another radical change in pro football, beyond the greening of younger quarterbacks. Pete Rozelle had been stressing something called parity. His utopia would be 8-8 finishes by all of the 28 clubs in the league.

It was no utopia, but pro football of the eighties was getting so the good teams and the bad teams were closer to either side of the mediocrity line, and excellent teams might lose several times a season. Teams won divisions with 9-7 records.

But this season, the 49ers were not alone in breaking into this new Rozelle rule stressing parity. Shula, Marino, and the Dolphins dominated the AFC as the 49ers had dominated the NFC. The Dolphins went through the season with a 14-2 record.

Then in the AFC playoffs, Marino drilled the Seahawks, 31-10. Dan threw three touchdown passes. The following week the Dolphins played the Steelers, who had been 9-7, for the championship. Marino was marvelous. He threw four more touchdown passes, and the Dolphins beat the Steelers, 45-28.

And there was a mark about Marino. Not only did he throw so many touchdown passes, but he was dangerous from all over. Five of his seven touchdown passes in the playoffs were from beyond 30 yards.

Going in, a colossus of a Super Bowl was in the offing, the finest match-up of any of the XIX. These were two giant teams, the two best. At no previous Super Bowl had both teams come to the game with such glittering records. It could be perfect in a sport of imperfections.

"You need a van Gogh to paint a picture of this game," said Sid Gillman, one of pro football's bright boys of the coaching craft from another era.

Speaking of imperfections—I'd covered every Super Bowl, part of a dwindling, elite group, but alas, my perfect record as a party mooch attending all of Pete Rozelle's glitzy spectacles was broken. Broken by my own clunking fingers. I was burning on Computer IV through a command piece on Super Bowl atmosphere and history the news side of my paper had asked me to do. It would be a couple of thousand words long, chock-full of anecdotes, pathos, mood. I was down near the end of it, sort of thinking about Pete's party and the milling 3,000 at the Moscone Center, when I punched some keys trying to edit out a word or two. I was in a hurry, I wanted to transmit back to the office. I went bang, bang and hit the wrong keys. The screen on Computer IV went blank. The entire story had vanished.

My technical knowledge was too limited. I didn't know how to bring back my words except by writing them all over again, 2,000 of them. So that's what I did.

By the time I had finished rewriting, trying to recall my wonderful phraseology, I was in no mood to party. Besides, it was too late. I sent the piece to the office and swore about a bloodbath if the editors cut it. Then I went off to the Washington Square Bar & Grill, which was jammed with the non-elite who did not qualify for Pete Rozelle's A list.

◆ ◆ ◆

Ever since the afternoon that Joe Namath rubbed their aristocratic noses in it 16 years earlier, the old NFL had been handed embarrassments in lopsided fashion in these January Super Bowls. The score was AFL/AFC 12, NFL/NFC 4 over that spell of time. It had to be more than a fluke for one conference to dominate the other at a three to one ratio over what amounted to four pro football generations. Even though they mixed in the same draft circles, and in the same social circles, the differences showed in the pudding on Super Bowl day.

There were reasons for this phenomenon. It has been my theory all along that too often coaches who were fired were not to blame for constant mediocrity. Most coaches were not in total charge of procurement. Those who were blessed with the responsibilities of drafting and trading had the best chances for survival. Men such as Don Shula and Chuck Noll, coaching exceptions. Most often it was the general managers who deserved the blame, and the coaches who got it. The GMs wouldn't fire themselves. Each club had its distinctive character. The AFL/AFC managed to acquire the superior quarterbacks from Namath's time on—Griese and Bradshaw and even Plunkett. The AFL/AFC had more smarts in the procurement department—Al Davis, Don Shula, Chuck Noll.

But now Bill Walsh believed he could alter this trend. Walsh had come out of the AFC, had been groomed there in San Diego and Cincinnati. And he had Joe Montana.

My theory could now be tested.

◆ ◆ ◆

It was a tedious bus ride from the Hyatt in San Francisco on a gray Sunday morning to the Stanford campus with its Spanish architecture and its antiquated stadium. We sloshed through mud to the gates of Stanford Stadium.

The Super Bowl had grown from its primitive beginning, hastily arranged in Los Angeles, with unoccupied seats, to this: tents strewn across the landscape for corporate parties tossed for favored customers and the company brass, game tickets at 60 bucks a pop with the scalpers' markup to $600.

We writers, lugging our portable computers and loaded Super Bowl XIX souvenir briefcases, plodded past the drinking swells.

◆ ◆ ◆

Ronald Reagan's second inauguration was scheduled for the following day. The president participated in the coin flip, but from a distance far enough away to please the NFL's muckamucks. He flipped the coin from the White House, via a TV hookup. So it was that the 49ers won the toss and messed up early and had to punt the ball away to the Dolphins. Marino came out gunning, hit Tony Nathan with a 25-yard pass, and took the Dolphins to score. But he was the touchdown master and the Dolphins had to settle for a field goal, 37 yards, by Uwe von Schamann.

Montana fired back. The 49ers went 78 yards in eight strikes. On the drive, he passed short to Roger Craig, exposing the Dolphins' linebacking weaknesses. Montana scrambled, and then he passed 33 yards to back Carl Monroe for a touchdown. The 49ers were in front, 7-3, and a pattern had been established.

Back came Marino. Shunning the huddle on several plays, the Dolphins neutralized the 49ers' pass rush. The 49ers were unable to shuttle their pass rushers in and out. Marino hit Nathan short, Mark Clayton twice for decent gains, Mark Duper for a short gain, then Dan Johnson deep for 21 yards. Then Marino connected with Johnson again for two yards and a touchdown. It was a wild beginning, exactly as advertised, with the teams swapping the lead. It was Miami's now, 10-7.

But not for long. Scrambling himself, passing 16 yards to Dwight Clark, Montana brought the 49ers back. He hit Craig with an eight-yarder over the middle and Craig bulled the final three yards on his own steam. It was 14-10, San Francisco. The defense began attacking Marino with its pass rush. The Dolphins had to punt. Montana fired two passes to Russ Francis. Craig carried once. Then Montana himself scrambled six yards for another touchdown. It was 21-10, San Francisco. Again the defense halted Marino, breaking in on the most dangerous offensive weapon in football. Once again Montana had the ball and passed it 20 yards to Craig. The 49ers stuck to the ground, Montana and Wendell Tyler gaining yardage to the five. Then Montana handed off to Craig, who crashed over from the two for the 49ers' fourth touchdown of the first half. They led, 28-10.

Marino managed to produce two field goals before the intermission. Von Schamann booted one from the 31 and then after a fumble recovery on the kickoff, another from the 30. They'd made a dent, but the 49ers were high in command, 28-16 at halftime.

The 49ers retained command in the second half. Ray Wersching kicked a 27-yard field goal for a 31-16 lead. Later Montana connected with Tyler on a 40-yard pass and 14 yards to Francis. At the 16, he passed to Craig, who scored his third touchdown. The 49ers' lead was 38-16, and that was the final in Super Bowl XIX.

The 49ers had broken Marino, and they had broken the Dolphins' suspect defense. Marino, sacked only 13 times all season and not at all in the playoffs, was barrelled over four times in the Super Bowl. Otherwise, he managed to get off 50 passes in the futile effort to stick with the 49ers' all-around mastery. Marino was intercepted twice. Montana's offense, meanwhile, produced 537 yards. He had befuddled the Dolphins with his agility, his daring dashes out of the pocket, running the ball himself. And he had three touchdown passes. Bill Walsh went off the field with an awesome grin.

PALO ALTO—This is the way he wins, and it is with a pump and a fake and a flash dance. This is Joe Montana, doing a quick jitterbug and tucking the football and scooting off with it. This is Joe Montana defying all the rules of pro football purity, the quarterback who wants to have a hole in his pocket.

This is Joe Montana—winner.

There have not been many like him in this pro football sport. Not Sid Luckman, the original, not Slingin' Sammy Baugh nor Bobby Layne nor Unitas, Starr, Tittle, and Namath, too. Not Terry Bradshaw nor Jim Plunkett.

Not Danny Marino, either.

These are candy quarterbacks—and they stood back and let go. They seldom ran and danced into the jaws of the defense.

There have been none—no championship winners—quite like Joe Montana, the dancing quarterback.

Quarterbacks are put on the field to pass the football—or hand it off. The rules protect them as if they were made of Venetian glass. Do not fold, spindle, or mutilate—or it's an eager-beaver zebra, a yellow flag, and 15 yards.

"Look, running is not a lot of fun most of the time," Joe Montana said. He had some smudges on his uniform. There was a little bit of red from the paint on the ground, some green from the grass. Joe Montana had done some hand fighting in the trenches.

But, of course, he'd won again. He usually does. There was a smile highlighting the dimple in his chin. There was mirth in his blue eyes.

He'd run—and passed—the 49ers to another victory in the Super Bowl. It was 38-16—San Francisco over Miami, Bill Walsh over Don Shula, Montana over Marino.

"Running is not high on my list of priorities," Montana said. Like the devil it isn't.

He stands back looking for an open receiver for all of three-fourths of a second most of the time. He taps his toes, hoists the arm, pumps once, twice, a third time. Then he skedaddles—and he loves it.

"None of my runs were planned," he said.

He busted off five runs in the Super Bowl. They netted him 59 yards. The first run of 19 yards set the tone for the whole day. It got the 49ers winging toward a touchdown.

"It's not scary," Montana said after the Super Bowl ended in the dark and fog.

"When I'm going up the middle and have to slide, then it's scary."

That's how he scored his touchdown. He danced a fast step. Joe Montana definitely does not waltz. Then he took off right through the gut. He had to head-butt through a couple of Dolphins before he dove into the end zone. His shoulder pad was ripped out of his uniform. He looked like he'd been mugged. He threatened to spike the ball. Then he dropped it.

. . . Joe Montana gloated. The champions get all the bragging rights.

"The last two weeks all we heard was how good Marino, Clayton, and Duper were," Montana said. "Nobody said anything about our offense. It was all stop Miami, stop Miami, stop Miami. Nobody said that we would have to be stopped. Our offense was overlooked through the whole thing.

"It motivated us. I wanted to prove that we could match up against anyone."

———

XX
The Unmentionable Moon

Chicago Bears 46, New England Patriots 10
January 26, 1986
Louisiana Superdome, New Orleans
Attendance: 73,818

The town is hog butcher for the world. Al Capone sprayed it with bullets and vice. The mob plundered it. A cow kicked over a lamp and gutted it. It is a town that was smeared with blood on St. Valentine's Day.

That is what Chicago is. It is romanticized in poetry and in history and in song. It is that toddlin' town. Once a man was seen dancing with his wife. It is the town of the Bears.

Chicagoans said it was a town burdened with a curse.

The home teams flirted and tantalized and nuzzled to the precipice of triumph. Then they fell. They lost. Some disaster happened. Always.

Chicago knew this. It was ingrained in the heartbeat of the city. The people were always faithful. They were always simplistically loyal. But they lived with the constant death wish that their teams carried into games.

But in January of 1986, they had the Bears, the best football team in captivity. And the town was agog.

The Bears were flavored with the strong grit of the city. The quarterback was Jim McMahon, and he played with Chicago in his soul. He stepped to his own drummer with his own cadence. He was out of tune, except in Chicago.

And now the Bears were in Super Bowl XX. It would be a team of history and tradition against the wild-card New England Patriots. The Pats were

247

a team with a bizarre background, built as the perfect Super Bowl foil to the zaniest group ever to plop into Pete Rozelle's postseason festival.

It was with relish and expectation that I shuffled off to New Orleans again for another week-long toot.

"See you on Bourbon Street," Jim McMahon had said. Jimmy the Greek could make book on that.

George Halas was dead. But the Bears lived in his image, in the image of his city. Halas had been one of the pioneers, one of the men of vision who had sat on running boards in the Hupmobile agency in Canton, Ohio, that day in 1920 when they formed a professional football league. It would be called the National Football League. Halas placed his team in Decatur, Illinois, and called them the Staleys after an industrial plant in town.

A year later, with more vision, he transferred his franchise upstate to Chicago and renamed the team the Bears. America was booming. The era was called the Roaring Twenties. It was the time of Babe Ruth. A bit of modern trivia is the question: Who played right field for the Yankees before Babe Ruth? The hint is: He was an obscure athlete who became more famous in a different sport. The answer is: George Halas.

In the Roaring Twenties, the American love for baseball grew more and more passionate, as Babe Ruth revolutionized the game with the home run. But there was little passion for professional football.

George Halas coached his own football team. He signed the players. He played for it on Sundays. During the week, after conducting his scrimmages, he typed up his own press releases to publicize the games. No writers bothered themselves to attend practice and interview the players and dig up stories. Halas himself delivered the press releases to the Chicago newspapers. Sometimes, he was rewarded with a rewritten paragraph or two. If he was lucky, and as his own press agent, he'd manage to come up with an adequate story angle.

Then he signed Red Grange, the Galloping Ghost. A publicity, and artistic, coup.

Through the years the Bears won frequent NFL championships—in 1921, 1933, 1940, 1941, 1943, 1946, 1963. The team had some of the great leather-helmeted players of the game: Sid Luckman, who revolutionized the sport as the first T-formation quarterback; Bill Osmanski, the mighty runner; Ken Kavanaugh, the spectacular pass receiver; George Musso, Bulldog Turner, terrifying linemen. They were known as the Monsters of the Midway. In 1940, in the NFL championship game, Halas's Bears beat the Washington Redskins of Sammy Baugh by the score of 73-0.

The championship in 1963 was won with blood, an interval in the Green Bay dynasty of Vince Lombardi. And three years later the NFL merged with the AFL, and great minds thought up an event that ultimately would be known as the Super Bowl.

The Bears had more great players. Dick Butkus. Gale Sayers. But concurrently with the NFL-AFL war and then its peaceful merger, the Bears dropped into a deep decline. Perhaps they were strangled by their own roots, trailing back to the league's formation. The organization was unable to cope and compete in post-merger football. Halas's franchise, begun on a running board for a pittance, was now worth millions. But artistically it was a loser. There was a 1-13 season, and the Bears lost the coin flip for Terry Bradshaw. So into the seventies, there were 3-11, 4-10, and a number of 6-8 seasons. The Bears went 11 years through the late sixties and most of the seventies with one winning season.

And then they started to flirt, tantalize, nuzzle to the precipice of triumph.

◆ ◆ ◆

The joy of the Super Bowl comes early in the week, before the hicks hit town and clog the restaurants and march along Bourbon Street with their plastic cups of booze. It was a tense week of work, pack journalism at its nastiest. Each year it became more difficult, more challenging. More TV people, with more elbows to jam into your rib cage. It was no longer exclusive to America. Writers came in from London, Tokyo, Rome. Pete Rozelle's little slice of American culture had turned international.

It was an annual grind, full of high-pressure coverage—reporting, interviewing, writing. You were always scared that out of this mob scene one hot shot would come up with a story nobody else had and make headlines with it around the world.

Still, it was my favorite week of the year. Perhaps because I felt so relieved when it was over.

At my 20th Super Bowl, I felt pride, some elitism. I also felt I had changed, too. I had learned to pace myself. I wouldn't be out at the Old Absinthe House every night for hours after midnight. I'd pick my nights. Jim McMahon could have Bourbon Street all to himself, for all I cared. So long as he didn't create some crazy story I'd rather not miss.

I now preferred the leisurely fine meal. I loved the camaraderie of the week. So it was that a bunch of us piled into a couple of cabs and rode across one of those steel girder bridges over the Mississippi to the town of Gretna. To LeRuth's, and the haute cuisine of, probably, one of the three finest restaurants in the United States. We talked about the changes in football, in newspapers, in life. It was a happy party that included a sweet, wonderful newspaperman from Dayton named Si Burick, who, like myself, had covered every Super Bowl. He was getting on in years. It was fun being with him. A night and a meal never to be forgotten.

◆ ◆ ◆

Like the Bears, the Patriots came to Super Bowl XX with a certain wackiness—but minus the tradition.

They had been the defeated in the first AFL game ever played in 1960, as the Boston Patriots. As the years advanced, the Patriots moved down the pike from Boston to the hamlet of Foxboro and were renamed the New England Patriots. They had an inglorious past. In their first quarter-century, they'd never won a championship. Once, they had reached the AFL championship game. They lost, 51-10, to San Diego.

Now they were champions, at last. As a wild-card team. But they could never scrub away the quaintness from their history, this team that wore the image of George Washington's Minutemen on its helmets.

Once, for example, the Patriots almost had a game canceled when their stadium started to burn. A spectator, perhaps influenced by what he was watching on the field, dropped a cigarette over the side into a pole vault pit and ignited the canvas and foam rubber. As firemen battled the blaze, the players stopped playing. Some signed autographs. The fire was eventually doused, and the Patriots finished as they customarily did—they lost.

There was another time when the stadium maintenance man at Foxboro drove his tractor onto the field in midgame to clear an area in the snow. Then John Smith proceeded to kick a field goal from the only bare spot on the field. This game the Patriots did win, 3-0, over the Dolphins. Don Shula screamed bloody murder.

The Pats did have a large group of coaches. One was Clive Rush. One day Rush was introducing a new general manager. Rush gripped the microphone, and as he did, there was a surge of electricity. Rush's eyes sparkled, and he was unable to loosen his hand from the hot mike. Finally, somebody pulled the plug, and Rush collapsed on the floor. Not long afterward he was fired. He was the only coach who was ever canned because of problems with his mental stability.

Similar episodes trailed the Patriots into their Super Bowl season. They were the team whose general manager, Patrick Sullivan, became famous for trying to punch it out with the Los Angeles Raiders. On the field, as the teams left.

◆ ◆ ◆

Now it was too bad for the Patriots, second fiddlers since the day they started. They could have been squeezing into American culture at this Super Bowl. If only they weren't being squeezed out by Jim McMahon.

Out of his football uniform, Jim McMahon did Chicago town with white-rimmed sunglasses across his face. They were there day or night. His hair was sliced into spikes.

In uniform, with his helmet off, Jim McMahon could be spotted on the sidelines with a white headband around the spikes. He wore the headband for a simple reason: He was ordered not to by Pete Rozelle.

Pete thought McMahon looked something like a race car festooned with motor-oil advertisements when he wore a headband marked *Adidas*. Not that Pete had anything against McMahon working as a huckster for Adidas. It was just that Pete didn't want him peddling Adidas when the TV cameras focused in on the bench and found Jim with his helmet off. So Pete threatened McMahon with all sorts of corporal punishment if he wore the Adidas headband again. McMahon complied.

For the next Bears' game, which happened to be for the NFC championship, McMahon took a magic marker and wrote onto his headband the letters: *R-o-z-e-l-l-e.*

"I got a big fine from Pete," said McMahon. "Five grand. Whatever that is. I thought maybe if I gave Pete a little publicity, he'd like it.

"They're taking all the fun out of the game. Well, that's football. I mean politics."

McMahon had another ritual that he performed whenever the Bears scored a touchdown, which was frequently. He butted helmets with his linemen. He ran up to them, jumping, and banged his head into theirs. Like goats. "We try to knock each other out," he said.

This was Chicago. It was always trying to knock itself out. In the saloons on the Loop, with the thunder of the El trains above, McMahon drank with Chicago. It was one beer, then another.

The Bears had drafted McMahon out of Brigham Young's pro quarterback prep school. The day he flew into Chicago to meet Mike Ditka, the Bears' coach, McMahon was picked up by a limousine. He was driven in style to the Bears' facility in the plush suburb of Lake Forest.

"He came into the office out of the limousine drinking a Budweiser," Ditka told reporters of their first meeting. "I thought he was thirsty. I knew he wasn't out to impress anybody with good manners and good behavior."

"I was thirsty," said McMahon.

◆ ◆ ◆

On picture day in the Superdome, reporters from the world over gathered around McMahon, circle after circle after circle, mikes taped to booms, cameras whirring, Super Bowl XX ballpoints scribbling in Super Bowl XX notepads.

Jim McMahon had arrived in New Orleans with a pain in the ass. He had taken a hit with a helmet in the NFC championship game. It hurt like hell. McMahon went to an acupuncturist in Chicago for treatment, a needler named Hiroshi Shiriashi from Tokyo. When the Bears flew off to New Orleans the Monday of Super Bowl week, McMahon wanted to take Hiroshi along on the plane. The Bears refused.

"I'm going to fly the acupuncturist down here," McMahon said on his arrival in New Orleans. "I need more if I'm going to play on Sunday. I didn't come here to watch. I'm going to try to stay on my feet and off my butt."

NEW ORLEANS—Everybody who is interested by now knows Jim McMahon has a sore and tender unmentionable. It has become the most famous and most written about unmentionable since Madonna appeared in those magazines.

Too, it has been recorded that McMahon's sore unmentionable prevents sitting down on hard chairs and inhibits other vital functions—such as playing football for the Bears. It is nice to know that the greatest issue of the upcoming Super Bowl has been resolved. The specialist imported from Japan to stick needles into the aforementioned unmentionable has been officially sanctioned to perform those duties by McMahon's employers.

So it is that McMahon appears at this Super Bowl site to give daily reports on the progress of the cure.

"My unmentionable still hurts," McMahon said yesterday. "It is getting better. I can't drop back to pass now. But I can backpedal. The closer we get to game time, the better it'll feel. I will play Sunday."

McMahon appeared to deliver this latest medical bulletin dressed in a white peaked cap with an Adidas symbol. This was stationed squarely above the sunshades that he always wears indoors. The pair selected for this occasion had sequins around the frame.

McMahon's shirt was red, white, and blue with an insignia proclaiming *Kingston Lions* below an array of red stars and above a sketch of some sort of blurry lion.

His unmentionable and legs were packed into tights sewn of stretch nylon. The tights, consisting of panels of red, white, and blue, were the latest thing.

"So many people think I'm a nut," McMahon said. "That's what's written and seen in the papers. That's all they see."

Somebody asked McMahon how he characterized himself.

"Normal," said McMahon. "I'm normal because I don't give a damn what people think. I don't care what people think of my lifestyle. I'm here to play football. . . ."

Somebody else asked if McMahon ever worried about playing a half-unmentionabled game.

"You do comedy, too?" McMahon asked the guy.

The conversation somehow switched to motion pictures.

"*One Flew Over the Cuckoo's Nest* is my all-time favorite movie," McMahon said. The Super Bowl hype has bored him to fits.

"You've got to print papers," McMahon said with a push toward cooperation. "Cover news. I guess this is news. It's a pain in the unmentionable, really. . . . We worked our unmentionables off to get here."

————

Also unmentionables in this Super Bowl were the Patriots out of New England. They might have managed to hit headlines. But the Boston press covered up the club's scandal with the drug scene. That would break after the game.

The other quarterback in this Super Bowl would be Tony Eason, a likeable chap who did not sport sunglasses in dark rooms and did not hurt when he sat down.

"I don't really care about image," Eason told the few writers who, perhaps from pity, interviewed him. "I'm just plain me."

He was asked how he might describe himself.

"I wouldn't," said Eason.

The Patriots had a talented running back, Craig James. But in this Super Bowl, he was matched for attention by the Bears' Walter Payton, the legendary Sweetness.

James attracted some press notice during the early week because, among other reasons, he was an escapee from the dying USFL. He had played on a team called the Washington Federals.

"It's funny," James said. "We're talking about one of the two best teams in football. In Washington we were one of the two worst teams, franchises, in sports. We were 3-and-15. That's why a lot of guys improved in speed—to get to the bank with their checks."

But the thrill of a Super Bowl flashed across his face. He was the basic runner who was not basic himself.

"Throughout my career, I've had to work and work," he said, "and then it happens for me. All those things they say about runners. That I didn't fit. That I wasn't a fullback. That I wasn't a halfback. That I was in between.

"That I was white. I had to overcome that. I can run as fast as most guys on this team."

There were still certain noxious prejudices existing in this game of pro football. Many black guys, who could have, didn't get the chance to play quarterback in the NFL. They didn't receive head coaching jobs. The rules were unwritten. Pro football said it just seemed to happen that way. The coin flip.

"There are not many white halfbacks in the league," said Craig James. "It's natural to assume if you're white you're a bulldozer. John Riggins.

"O.J. Simpson said all white running backs he classifies as dump trucks. But he said to me, 'You're not in that category.' I said, 'Thank you, O.J.'"

A helicopter, transporting a TV film crew, buzzed through the forbidden air space above the Bears' practice field at the Saints' facility. Jim McMahon lowered his drawers and bared his pin-pricked unmentionable for the cameras. Moon over the Super Bowl.

◆ ◆ ◆

Two years before those wealthy, self-styled fools started up the American Football League as a challenge to the long-established faction, the NFL played what historians decreed: *The Greatest Game Ever Played*. It was a game of super competition long before any imaginative soul dared dream there would ever be an event called the Super Bowl. This game pitted the New York Giants and the Baltimore Colts in Yankee Stadium with the NFL championship the prize. The Colts tied it with seven seconds left. So, the Giants and Colts played into overtime, all square.

It was the first overtime game in history. And then young John Unitas, with horseshoes on his helmet, marched the Colts downfield with the precision of a surgeon. He sliced the Giants, he nipped at them, he used the sidelines with skill, until he sent Alan "The Horse" Ameche plowing into the end zone to win the game and the championship.

On the drive to tie it, Unitas had passed three times at the sidelines to the same slow, poor-visioned receiver whose legs were different lengths. For 25 yards, for 15, for 22, into field goal range. The ball was caught, the feet went out of bounds, the clock was stopped.

On the drive to win it, Unitas utilized the same receiver on much of the 80-yard march. For 21, for 12.

The pass receiver was Raymond Berry. And now this mild, pious man was coach of the Patriots and in the Super Bowl. His exploits as a receiver placed him in the Pro Football Hall of Fame.

Berry played with finesse and deftness. He faked the defenders out of their booties.

In the same era, the Chicago Bears had a tight end who reflected the image of the brutish city. He caught passes with pig iron hands and used iron shoulders to crush the defenders, belting and boffing his way forward with the ball. His name was Mike Ditka. He now coached the Bears.

The rival football teams reflected the personalities of their coaches. Berry, slow, quiet, refined, was an overachiever. So were the Patriots, the wild card that made it. The Bears were boisterous and earthy, Ditka personified.

Ditka was the tough guy with a square head and a fiery mustache and the heavy fists. Yet, by Super Bowl XX, the savage in Ditka had been partially tamed. He no longer raved throughout the 60 minutes of a football game. He'd quit tearing clipboards in half and firing the pieces at his uniformed targets.

Once, in his earlier days as coach of the Chicago team, Ditka punched out a locker after a loss. The locker had a huge dent. Ditka had a broken hand.

The next week he exhorted his players: "Win one for Lefty." They did.

Ditka now had stopped punching. Instead, during the Super Bowl season, he celebrated a victory over the 49ers by weaving his car along the freeway after the plane ride home. The cops stopped him. Ditka was cited for drunk driving. Chicago cops are very tough. Some believe they are tougher than Ditka.

The population of Chicago was outraged. At the cops.

◆ ◆ ◆

We're Not Here to Start No Trouble
We're Just Here to Do the Super Bowl Shuffle.
Tum-te-tum-tum.

Through the fall of '85 and into January of '86, America rolled and rocked to the Chicago Bears and the *Super Bowl Shuffle*. The Bears—McMahon, The Fridge, Sweetness Payton—jived at a nationwide audience with their own video.

This was the cockiest team ever to show up at Pete Rozelle's Super Bowl. And the Bears earned that right.

They had the great, great Walter Payton running the ball. After all these years, Payton was in a spotlight situation. If his teammates would only let him. He had run farther, for more yardage, than any other running back in the history of pro football. And still he couldn't get the ink he deserved.

He spoke earnestly when interviewed, when the media folks could turn away from McMahon. And there was some sadness to his words, now that he had reached a Super Bowl.

"When you're on the outside looking in, you envy the people there," Payton told the writers. "You wish you could be there instead of them. But once you get there, it's not all you think it is.

"The game is supposed to be the ultimate in football. But at this point it hasn't escalated to that."

The rest of the Bears, swaggering, smirking, reveled in the atmosphere —Ditka; McMahon; Steve McMichael, the onetime strip-joint bouncer; William Perry, renowned as "The Refrigerator," 308 pounds, a slab of Americana as a rookie; Richard Dent, sulking through his contract battles; Mike Singletary, his eyeballs mesmerizing like bright headlights; Gary Fencik, the headhunting assassin out of Yale with the penchant for invest-ment banking and running with the bulls at Pamplona.

It was some team. Papa Bear Halas would have been proud as hell. The Bears clinched their spot in the playoffs weeks before the end of the season, going 15-1. They lost only to the Dolphins, on Monday night, and the defeat bridled them. They were destined for the Super Bowl before the playoffs ever started. And with McMahon, wearing his headbands, they beat the Giants, 21-0, and then the Rams for the NFC championship, 24-zip. Two shutouts.

"Bleep the champagne," said McMahon. "I want a beer."

Informed that the Bears would be playing the Patriots in the Super Bowl, McMahon said: "Bleep. I wanted to play the Dolphins. They gave us the only blemish on our record."

Right away, Jimmy the Greek made the Bears 10½-point favorites to beat the Patriots.

◆ ◆ ◆

While America was amused by the Bears, much of its population could identify with the Patriots. These were the heroes of the downtrodden, the working stiffs who lugged lunch buckets to the plant and struggled to meet the next payment on the car. Tony Eason, with no flash to him, started most of the games at quarterback. Steve Grogan, who had played with the Patriots through years of lackluster football, often replaced him. Stanley Morgan caught passes with a flair. Tony Collins ran and caught. Junius Adams had been with the Patriots for 15 years, and at age 37 would be playing in his final game at the Super Bowl. The Patriots went 11-5 during the season. They finished behind the Dolphins in the AFC East, with the same record as the Jets.

Pete Rozelle's trick of putting two wild cards into a playoff game and providing an extra weekend for television enabled the Patriots to enter the postseason. They went to the Meadowlands underdogs and upset the Jets, 26-14. They went to L.A. underdogs and upset the Raiders, 27-20, the game after which GM Patrick Sullivan, who also happened to be the son of the owner, sought to slug it out with the beaten foes. They went on to Miami underdogs and upset the Dolphins, 31-14, for the AFC championship.

To reach the Super Bowl, the Patriots had to win all three playoff games on the other teams' fields.

◆ ◆ ◆

To reach the lobby of the Hilton, on the final day of player interviews, it was necessary to push through a mob scene of women pickets.

Upstairs, where the press mob was headed, there was gossip and innuendo. Pssst.

Jim McMahon was in the eye of another brouhaha. A New Orleans TV announcer, in his Cajun mumble, had accused him of slurring this princely city alongside the Mississippi mud and its fair ladies. Thus, for the first time in 20 Super Bowls, a mob of chanting females had gathered outside a team hotel bent on lynching a quarterback. Thus, for the first time, other irate citizens threatened to bomb or put the torch to a participating team. The night before, on WDSU-TV, Buddy Diliberto, the station's sports director, had told his enrapt audience: "Jim McMahon, apparently on a radio interview with WLS, the Chicago radio station, really ripped New Orleans. He ripped the people, he ripped the ladies, he ripped a lot of things.

"Basically, I understand he said most of the ladies he ran into were sluts. He said most of the people he ran into were stupid."

The audience, especially the female segment attracted to the station, was quite ticked off at McMahon. Trouble was, Jim McMahon never uttered such words. Further trouble was, WLS in Chicago denied that any of its people had interviewed McMahon during Super Bowl week. Additional further trouble was, WLS wondered who Buddy Diliberto was. So we had one local telecaster beating a terrible retreat to wipe a coating of egg off his pancake makeup. Diliberto was made to go on the air to renounce his unchecked story and say he was sorry. Then WDSU stripped off his medals and his Super Bowl credentials and suspended him for the duration, so he could study the ethics of journalism. And 2,000 print journalists packed off with pithy stories to write.

◆ ◆ ◆

That night, Jim McMahon's needle-pocked unmentionable started to feel better. And Pete Rozelle convened his semi-private party of the Super XX Club, those of us who had covered them all. We stripped the shells off Gulf shrimp and wondered why everybody else looked 20 years older. Two decades of Super Bowl coverage, and going strong. From Starr to Mc-

Mahon. From Lombardi to Ditka. From Red Smith and Jimmy Cannon to us.

The next night, Pete Rozelle's annual party was larger and more crowded than ever, in the New Orleans Convention Center. My computer did not screw me up. I was back, starting another streak.

But it was the Saturday night party that had me enchanted. Dick and Trish Schaap had a tradition going. Dick would invite a few media friends, a few current and former players, a few notables, and mix them at some exclusive party place. On this night, I left the Hyatt and found a taxi and directed the driver to K-Paul's in the French Quarter. It was the hottest restaurant in the country. And on the night before the Super Bowl, in New Orleans, it was closed for a private party.

Inside, Paul Prudhomme, wearing, a chef's topper, cooked the Cajun dinners for the guests. Schaap introduced me to Gary Hart, whose hat had already been tossed out for the presidential election more than two years distant.

I sat down at an empty seat filled with Hart's supporters. A young woman at the table introduced herself. "I'm with Gary Hart's group," she said. "One of the campaign workers." She said it with a lilting voice.

◆ ◆ ◆

Refrigerator Perry, 308 pounds of avoirdupois, had become an American cult figure. He could be seen peddling something or other during every commercial break on every network. Ditka, with a puckish sense of humor, placed The Fridge in the backfield on offense in a midseason game. Perry got the football and was unstoppable. He became a vital part of the Bears' goal line offense. Less than a year earlier, the Bears had drafted Perry out of Clemson on the first round. Buddy Ryan, the Bears' defensive coordinator, took one look at Perry and proclaimed: "We wasted a draft choice." Ryan, a crusty figure with his own ambitions, was not Ditka's favorite assistant. The night before the Super Bowl, Ryan gathered the defense in a room. It was billed as Ryan's farewell address. He was in line to become head coach of the Eagles.

"You'll always be my heroes," Ryan told his defensive players, Dent, Singletary, Otis Wilson, Dan Hampton, Fencik, Wilber Marshall, Perry, McMichael. Ryan's words put an emotional charge into the Bears. After Ryan left the room, McMichael seized a chair and threw it at the blackboard.

NEW ORLEANS—Everybody's laughing because I'm picking the Bears to win the Super Bowl 73-0. They tell me I'm nuttier than Jim McMahon and I ought to wrap my head in a *Rozelle* straightjacket.

It was with a sense of history that I went to Sid Luckman's 73-0 score. And I courageously backed it up with a frayed buck bill in the pool in the pressroom where the sportswriters performed this annual ritual. I'd never been close to the wealth that goes with winning the pressroom pool. But . . .

◆ ◆ ◆

Walter Payton fumbled on the second play after the pregame stuff. The Patriots got the ball. On their first play, John Hannah belted Richard Dent on his seat. That knocked the Bears awake. The Patriots started moving— backwards. Not far enough this first time, so that Tony Franklin managed a 36-yard field goal. The Patriots were actually ahead.

McMahon, needled one more time in the unmentionable by Hiroshi before the game, promptly connected on a 43-yard pass to Willie Gault. Kevin Butler tied it with a 28-yard field goal. Now on their next three possessions, the Patriots tried nine plays. They lost 22 yards, had two sacks, and lost two fumbles. The Bears scored again, on a 24-yard field goal by Butler, for a 6-3 lead. Then, after the second fumble, the Bears scored their first touchdown. Payton was the decoy. Matt Suhey cut around right end from the 11 for the TD. It was still the first quarter, and the Bears were commanding, 13-3.

The Patriots did not gain one yard forward until the final play of the first quarter. By the second quarter, Eason was sitting on the Pats' bench all alone. His helmet was off. The gray look of defeat was engraved on his boyish face. He had gone 0-for-6 on his passes. He was out of the game. Steve Grogan was hardly the solution.

In that second quarter, McMahon took the Bears 59 yards, battering across himself for the touchdown from the two. That put the Bears ahead, 20-3. Then McMahon went to the bench and changed headbands. He had made out a bunch of them before, all aimed at charitable causes. That must have made Rozelle happy, even if he didn't care much for the drift of the game.

Just before halftime, McMahon staged another drive finished off by Butler's third field goal, a 24-yarder. The Bears had a 23-3 lead when they yielded the turf to the halftime performers. Early in the third quarter, the Bears started from their own four. McMahon retreated into the end zone and connected with Gault on a 60-yard pass play. That drive went 96 yards, and McMahon again scored the touchdown from the one. Bears ahead, 30-3. Next, Reggie Phillips picked off a pass by Grogan and ran it back 28 yards for another TD. Bears ahead, 37-3.

McMahon came at the Patriots again. They got down to the one. The crowd chanted for Payton. Walter hadn't scored in the Super Bowl. Ditka put Perry into the game. The Fridge got the ball and crunched ahead for the touchdown. Bears ahead, 44-3.

The Patriots did manage a touchdown in the fourth quarter. Grogan passed eight yards to Irving Fryar. But later Grogan was trapped and tackled in the end zone by Henry Waechter for a safety. The final was 46-10 —not 73-0, close, but not close enough to win me the pool.

The Bears trooped off with hardly any jubilation after hoisting Ditka and Ryan for short rides.

NEW ORLEANS — Walter Payton suffered more than the other Bears. He has played in the pro football league 11 years. Most of those years, he was the most dangerous back in the league. And the Bears were one of the weakest teams.

They were chronic losers through most of his career. And on the day the Bears won the Super Bowl to make good riddance of the frustration that grips Chicago sports, Payton looked like a loser again.

He did not play well at all. He did not score a touchdown. William Perry, the rookie Refrigerator, scored a touchdown, but Walter Payton, whose goose-stepping legs have carried him for greater distances than any other runner in NFL history, did not score. It hurt him . . .

Payton carried for 61 yards on 22 carries, something like a day off on Super Sunday. He fumbled once. He failed to catch a pass. But he dropped some.

And when William Perry scored, crunching over the line in a whirling glob of bacon fat, Payton was the decoy. . . . "Was I upset?" said Payton. "Yes, I was upset. Was I disappointed? Yes, I was disappointed. Maybe in time it'll become better for me. But now it's just another game.

"The championship ring. I can't even wear it."

XXI
The Blue Collar Team

New York Giants 39, Denver Broncos 20
January 25, 1987
Rose Bowl, Pasadena
Attendance: 101,063

The picture book cost a dime and was the best bargain on the stand in the candy store at the corner. The photographs in the magazine's innards were printed in the old gravure style and had a brownish cast. But they were clear and sharp, and for 10 cents you could see the shots of your favorites.

Tuffy Leemans's picture was near the back of this 1938 football publication. He was the most famous Giant of his day. He ran for them before Frank Gifford, most famed of the Giants, who was also credited with the invention of television.

You could see Leemans with the football tucked in his arm. His knee was lifted high. His arm was jabbed out in a traditional stiff-arm. He wore a leather helmet that was battered and scraped. This was the classic football pose of the era.

Every running back in the book was snapped in the same maneuver. But this was Tuffy Leemans. He was special. He was the tailback for Steve Owen's New York Football Giants. The papers called Owen "Stout Steve."

The image of Tuffy Leemans remained sharp and clear. For some reason, the memories from boyhood were beautiful and stayed in focus long after the current season's madcap dashes by Joe Morris would be blurred.

Once the football Giants had been thick in my blood. Many years before, they had been the team that stirred my passions.

Now I was back in California in January 1987 to cover Super Bowl XXI. For the first time, the Giants would be at the Super Bowl; they would be playing the Denver Broncos. The Giants were champions, after three decades of inertia. But through the years of forced impartiality as a writer, of haughty professional neutrality, my ancient passions had faded away— but never the loving memories.

There was a November Sunday that came back in keen detail as I sat down to write about my first day at Super Bowl XXI. I was in a room at the Marriott in Anaheim, Super Bowl XXI headquarters, but my mind was caught in the depths of nostalgia—in the Polo Grounds in upper Manhattan. The old baseball park.

The jury-rigged bleacher bench was hard on the tender bottom. And on the field, the football Giants were playing the Green Bay Packers, Don Hutson's team. The captioned names in the football picture book turned into flesh.

Tuffy Leemans was in the backfield. It was late in the game. The time was vague after too many years. Probably the third quarter. But the rest had been etched in my mind for most of a lifetime.

Leemans took the direct snap from center and cut hard toward his right. He was at the Giants' 25 on the uncovered skin of the infield. Leemans veered and suddenly he was open, running upfield. He ran past Green Bay tacklers, and he kept running. He crossed the 50 and still nobody grabbed him. He was at the 30, the 20, and it was there that he quickly turned his head to the right, saw something, dodged to his left, and kept on going. He went 75 yards for the touchdown that won the game. It was the boy's first pro football game. What he saw would never perish.

In a bit, the boy collected background on Tuffy Leemans, his first football hero. He had played college football for George Washington, and his true name was Alphonse Leemans. He needed a nickname, Tuffy. After football, he operated a laundry in Washington.

What happened to Leemans in the intervening years became gray, obscured. But many years later, the boy went to a Super Bowl, and there he sat on the 28-member selection board of the Pro Football Hall of Fame. His vote helped. Leemans was elected to the Hall of Fame.

Now the boy, grown up, was covering the Giants at another Super Bowl. The franchise had not won a championship for 30 years. The current Giants growled and grumbled about the emphasis on history. For many lean years, they had battled against tradition.

"The Giants have now moved out of the Dark Ages," said Joe Morris, who ran for the Super Bowl Giants in the position once worked by Tuffy Leemans. "All they talk about is the old days. This is the present."

And so it was. No more hard seats.

◆ ◆ ◆

The logistics for a southern California Super Bowl are the most difficult because of the vastness of the territory, the gridlock on the freeways, the smog, the noxious fumes. This time the NFL—with a piquant touch of irony—billeted the Super Bowl press down the street from Disneyland.

We were handy to a variety of interview subjects—John Elway, Phil Simms, Donald Duck. In the evening, we had our choice of Mexican restaurants.

The first thing you noticed about John Elway was his teeth. In NFL circles, there was occasional debate about the might of his arm. But there was total agreement about the dazzling quality of John's enormous smile.

New York, chic and smart, was in this Super Bowl versus Denver, which was nestled into the Rocky Mountains, a lost city of yahoos dressed in bright orange with deep emotions for a collection of football mercenaries. There was nothing blasé about Denver. Nine years earlier, Denver had brought its ever-loving hordes of pumpkin-tinted bumpkins to a Super Bowl and had gone away embarrassed.

Through the years, the Broncos managed to remain competitive; they were a challenging team that yearned to return to a Super Bowl. They made the annual changes football teams must make to prevent decay. There was a coaching change. Red Miller, the old fist-faced fighter, was gone.

Dan Reeves, sophisticated protégé of Tom Landry, had become the Broncos' head coach. He was experienced in winning. He was experienced in Super Bowls. Once upon a time, a forward pass from Craig Morton had been misfired and intercepted in Super Bowl V as Reeves came out of the Dallas backfield. The interception had resulted in the field goal by Jim O'Brien that won for the Colts, over the Cowboys.

The thread connecting the Super Bowls through time remained. But Craig Morton, of course, had long ago left the Broncos.

The basic reason the Broncos kept their edge through the seasons was John Elway. He had been drafted tops off the board out of Stanford by the Baltimore Colts in 1983. It was the year Dan Marino almost got lost. John, educated, California-raised, did not quite recognize the appeal of Chesapeake Bay crabcakes and flatly refused to play pro football in Baltimore. The town would soon be abandoned anyway when the entire load of property owned by the Colts would be dumped aboard moving vans in the middle of the night and taken to Indianapolis. The Colts had been forced to trade Elway's rights to Denver. His toothy caricature promptly became as significant to pro football as the NFL's badge-shaped logo.

Elway was a pro football star the first day he dressed in Denver's pumpkin orange with the Number 7 on his chest. Magazine, television, and newspaper media from as far away as America's command center in New York gravitated to the Broncos' Rocky Mountain hideaway. Just to smooze with Elway.

Elway started as a rookie. His arm threw passes with the velocity of a fired cannon shell. But without the accuracy. Not to worry, there was no NFL quarterback with more potential. John played with derring-do. He scooted out of the pocket. He ran the ball, daring linebackers to belt him. He slid across the turf. His passes singed the fingers of his receivers. And as the seasons passed, John developed a tendency for the absurdly dramatic on the football field. The Broncos were in Super Bowl XXI simply because Elway had managed to succeed on a 98-yard march against the clock in frigid conditions in an enemy town—to survive in the AFC championship game.

"You can't believe the pressure John has been under ever since he joined our team," said Reeves.

Now Elway, his teeth, his arm, his personality, his characteristics, were under the magnifying glass of a Super Bowl. New York, where all the publicity drums were in business, was in it. But the show in this Super Bowl prelude would be a kid who played in Denver. Somewhere across the Hudson River—America's continental divide—out there in the mountains.

♦ ♦ ♦

The Super Bowl 2,000 milled around on the parking lot at Cal State-Irvine. It was another Super Bowl picture day. The sun beat on us as we were kept captive on the bubbling asphalt of the parking lot. My mind retreated to another picture day, five years earlier, when we had been corralled to wait for the players to be uncaged for our grilling. We'd nearly suffered frostbite that Super Bowl day in Pontiac. Now we risked sunstroke as we awaited the Giants.

The Giants were this season's Chicago Bears, remodeled. They played football with that much gristle. Their game was bloody noses and sticks in the gut. And they had peaked when it was best to peak. The Giants were on a roll—rolling toward the Super Bowl. This mighty roll made them true successors to the Bears of the year before. There was no doubt in my mind that the Giants would be able to tease, to toy, to frolic with the Broncos, just as the Bears had with the Patriots.

But as another Super Bowl week started, the Giants were there, and they hadn't been immortalized on videotape. They went to the Super Bowl— but without a Refrigerator. Their defensive celebrity did have a nickname. Lawrence Taylor was called by his initials.

Their quarterback did not sport headbands and punker's eyeshades and show up in stretch jumpsuits with advertisments on his chest. He did not transport his acupuncturist to California. Phil Simms came out of Kentucky, and he was full of "Aw, Shucks."

"We didn't make the Super Bowl Shuffle," said Bart Oates, the Giants' center. "We may be boring—boring from a Fifth Avenue standpoint. We don't have anybody endorsing clothes. But what we have here fits perfectly."

There was no trickery to the plays when Joe Morris was handed the football. He was as subtle as the guy lugging a lunch bucket into a factory on the morning shift.

"This team is very blue-collar," Morris said. "That's because Bill Parcells is a blue-collar coach.

"When I started out here with this team, we were 4-5. Then we were 3-12-1. For somebody who's been here through the lean times, this means a lot. They said we'd never do it."

It was a grinder's team. Joe Morris did not wear Calvin Kleins in Calvin Klein's own town. Joe wore Levis.

The Giants had been put down, knocked down, for a generation. All they heard through the years of travail was the glorious history of the old Giants.

They heard the comic stories. How one Sunday the Giants were endeavoring to run out the last minute to preserve a victory over the Eagles. How Joe Piscarcik, the quarterback, fumbled a handoff. How the Eagles grabbed the fumble and ran it back for a touchdown, the touchdown that beat the Giants. How an airplane flew over Giants Stadium trailing a banner: *Fifteen years of losing football—we've had enough.* How the fans booed Phil Simms the day he was drafted from college.

◆ ◆ ◆

The Giants hadn't been champions since 1956, when Frank Gifford lugged the ball. It was a decade before the creation of the Super Bowl, back in the Dark Ages, as Joe Morris called that time in history. The days of Gifford and Charley Conerly and Y.A. Tittle, and before them Leemans and Ken Strong and Ward Cuff.

The Giants, just as the Bears, came to the Super Bowl with a rich tradition, followed by years of poverty. "All they used to talk about was the old days," Morris said. "Now people are going to talk about this team."

Among those talking would be Gifford, who wore a fur coat to the New Jersey Meadowlands the day the Giants qualified for the Super Bowl.

The Giants permitted themselves only one escape from normalcy. When they won, which was practically every Sunday, they committed the juvenile delinquent's act of drenching their coach with Gatorade. Bill Parcells always laughed as he dodged Harry Carson's splashing bucket.

Somehow, the TV cameras always had Carson and Parcells in focus when the bucket was turned over. Somehow.

Alert media are the salvation of a bug-eyed nation.

◆ ◆ ◆

The NFL put John Elway and the Broncos up in Newport Beach. This slice of swank had grown in snootiness since Super Bowl VII and the press stayed there. We came, as always, by bus. And every morning Elway would arrive, flashing the grin in his boy's face. And 200 TV cameras would trail him, their operators banging each other for position. For the welfare of the bug-eyed nation.

Elway would pop out the platitudes. "I've always wondered," spoke John to the vast assemblage, "does anyone ever reach his potential?"

It would have been a disservice to the clientele not to write about Elway.

NEWPORT BEACH, Calif.—QB VII went to Hollywood by limousine to meet Eddie Murphy filming *Beverly Hills Cop II* during hype time of Super Bowl XXI.

"I got up there and said 'I'm sure glad I'm a football player and not an actor,'" said John Elway, QB, with No. 7 on his football shirt. "It takes forever to set up one shot."

Elway, it is recalled, can move 98 yards lugging a football and an entire team in barely a minute and some fractions. He speaks cleaner than Eddie Murphy, too.

"I like to go out and have a beer with the guys," said Elway, getting about as raunchy as he can get.

Super Bowl XXI is about to drop on us with its glitzy thud. John Elway is the star. He's the attraction. They've put his name on the marquee at the Rose Bowl: *John Elway vs. the Giants, Sunday, 3 p.m.*

What the Giants will do to John Elway is something else. But this is the Super Bowl. He appears with a cast of . . . well, 44 (XLIV). It is John Elway and the spear carriers. Those extras who are role players for the Broncos.

The guys, as John Elway calls them.

This is a rare football team, the Broncos. There is no resentment. It lacks jealousy. The Giants may be brutes, tough guys who want to kick in Elway's mouthful of teeth. The Broncos are class.

"John's won a few ball games for us," said Steve Watson, who gets so little publicity for making his acrobatic pass catches. "We're excited for John. We never look at it with jealousy. We know his attitude. He wants to be one of us."

The Broncos went to the Super Bowl once before. It was nine years ago . . . Denver reached that Super Bowl by virtue of its defense. Orange Crush, it was called. After that Super Bowl, the Denver team was divided. The Denver defense hated the Denver offense. The guys didn't go drink beer together.

Now the Orange Crush defense adores John Elway. . . .

The day John Elway marched the Broncos 98 yards against vanishing time all the way to Super Bowl XXI he did it without the limo. He did it in hostile conditions in Cleveland.

"We kept getting hit with dog bones," said Watson, referring to the Clevelanders who brought along Ken-L-ration to spur on the Browns' Dawg Defense. "One end zone was littered with dog bones. It's a shame I didn't have my dogs there."

Elway was there, though. And he reached the end zone.

"No wonder we all love him," said Watson.

New York, New York, it's a wonderful town—sort of.

But there were those in New York who would never forgive the Giants for abandoning the city and moving across the Hudson River divide to New Jersey.

"Foreigners," Ed Koch had proclaimed before the Giants reached the Super Bowl. Koch was the lord mayor of the city and spokesman for all that ailed the world.

But somehow Lawrence Taylor convinced Koch that a lot of New Yorkers still rooted for those foreigners. "And a whole lot of them vote," L.T. said. It was then that Koch decided that the New York Giants were—hurrah for them—New York's team. They'd kept the city's name, after all.

"Mr. Koch, or whatever he calls himself . . . he's a great bandstand player," said L.T.

Thus, one New York City government crisis was solved, with even a promise of a parade for the Giants from Wall Street to City Hall, New York.

But another crisis threatened as the Super Bowl neared. A Bowl Warning was issued to the citizens of New York by the commissioner of the city's Department of Environmental Protection. "Think before you flush," Harvey Schultz declared as he decreed that the day of Super Bowl XXI would be *Super Flush Sunday*.

"We could experience a temporary drop in water pressure in some areas of the city if the game should be a close one," the commissioner warned. "A surge in water could occur at the final gun."

Thus, Schultz managed to get his name in the papers with the rest of the Super Bowl hype.

♦ ♦ ♦

At the Giants' hotel in Costa Mesa, Lawrence Taylor tried to avoid the hype. He chose silence, as Duane Thomas had, as John Riggins had. He preferred to hide and study game film highlights.

One New York reporter managed to get L.T. to utter a few words about quarterbacks, such as John Elway: "I can be an SOB. Nasty, lousy, mean people are the guys who get the farthest. I love the contact. It makes the game real enjoyable. I can go two or three games without a kill shot. That's when the snot comes from his nose and he starts quivering on the ground. You want to run that film again and again."

Bill Parcells had some choice words, too: "The press are all communists."

We started to yearn for Jim McMahon and Joe Theismann. Instead, we had to settle for Phil Simms.

COSTA MESA, Calif.—This is Broadway Joe's game. The Super Bowl is Joe Namath stepping out of a Fort Lauderdale bar and guaranteeing victory. It is Mr. Laff's saloon and Joe and his ladies and his llama coat.

Phil Simms plays in the same town Joe Namath did. It was Joe Namath who established the Super Bowl as a fixture of Americana. The town is New York. They loved Joe there.

And Phil Simms? The first time anybody in New York ever heard of Phil Simms they booed him. It was NFL draft day, 1979. The NFL does it live in New York. The league rigs up bleachers and sets up a time clock and invites in the public. Pete Rozelle reads the names.

First Round: "The New York Giants select Phil Simms, quarterback from Morehead State."

Two thousand New York voices erupted as one. *Boooooo.* It might have sounded like *Whooooooo?* But it was boo.

Welcomed, Phil Simms proceeded to play as a rookie for a flop team. He did OK, but the team gasped.

"A lot of times my rookie year, I had flashes of greatnesss," Simms said. "I said this game isn't as tough as it looks, next year I ought to be a helluva player.

"Then things kind of went backwards."

The boos never stopped for Phil Simms. They didn't until this season.

. . . He is a Kentucky kid with strawberry blond hair and an innocent look. He could live next door and play for the high school down the street.

The Super Bowl is a quarterback's game. It was Joe Namath's game. It belonged to Starr and Stabler and Bradshaw and Montana and Plunkett and Theismann and Griese and Staubach and Unitas and McMahon.

Now it is John Elway's game.

Elway is the glitter at Super Bowl XXI. He brought the Broncos here on his historic, heroic 98-yard drive.

The Giants brought Phil Simms to the Super Bowl. He came along, like the baggage with the shoulder pads. But the game has to be played with somebody taking snaps and handing off and throwing the ball sometimes. So it's Simms, the plugger quarterback.

"I'm not pretty or exciting," said Phil Simms. "I'm not flashy like John Elway. I'm just a lunch bucket kind of guy.

"Elway—he's an executive quarterback."

. . . The bad times went on for years after Phil Simms arrived with his ceremonious welcome. The Giants were able to string together a bunch of three- and four-victory seasons. The fans got to pelting Simms with golf balls, eggs, and rotten oranges. Unlike Phil's, the fans' throws were never intercepted.

Simms suffered injuries. He was benched . . .

"I thought, 'Hey, this was never meant to be,'" he said.

He considered quitting.

Now he's the other quarterback at the Super Bowl. No victory guarantees for Phil Simms. Just a day's work under a blue collar, plugger's style. The Super Bowl is destined to become Phil Simms's game, too.

Tom Jackson was haunted by the memories of Super Bowl XII. It had been a galling loss to the Cowboys nine years before. Jackson was the senior member of the Broncos. The constant requirement for changes, for new talent, in the banging sport of pro football had caused a massive turnover among the Broncos. Only three starters remained from Red Miller's first Denver Super Bowl team.

Now before Super Bowl XXI, America was laughing at the Broncos. Jimmy the Greek had made the Giants the favorites by eight and a half points. Or, in the Denver psyche, he had made the Broncos eight-and-a-half-point underdogs.

The smart guys in the press figured America had been set up for another Super Bowl comedy. The past three years, television sets had been clicked off long before there was any danger of a simultaneous national toilet flush at the final gun. And now we figured Super Bowl XXI would be little more than the Raiders over the Redskins, the 49ers over the Dolphins, the Bears over the Patriots. Routs.

Ticked off by our fears, our jokes, our predictions, Tom Jackson spoke for his team: "The hype and the glamour are what created the game. Guys who are never talked to have 100 people asking them questions this week. That creates a different intensity."

There was no balance of power in the NFL. Power rode a teeter-totter. After Vince Lombardi, the AFL/AFC had won 11 of the next 13 Super Bowls. But now, before Super Bowl XXI, it had tipped the other way. The NFC had beaten the AFC in four of the past five.

All of which made the Broncos appear as choice victims.

They resented these thoughts because they had remained contenders, which few franchises had managed during rebuilding years. In 1986, the Broncos went 11-5 in winning the AFC West. They won with a wildly productive offense. But toward the end of the regular season, the Broncos went into a fade and lost three of their last five games, including a 19-16 loss to the Giants.

In the playoffs, Elway took them to a 22-17 victory over New England at Mile High Stadium in Denver. That put them into the AFC championship game. But they would have to play in Cleveland—with the wind whipping off Lake Erie, on the lumpy field, before the vulgar, emotional fans. The Browns had the better record, 12-4, and had Bernie Kosar at quarterback. After 20 years of frustration, the Browns were aimed toward the Super Bowl.

The Cleveland fans barked and howled when their club went up on Kosar's 48-yard touchdown pass with less than six minutes to play. The score was 20-13, Cleveland. And they barked louder when the Broncos screwed up the kickoff and finally recovered it back on the two.

Elway conducted his huddle in his own end zone. The clock read 5:34 left. The drive began with an inauspicious pass. Elway hit back Sammy Winder for five yards. Along the way, Elway, trapped going back to pass, escaped for an 11-yard gain. Moments later he hit Steve Sewell for 22 yards and Watson for 12. The Broncos had reached Cleveland's 40 at the two-minute warning. Now Elway was flipped for an eight-yard loss. It was third-and-18 with 1:47 on the clock. Elway went for the entire glob on one play. He hit rookie Mark Jackson for 20 yards. At the 28 now, 1:19 left, he hit Sewell again for 14 yards and then chugged nine more yards himself. The Broncos were at the five with 42 seconds left. With dog bones bouncing all around, Elway passed once more and Mark Jackson, sliding on the end zone dirt, caught the pass to tie the score. Elway had driven the Broncos the 98 yards in 15 plays.

In the overtime, he drove them again, from their 25 to the Cleveland 15. There Rich Karlis kicked the sudden-death field goal, a 33-yarder, to put the Broncos in Super Bowl XXI, by a 23-20 count.

◆ ◆ ◆

The Giants needed no heroics to reach their first Super Bowl. Playing with blue-collar might all season, they finished their schedule with a nine-game winning streak. They were 14-2 for the season. Simms had emerged as a productive passer; Joe Morris, after a contract holdout until four hours before the opening game, had gained more than 1,500 yards. The linebacking trio of Taylor, Carl Banks, and Harry Carson had slaughtered the enemy with their brutish tackling and blitzing. The Giants were at a peak when they entered the playoffs.

In their first playoff game, they destroyed the 49ers of Bill Walsh, 49-3. Simms threw four touchdown passes; Morris ran for two touchdowns; Taylor ran a pass interception back for a touchdown.

The Redskins were the Giants' opponents for the NFC championship game in the Meadowlands. It was a raw day in New Jersey, with the wind whipping confetti into the faces of the athletes. Parcells elected to kick off when the Giants won the toss. The Redskins could do nothing with the ball. The Giants were quickly ahead, led 17-0 at the half, and that was the final score. They were champions—for the first time since the Giffer played in their backfield.

◆ ◆ ◆

Pete Rozelle tossed one of his best parties in years. It was a victory party, sort of. The courts had destroyed the USFL. Given a plan by Donald Trump, the new league schemed to switch its games from spring and summer to fall. Trump, who had the New Jersey Generals among his properties, planned to go eye-to-eye, throat-to-throat, buck-to-buck against the NFL. The USFL sued for millions in claiming that the NFL was in violation of antitrust, a monopoly.

Sure enough, the NFL was a monopoly, or so the jurors decided. Then they awarded the USFL one U.S. dollar, trebled for damages, for winning the court case. The USFL was left without the legendary pot.

Pete's party was at Universal Studios in Hollywood. A tourist attraction, it was equipped for mobs. We were transported in trams through the sets, treated to the make-believe of Hollywood, taken back into history and back to the future.

Rozelle had just one wish, that only a Hollywood script could provide: icy cold in the East, forcing folks to remain inside their homes; dusk gathering in the West; a football team driving in at the last moments of a tight game; the TV camera flashing on a placekicker flexing his leg; a time-out and the kicker rushing onto the field. America pausing to catch its breath.

"What I want is a close game," said the lord high commissioner. "With cold weather in the East, we'd have a chance for record TV ratings." It was an annual wish. And he hadn't had a true, close Super Bowl game for five years.

♦ ♦ ♦

On Saturday afternoon, I drove out of Anaheim toward the Pacific as the sun set, a burning disk, on the ocean, to the traditional party tossed by Dick and Trish Schaap. I had stopped in Beverly Hills on the way to people-watch along Rodeo Drive. The sidewalks of this fantasyland were full of people in burnt-orange T-shirts. They all had funny fantasies about the Broncos beating the Giants.

The Schaaps' party was far up along the ocean in Malibu. I dropped down a dirt road to an isolated beach. Dick Schaap introduced me to one of the Giants' fans, Billy Crystal. He was serious about the game. Then, over a tub full of ice and beer, I ran into Jim O'Brien, a genuine hero of Super Bowls past. We relived—several times—the drama of the final moments of Super Bowl V. O'Brien's kick. It was a moment Pete Rozelle should have put into a time capsule.

♦ ♦ ♦

The buscapade left early from Anaheim, on the serendipitous freeway route plotted by Pete Rozelle's planners. We did get to the Rose Bowl. It was a glorious California day and Neil Diamond sang a glorious version of "The Star-Spangled Banner."

The folks dressed in burnt orange were the first to show ecstasy. Elway guided the Broncos to a score on their first possession. Rich Karlis barefooted a 48-yard field goal for a 3-0 lead. Karlis was hot, first winning the game in Cleveland in sudden-death and now making this accurate kick that tied the Super Bowl record for field-goal distance.

Now Phil Simms, the jeered, ridiculed, blond quarterback, trundled onto the field and marched the Giants 78 yards. They scored the touchdown on Simms's pass to Zeke Mowatt for a 7-3 lead. Elway responded immediately, marching the Broncos 58 yards. Improvising near the goal line, Elway scored the touchdown himself on a four-yard draw. Denver was back in front, 10-7, and form was being tossed into the ashcan.

The Broncos threatened again as the second quarter started. Elway, scooting to escape the Giants' rush, passed deep to Vance Johnson for 58 yards. Denver moved forward to a first down on the Giants' one. Their fans were going bananas, if not oranges. Elway kept the ball on the first play, rolling right, shooting for the end zone. He met Mr. Lawrence Taylor and was flipped back for a yard loss. On second down, the Broncos tried a trap with Gerald Willhite carrying. Mr. Harry Carson stopped him for zero gain. It was third down at the two. The Broncos tried the left side, wide this time, with Elway pitching to Sammy Winder. Mr. Carl Banks hit Winder behind the line and dragged him to the grass for a four-yard loss.

The introductions were completed. The Broncos had met the Giants' three linebackers. The dependable Karlis went back to try the chipshot field goal so the Broncos would not forfeit this drive without any points. Karlis missed—from the 23.

The look of the game changed. The Giants kept misfiring on offense, despite Simms's accurate passing. But the Giants' defense was nailing Elway. George Martin, the DE, loped in and trapped Elway in the end zone for a safety. The Broncos' lead was cut to 10-9. As the half ended, Karlis tried another short field goal and missed from the 34. The Broncos would have only a one-point advantage entering the second half.

Protecting that appeared impossible.

Early in the third quarter, the Broncos stopped the Giants on the far side of midfield. It was fourth down, a half-yard to go. The punting unit went onto the field. But Parcells had a trick. Backup quarterback Jeff Rutledge, on the field to block, took the snap and gained the first down. Simms capitalized immediately. He passed 12 yards to Morris, 23 to Lee Rouson, then 13 to tight end Mark Bavaro for the touchdown. Bavaro went to his knees and genuflected in the end zone. The Giants were in front, 16-10.

Simms would not miss. The cheers were for him. It might have sounded like music. He kept his offense going. With the lead, he marched the Giants to another score on Raul Alegre's 21-yard field goal. The Giants were ahead, 19-10. The defense was now attacking Elway, halting him. Simms got the ball again. Flipping to Morris, getting the ball returned on the flea flicker, Simms passed deep on the old Super Bowl play that had failed once for Earl Morrall. Simms made it go, 44 yards to Phil McConkey. Morris busted over from the one on the next play. With 17 points in the third period, the Giants were up, 26-10, entering the last quarter. Simms had passed eight-for-eight in the outburst.

And Elway couldn't hit.

Early in the fourth quarter, Simms hit the target again—Stacy Robinson for 36 yards, then McConkey for six, on a pass that ricocheted off Bavaro, for the TD. The Giants had a 33-10 lead.

Karlis finally clicked with a 28-yarder to make a dent, nothing more. Giants, 33-13. Simms guided the Giants the distance again, with Ottis Anderson scoring on a two-yard run. Giants, 39-13.

Harry Carson edged toward the Gatorade bucket to perform the ceremonies on Parcells. Only then could Elway strike back. He hit Vance Johnson for a 47-yard touchdown before the two-minute warning. Carson edged closer, grabbed the bucket, and poured it over his coach. The final was 39-20, Giants, another flop for Rozelle.

But it was a piece of fine sculpture for Simms. The once-sneered-at quarterback had hit on 22 of his 25 passes in the Super Bowl. He had thrown for three touchdown passes, 268 yards.

"That might be the best game a quarterback has ever played," said Parcells.

And the quarterback who had been the target of rotten fruit on his home field? He said: "When you think of the Denver Broncos, you think of John Elway. When you think of the Giants, you don't think of Phil Simms."

It still burned him. But he had burned out a segment of Giants' history for himself in the town that once cheered Tuffy Leemans, Frank Gifford, and Joe Namath. Phil Simms did not leave his Super Bowl as Namath had, with the cops, the dogs, the ladies. He left in a bus. But the unlikely happened—the New York fans were pelting him with kisses and cheers.

XXII
The 15 Minutes

Washington Redskins 42, Denver Broncos 10
January 31, 1988
Jack Murphy Stadium, San Diego
Attendance: 73,302

Perhaps a billion words would be written and read, or spoken and heard, during this wonderful week in advance of Super Bowl XXII. Who can count that high? Maybe more than a billion words as the writers, the TV men, the radio probers crunched and skittered around the athletes who played for the Redskins and the Broncos.

It was picture day in San Diego, a city that Pete Rozelle had discovered and made into a new Super Bowl location. A thousand or so reporters clustered around the Redskins' tall quarterback, Doug Williams, on this photo day. From one of these elite of the world media came a voice that spoke nine words: "Obviously, you've been a black quarterback all your life . . . "

Doug Williams just looked at the person forming this question. *Damn the torpedos, full-speed ahead. Don't give up the ship. Nuts. Fourscore and seven years ago. One small step for man, one giant step for mankind. I have a dream.* Some words, once spoken, are etched in history.

Williams had learned that intellectual capacity in a journalist was never required for the assignment to cover the Super Bowl.

"If you're white, black, yellow, or pink, it means a lot to a quarterback, if you can take a team to the Super Bowl." Those words had been spoken by Doug Williams.

"Martin Luther King didn't change it, John F. Kennedy didn't change it. All I can do is live my life the way I'm living it and be an example of how you can overcome." Those words, too, had been spoken by Doug Williams.

Doug Williams guided his team to the Super Bowl much the way Joe Montana, Jim McMahon, and Phil Simms had taken their teams to the ultimate event—with passing, leadership, motivation, and skill.

But Williams gave us a different issue, an issue heightened by Jimmy the Greek and his words—myths, lies, bumbling, bigoted statements.

The Friday before Williams would be playing in the NFC championship game, winner to go to the Super Bowl, the Greek sat down for lunch at Duke Zeibert's restaurant in Washington. A crew from WRC-TV, Washington's NBC outlet, stuck a microphone in the Greek's face. He was asked to say something to commemorate Martin Luther King's birthday. And the Greek spoke, delivering his theories and philosophies for all us TV viewers.

Among other things, he said: ". . . the black is the better athlete, and he practices to be the better athlete, and he's bred to be the better athlete because all this goes way back to the slave period, the slave owner would breed this big black with his big woman so he could have a big black kid. That's where it all started."

He also said: "If they take over the coaching jobs like everybody wants them to, there's not going to be anything left for the white people. I mean, all the players are black. The only thing the whites control is the coaching jobs. Now I'm not being derogatory, but that's all that's left for them. Black talent is beautiful, it's great, it's out there. The only thing left for whites is a couple of coaching jobs."

Suddenly, every network was showing footage of Lunch at Duke's, Noontime with the Greek. The news wires blistered. CBS was appalled. The network had employed the Greek for a dozen years, used his opinions, permitted him to deliver his ass-backwards scoops, provided a forum for him to deliver to us his point spreads.

The Greek apologized. Next day, CBS fired him. The following day Brent Musburger, the Greek's long-time colleague, apologized for CBS. Brent reminded America that the Greek's words did not reflect the thinking or attitudes of the rest of the people at CBS. Thus, pleading itself innocent, CBS permitted the games to go on.

Doug Williams's biography became the story of Super Bowl XXII. As the first black quarterback to start in the event devoted to excess, gluttony, avarice, corporate buffoonery, lechery, sporting pomposity, journalistic incest, Doug Williams's every mouthful was headlines material.

"I used to see crosses burning every Friday night," Williams told the writers about his boyhood in Louisiana. "They burned a cross at every intersection. We couldn't go out of the house after dark."

He had lived through hard days—in his boyhood and in his professional manhood.

"Articles say I'm vindictive," Williams said. "They say I have something to prove. I have nothing to prove . . . except to Joe Gibbs and my team."

Gibbs was the only NFL coach to give Williams a decent chance.

Williams had gone to the NFL a decade before Super Bowl XXII. He came out of Grambling, a top-rated quarterback. He was drafted in the first round by the Tampa Bay Buccaneers.

Then, too, he was cast as a man destined to crash through a color barrier. The NFL had never had a premier quarterback whose skin was anything but white. Blacks—James Harris, Joe Gilliam, John Walton— had played quarterback before in the league, but they were backups mostly, seldom used.

Williams was brought to the NFL to play for a downtrodden expansion team, to lead it in its development, to crumble the myths and the stereotypes. The Bucs, the pro team that had lost its first 24 games, quickly flourished with Williams on the team. Williams was the Bucs' quarterback for five seasons, during which time they went to the playoffs three times. With Williams, the Bucs reached the NFC championship game, the brink of an earlier Super Bowl, but lost.

It was then that the Bucs turned on their quarterback by being cheap in a contract offer. Williams jumped to the USFL, the Oklahoma Outlaws.

Then there was the terrible tragedy of the death of Williams's wife, Janice, who died of a brain tumor just after the birth of their daughter, Ashley. Williams went half-crazy. He wondered about life and the cruelty of it.

"I don't think it can get any worse," Williams told the Super Bowl press. "You think, 'Why me?' You think about the baby and its mother. You think, 'It should have been me.'"

The USFL went under. Doug Williams, once a number one quarterback in the NFL, was jobless at age 30. It was 1986.

"The only reason I came to this team in Washington is it's the only club that offered me anything," Williams said, "and that as a backup.

"Everybody says that Doug Williams is a better reliever than he is a starter. I've always been a starter.

"For a year I'd been all dressed up and nowhere to go. Go out for the pregame warm-up. Listen to the tunes. Go back to the dressing room. Come back out for the kickoff. Sit on the sidelines.

"Then somebody calls and says, 'Hey man, c'mon down here.' You feel wanted."

As successor to Joe Theismann, Jay Schroeder had been a near champion in 1986. Williams was allowed to play and feel wanted in one game, as a reliever. He threw one pass in the '86 season.

At the end of the '86 season, Williams went to Gibbs and asked to be traded to a place where he could play. A trade was fixed with Al Davis and the Raiders: Williams for a second-round draft choice. Then the trade was canceled.

The Redskins started the '87 season with Williams as Schoeder's backup, again. But in the season opener versus the Eagles, Schroeder was injured. Williams rushed in, the emergency quarterback, and threw two touchdown passes. The Redskins won.

The players walked off in another strike in the 1987 season, but this time the NFL did not cut off the games. The NFL hired non-union football players, rejects, the unemployed, camp cuts who had become bookkeepers and construction workers, and it played on. The NFL counted the games in the season standings.

Mickey Mouse II.

When the strike ended after several games and the genuine football players returned, Williams remained Schroeder's backup. But now there was a pattern. Schroeder would falter, Williams would rush in—and hail to the Redskins. In the season's final game, Williams came in again and helped save the Redskins from a loss to the Vikings. They produced a 27-24 victory in overtime.

Gibbs changed quarterbacks when the season ended, before the Super Bowl playoffs. Doug Williams was a starter in the NFL for the first time in five years.

Now he was at the Super Bowl in San Diego. He was analyzed, scrutinzed, critiqued. Thrust under a microscope, he was a football player forced to become protagonist in the hottest sociological story of the year.

Williams said it had all started back for him when he bailed out the Redskins in the season opener, when he produced the victory in relief of Schroeder.

"Even Ronald Reagan took a look at that game and said, 'By God, Jesse Jackson will love this,'" said Williams.

◆ ◆ ◆

The truth is the NFL never picked fleabag dumps to put up the elite media corps. A contented scribe is one who would be more inclined to write nice, sweet puff pieces promoting pro football. So went the rationale of Pete Rozelle, whose own origins were in PR.

Now we were in the new shoreside Marriott in San Diego. I had a neat room overlooking the San Diego harbor with its sailboats, ferryboats, great naval ships, and flocks of seagulls. It had a step-out porch, where I could bask in the afternoon sun after finishing my writing and read the freebie papers and magazines that were dropped in the pressroom to make us happy.

Our own newspapers, of course, had codes of ethics and paid for our hotel rooms and meals. At least they should have, the days of the total freeload having vanished with the demise of the leather helmet and the single wing.

We now had *USA Today* hanging on our hotel room door handles every morning. *USA Today* had created the world in 1982 and discovered the Super Bowl. Anything that might have happened before then did not count, because nothing ever happened before then. The stuff it wrote about was designed to be remembered for 30 seconds, the maximum length of its average reader's memory span.

Mike Lupica, the columnist from New York, was impressed by the writing. "Every story reads like a ransom note."

USA Today's contribution to sporting America was the television column. We learned what Brent Musburger said yesterday when he covered a football game. We learned what Bob Costas said today when *USA* discovered that a basketball, along with the planet Earth, was round. We learned what Dick Vitale had to say, in his well-chosen words. And then we learned which team Brent Musburger predicted would win the Super Bowl and why. My old bugaboo: The media interviewing the media. Nincompoop journalism.

A guy named Rudy Martzke assembled all this vital information and published it ransom-note style. He ran the ratings as though they were as important as the scores, and he scared the crap out of all the network bosses lest he write something that showed CBS didn't beat NBC the Sunday when the Cowboys played the Steelers.

◆ ◆ ◆

Bleep John Elway!

Being something of a traditionalist, I went out to the Broncos to hear what John Elway had to say, even though it was against the modern journalistic judgment.

Across John's face was a pair of blue-tinted sun shades. He was chewing gum. This might have been Elton John on tour in Australia, or General Eisenhower on the invasion beach. We—the traditionalists—jostled around him, straining to hear his words. He vanished from my view, from within the elbowing crowd. I squeezed in and craned my neck. I was able to see his white shoes, laces untied, and two white sweat socks. There was a voice, of which one of every four words was audible. I assumed the voice was Elway's.

"Underneath all the hype and hoopla, there's a football game," Elway said.

Somebody moved in and told Elway: "The Top Gun pilots of the U.S. Air Force admired your calm and performance."

"I admire what they do," said Elway. "My job is a lot easier than what they do."

"John," somebody else said, "were your struggles when you were a rookie, years ago, were they humbling?"

"Gee, I didn't know what I was doing," Elway said. "I didn't think it was humbling. I don't think I was an egomaniac when I came into the league. It damaged my confidence. I was shattered. People said my first year I was a bust."

"Were you a bust?" another guy asked.

"Yeah," Elway said.

Somebody—it looked like the guy from Dubuque—chimed in: "The Super Bowl, what is it?"

"The players are sort of sidelights here," said Elway. "It's the media. It's attention. Look at the stories. Most are about the media. It's the spectacle."

The prattle lasted for 45 minutes. Then an NFL PR guy blasted into his power megaphone that the session was history, that Elway was being freed.

"Time flies when you're having fun," said Elway.

"One more question," said a persistent snoop. "The game's in Jack Murphy Stadium. John, do you know who Jack Murphy was?"

"No," said Elway. "No."

"He was a sportswriter," said the sportswriter.

"He must never have written a bad thing to have a stadium named after him," said Elway.

◆　◆　◆

The bus carried a mob of gringo journalists. It rolled up to the border control south of San Diego, past the barbed wire fences. We rode into Tijuana, in Old Mexico, and stopped on the other side. A Mexican police officer climbed aboard followed by a man in civilian clothes.

"Welcome on behalf of the police department and our mayor to Mexico," the man said. The gringo journalists nodded.

A sign above the street said: *Tijuana Welcomes the Super Bowl.* The NFL's sanctioned Super Bowl XXII was on the sign. We were hot stuff in Mexico, too.

The bus moved onward, with a police escort. The sirens roared. Here come the gringo Super Bowl media. Mexican urchins stopped, for the moment, offering to peddle their sisters to Yankee tourists. The bus passed through a plaza dominated by a statue of Abraham Lincoln holding a broken chain.

It was the day of the Fiesta de Super Bowl in Tijuana.

The bus deposited us at the Agua Caliente Race Track, and we marched inside. The Tijuana Super Bowl Committee gave us miniature bottles of tequila and gracious smiles and sent us into the clubhouse. The dogs were running. It was shortly after siesta.

The committee told us that the caesar salad was invented in this part of Mexico. And to prove it, right in the Agua Caliente track, they brought in a super bowl, filled it with lettuce and croutons and cheese, and mixed up the world's largest caesar salad. It might have weighed half a ton.

Night came. We were taken to downtown Tijuana. The shops were open, offering their wares to the gringos who write about "Americano Futbol." Ceramic statues, leather bags, and switchblade knives were available at bargain rates. The Tijuana cops had closed off Avenida Reveluccion, the main drag, for La Fiesta de Super Bowl. Bands played. We wandered down the street, into the Jai Alai Fronton, where it was Super Bowl night, and back onto the Avenida. The good citizens of Tijuana wondered what was going on.

I jumped on a bus headed back to the San Diego Marriott. The U.S. customs agents at the largest land border crossing in the Western Hemisphere welcomed us home. This is a hot border, and they didn't give a hoot about a busload of American football writers loaded with contraband. They were after illegals.

SAN DIEGO—Joe Gibbs is at his desk at midnight. Sometimes it is difficult to sleep. He breaks out the machine and runs over the films.

Nothing unusual for a coach, viewing the films over and over, looking at familiar figures.

Gibbs, coach of the Redskins, believes a successful football coach must be a workaholic. Monday through Thursday nights, Gibbs sleeps in his office at Redskin Park.

He is being called the best coach in pro football history.

But the late-night films haven't always been of linebackers and running backs. Sometimes Gibbs has watched two lads at play. Throwing footballs. Marching with books in their hands. Not playbooks—school textbooks.

The films are of his two sons. Videotapes of the family from which he separated himself to do his job in his style. His wife, Pat, would operate the video camera at home. The boys, JD and Coy, would perform. Pat would ship the video out to the training facility. Gibbs would watch it on his machine.

This way, Gibbs could compensate for his gnawing conscience.

This is dedication.

He is back at the Super Bowl for the third time in his seventh season with the Redskins. He is here with the team that was not the most talented in its conference. . . .

Diligence pays off. To some, the result justifies neglect of family.

Gibbs had been decreed the top pro football coach of all time in a *Sport* magazine piece just before reaching Super Bowl XXII. Tons of esoteric data were force-fed into a computer by Elias Sports Bureau, official keeper of NFL numbers. Stuff such as improvement or deterioration of teams, how many games the coach won and should have won, how many games he won that he should have lost. The machine spun and whirred and coughed out Gibbs's name as number one. The Redskins had won more games than they should have.

Vince Lombardi was second to Gibbs and then came John Madden. Tom Flores was fifth. Don Shula was sixth. Tom Landry, if you could believe it, was tenth.

I disputed this entire notion in a column. Using heart and soul in preference to strange numbers and a computer, I decreed Lombardi tops of all time. And Vince never had to sleep in his office.

◆ ◆ ◆

The Redskins of 1987 were overachievers. That could not be disputed. In this asterisk-pocked season of more Mickey Mouse, they went 11-4. They did a good job of picking strike-breakers when the real guys went out. And Gibbs went against his image as conservative coach when he elected to switch quarterbacks between the finish of the regular season and the playoffs.

It was Doug Williams's time. The Redskins were underdogs when they went into Chicago for the first playoff game. They were quickly down 14-0. Williams brought them back to tie the score and then Washington won it on Darrell Green's 50-yard punt return. The game ended, 21-17, with Walter Payton trying to gain one more yard and being shoved out of bounds. It was his last game, his last play. He had hoped to go back to the Super Bowl for his last hurrah.

With Payton out and Williams in, the Redskins beat the Vikings, 17-14, for the NFC championship. Williams threw two touchdown passes.

◆ ◆ ◆

At La Jolla, where the Broncos were encamped, Dan Reeves spoke to clusters of reporters. Twice Super Bowl losers, beaten badly by the Giants the year before, the Broncos had started to acquire the rank, smelly image of the Minnesota Vikings.

"Our entire football team has been . . . " Reeves paused, searching for the proper word. "Haunted . . . is the word I come up with for last year's loss."

The haunted Broncos had gone through the '87 broken season with a 10-4-1 record. Nobody was more haunted than Karl Mecklenburg, the Teutonic linebacker with the mild persona and the high IQ. He remained tormented by the memory of how the Giants had beaten his team in Super Bowl XXI.

"We learned how to lose a Super Bowl," he said. "Now we have to learn how to win one.

"A loss is very hard to swallow. I think it's better not to make the playoffs than to lose the Super Bowl."

Mecklenburg was surrounded by writers at a table under a tent in La Jolla. One of them told him how the Redskins were changing the numbers of their players at practice. The idea was to confuse any peeping Tom spies.

"Pretty paranoid," said Mecklenburg.

And wasn't it paranoid to say better not make the playoffs at all than to get there and lose the Super Bowl?

The Broncos again rode Elway through the playoffs and back to the Super Bowl. They toyed with the Houston Oilers in their first playoff game. John flipped two touchdown passes and ran for another in a 34-10 victory.

They would be playing the Browns in a rematch of their epic of the year before for the AFC championship. The Browns arrived in Denver with bitter memories and vows of revenge, but all that seemed hollow. Elway took the Broncos to a 21-3 advantage in the first half. In the third quarter, Bernie Kosar fired an 18-yard touchdown pass. Elway fired back with an 80-yarder. Kosar fired back with a 32-yarder.

The rivals were slugging the bejabbers out of each other. By the end of the third quarter, the Browns had cut deeply into the Broncos' edge. It was 31-24, Denver, but Kosar was cranking. He produced a 31-31 tie score with another scoring pass early in the fourth. Elway fired back with his third touchdown pass for a 38-31 lead with four minutes left.

The year before, Elway drove the Broncos 98 yards to produce the tie at the end of regulation in the championship game. This year, the ball was Kosar's, and he drove the Browns downfield until they reached the Denver five. There Kosar handed the ball to Earnest Byner. Byner crashed across the five, headed for the end zone. Inside the three, a hand—Jeremiah the five, headed for the end zone. Inside the three, a hand—Jeremiah Castille's—reached out for Byner and stripped the ball away from him. Denver recovered the fumble. There were 65 seconds left. The Broncos used what they could, then took an automatic safety to save themselves. The final was 38-33. The Browns, torn emotionally, were frustrated again; the Broncos headed to the Super Bowl for the third time.

◆ ◆ ◆

A dash of verbal venom is always helpful when it gets dull for us. So it was a joyous occasion when Dexter Manley accused Mike Ditka of possessing the smarts of a grapefruit. This evaluation was offered before the Redskins and the Bears clashed early in the playoffs. It was awarded widespread attention in the football prose written in January. Dexter Manley was one of the most quotable athletes in the league.

Now at the Super Bowl, Dexter Manley, who manhandled quarterbacks for the Redskins, went into his mum act and refused to be interviewed. He was a no-show in the interview tent the NFL set up for the Redskins, lagoon-side, at the Hyatt in San Diego. Dexter's silence became another of those Super Bowl stories that get overkilled.

He actually wasn't hiding. Wandering through the Hyatt's swimming pool area, designed with a pseudo-Polynesian motif, I happened upon Dexter. He was talking with my old friend Moe Siegel, out of Washington. Dexter had some T-shirts with grapefruits on them.

"Did Mike Ditka send you those T-shirts, Dexter?" I asked.

"No," said Manley, "Mike Ditka sent us to the Super Bowl."

He would again be a no-show at the mandatory interview session that day. But he guaranteed his appearance for the next morning, under the tent in San Diego. So it was that he drew a maniacal mob of scribblers and electronitoids to hear his statements, usually directed toward quarterbacks he promised to maim.

Manley arrived late, convoyed by two security guards. He burst through and leaped onto a platform.

"Ho, ho, ho," said Manley. He had a sheet of paper and appeared to read a statement.

"There are so many questions . . . that in order to save your time and my time I suggest that you submit your questions in writing and I will study them overnight and I will submit my answers tomorrow." He leaped off the platform and left.

We waited. Jilted. Then minutes later he returned. He was handed the first question in writing. "Why did you come back?"

Manley broke up in giggles. "I'm sweating bullets," he said.

We fired questions.

"I don't need attention," he said. "That's why I wasn't here yesterday. I just like to go out and kick somebody's you know what," he said.

"There comes a point in time you got to take time for yourself," he said. "I sat in my room and meditated. The PR department was upset with me.

"People have a general perception of me," he said. "People make me out to be something I'm not. I'm only a defensive lineman, and you know we're not very smart.

"Why should I be fined for not coming here?" he said. "You got to be a man. You got to have some balls.

"Coach Gibbs had a talk with me," he said. "That's why I came back. When E.F. Hutton talks, you listen.

"I don't want to say some words that get somebody motivated," he said. "Bulletin board stuff. Coach Gibbs is always worried about me saying things. Now he wants me to say things.

"If we don't do the job up front, no question, Denver will be the world champions," he said.

"It's kind of getting kind of boring," he added.

◆ ◆ ◆

I'd be curious later on, when Dexter Manley went before a Congressional committee and said he'd never learned to read and write. If that were true, how did he read that statement to us?

◆ ◆ ◆

The papers came out and they were full of Dexter Manley. The San Diego *Tribune* had a long piece on Rudy Martzke and how he was at the Super Bowl, talking to all the TV people and finding out what they were thinking.

We'd reached the Super Bowl ultimate at last—the Martzke Mentality. The media interviewing the media about interviewing the media.

In midweek, the folks at the grandiose Coronado Hotel permitted the media within its hallowed confines when they threw a Super Bowl party just for us. It was a scene out of the twenties, for a bunch of guzzling journalists; certainly it ranked in the final four of quality Super Bowl parties. Pete Rozelle's party was pretty good, too. For this one, Pete had obtained use of the Naval Air Station at North Island. This time the only traffic on the runways was the NFL buses and limos for the more elegant.

◆ ◆ ◆

It was a quick haul to Jack Murphy Stadium on the morning of the game. The parking lot was enormous.

The stadium really was named for a sportswriter. Jack Murphy had been a grand writer. He had been a close friend of Red Smith and of Tom Callahan, who wrote splendid sports articles for *Time*. One night, years before, I'd been honored to go to dinner with Jack and Red and Tom at a Super Bowl. The years passed, and now America stopped to watch the Super Bowl. As I walked through the parking lot toward the stadium named in honor of Jack Murphy, I thought of departed friends. Jack had died. Red had died. Jimmy Cannon had died.

Herb Alpert, from the old Tijuana Brass, sang "The Star-Spangled Banner" with the customary pomp. Super Bowl XXII was permitted to begin.

The Redskins were quickly down 10-0. The Broncos, made three-and-a-half-point favorites by the odds makers still being listened to, scored on their first offensive play. John Elway masterfully fooled Barry Wilburn with an eye fake and enabled Ricky Nattiel, one of his Three Amigos receivers, to go streaking past the defender. In the open field, Nattiel caught the ball from Elway and dashed the distance, 56 yards. It was the fastest touchdown in any of the Super Bowls. On the next possession, Elway turned receiver after a flip to runner Steve Sewell. Sewell's trick-play pass to Elway gained 32 yards against the befuddled Redskins' defense. With the Broncos stopped at the six, Reeves entrusted Rich Karlis to try a 24-yard field goal. Karlis had been haunted for a year by his misses against the Giants. This time he was perfect. The Broncos were threatening to rout the Redskins.

The entire story was blowing up. Williams had four passes dropped in the first quarter. Then he went down in agony. He had been in the midst of his pass retreat when his foot skidded and he fell. The left leg, hooked oddly at the knee, crumpled beneath his body. The right ankle caught and bent in an unnatural direction. He was hurt, badly. Quarterbacks get damaged in football. All of them. Injury goes with the job. Williams rolled on the grass. He managed to get up, but then he collapsed and was assisted to the bench. Schroeder ran to the huddle. The doctor quickly examined Williams. It was a hyperflexed left knee.

What happened next was history. It was not just a black quarterback playing in the Super Bowl. It was a quarterback performing with exquisite skill, limping, with spasms of pain in his knee. A quarterback winning.

What happened next was the most stunning 15 minutes of the 22 Super Bowls, the most stunning 15 minutes in all the years of pro football. Perhaps the most astounding 15 minutes in all of sports.

"I've played with pain before," Williams told Gibbs at the bench. And Williams went back onto the field to play on his hyperflexed knee.

Williams stepped back gingerly and tossed a short pass designed to gain seven yards to Ricky Sanders. Sanders got behind the defense and caught the ball and ran off with it, 80 yards for a touchdown. It was 10-7, Denver.

The Redskins got the ball back. Williams moved them downfield. At the 27, he dropped back and passed to Gary Clark, behind the Denver secondary, for his second touchdown. It was 14-10, Washington.

The Redskins got the ball back after Karlis missed, this time on a 43-yard field-goal try. Williams handed off to Timmy Smith on a counter. Smith broke free and ran 58 yards for the third touchdown. It was 21-10, Washington.

The Redskins got the ball back. Williams pumped on a play-action pass and hit Sanders again beind the Broncos. This time Williams hit Sanders for a 50-yard touchdown pass. It was 28-10, Washington, with 3:42 to play in the half.

The Redskins got the ball back on Barry Wilburn's interception of Elway. Williams dropped back to pass and hit Clint Didier for eight yards and another touchdown. It was 35-10, Washington, with 64 seconds left in the second period.

In these 15 minutes of the second quarter of Super Bowl XXII, Doug Williams produced five touchdowns. He passed for four of them, on plays of 80, 27, 50, and 8 yards. He was 9-for-11 in the quarter for 228 yards. Smith ran for 122 yards on five carries. Sanders caught five passes for 168 yards.

All that on just 18 plays in the quarter, all that in just 15 minutes.

The second half was unnecessary. Pete Rozelle's prime-time Super Bowl became superfluous. Timmy Smith scored another touchdown in the fourth quarter, a four-yard run. Washington won, 42-10. With another long run of 43 yards, Smith totaled 340 yards, more than Csonka and Franco Harris and Marcus Allen and John Riggins and all the other backs who had run in the Super Bowl.

The Broncos kept coming back to get themselves clubbed. They were now 0-3 in Super Bowls. They'd never even been close. "We know how to get here," said John Elway, "we've got to figure out how to win one."

You bet Doug Williams was history. He was history the way Bart Starr was history. The way Namath and Bradshaw and Griese and Plunkett and Montana and McMahon and Simms were history. Doug Williams, the quarterback who delivered a bravura performance in the ultimate football game, the quarterback who was unwanted by 27 of the 28 clubs when he hunted for a job, was 18 for 29 on this day, for 340 yards and those four TD passes. Williams outproduced all the others. And when he was mobbed in the locker room he said, simply: "I'm not Jackie Robinson."

XXIII
The Dancer

San Francisco 49ers 20, Cincinnati Bengals 16
January 22, 1989
Joe Robbie Stadium, Miami
Attendance: 75,129

O nce upon a time a guy used to put on a jock and shoulder pads, cover his head with a thick helmet, and become a modern warrior. Football is full of warfare lingo: *The trenches. The blitz. The bomb. Attack. Defend. Territory.*

But I discovered that pro football is not a battleground for some mock war. Rather, it is a training ground for broadcasters.

The proof of this is that Dick Butkus went into television. I had never seen a more militant athlete than Butkus. He was a killer of a middle linebacker when he played with some rotten teams in Chicago.

Butkus was the subject of a TV special in the sixties. He was asked about his favorite movie. "I sort of liked it when Richard Widmark sent the old lady in the wheelchair down a flight of stairs," Butkus said.

Now CBS had polished him up, taught him how to pace his diction. Butkus came across as a guy out of charm school.

John Madden, I suppose, made the most famous charge from the football field to the field of the broadcasting booth. Dick Vermeil followed when he self-sizzled as a coach. And there were mobs of others: Alex Karras; the Giffer; Fred Williamson, The Hammer himself; Joe Namath; Dan Dierdorf; Merlin Olsen; Terry Bradshaw; Joe Theisman; Harry Carson; Walter Payton; Rocky Bleier. Now there were hot rumors, as we

288

gathered in Miami for Super Bowl XXIII, that Bill Walsh was gearing to take his genius and his ego to television.

It helped to know how to operate a tape recorder.

These were all reflections as Walsh delivered his commentaries on picture day before Super Bowl XXIII that would feature the 49ers and the Bengals in a rematch of the Pontiac affair. Walsh was in field center at Joe Robbie Stadium.

Then across the way I saw Wayne Walker grinning on the sidelines.

Walker was the pioneer in this trek from jockstrap territory to the lights, pancake makeup, and microphone. He worked hard at learning his new profession. He had been an All-Pro outside linebacker with the Lions when he started in TV as a weekend sports anchor at Channel 2, Detroit. He would go on to become the top sportscaster on the San Francisco station with the highest ratings. He did NFL game work from time to time. It was good to see him, because he was always a favorite of mine when I was covering the Lions beat.

We laughed again about the day Walker was kicked out of a game in San Francisco, at Kezar Stadium. He had been caught punching Monty Stickles, the large tight end of the 49ers.

"He was holding me," Walker said he had said that day in the heat of combat, to Joe Muha, the umpire.

"Muha told me to take care of it in my own way. So I did. I punched him."

Being an intrepid reporter, I had gone into the 49ers' locker room that day to get Stickles's version of the fight.

"Go ask the guy who hit me," said Stickles, with a heavy look of hostility and a growl.

A number of years later I was back in San Francisco covering a playoff game. Walker was the TV star in town. We had dinner together one night.

Then I covered the game. Afterwards, I went into the Vikings' locker room with the other guys with tape recorders and notepads. We mobbed around Francis Tarkenton and I asked him a none-too-profound question. One of the radio guys stuck his microphone in front of my mouth to pick up my question.

I looked over to see who was holding the mike in my face, stealing my words. It was Monty Stickles.

◆ ◆ ◆

Bitch not. My basic role at Super Bowl XXIII was a daily gig on the radio. I was on each morning with J.P. McCarthy on his highly popular morning show on WJR, Detroit, talking about Bill Walsh, Sam Wyche, Boomer Esiason, and Ickey Woods and his touchdown wiggle.

Pete Rozelle brought us back to Miami in January 1989, for the first time in 10 Super Bowls. The gouging on the Beach, the town's general don't-give-a-damn attitude, the snatching of game tickets from patrons outside the stadium, the rotting condition of the Orange Bowl—these matters forced Rozelle to move his moveable feast into different environments. Since the Steelers and Cowboys had fought to the finish at Super Bowl XIII, Miami had built a new pro football facility. Super Bowl XXIII would be at Joe Robbie Stadium, named for the owner of the Dolphins.

In the decade that Miami missed out on Super Bowl action, the city amazingly started caring about the visitors who wrote for newspapers and spoke into microphones and took video pictures for the 11 o'clock news. It opted to outdo all the other Super Bowl cities in the thick spreading of wretched excess.

Miami—South Florida—was being given another chance, the opportunity to deliver a new message, to rebuild its image. But Pete's people didn't dare put us out on Miami Beach as in other years. There were too many ripoff memories. We stayed downtown at the Hyatt. The Miami Super Bowl hospitality group had its battle plan—to provide a dream-week Super Bowl and lure the game back on a regular schedule.

The first night that most of us were in town, the eve of picture day, we dined, unfashionably, at a restaurant near the hotel. Ray Buck, a writer from Houston, decided to use this Monday night to go to the track with his wife. On the way, a rock smashed the window of their car and they were set upon by a mob. They heard gunshots. Buck was bleeding, and he and his wife were lucky to get away.

Those of us who stayed near the hotel returned to the press hospitality room. We started hearing whispers about trouble. The news at 11 confirmed it.

Miami was burning, and the poor souls who lived in the Overtown section didn't give a damn about a Super Bowl. They didn't give a damn about the city's image with the cream of American—and global—journalism there to cover a game.

A black motorcyclist had been shot to death by a light-skinned Hispanic police officer. What amounted to a minor traffic violation escalated into violence. There was shooting and rock throwing and bottle throwing. Cars were torched. Citizens bled.

The Bengals were in the Omni Hotel six blocks from the flames. The press, in the Hyatt, was perhaps 10 blocks away. Sportswriters used to fawning over athletes and sniffing jocks turned into battle correspondents. Some were set upon.

Stanley Wilson, a football player with a history of taking wrong turns, took one in his car while he was driving back to the Bengals' hotel. Rioters threw rocks at his car. Wilson didn't get out and say: "Hey, I'm playing in the Super Bowl, stop it." Instead, he went like hell.

"It was very intimidating," Wilson told the writers. "And I'm a guy who is not easily intimidated. It was very scary. I think I'll wear my uniform next time I go driving."

◆ ◆ ◆

The next night the visiting media were loaded into Super Bowl buses and taken to the Vizcaya Palace and Gardens in Coconut Grove. Rioting, heck, this was Super Bowl time. And Miami was tossing the week's first party. The printed invitations read: ". . . in honor of the 1989 Super Bowl Media—Business Attire . . ." That meant most of us wore our best blue jeans and Reeboks to the enormously plush mansion on enormously well-groomed grounds. We marched in, past flowing fountains, along an esplanade, to a trumpet fanfare tooted by musicians dressed as Renaissance heralds. We stuffed ourselves with shrimp and oysters out of enormous vats of bouillabaisse, we gorged on Cuban roast pork and black beans and conch fritters and Key lime pie. We listened to violinists playing in white tie and tails, and we topped off our free meals with ice cream and goodies as we watched the stars twinkle over Biscayne Bay. It was a terrific party.

That night, Miami still burned. Looters and arsonists and gun-toters hit the streets. Hey, the Super Bowl is coming. The violence spread from Overtown to Liberty City and Coconut Grove. Of course, not the part of Coconut Grove where we were munching shrimp. Never.

◆ ◆ ◆

The buses took us to the Omni and the Bengals' interviews in the morning, precisely on schedule. We slopped up the NFL's standard vittles. And then we piled into the press conference room to attend Sam Wyche's magic show.

Wyche had been a magician in his time. He could pick a nickel out of your nose, or tell you to go ahead, take any card, and he would name the one you picked.

Wyche also had been a lifelong football roustabout. To play college football at Furman, he had to try out as a walk-on. To reach pro football, he had to play for the Wheeling Ironmen in the Continental League. When Paul Brown formed the Bengals in the AFL in 1969, Wyche asked for a tryout as quarterback and got it. He played for the Bengals with Bill Walsh as his quarterback coach. Wyche then moved on as a backup, to the Redskins, to the Lions, to the Cardinals, and to the Bills.

During his travels he made it to Super Bowl VII as the backup to Billy Kilmer on the Redskins. Wyche got into the game—to hold for the extra point after Garo Yepremian's intercepted forward pass.

"Before the end of the 1977 season," Wyche said, "I officially put everybody out of their misery. By retiring."

He moved on, went into business. He opened a sporting goods store in South Carolina. He yearned to go into coaching and applied for a high school job in Carolina but was rejected. Lack of experience, he was told. Bill Walsh, at last a head coach in San Francisco, was looking for somebody to tutor his quarterbacks and he hired Wyche. Wyche's task his first year with the 49ers was to train a rookie quarterback Walsh had drafted on the third round. The rookie's name was Joe Montana.

Wyche was on Walsh's staff when the 49ers beat the Bengals in Super Bowl XVI. Then he journeyed on again, to become a college head coach at Indiana in 1982. Indiana went 3-8. After that season, Paul Brown hired Wyche as head coach of the Bengals. The Cincinnati papers reported that Brown had hired a head coach he could control. That he was Paul's puppet.

Asked to comment, Wyche turned to Brown and said: "What do I say about that, Paul?"

Now Wyche was coaching in the Super Bowl. But fitting in the mood of the Miami environment outside the hotel, Sam discussed some brickbats thrown at him.

In 1987, the strike season, the Bengals had collapsed to 4-11. During the strike, he had feuded with Boomer Esiason, his quarterback. Boomer was a million-dollar-a-year, 100-percent strike leader.

It was in this season that Wyche and the Bengals seemed to have Walsh and the 49ers beaten 26-20 in the final minute. The Bengals had the ball and needed only to run out the clock. But rather than calling for a punt, Wyche ordered Esiason to run a time-consuming reverse, which used up all but the last two seconds. In the time left, Montana threw a 25-yard touchdown pass to Jerry Rice and the 49ers won, 27-26. All of Cincinnati demanded Wyche's jugular. Other coaches, familiar with Sam's quaint decisions, sometimes referred to him as Wicky-Wacky. Paul Brown castigated his coach. The press, the TV commentators, the people wanted Wyche fired. Wyche himself figured he'd be fired when he was called into Brown's office at Christmas time. Instead, Brown lectured Wyche for two hours and then gave his beleaguered coach a reprieve.

It was a near ziggy, and Wyche realized he was endangered as he assembled his Bengals at training camp 1989. At their players' first meeting, Wyche had all the seats in the classroom turned around in the opposite direction, reverse of focus.

Wyche turned out to be half Walsh, half Houdini. He spoke of his personal hell as the Super Bowl ritual went on in frightened, frightening, burning Miami. He talked about the cruelty of defeat, the jeers and gibes, the verbal stabs at his families, the dangers of December dismissal—all the perils of coaching and losing.

"They were saying 'Get rid of the bum,'" Wyche said. "If I'd been the owner, I'd have been questioning myself. I'd have had to make a judgment. Can he win? Should we change coaches and change the system now and waste a year? Paul Brown's been a coach. If the owner hadn't been a coach, he might have made a change.

"You try not to let it eat away at you. You're not going to expose yourself. I read too much in the papers. It was on every TV station. I kept seeing and hearing the unfair things they said.

"So, I'm not reading much now. I don't watch much on TV. I'm just happy Ronald Reagan was elected."

Wyche let his last sentence sink in. Slowly. There was silence. Then dawning.

"That's a joke," said Sam Wyche.

While George Bush was campaigning for the presidency, Sam Wyche was coaching a turnabout team toward the Super Bowl. The Bengals had the hottest turnabout in all pro football in the fall of 1988. They went 12-4. Sam Wyche introduced a no-huddle offense that had genius Bill Walsh concerned. Boomer Esiason, the lefty, patched up the disharmony with Wyche and took on the glorious status of NFL icon. Ickey Woods, the rookie runner, wiggled his bootie at the bench every time he scored. The Ickey Shuffle became America's new dance rage.

Now, in the same week, George Bush and Sam Wyche were achieving the objectives of their lifetimes. Presidential inauguration and the Super Bowl. The Super Bowl drew more press.

◆ ◆ ◆

In college, Jerry Rice caught forward passes for Mississippi Valley State. His acrobatics seldom, if ever, were shown on the TV screens across America. Rice didn't play for Alabama or Ole Miss. But pro scouting had become more sophisticated since the time when clubs guided themselves at the draft by page-turning through the *Street & Smith Yearbook*. Jerry Rice's record college stats, his foot speed, his size were fed into the computer. Bill Walsh, the genius, had visions of Jerry Rice dashing downfield, dance-stepping past two defenders, catching the ball thrown by Joe Montana, and running onward to the end zone.

So it was that Walsh traded three draft picks to advance the 49ers in the first round of the 1985 pin-the-tail-on-the-donkey session. Jerry Rice was selected as the 16th player taken in the first round, the third receiver of the group. A who-is-he unknown!

And every one of Walsh's visions became reality.

In his first four pro seasons, Rice became the most prolific, most productive, most dangerous wide receiver in the sport. He made the touchdown catch, the long-distance spectacular, the swift grab in traffic.

In 1987, Jerry Rice caught 22 touchdown passes in the 12 non-strike games and was the NFL's MVP. But in 1988, his touchdown production dropped to nine in the 16-game schedule. He'd sprained an ankle in the early season. He'd been hurt trying to escape a defender whose only method of stopping him was to grab his face mask and twist.

Rice had told the visiting press during the playoffs: "I played a little every game, but I couldn't be Jerry Rice. I couldn't get away from the bump-and-run . . . I really kept my mind in the game mentally. I would say I was competing against myself."

By the time Walsh rallied the 49ers into the playoffs after a mediocre start, Rice's ankle was better. He blazed in the two playoff games and caught five touchdown passes.

Now at Super Bowl XXIII, there were horror stories that Jerry Rice's ankle was wounded again. On Monday, when the 49ers arrived in Miami, the NFL's official injury roundup listed Rice as questionable for the Super Bowl.

The Las Vegas odds makers watched with high interest; the media went crazy with bulletins.

Wyche's woes, Rice's pains, were vintage Super Bowl stuff. But on Thursday night, there was another party to attend. Riding the bus across the causeway to Miami Beach and the spot called Penrod's on the Beach, I wondered if Miami would be burning for another night. I thought about this terrible contrast—the excess of the Super Bowl and the poverty of the people. This same week, as the city celebrated the return of the Super Bowl and as the same city burned, several hundred refugees from war in Nicaragua were in the Miami baseball park, sleeping in the ramps, in the dugouts, in the runways, where rats had lived at large for years.

I wandered on the beach at Penrod's, drank a beer or two, and watched the mobs of young things on the eternal hunt for beefy football players. Life must continue.

Suddenly, there was a commotion for the arrival of a celebrity. Accompanied by his entourage of cooing models, protected by his mob of bodyguards, wrapped snugly in the arms of a guardian, Spuds McKenzie was making his entrance to the party. I wished the bewildered Bud Light mutt would pee in the pool.

I got on the next bus back to the Hyatt. The Nicaraguans trying to sleep at the ratty ball park, and the dog spotlighted to sell America more beer crossed my mind.

Miami had quieted down that night. The Miami Heat played their NBA game within the violence area, after a postponement of only one night due to the rioting. At halftime of the basketball game, Ickey Woods came out of the stands to entertain the crowd with an impromptu version of the Ickey Shuffle.

Life, indeed, must continue.

◆ ◆ ◆

In the Hyatt's press hospitality room, we talked football now. Outside the door, Miami TV stations set up to do the six o'clock news from there. It was peacetime again in Florida.

We wondered about Jerry Rice's injury.

We discussed whether Bill Walsh would really chuck coaching after the Super Bowl, as Vince Lombardi once did. Eddie DeBartolo, the 49ers' owner, had gone public with his gut feeling that Walsh was a goner. "He's the best coach in football, but sometimes people lose their desire," De-Bartolo said to some California papers.

Walsh seemed uptight. When DeBartolo donned the old bellhop disguise at the 49ers' hotel and tried to grab Walsh's attache case, the coach didn't even appreciate his boss's spoof.

Through all the conversation and the haze in the room, I spotted the familiar face with the weak chin and smile. Super Bowl Sally had come back. For the first time in years, she was at the Super Bowl, working her beat. She wasn't alone for long.

◆ ◆ ◆

Super Bowl headline: *Rice Dances!*

Super Bowl practices are shut down to the media. One pool reporter is permitted inside the gates to make a report for the other 2,500 human beings covering the game. The league-approved skinny from the pool reporter was that Jerry Rice was not participating in the 49ers' practice sessions. Walsh said Rice had trouble cutting, but thought his prize receiver would be all right.

The other skinny, from witnesses with huge eyes not bound by the NFL imprint, was that Jerry Rice was dancing on his questionable ankle at Penrod's on the Beach.

"I'm down here to have fun," he said when questioned by writers about his nocturnal activities being more demanding than practice sessions. "I'm not going to sit in my room just because I have a sore ankle. I danced, but I didn't do anything fancy. Everything was straight ahead.

"No way could I do the Ickey Shuffle. That's too hard. The bottom line is I had a great time."

The bottom line was that the Bengals smelled a scam.

◆ ◆ ◆

Boomer Esiason surveyed the mob scene at the Super Bowl and jumped right in, vocal cords blazing.

"Some quarterbacks are smooth and picturesque," Boomer told the media. "I'm a little bit different. I'm supposed to drop back five steps. I might drop back five and a half or four and a half. I'm at my best when I improvise. It's always been that way since I've been a white quarterback."

Boomer addressed the dispute he'd had with his coach the year before, when the Bengals went 4-11 and when the townspeople of Cincinnati wanted to run him out along with Sam Wyche.

"It's funny," Boomer said to the writers. "Last year they wanted to fire him and this year everybody wants to hire him. He's gone from Wicky-Wacky to Genius."

When the Bengals signed Boomer to a $6 million contract for five years, management insisted on a special clause, referred to as a Big-Mouth Clause. Esiason would be forbidden to have his own television or radio show, and he would not be permitted to write a book. The gag restrictions were written into the contract, the Bengals said, so Boomer could concentrate on playing football. Management, actually, was scared about what Boomer would say.

The 4-11 disaster had caused Boomer to ask for a trade from Cincinnati after the '87 season, when Wyche was receiving his reprieve. Esiason then took a four-month sabbatical, effectively vanishing, to mull over his situation. When he resurfaced, he was determined to rededicate himself to his profession.

Now he was at Super Bowl XXIII, preaching the values of concentration, dedication, a work ethic, excellent pass receivers, and a snaky left arm.

"I made up my mind I wasn't going to let anything get in the way of playing football this year," said Boomer. "I turned down endorsements. I turned down requests for interviews. I turned down being the player rep."

Boomer established himself at the beginning of the '88 season as the top-rated quarterback in the NFL. The Bengals, last year's patsies, became this year's invincibles. They started off 6-and-0, the last of the league's unbeaten teams. Cincinnati had football romance instead of fourth-quarter gaffes. Wicky-Wacky had turned genius. The Ickey Shuffle entranced the nation, and the Madison Avenue advertising agencies spouted profit-endorsement ideas. The Bengals, sometimes shunning the huddle to dash off plays, had the most productive offense in the entire league. Boomer finished as the number one passer and the most valuable player in the entire league.

The Bengals finished 12-4. No team in the league had a better record—one year after Sam Wyche heard the city asking to get rid of the bum.

The playoffs were quick and decisive. Boomer and his teammates beat the Seahawks in round one of the AFC playoffs, 21-10. The next week they did the same thing to the Bills with Ickey Woods scoring two touchdowns, dancing the Shuffle twice at the bench, again winning by a score of 21-10. Boomer and Wicky-Wacky were in the Super Bowl. And the people of Cincinnati were muttering some strange motto—*Who Dey?*—about the football team that had transformed hate into love.

◆ ◆ ◆

Jimmy the Greek was a long goner. Never mind, the Bengals were installed as the favorites by Dr. Ruth.

Sure, there are novel angles in Super Bowl coverage. A guy from Associated Press called Dr. Ruth Westheimer and fed her all the important details about the Super Bowl. Dr. Ruth fed this material into her mixmaster gizmo and declared that the Cincinnati club would be Super Bowl XXIII champions.

She ignored the season records, but took into account certain statistics. To wit, Bill Walsh had split the 49ers from their wives or special ladies; players stayed at the Airport Hilton, wives/friends at a hotel in downtown Miami. Sam Wyche believed in connubial togetherness, even at Super Bowl time.

"I think in many cases couples being apart will create more tension than good," Dr. Ruth proclaimed for the benefit of America's football curious.

"I do believe that if it's a steady relationship . . . that to be together the night before a game can be very helpful. Even if they have what is called a quickie. It relieves tension."

It was not known if Dr. Ruth consulted Joe Namath's book on Super Bowl conquest before favoring the Bengals.

The odds makers thought Ruthie didn't know what she was talking about. Using factors other than quickies, the Las Vegas line made the 49ers seven-point favorites.

◆ ◆ ◆

From the time of The Hammer, the loudest mouths collected the most ink at the Super Bowl. Now we had Tim McKyer, who played cornerback for the 49ers. He stood on a platform every morning at the 49ers' interview sessions and waved a hand at the clinging mob, scribbling away.

"That's the finger the Super Bowl ring will go on Sunday."

"Which finger was he using?" inquired Bill Walsh.

Walsh resisted flipping a finger himself. The daily speculation that he'd give up coaching after the Super Bowl had become a personal pain. He almost had quit before, and his owner had talked him out of it. Now DeBartolo was fueling the rumors himself.

"Obviously, you guys are at the stage you're looking for things," Walsh said late in the week.

The word *burnout* was flipped his way.

"*Burnout* is an overstated buzz word," Walsh said. "My nerve endings aren't shot. It's a matter of what's right at the time."

Somebody flipped the subject to Dr. Ruth's prediction and her reasons for it.

"That has merit," said Walsh.

The 49ers were in this Super Bowl themselves on a reprieve. In mid-November, they were 6-5. A year before, the 49ers had been 13-2, and then had been blown out of the playoffs in the first round by the Vikings. The malaise carried over into 1988. Walsh's genius had turned to poop. Joe Montana's mystique had turned to myth. Joe was benched with a hurt elbow. San Francisco started to believe that Steve Young should be the regular quarterback. Walsh put the fuel on this one.

There were odd rumors that Montana would be traded. There were funny stories in the papers that Walsh was about to be fired. There were funnier stories that claimed Walsh was outdated, that the game had passed him by. He burned.

"I'm consistently analyzed by people trying to find some secret that doesn't exist," Walsh had once told reporters. "The real Bill Walsh is the one people see. They don't see me in a social atmosphere, just in the role as head coach of the 49ers, where it can appear that I'm cold and calculating, which is an error.

". . . I'm definitely not a good, easy-going, swell guy. Anytime you see an old guy, a relaxed, unperturbed, steady guy, you're going to have a steady, mediocre team."

And suddenly, the 49ers, who had been steadily mediocre until the 12th game of 1988, rediscovered whatever chemistry made Walsh's teams special. They whipped the Redskins to start a four-game streak. They finished 10-6 for the season, winning the NFC West on Pete Rozelle's unfathomable numbers formula, although the Rams and Saints had the same records.

In the first playoff game, the 49ers beat the Vikings, 34-9. Rice caught three touchdown passes. The next week the 49ers had to go to Chicago to play the Bears for the NFC championship, in the dead of wintertime. Montana hit Rice for two quick touchdowns, 61 and 27 yards. The 49ers won, 28-3. Bill Walsh and Joe Montana were in their third Super Bowl in eight years.

◆ ◆ ◆

The day the 49ers left for Super Bowl XXIII, Les Boatwright planned to contact his bookie. Boatwright was a long-time 49ers fan. He had purchased two tickets to the game, and his plane trip from San Jose to Miami was set. That day Boatwright had a heart attack and died, and his body was cremated.

Boatwright's sons decided to take him to the game anyway. His ashes were placed in an urn, which his sons took to Florida and planned to take to Joe Robbie Stadium on Sunday.

"It was my brother who said we should take Dad to the Super Bowl," Marc Boatwright told writers when he reached Florida with his father's ashes. "Everybody thought it was the greatest idea they ever heard. He'll be there in spirit."

◆ ◆ ◆

Safe now that the flames in Miami had died, Stanley Wilson discussed himself at the Bengals' headquarters. The NFL had suspended him three times for drug abuse. He had missed all of the '86 and '87 seasons and returned to run the football for the AFC champions in '88. He excelled in the playoffs.

"I don't think anyone appreciates being in this game more than I do," Stanley Wilson said late in Super Bowl week.

On Friday morning, Pete Rozelle conducted his annual State of the NFL press conference.

He promised Miami that the week's riots, in the face of the world's media, would not be held against the city in bids for future Super Bowl staging.

"I don't mean to minimize the situation," Rozelle said. "But we can't stop these things from happening. And we don't know when they will. If we were aware of these things, we'd never have Super Bowls in California because of its earthquake history."

At the moment Rozelle was speaking, telling Miami not to worry, George Bush, effectively made unwelcome as a Super Bowl spectator, was being inaugurated as president of the United States.

Rozelle was in fine form, as though he had beaten some terrible pressure from his mind. Somebody asked him about the new trend in which college bowls were accepting corporate sponsorship. We were considering the Trump Castle Super Bowl," Rozelle said.

Rozelle's annual party was that night. We could see colored lights, formed in the shape of giant football players, flashing off high-rise buildings near the Hyatt. The party would be held at the Convention Center in Miami Beach. Xavier Cugat's orchestra would be providing the Latin beat for the Latin mood.

The transportation dispatcher from Rozelle's office had bare feet and a bossy demeanor.

"You do a helluva job ordering those bus drivers around," I told her as I climbed the steps.

"Wear a short skirt, you can do anything," she said.

The buses ran well to Joe Robbie Stadium on the afternoon of Super Bowl XXIII. It was a fine Florida day. I climbed the ramp to the press box and was handed an NFL press release along with a glut of other Super Bowl stuff: "Stanley Wilson of the Cincinnati Bengals will be ineligible to play in Super Bowl XXIII due to a violation of the NFL's substance abuse policy. No other information will be made available at this time due to the confidentiality of the policy."

◆ ◆ ◆

The pregame show—the balloons; Billy Joel's rendition of "The Star-Spangled Banner," exquisitely lip-synchronized—Rozelle had it perfected. What he had never had perfect was the quality of the football game. It started off as another dud. The score was 3-3 at halftime. Mike Cofer got the 49ers ahead with a 41-yard field goal late in the first quarter. Montana got the 49ers to the Bengals' two in the second quarter. But then Randy Cross, his retirement announced during the week, goofed up on the center snap on another field goal attempt from 19 yards, which caused Cofer to miss. A bit later Roger Craig fumbled the ball away to ruin another San Francisco threat.

For the Bengals, Esiason kept misfiring on his passes. Tim Kumrie, the Bengals' toughest defensive lineman who had beat up on some of his teammates to enliven Super Bowl week, broke his leg early in a frightening injury and was carted off the field. Just before the half, Jim Breech kicked a 34-yard field goal for the Bengals to level the score at 3-3.

"Typical Super Bowl football," I muttered to my friend Green Bay as we tried to figure out what was happening during the halftime show that TV-America was able to watch in 3-D.

Esiason was sharper in the second half. He passed to Chris Collinsworth for 23 yards and to James Brooks for 20. Esiason then hit Collinsworth again for 11. The 49ers stopped the Bengals there. Breech kicked a 43-yard field goal, and the Bengals led, 6-3.

The exchange of field goals went on. After linebacker Bill Romanowski picked off a pass by Esiason, the 49ers tied it again. Cofer kicked a 32-yarder to make it 6-6 in the last minute of the third quarter.

The 49ers kicked off. Stanford Jennings caught the ball at the seven. He streaked up the middle—dead, solid, perfect through the 49ers on a 93-yard return. It was the game's first touchdown. The Bengals led, 13-6, going into the fourth quarter.

The fourth quarter, history has shown, was Joe Montana's finest 15 minutes. Needing a touchdown to catch up, Montana passed 31 yards to Rice. On the next play, he passed 40 yards to Craig. The 49ers were at the Bengals' 14 in two strikes. Moments later, Montana passed left for Rice, who was dancing inside the sidelines. Rice caught the ball, and just as he was about to go out of bounds, he stepped inside the end zone, hanging the ball around the goal-line pylon. It was tied again at 13-all, with 14 minutes to play.

The 49ers had the next scoring chance. Cofer missed a field goal from 49 yards. Esiason marched the Bengals back and hit Ira Hillary for 17 yards. Ickey Woods ran for 10. Esiason connected with Brooks for 12 yards. Then Breech kicked his third field goal, from 40 yards. The Bengals led again, 16-13, with just three minutes and 20 seconds to play.

Joe Montana huddled up the 49ers at their own goal line. They had the ball at the eight. The length of the field was in their faces, and time was vanishing. "Let's go, be tough," said Montana, no bravado in his command. He was thinking field goal, tie the game. Overtime.

Montana took the snap from Cross. He passed eight yards to Craig. He took the snap again. He passed seven yards to John Frank, the tight end. He took the snap again. He passed seven yards to Rice. Then he handed the ball off to Craig for one yard. On third-and-two, he handed off to Craig again. Craig plunged for four. Montana took the snap again. He passed to Rice, down and cutting out for the sideline, for 17 yards. Montana took the snap again. He passed to Craig this time, for 13 yards. The 49ers had reached the Bengals' 35 with two time-outs left, inside two minutes.

A penalty against Cross cost the 49ers 10 yards to the 45. It might have been death for San Francisco. Montana took the snap again. He aimed for Rice slanting, dancing among three defenders. Rice caught the ball and ran until he was swarmed down. It was a gain of 27 yards, more than half of it created by Rice's running after the catch. The 49ers had reached the Bengals' 18. Montana took the snap again. He passed to Craig over the middle for eight more yards to the 10. Thirty-nine seconds remained. Montana used the second time-out. Then the 49ers huddled. When they broke the huddle, Tom Rathman took the wrong side in the set. Craig couldn't argue and took up the opposite position, wrong also. Montana took the snap again. He looked for Craig, coming out of the screwed-up alignment. Craig was covered. Rice was covered, a decoy. John Taylor, the other wide receiver, was dashing toward the end zone, open. Montana threw the ball. Taylor caught it in stride in the end zone and spiked it over his shoulder. Montana raised both arms high. Touchdown. The 49ers had it, 20-16, victors on the first winning touchdown drive against the clock in all the Super Bowls.

Jerry Rice had caught 11 passes, five in the fourth quarter, and had made history with 215 yards. Bill Walsh had won his third Super Bowl in seven years. Montana had won his third.

"Finally," said Randy Cross, "after 23 years, the Super Bowl is super."

XXIV
The Monkey

San Francisco 49ers 55, Denver Broncos 10
January 28, 1990
Louisiana Superdome, New Orleans
Attendance: 72,919

John Elway came into pro football with a reverie. Celebrated, fought over, flushed with a media overkill before he ever launched his first forward pass in the NFL, Elway fancied himself as Terry Bradshaw reincarnate.

"My goal is to beat Terry Bradshaw," Elway had once said, listing his ambitions. "He won the Super Bowl four times. I want to win it five."

Now, in January 1990, Elway was a double loser, 0-and-2 in Super Bowls. Instead of being another Terry Bradshaw, Elway was in dreaded danger of becoming another Francis Tarkenton, the three-time Super Bowl loser quarterback. The Broncos did not remind America of the Pittsburgh Steelers in character. They had the odor of the Minnesota Vikings about them.

"We know how to get here," said Elway. "But we got to figure out how to win one."

Beaten, humiliated, in three Super Bowls, the Broncos were back at Super Bowl XXIV in New Orleans. The 49ers were back, too, victors in three Super Bowls in eight seasons with the opportunity to match the Steelers. And it was Joe Montana, 3-and-0 as a Super Bowl quarterback, who had the chance of equaling the feats of Bradshaw.

◆ ◆ ◆

Harping, controversy, barking, bickering, rioting, pushing, and media overkill had been part of the Super Bowl since Pete Rozelle had squatted on the sideline late that afternoon in Dallas 23 years before and watched the Packers escape into Super Bowl I.

But this, Super Bowl XXIV, would be different from all those that had gone before because Pete Rozelle was no longer lord high commissioner of professional football. He had stood before the owners the previous March at their meeting in Palm Desert, California, and told them something they were not expecting to hear. He was resigning, leaving the NFL, delivering the self-ziggy. He had convinced himself to take this action six months earlier, and he had kept his secret from leaking. The owners were rocked. The media were shocked.

Rozelle had come in as commissioner of the NFL with clean hands in January 1960. History had captured that era with one word: Camelot. John F. Kennedy, a former Harvard receiver, would defeat Richard Nixon, a self-styled play caller for pro coaches, in a major match-up for the presidency later that year. The Super Bowl had not yet been concocted. America had not yet become divided by a war in Vietnam. The Beatles were still juveniles living in Liverpool blight.

Pete would be commissioner for 29 years. During his years, pro football soared in popularity, in wealth, in size, in shape. He cajoled the TV networks; he fought a war and handled a merger; he was attacked by some of the owners, Al Davis and others; he was mocked on occasion by the media; he was faulted, at times, by the players and their association; he was grilled in Congress; he created the most-watched, most-successful sporting enterprise in America.

Now Pete Rozelle would be another slice of history. What he constructed in pro football had been imitated by the other pro sports, all envious at the marketing acumen and appeal of the NFL. Rozelle was the best commissioner who ever lived, who ever bossed any sport. And now he wanted to sniff the daisies while he still was able, at age 63.

"I won't miss the power," Rozelle told me when I went to New York to interview him in his office overlooking Park Avenue two months after the Palm Desert proclamation. "I'll miss the action. So much has happened in the last 29½ years. It's been exciting to be part of the growth. But I won't miss the power. I'll miss the Super Bowl Sunday."

We were seated near the window. The sun was streaming through. I asked Pete how he would like to be remembered.

"That I did my best," he said. "I was fair. A lot of owners have written me to that effect . . . and that I was part of the great growth of the National Football League. This was a very exciting period."

The owners procrastinated in determining Rozelle's successor. Jim Finks, the president of the New Orleans club, almost made it. But then some of the newer club owners rebelled. There was battling, fighting, and trashing. Once again, a compromise man was needed. That's how Pete Rozelle, 29 years earlier, had been selected commissioner.

The owners eventually settled on Paul Tagliabue as their new commissioner. Tagliabue had been the league's attorney. He had been a basketball player at Georgetown. And he would be at Super Bowl XXIV as a curiosity, as the man elected to follow the master, a man, perhaps, with some new ideas.

From now on, the Friday night parties before the Super Bowls would be Paul Tagliabue's parties. Pete Rozelle had a standing invitation to them.

There would be one more dramatic change at this Super Bowl XXIV: Bill Walsh was not coach of the 49ers anymore. Eddie DeBartolo's gut feeling the previous January had been more than just that. Super Bowl XXIII and the 49ers' last-minute victory were Walsh's last hurrah. He went to work as an analyst for NBC, a genius in the booth.

George Seifert, Walsh's defensive expert, was promoted to the head coaching job. So there would be a rookie head coach at Super Bowl XXIV.

◆ ◆ ◆

The New Orleans hospitality folks had buses at the airport to meet the invading reporters. Riding into town, the hostess spoke to us in pure New Orleans.

"There's a *pahty* tomorra night, and anooother *pahty* Fri-dee. . . ."

Then we were handed dubloons, coins minted for flipping into the crowds at Mardi Gras. The dubloons could be exchanged for three beignets, which are globs of dough covered with powdered sugar and considered a New Orleans delicacy.

The hostess went into a spiel about the virtues of New Orleans. By then we were tooling outside the airport, and I spotted my first Super Bowl balloon. It bobbed and floated, sort of like John Madden. It was a Miller Lite balloon, and it was rigged to the roof of a roadside shack belonging to A&L Auto Supply.

The Super Bowl had become a war of beers as well as football teams. Miller had the NFL man of the year. Budweiser had its Bud Bowl. We were supposed to be pitchmen now.

◆ ◆ ◆

The Super Bowl had become so hot that the sportswriters and the guys with the electonic gizmos could no longer repress their anxieties until the scheduled media day on Tuesday morning. Press conferences were arranged for Monday evening. The NFL media men conscripted the Broncos for a pre-media day press conference under a huge tent on the parking lot of the Intercontinental Hotel. Something like 47 TV trucks were parked outside. Each had thick cable wires taped onto the sidewalk from the street into the big top. Lights blazed.

Dan Reeves, the Denver coach, spoke. He was at his eighth Super Bowl, as player and coach. Most of his appearances were losses.

"I do believe in the law of averages," Reeves said. "And hopefully, if I'm here long enough, the law of averages will catch up, and I'll win.

"We realize the task in front of us. We're reminded of it every day by the press who tell us we don't have a chance."

◆ ◆ ◆

It was New Orleans and dinner time. We went off to a place called the Old N'awlins Cookery and ate dinner in a courtyard and talked about football. The conversation was mostly about Elway and Montana, and the fact that the 49ers already were 12½-point favorites and the spread was getting larger.

"Remember Super Bowl III," I cautioned, digging back into my history. "Joe Namath." The other writers scoffed.

We all walked back to the hotel, the Hyatt. I stopped off in the pressroom, by habit. There were always all sorts of goodies there for the media—canvas bags with advertising, football magazines, newspapers, city tour tips. They had something new for us this time—free packets of Bayer aspirin. Years ago, I might have wanted it.

◆ ◆ ◆

It was media day, and we'd marched across the bridge from the Hyatt. John Elway was the picture of the nonchalant hero, his audience of hundreds at his feet. Those dancing feet were up on a railing in front of the first row of the Superdome grandstands. He cupped his hands on his blond head. His voice was husky.

John floated in the fishbowl atmosphere. He lived in it. The previous Halloween a couple of reporters from Denver's Rocky Mountain *News* bundled up their kids in costume and rang the bell at Elway's house. Trick or treat. John gave the kids treats. He handed out Reese's Peanut Butter Cups and KitKat bars.

It was trick.

The reporters wrote in their paper what John Elway gave away for Halloween. It so happened Elway was being paid to endorse Nestle's Crunch bars.

A few days later, Elway told *Sports Illustrated* that he was about to suffocate—his word—as quarterback in Denver.

Now he was suffocating at the usual Super Bowl interview with the mob jostling below him. "There's pressure in every game," he said, "so there's no more for me in this.

"Any time your team's been to the Super Bowl three times and lost, and this is your fourth time, there's a little bit of a monkey. You win, and you lose that monkey. You can be 1-and-8, and you don't have that monkey on your back like 0-and-4.

"For me to be the quarterback I want to be, we've got to win this game. I've been twice and haven't won.

"If we win, it'll be the greatest upset of all time."

I managed to squeeze and push into the second rank below Elway. "You want to guarantee it?" I piped up.

Elway grinned.

"Get us another point and a half, and I'll guarantee it," said John Elway.

He pondered.

"I guarantee we'll cover the spread," he said.

A bit later I stood in a line of about a million sportswriters and broadcast journalists. We were beneath the Superdome, watched over by the yellow-jacketed NFL security to make sure we didn't misbehave. We were awaiting the NFL-catered breakfast that would cause my cholesterol level to soar.

I returned to the field after breakfast. The NFL already had the game clock running on the scoreboard, the countdown to the moment when the 49ers would be trooped out to meet the media.

Bubba Paris, weight listed at 299 pounds but looking heavier, lugged out his camcorder and seated himself on the platform. A reporter started to question Paris about his weight.

"I'm going to interview you," said Paris, pointing his zoom lens down at her. "How does it feel to know that you have to go someplace and ask a person the only question that aggravates him?"

The reporter persisted. "Why do you have to lose weight if you're playing so well?"

"I can't fit in Porsches, and my kids don't have anything to eat," said Paris, not softly. "I'm eating their food. You got any more questions?"

"I'm too embarrassed to go on," said the reporter. "I'm going to leave now." She walked away. "See, I'm not fat," said Paris. "I'm big."

I walked back to the Hyatt and went to the front desk. A TV crew from Sacramento came to the desk. The little red light went on. The camera whirred. I was a prop, making believe I was registering at the press hotel. At Super Bowl XXIV, I'd become vital news at six in Sacramento.

◆ ◆ ◆

That afternoon there was a press conference for Bud Bowl II. This scripted game between animated bottles of beer, butting into each other like jocks, would be contested during commercial breaks of Super Bowl XXIV. Bud Bowl I presumably had been worth the expense. So we were going to have Bud versus Bud Light again, with honest-to-goodness TV announcers. Budweiser introduced Brent Musburger and Terry Bradshaw as the men who would describe and analyze the bottle-butting during the breaks when America used to go to the bathroom on Super Sunday.

Terry had learned to spell TV among his readin' and learnin' accomplishments. He had graduated to CBS, as a thinking head. Now the writers at the press conference wondered about Terry's opinions of John Elway.

"I think John's problem is he's been babied by the fans, the media, and, to an extent, by the coaches," Bradshaw said. "It's really too easy for him."

Bradshaw mentioned that Elway was 0-and-2 in Super Bowls and was about to be 0-and-3.

". . . he's too inconsistent. He lets too many things bother him. He's got to get a little tougher emotionally. Things like that shouldn't bother you when you're making two million dollars a year."

This was better stuff than promotional piffle about Bud against Bud Light.

"Is he a great quarterback?" said Bradshaw. "Nope. A good one. When you choose a profession, and if you don't reach a pinnacle, you can't consider yourself a success."

There was one standard of greatness to Bradshaw: Super Bowl rings. John Elway, the man who'd wished for five, had none.

◆ ◆ ◆

I called J.P. McCarthy back at WJR in Detroit early every morning to talk Super Bowl on his radio show. We discussed the scene. The NFL was upset by the scalping of hotel rooms in New Orleans. The problem was, the NFL coppers said, rooms that sold for 125 bucks a night, plus tax, were being reserved and paid for, then sublet via travel agents for 400 or more a pop.

J.P. told me the wires were full of stories that the London bookies, with the 49ers huge favorites, were taking British action on the coin toss and on who'd flub the first field goal.

He asked about Bourbon Street. I made it there one night. I walked into the Old Absinthe House through one door and surveyed the crowd. I didn't know anybody. I left through another door and walked back to the Hyatt. I had to be up early to go on the radio before going to the 49ers.

"I used to go to bed at 4 a.m. at the Super Bowl," I told the listeners back in Detroit. "Now I wake up at 4 a.m."

♦ ♦ ♦

A few days after the 49ers won Super Bowl XXIII, George Seifert boarded a plane in San Francisco. He was going to Cleveland, but he was unable to get a direct flight and had to change planes in Dallas. Seifert had been Bill Walsh's long-time defensive coordinator. Now he was going to Cleveland to be interviewed for the head coaching job of the Browns, which had been vacated when Marty Schottenheimer was pushed out.

Seifert had dreamed of being a head coach in the NFL, as Bill Walsh had dreamed in the 1970s. Seifert's roots were with the 49ers. As a boy, in the 49ers' early seasons, Seifert was an usher on Sundays at Kezar Stadium. He went to Utah and majored in zoology and played football in the non-glamour positions of offensive guard and linebacker. Then he went into college coaching and got a head coaching job at Cornell. It was Ivy League football, no pressure, no alumni pounding. Right. His teams won three games in three years and Seifert was fired.

He then took an assistant's job at Stanford, where his boss was Bill Walsh, the NFL coach-in-waiting. When the 49ers, at last, summoned Walsh, Seifert rode up with him.

Because of what had happened at Cornell, Seifert didn't seek another head coaching job for many years. He had lost his confidence. And then, in the last week of January 1989, he was aboard the airplane headed for Cleveland. He landed in Dallas and looked at the board to find the gate of his connection.

He went to a pay phone and called home. There was a message to call the office back in San Francisco. Walsh had quit. Eddie DeBartolo was offering George Seifert the 49ers' head coaching job, the opportunity to succeed Bill Walsh, the genius.

Seifert called Cleveland, apologized, and caught the next plane back to San Francisco.

Now he stood before a ballroom full of curious media people at the Hilton near the Mississippi River in downtown New Orleans. Seifert had gray hair, and he wore wire-rimmed eyeglasses. He looked professorial.

He spoke. He charmed us with the best fish story since Hemingway.

He was fishing, he said, off the California coast in the Pacific. His hook caught, and he brought in his catch. He heaved it into his boat. He was happy. He figured it weighed 27 pounds.

Then he realized the boat was taking on water. He started rowing toward the shoreline. The boat was sinking and he had to abandon it. He tried to save the fish, as Hemingway's fisherman had. Seifert went into the drink, holding the fish. He tried to swim with it, but he had to let go.

"That was the biggest striped bass I ever caught," Seifert told us. "I hated to give it up, but my pants were filling up with water."

Seifert told us he'd returned to the spot where he'd surrendered his fish.

"I still enjoy being on the edge," he said. "I like to gamble a little. I've returned to the scene. Like if you're in a trampoline accident, if you fall off, you get back on. And I did that some in football."

◆ ◆ ◆

I jammed into the first of the week's media parties, in a tent between the hotel and the Superdome. N'awlins jazz ricocheted through the tent. They stuffed us with gumbo and beef.

I pushed through the mob and encountered the folks from Denver, faithful still. One guy was stuffed into an orange metal barrel, which was held up by suspenders. His gut rolled over the top. He looked as if he were otherwise stark naked, except for the orange cowboy hat on his head.

To pump the card show in the adjoining tent, each media person was given a packet of Super Bowl cards. I roamed into the next tent to look at the football and baseball cards and magazines assembled by the traders and collectors. I was offered eight bucks for my packet of free Super Bowl cards. I rejected it. Somebody else offered 10 bucks. I rejected that, too. Later, the price was raised to 25. I kept mine.

In the interview tent at the Intercontinental, John Elway responded to Terry Bradshaw. "Terry Bradshaw has been bashing me since I got in the league. He didn't like the money I make. He still doesn't. He can stick it in his ear."

Dan Reeves responded: "I played against Terry Bradshaw, and John Elway is as tough as Terry Bradshaw ever was. Terry Bradshaw had a helluva supporting cast, and he better be thankful for that."

Overnight, the Bradshaw-Elway controversy dwindled to zero. In Washington, television station WJLA hit the air with a report that three quarterbacks, all white, had tested positive for high levels of cocaine usage. No names were mentioned. But the NFL was charged with a coverup, with racism, and with playing favorites. On the air, the station questioned the competence of the testing laboratory operated by Dr. Forest S. Tennant, the NFL's drug advisor.

Because the station had not identified the three supposed users, rumors spread through New Orleans. Reporters chased around, whispering, mentioning station WJLA and the reporter who had gone on the air with the piece, Roberta Baskin. She had said the three quarterbacks or their agents had confirmed the allegations. Ted Koppel discussed the report on the ABC network.

The station had obviously sat on the story until Super Bowl week. Then, it could make the heaviest impact, catch the most publicity for the station. The standards of professional journalism decreed that this station identify the quarterbacks it accused. Otherwise, every white quarterback in the league was suspect. Otherwise, the news value was reduced to innuendo and common gossip. No names, no story.

One name mentioned in the subsequent rumor-mongering was Joe Montana. "Did you ever fail a drug test?" Montana was asked on ESPN.

"No, only an accounting test," said Joe.

Joe Browne denied the story for the NFL, denied that the league played favorites, and said the station was on a witch hunt.

None of the Super Bowl reporters could confirm the Washington TV story. But as Ted Koppel said, the drug story had altered the Super Bowl's focus, just as the unsubstantiated TV gambling accusations against Lenny Dawson had altered the focus 20 years earlier at Super Bowl IV, just as a TV reporter's imagination altered the focus when he thought he heard somebody say that Jim McMahon had referred to New Orleans womanhood as sluts.

◆ ◆ ◆

When Vince Lombardi gave up coaching in Green Bay after winning the first two Super Bowls, he was replaced by Phil Bengtson. Bengtson had devised the defense that turned Super Bowl I, that enabled Lombardi to flip the football in the Packers' locker room and preen about the NFL's superiority in running with it and catching it. The Packers had flopped miserably after Bengtson succeeded Lombardi.

The most difficult job in coaching sports might be to follow the man who has built and led a dynasty. The footsteps mentality. They are almost always too huge.

"On the contrary," said Seifert at Super Bowl XXIV when asked whether he wanted to deliver his own impact after he replaced Walsh. "It was a matter of continuity. Keeping what Walsh left here."

With Joe Montana and Jerry Rice and Roger Craig and Ronnie Lott —plus the addition of Matt Millen, who was cast off by Al Davis and the Raiders—the 49ers steamrollered through their season. They finished at 14-2, the best record in the league. They entered the playoffs powerful, dominant.

Montana threw four touchdown passes in the first playoff game against the Vikings, completing 17 of 24 for the day. The 49ers won, 41-13. The next weekend they won their fourth NFC championship of the decade by devouring the Rams, 30-3. Montana threw two touchdown passes. He completed 26 of 30.

Continuity! The 49ers were better than ever as they hit their fourth Super Bowl in eight years, their first with George Seifert.

Bill Walsh, certified genius that he was, had never beaten the Broncos in four meetings while he was a coach.

♦ ♦ ♦

Dan Reeves took the Broncos into the Superdome for practice Thursday. Looking around, he noticed that they had painted all the previous Super Bowl scores on the rim of the mezzanine. Winning teams' helmets first, to the left side, losers' to the right.

"They had Super Bowl XXIV up there with the place for the scores blank," said Reeves, "and they already had a San Francisco helmet painted on the left and a Denver helmet painted on the right. They expect us to lose.

"We're going to do our damnedest to make them change it."

There was cause for paranoia for Denver.

The Broncos could handle the AFC well enough, playing well in the season and winning four conference championships, three of these in four years. With Elway excelling, with Bobby Humphrey providing strong running as a rookie, the Broncos went 11-5 during the season. Again, it was the best record in the conference entering the playoffs.

In the first playoff game, the Broncos were behind the Steelers through most of the game, but Elway rallied them twice. The second time he took them on another long drive, 71 yards, to a touchdown with less than two and a half minutes to play. The Broncos survived, 24-23.

The next week, the Browns, now coached by Bud Carson, were the Broncos' opponents in the AFC championship game. For the third time in four years, the two clubs bashed each other, first the Broncos, then the Browns rallying. Elway drove the Broncos 80 yards for a decisive touchdown in the fourth quarter. The Broncos won it again, 37-21—and pity the Browns and Art Modell.

♦ ♦ ♦

Super Bowls make for gleeful owners. As the Broncos geared for the Super Bowl before leaving Denver, their owner, Pat Bowlen, took some swats at the 49ers.

"Those guys have got a great owner," he said. "They got God for a quarterback. They got a Chinaman who plays wide receiver whose feet never touch the ground."

"Huh?" said the Denver guys.

"That Chinese guy," said Bowlen. "What's his name? Rice?"

The Broncos' PR guy had to explain that Bowlen was just playing on words, that, hey, this was no ethnic slur.

"We're just a bunch of Palookas from the mountains who wear funny uniforms," said Bowlen. "So maybe we've got a chance. We're going to sneak up on them."

John Madden now had his own Super Bowl TV special.

"There's one word to describe them," Madden said, speaking of the 49ers. "Efficient.

"You go in their locker room, and it doesn't even stink."

I heard a good story. In 1988, when Bill Walsh benched Joe Montana, Eddie DeBartolo had traded his quarterback plus a first-draft choice for Billy Ray Smith. It was a done deal, but the Chargers backed off, and the 49ers were stuck with Joe Montana.

◆ ◆ ◆

As I waited for the glass capsule elevator on the 18th floor of the Hyatt, I spotted the visiting Pete Rozelle. I walked over to greet him, and he introduced me to the man with him, Paul Tagliabue.

Tagliabue held his first Super Bowl press conference Friday at noon in an overflowing ballroom. The focus was on the drug story. This would be the first battle-testing of the new commissioner.

He went for the issue.

"A smear and a gross distortion," Tagliabue said. "It is a journalistic Molotov cocktail. It takes two of the most volatile issues in America, mixes them, and throws it against the wall."

Tagliabue told us that Dr. Tennant's lab did not conduct the testing for the NFL during the '89 season. But the TV story, he said, omitted that information.

"You would think," the new commissioner said, "that Dr. Tennant were under the podium here testing me."

Clean hands? The NFL would continue to be in good hands. Paul Tagliabue showed to be smooth and slick as Pete Rozelle's successor. The NFL had its continuity, too.

Sure did. Paul Tagliabue's first Super Bowl party down at the Convention Center near the Mississippi River was the same kind of thing that Pete Rozelle had tossed. Folks begged for invitations, offered high prices for them. The party theme was LaFete, like out of Mardi Gras.

Powder-wigged performers made out to be plantation aristocrats danced to a flute and string sextet inside the front door. It was the Old South, recreated. Then were the long lines, the taste of gumbo, sushi, oysters, clams, and mussels. As usual, I got out of there early, in a bad mood.

Jazz combos played in the middle of the streets of the French Quarter on Saturday afternoon. Mobs of visitors in 49ers red and Broncos orange paraded along Bourbon Street in the sunshine, gripping the customary plastic cups filled with booze. Football seemed to be America's excuse to get drunk.

I went to the wharf and took a paddlewheel ferry across the Mississippi. Then I drove out to Dick Schapp's party along a bayou, where it was quiet, and pigged out on ribs and jambalaya. It seems there's always an old placekicker at Dick's party, and this one was no exception. Jan Stenerud was there, and he relived Super Bowl IV for me, especially the three field goals he kicked to send the Chiefs ahead of the Vikings, 9-0.

That had been the Other League's last game, and the Chiefs had played with AFL-10 patches on their shoulders. Through the seventies, the AFC's successor had dominated this Super Bowl. Now the NFC, with its roots to the old NFL, dominated again. NFC clubs had won five Super Bowls in succession, seven of eight. It was an imbalance to concern the new commissioner.

◆ ◆ ◆

On the footbridge outside the Superdome, memorabilia collectors eyed our Super Bowl XXIV press badges. They were offering $100 for a pin.

Someplace, scattered at home, I had them all, 24 of them, the little medallions they gave us at Super Bowls I and II, and the pins, I thought. I wondered what the whole set would be worth.

Nope. Just a flash thought. Priceless. They symbolized so many good memories to me.

◆ ◆ ◆

This year there were no bolting horses. No booming cannons. No recreation of the Battle of New Orleans. No New Orleans stripper prancing topless along the sidelines. All these memories of Super Bowls past flashed by.

Instead, there were just the usual twinges of patriotism. A copy of the Statue of Liberty was wheeled in, and an enormous American flag descended from the roof. The crowd gave a standing ovation for the Panama invaders. Then Aaron Neville lip-synced "The Star-Spangled Banner."

Denver won the toss, as the London bookies watched in the middle of the night in England.

And then John Elway took the first snap from the Denver 23. He passed and threw wild low, yards from his receiver, Mark Jackson. Oooops. An omen, I thought. Then Elway tried a pass on second down. Wild low a second time. Denver had to punt.

Joe Montana missed his first pass, too. Then Roger Craig ran around the left end for 18 yards. You could sense the angry talking on the field. The Broncos seemed to want to fight. Montana guided the 49ers down to the Broncos' 20. Then he looked right—no receiver open—left, no receiver—then over the middle. Jerry Rice was drifting free, and Montana hit him. Rice broke off the Broncos' shoddy tackle attempts for a touchdown.

Elway managed to bring the Broncos back to the 49ers' 25. Then he missed three passes. David Treadwell, the Broncos' new kicker, booted a 42-yard field goal. It was 7-3, San Francisco, midway through the first quarter.

Next, the Broncos stopped the 49ers. They had the ball at their 49, starting with decent field position. Bobby Humphrey fumbled the ball away on the first play.

Joe Montana had the ball again and passed to Rice for 20 yards. A few plays later he passed to Rice for 21. The 49ers moved to the seven. Montana passed to Brent Jones, the tight end, for the touchdown. Mike Cofer missed the point after. San Francisco was up, 13-3, when the first quarter ended.

Elway threw some more incompletions as the second quarter began. Denver punted again. Montana had the ball again and passed to Tom Rathmann for 18 and then 12. Craig ripped off some runs. At the one, Montana handed off to Rathmann, who bashed in. San Francisco was up, 20-3.

With 1:38 left before the halftime show, Montana had another chance. He worked the 49ers from their 41 to the Broncos' 38. Forty seconds showed on the clock. On second-and-one, Joe went the distance and hit Rice for the 38-yard touchdown. It was San Francisco 27-3 at the half. Elway had gone 6-for-20.

The halftime show featured Snoopy on his 40th birthday.

On his first pass of the second half, Elway missed his receiver again. Michael Walter intercepted. Montana, on the first play, hit Rice again for the touchdown, 28 yards. It was Rice's third TD. San Francisco was up, 34-3.

On Denver's next series, Chet Brooks intercepted Elway. Brooks ran the ball back 38 yards. Montana threw this time to John Taylor, for 35 yards, for his fifth touchdown pass. San Francisco was up, 41-3. And we were just a bit into the third quarter.

But . . . but . . . John Elway took the Broncos on a drive now. They went 61 yards, with Humphrey running 34 in one burst. Elway scored the TD himself, running in from the three. The Broncos had cut the 49ers' lead to 41-10.

On the 49ers' next series, Montana completed four of five passes. Rathmann scored the touchdown from the three on the first play of the fourth quarter. San Francisco was up, 48-10.

On the field, Matt Millen, the refugee from the Raiders, stuck his tongue out at Elway. Elway barked back.

Millen said something. Joking later, he said he'd said: "'Now that I'm in San Francisco, I'm a closet homosexual and I can come out.' He laughed. "No, I told him to keep his spirits up."

The 49ers chased Elway as he tried to flee their pass rush. He was hit behind the line and fumbled. Daniel Stubbs picked it up for the Niners and rumbled 15 yards to the one. Roger Craig scored on the next play. San Francisco was up, 55-10.

Montana left the game to a standing ovation. When the Broncos got the ball again, Elway was out of the game, too.

Elway knelt near the bench and rested his hand on his helmet. A memory flashed back of the thrice-beaten Francis Tarkenton years before sitting on his helmet at another Super Bowl.

The final was San Francisco 55, Denver 10. That made it six straight Super Bowls for the NFC. San Francisco 4-0, and Denver 0-4.

America bemoaned another lopsided Super Bowl. I thought back to what I had written years before, before Pete Rozelle's first Super Bowl. The game was another resounding dud. But the 49ers, they were the colossus.

The greatest quarterback ever, they said to Joe Montana.

"As I've been saying," Montana said, rejecting the notion, "those things are reserved for the guys who are no longer in the game."

The next morning, George Seifert, with his gray hair and wire-rimmed eyeglasses familiar to all of TV-America, was hailed as a hero, as he conducted the winning coach's press conference. When it was over, he went to rejoin his team to fly back to San Francisco and the victory parade on Market Street.

But now he was standing outside the Hyatt, alone, a forlorn figure in the New Orleans gloom, hands in pockets, unnoticed, looking lost, waiting for his ride.

XXV
The Real War

New York Giants 20, Buffalo Bills 19
January 27, 1991
Tampa Stadium
Attendance: 73,813

Bombs! Blitz! Trenches! Jets! Bullets! Battle! Offense! Defense! Attack! *Field General! March!*

These are the words of war-speak—and the graphic terms used to describe football games. They had been part of my vocabulary through 24 Super Bowls. To describe Joe Montana collaborating on a deep forward pass to Jerry Rice; to provide an image of Jack Lambert charging from linebacker toward Roger Staubach; to picture the action along the line of scrimmage when Lombardi's Packers played a football game against Stram's Chiefs.

George Allen, recently deceased, once said: "Losing is worse than death!" His words imply that a football game—two teams playing in colorful uniforms and heavy plastic pads before a stadium crammed with passionate spectators—resembles war.

But this year the metaphors of war paled as the New York Giants and the Buffalo Bills engaged in the simple routines of Super Bowl XXV at Tampa. I could not use any war-speak at this Super Bowl, not when Americans were fighting a war that had begun 11 days before in the Persian Gulf against Iraq. Not when Americans were seeing the bombs and tanks and guns of that war on their television screens every day. This football game was insignificant, its borrowed language blasphemous. The Gulf war was reality, the death it brought about real and terrible.

317

As I arrived in Tampa, I could not believe how much of a fuss we as a nation have made for a quarter-century about an event, a game, given the name *Super Bowl.*

The mood was somber as we checked into the Hyatt Downtown. It was Super Bowl week, and I'd always loved it. *Time* magazine, in its continual urge to provide perspective, had once capsuled the atmosphere of this week as "The Great American Time-Out." Now I didn't give a damn. There was work to do and it would be done. But not with the relish of my first 24 Super Bowls.

I agreed with Paul Tagliabue's decision to let the game go on. I had grown through adolescence during World War II, and the games had been played then. NFL football had gone through its motions, and so had baseball and hockey, with inferior athletes who could not pass military physicals. The games went on because President Roosevelt believed they could boost wartime morale.

And now, in another bloody war, Commissioner Tagliabue had opted to play the championship games and then Super Bowl XXV as planned. That would be fine. It didn't have to be party time, as before, with the plastic cups and the goofy hats that fans believed were a display of loyalty to their hometown football teams.

◆ ◆ ◆

Airport security was tight and welcome on the morning I flew out of Detroit. So secure, as the threat of terrorism gripped America, that the mailboxes at the airport had been sealed over. So secure that the potted plants in the lobby of the Airport Marriott Hotel had been removed by federal officials, lest one become a hiding place for a terrorist's weapon.

So now I thought of the movie *Black Sunday,* which had been filmed at Super Bowl X. The plot, simply, was a group of Mideastern terrorists arranging for killer darts to be fired at the football crowd from the Goodyear blimp overhead. It was fiction then, but it made me shudder now. What likelier place for Saddam Hussein to arrange for an act of terrorism to make a statement to the world!

Tagliabue, persuaded by the networks in the new TV contract, opted to extend the season by an additional week, putting in yet another set of wild-card games. The casualty was the usual two-week interval between the championship games and the Super Bowl. So the Giants and the Bills arrived in Tampa on Monday, the day after winning their conference championships, ready for the Super Bowl week grind.

Paul showed his smarts right away. On Monday night, our first night in Tampa, the NFL proclaimed that the Commissioner's Freeload had been called off. It was no time for excessive gaiety, not when Americans were ducking anti-aircraft fire while flying sorties over Iraq.

On that same night, another of those opposing team confrontations occurred in a nightclub. Not Joe Namath versus Lou Michaels this time, but Lawrence Taylor and Jim Kelly at a joint named The Dollhouse. They were there as judges of a topless contest, with all amateur entrants. War or no war, this Super Bowl would have its prize moments.

◆ ◆ ◆

We had early reveille Tuesday morning for media day, now the pushing, shoving tradition that allowed the cream of American sports journalism to wind up asking their best questions. Like, How do you feel playing a game when there's a war on? With watches synchronized at 7 a.m., as always, we boarded buses at the new Tampa Convention Center. The NFL had commandeered this cavernous structure because a hotel no longer could handle the mob of working media. With our SBXXV press pins and dangling picture ID badges properly displayed, with our arms packed with the gratis newspapers shoved beneath our hotel room doors, we bounced onto the buses out to Tampa Stadium.

Tampa public safety officials had already encircled the stadium with a thick concrete anti-terrorist barrier. They didn't want any crazy driving a car loaded with explosives, Beirut style, through a stadium gate. We dodged through a break in the wall, watched over by security men in the usual yellow jackets. We clogged our entrance, as always, to wait, and we shivered in the chill of the Florida morning.

The NFL was at full alert. "Raise your arms," a guy said to me. He frisked me with one of those wands to make sure I was clean. Every writer got it this way. Every cameraman had to send his photo gear through an X-ray machine. Every guy lugging one of the NFL's silver-colored Super Bowl XXV freebie briefcases had to send it through the machine.

You never know when an NFL bag might be used to cover up a terrorist's Kalishnikov.

◆ ◆ ◆

We were inside the wartime security—and it was the same as always.

Five video cameras with microphones on booms enveloped Bill Parcells, the Giants coach, on a bleacher bench to learn if his intelligence had diminished since the Giants won Super Bowl XXI. TV journalists popped obvious questions to him. They asked about the risks of using Jeff Hostetler, who would be starting at quarterback against the Bills. Hostetler was a career backup who had rushed in in the long-ago style of Earl Morrall and guided his team to the championship after Phil Simms was badly injured in December.

"I've been real pleased with him," said Parcells, providing the obvious answer. "He's played error-free football, basically, one turnover in the four games he's started for us. That's probably the reason why we're here." In seven years, Hostetler's job, basically, had been to hold the ball for the placekicker. He had started all of seven pro games in his life, only three before the '90 season.

Another mob gathered around Hostetler. "Everybody's got their own opinion," Hostetler told the Super Bowl cynics. "They keep telling me I can't. I'm going to the Super Bowl."

A group stood on the sidelines listening to Mark Bavaro, the quiet tight end. As he spoke, a helicopter fluttered past the rim of the stadium.

"Ours or theirs?" Bavaro mused to his questioners.

A sleek young woman with proper press credentials marched around with a proper bowler on her head, a skin-tight micromini skirt, and an entourage. Somebody identified her as Downtown Julie Brown from MTV. "Nice buns," Julie Brown kept saying about the Giants.

◆ ◆ ◆

The Bills intrigued me. An original franchise in the AFL, the team with Jack Kemp, Cookie Gilchrist, and O.J. Simpson in its heritage, Buffalo had been one of ten teams in the greater NFL that had never reached the Super Bowl. The Bills had had a chance to make it to Super Bowl I against Lombardi's Packers, but they had been crushed in their AFL championship game by the Chiefs. They became one of the sad sack teams in football with a history of clownish pratfalls.

Now the Buffalo Bills—from that iceberg of a city near Niagara Falls— were in the Super Bowl for the first time. The Bills had become a mighty ball club, AFC champions favored to break the NFC's string of six successive victories in the Super Bowl.

I stood next to Ray Bentley. Bentley played linebacker for the Bills with his face covered with war paint. We wondered what possessed him.

"I started doing it in high school in 1978," Bentley said, repeating himself perhaps 100 times. "We had a game on Halloween and I was a big Alice Cooper fan. There happened to be some watercolor paints there. The team just went crazy. We killed the other team that night, 41-0, so I've been doing it ever since."

"Your favorite Alice Cooper song?"

"'Welcome to My Nightmare,'" said Bentley.

The conversation switched to Bentley's books. He writes children's books in which the main character is named Darby the Dinosaur, and with cartoons drawn by former teammate Mike Hamby.

"I try to teach a lesson with them," Bentley said. "All kids want to do is play Nintendo and watch cartoons. That's what I like to do. There needs to be an emphasis on reading." He added: "I have a copy for all of you guys."

Most of the media gathered around Jim Kelly, the Giants' quarterback who had been in the USFL and had become one of the NFL's best, and Thurman Thomas. Or they hit Bruce Smith and Cornelius Bennett of the Buffalo defense. Smith spit at the Giants. He wanted Joe Montana, not Jeff Hostetler.

"The 49ers are famous and everybody says they are this and that," Smith told the media. "It makes me sick. I wanted the 49ers."

Bennett took note of the Bills' historic futility, the 2-14 records of '84 and '85, and the 4-10 of '86.

"I think the turnaround began when they got Cornelius Bennett," said Bennett, obtained by the Bills in '87, to a gaggle of press.

Nobody gathered around Marv Levy, the erudite Buffalo coach. Nobody could find him. Marv didn't bother to show up on media day

◆ ◆ ◆

Lisa Olson was not one of the reporters at the Super Bowl. Yet she had been involved in the most dominant, most disgusting story of the 1990 season. Like most of the writers at Super Bowl XXV, Lisa Olson had been assigned by her newspaper as the daily beat reporter covering a local pro football club. She worked for the Boston *Herald,* and her job was to go into the Patriots' locker room, interview the players, and write an article for the next day's paper.

One afternoon early in the season she was talking to a player in the locker room. It was then that five of the Patriots surrounded her. They were buck naked.

"Is this what you want?" she quoted one of the players as saying. She identified him as Zeke Mowatt. She wrote that the five players "approached me, positioned themselves inches away from my face and dared me to touch their private parts."

Victor Kiam, who had liked Remington razors so much that he bought the company, spoke up with tender concern. Kiam had also liked the Patriots so much that he bought the franchise.

"I can't disagree with the players' actions," Kiam said in an interview published in the *Herald.* "Your paper's asking for trouble sending a female reporter to cover the team. Why not stand in front of her [naked] if she's an intruder."

Another reporter cornered Kiam and quoted him as saying about Lisa Olson: "She's a classic bitch."

The furor had begun. It would continue in the daily press through September into October to late November. The Sunday football games became secondary. The alphabet soup of the media—CBS, NBC, and ESPN—refused to let the sexual harassment story fade away. It made the network news, Tom Brokaw; the pregame shows covered the story from almost every angle. The National Organization for Women somehow made Kiam realize he peddled Lady Remingtons.

It was a mess for the public relations professionals to clean up. They placed ads in the Sunday Boston and New York papers in which Kiam issued an apology. Then the alphabet soup people picked off Kiam live on their pregame shows. TV critics, who keep score of such engagements, decreed NBC the clear-cut victor in interviewing Victor. Live, Bob Costas asked Kiam if the ads in the Sunday papers were an honestly contrite apology or if he was trying to smooth over a PR catastrophe.

Responded Kiam, "This is more than a public relations disaster. This is a grievous injury to a lovely young lady. What is more disheartening perhaps than anything is that my response to this whole terrible, terrible situation has been done on the basis that I knew nothing—absolutely nothing—about this incident until six days after the event."

Victor denied that he had ever referred to that "lovely young lady" as "a classic bitch."

Of course, America liked the words the recanting Kiam spoke so much it bought the argument.

America took sides: the people versus the press. Newspapers ran polls to learn if the citizenry favored permitting women reporters to enter men's locker rooms in the legal efforts to do their assigned jobs. The polls showed, mostly, that there are a lot of press bashers out there in the hinterlands. A lot of folks figured that male reporters ought to stay out of the locker rooms, too, that capturing the moods and emotions of the athletes, the smells and the scenes, was not part of the right to know that Americans claim to have.

And the furor went on. The *Herald* switched Lisa Olson to pro basketball, covering the Celtics. Tagliabue ordered a probe.

And Sam Wyche, Wicky-Wacky in person, decided that this was the very best time to bar women reporters from the Bengals' locker room. After the Bengals were skunked in a Monday-night game in Seattle, Wyche prevented Denise Tom of *USA Today* from going into the locker room. The press, antennas waving due to the newsworthiness of the Olson case, jumped onto this new incident. Newsmen quoted Wicky-Wacky as saying: "Sam Wyche was not letting a woman into his locker room with all his players naked . . . I'll be out of business before I do that."

Tagliabue did what he could to Sam's business—he took away 1/17th of Wyche's salary. The fine was a socking penalty of $27,941.17. American journalism tuned in to discover what Wyche would do at the Bengals' next game against the Rams at Anaheim. Wyche did not disappoint. He started his postgame press conference with a striptease. When Wyche yanked off a shirt and a towel, he was left with a mock bare chest and . . . er, mock fig leaf. Then he divulged his modified locker room policy.

"What we've got in there is a curtain, behind which is the crapper, the shower and a separate room where the players can slip on their pants," Wyche said. ". . . They'll dry off, slip on their pants and come out and cooperate with you."

Wyche's enlarged, enrapt audience consisted of reporters of all persuasions.

During the last week of November, the results of Tagliabue's Olson inquiry were announced. The investigation had been conducted by special counsel Philip B. Heyman, from the Harvard Law School, a dignified man whose background included work as prosecutor in the Watergate hearings. His probe had taken five weeks, and when it was done, the findings covered 60 pages plus three appendices. Tagliabue fined Mowatt $12,500 to pay for instructional material on just how to get along with the media. Thus it was that Paul Tagliabue established himself as the wrist-slapping commissioner.

♦ ♦ ♦

My old Washington friend Moe Siegel hit me with a stumper in the press hospitality room. We were eating a bowl of Fisher Sports Nuts, which was staging its fourth annual Fisher Nuttiest Sports Nut Contest, emceed by Terry Bradshaw, later in Super Bowl week.

"What are the most important things that ever happened in Buffalo?" asked Siegel, in search of an angle.

"Huh?" I responded. Moe already had jotted down a few notes.

"President Millard Fillmore lived there," he noted. "President McKinley was shot there. Grover Cleveland was mayor there. Joe McCarthy (the baseball manager) was born there. Chicken wings were invented there."

"That it?" I asked. That was it.

"Oh," said Moe, "Jim Kelly gets $150,000 extra in pay to come back to Buffalo to work out in the off-season."

♦ ♦ ♦

Vince Lombardi had been available to the press at the Super Bowl. Don Shula and Bill Walsh and Tom Landry always showed up, on NFL orders, to smile and answer questions at media day. Shoot, even George Allen was there, squawking, of course, but he was there. Marv Levy was the first head coach to thumb his nose at this nutty gathering of pushy reporters and defy the NFL as a no-show. He should have known what it was like: another repetition of the old Super Bowl linkage.

TAMPA—Marv Levy was an obscure assistant coach for George Allen when the Washington Redskins made it to Super Bowl VII, long ago in the history of this media/football circus.

That was 1973, and Allen, complaining bitterly about the distractions in his secretive practice routine, was required to troop his Redskins around Anaheim Stadium for the annual Super Bowl Photo Day. The players and coaches were on the field, available to the ink-stained wretches and electronic media marvels to answer the usual probing questions. In its quest for more public attention, the NFL permitted some 2,000 spectators into the grandstands of the baseball park to observe this traditional scene that opens Super Bowl weeks.

It was a very few minutes into the Redskins' photo day that the hordes from the stands stormed over the fences and overwhelmed the cops protecting the press and Redskins and George Allen from such intrusions. In a panic, Allen ordered the Redskins to flee to the locker room. . . .

Marv Levy, back at Super Bowl XXV as head coach of the Buffalo Bills, is more than a chip off the late George Allen.

"Anaheim," said Levy, "I stood around with the assistant coaches, two hours a day, five days a week, and I'm still waiting for somebody to talk to me." The lesson of the mob scene of super Bowl VII remained vivid at Super Bowl XXV. Marv Levy became the first head coach in the history of the Super Bowl to snub the mighty media on the now-traditional media, or photo, day, thus risking the wrath of the NFL and Commissioner Paul Tagliabue. The appearance by both participating head coaches is mandatory. Any defiance of that rule is punishable by a healthy fine.

Levy skipped anyway. George Allen would have loved it. And the issue of Levy's absence from Tampa Stadium last Tuesday morning at 9:30 has become a major story this grim, somber Super Bowl week.

"I was so immersed in the game plan," Levy explained the following morning when required by the NFL to issue a forced apology. "I made the decision that our first priority was to prepare for the game.

"I've been in coaching 40 years. This is the game I've been preparing for all that time. That entered my thinking. I apologize to you. All my players were there.

"I didn't know it was an issue. I'm finding out it is."

At age 62, Levy, the itinerant career coach, the only NFL coach eligible to wear a Phi Beta Kappa key, has reached the top moment of his life.

"I don't think I'm consumed by it," he said. "I'm involved in it.

"I'm thrilled by it. Any coach is, even if he's blasé. You don't have to be giddy.

"Getting here is not the important thing. Winning is.

"Anything that happens outside that 100-yard rectangle—whether you've played here in the Super Bowl before [as the Giants have], on grass, the weather—you're fuzzing up the focus."

Levy talks that way, when he does talk.

Born in Chicago, a running back and sprinter in track at Coe College in Iowa, Levy got into coaching via a detour.

"I wanted to be a lawyer," Levy said. "I went to Harvard. After about four weeks there, I said this wasn't for me. I wanted to get into coaching."

He switched to English history and earned his masters degree at Harvard. Then Levy's travels began.

(St. Louis Country Day in 1951, back at Coe as an assistant, then at New Mexico as an assistant, then head coach; then California, then William & Mary; then pro football as an assistant with the Eagles; then with George Allen on the Redskins; then as head coach in Canada with the Montreal Alouettes; then six seasons as head coach of the Chiefs; then the Chicago Blitz in the USFL; then to Montreal again as director of player operations.)

. . . He was there in 1986 when the Bills went on a manhunt in midseason for a new coach.

Now speaking, finally, at the Bills' first Super Bowl, Levy, as George Allen would have, told a story.

"The Blitz were a good team when I got there. Then right after that, I found out they traded all their players to the Arizona Wranglers, who had been 2-14, for all the Arizona players.

"This was a team devoid of funds. They didn't even supply the restrooms with toilet paper. One of our coaches wrapped about 40 cases of toilet paper in Christmas wrapping and distributed them around."

What Levy left out of the story was that the man who engineered the swap of ownerships and franchises of the Arizona Wranglers for the Chicago Blitz was a wily head coach—named George Allen.

". . . George Allen was fun to work for. He was a little bit
transparent. You could see through him. But no matter if it was junior
high school, high school, college or the pros, he had a sense of
priority. He prepared to win."

Bruce Smith's taunting boasts had the makings of a hot Super Bowl
feud. Early in the '90 season, Smith became embattled with Levy when
Kelly was yanked from a game in which the Bills were being destroyed
by the Dolphins. In essence, Smith accused his coach of quitting during
the game.

It was a dangerous dispute because the Bills had been split into factions
regarding Kelly the year before, in the '89 season. The club stumbled to a
9-7 record that season and was kayoed from the playoffs in the first round.
But this time the flap unified the Bills. And as the season progressed, Smith
could commit himself to other topics—to wit, publicizing Bruce Smith,
defensive end.

"I think I have emerged as the most dominant player in the league,"
Smith said. "Over the last 10 years, Lawrence Taylor has been the most
dominating player in the league. But I think I've taken it a notch above
that. Right now, It's time I give credit to somebody who deserves it. It
would be an injustice if I didn't get the MVP [this year]." His comments
made every sports section and sports TV show in the country.

◆ ◆ ◆

The Bills did their midweek press conferences under a tent at the Holiday
Inn, where the NFL had made arrangements to billet the AFC champions.
But the Bills ignored the NFL's painstaking logistics specialists, who had
years of Super Bowl experience. They went off on their own hook, at their
first Super Bowl, and moved as a team into the Hilton. So it was that on
Wednesday and Thursday mornings they had to be bused to the Holiday
Inn, where the interview tent had been pitched, to see the media.

It was here that Levy apologized for being a no-show, and that Smith
talked less of himself and more of his father being ill in Virginia. "My
father's illness has affected me in a major way, Smith told the journalists.
"I'm still trying to have fun. But this is no longer fun. It's rush here, rush
there, rush, rush."

We rode the bus to the Giants' interview sessions at the Hyatt Regency
Westshore—on the causeway toward Clearwater, take a left at the Tonga
Lounge, where the marquee proclaims *Nude Girls*.

Lawrence Taylor sat in a corner of the tent on the Hyatt parking lot, with a thousand or so guys around him. He wore a straw planter's hat and a diamond stud in his left earlobe.

He indeed had been the most dominating, most intimidating defensive player in the league. And now L.T. was being challenged by words.

There had been braggarts at the Super Bowl before—The Hammer, Hollywood Henderson, and, hey, Joe Namath. Now Bruce Smith was presented to Lawrence Taylor as another.

"I got nothing against Bruce Smith," said L.T., as we strained to get closer to hear better. "Right now I think he is the greatest player on defense. At this stage of my career, I'm not Superman. I'm Clark Kent. Clark Kent can get the job done."

And there went that feud.

The somber atmosphere stuck all week. I went to the interview sessions and rushed back to the room at the Tampa Hyatt to catch the war news on TV. I went to dinner at the Columbia, to Berns, and rushed back for more war news. That's what mattered at this Super Bowl.

Bud Bowl III canceled its bash. The Players Association decided, across the bay, to cancel its fancy party. Some parties went on. St. Petersburg staged a huge Super Bowl press party. A lot of us skipped it. Ybor City, the quaint Cuban section of Tampa, tossed a shindig at which it advertised the world's longest conga line. One-two-three SICK.

One party would do it for the entire week. We were now the Super Bowl 25 Club, the 13 grizzled writers and seven photographers who had covered all the Super Bowls, I to XXV.

They honored us with miniature copies of the Lombardi Trophy. They honored us together with the Silver Anniversary Super Bowl team—among them Franco Harris, Larry Csonka, Lynn Swann and Forrest Gregg and Jan Stenerud, Joe Greene and Jack Lambert, Ted Hendricks and Gene Upshaw and Jerry Kramer, and Joe Montana, who couldn't make it.

Pete Rozelle was there. He had flown from his retirement home near San Diego. He was one of us.

Paul Tagliabue skipped the party. But then, he wasn't eligible.

TAMPA—Among the souvenirs of the Buffalo Bills are an ancient, misshapen stadium full of cobwebs, broken bricks and rotting wood and a vagabond placekicker named Booth Lusteg.

"The story's true," said Ralph Wilson, the Detroit industrialist who founded the Bills 31 years ago and stayed until they at least reached the Super Bowl.

"Lusteg, we had him in 1966. He had a cinch field goal against the Chargers. He missed it at the end of the game. He goes inside and gets dressed. Then he goes into downtown Buffalo, and three tough guys run over a curb and get out of their car and beat him up."

The facts are that the field goal Lusteg missed was a 23-yarder and the Bills took a tie in the game. . . .

Years later Lusteg was asked by *Sports Illustrated* why he didn't get the license plate number of the mugs who beat him up.

"Because I deserved what I got," said Lusteg.

Tough town, Buffalo. Roughneck fans. The place they played in for a dozen seasons reflected the city. It was called War Memorial Stadium. It was cockeyed in shape, jerry-rigged with a number of additions. Originally, it was a WPA project, the product of a Depression work program during the presidency of Franklin D. Roosevelt.

It was there that the Bills won some early American Football League championships with Jack Kemp at quarterback and lost a championship game when they could have advanced to Super Bowl I. From that defeat on, the Bills went through years of depressed seasons, some scratching down to 1-13 and 2-14. Among O.J. Simpson's souvenirs are memories of running in his early pro years on the clumped grass in War Memorial Stadium before the hostile roughnecks.

"We called it the Rock Pile," O.J. told me this Super Bowl week. "My rookie year, after the first game, all my teammates rushed off the field as soon as the game ended. They didn't even stop to talk to our opponents, like you usually do. Paul Maguire was really cooking off the field with purpose. I thought it must be a team tradition.

"When I got to the locker room, I could see why. They had only about two minutes of hot water in the locker room. It wasn't so bad early in the season. But when it started to freeze . . . you found out how important a lukewarm shower was.

There were times we got in a bus and drove around to see where we were going to practice. We practiced in a silo, once in an equestrian stable area, in a horse ring. It was indoors. It kept the snow off.

"We practiced in an ice rink on ice. They put a cover on it."

Those early years, when they had the mightiest runner of the era, the Bills went 4-10, 3-10-1, 1-13, 4-9-1.

"One year, John Rauch was fired or quit as our coach," said O.J., now an NBC telecaster and cinema actor. "Harvey Johnson took over. He was a scout. We had to play a whole year with a guy who wasn't a head coach and made no pretenses about wanting to become one."

Paul Maguire, O.J.'s teammate now at NBC, has seven seasons with the Bills among his souvenirs.

"War Memorial was the only stadium where you could come out of the locker room and get hungry," Maguire said. "You passed where they cooked the hot dogs and the popcorn for the games. My stomach went crazy.

"During the summer we played exhibition games with the pitcher's mound up. That's how Jack Kemp developed that jump pass.

"Those were wonderful years . . . War Memorial Stadium . . . where they filmed *The Natural.*"

Reggie McKenzie had one season in War Memorial Stadium among his souvenirs before the Bills moved to the chic, modern Rich Stadium in 1973.

"I started out with a laugh," said McKenzie from Seattle, where he now works for the Seahawks. "They still played the College All-Star Game when I played St. Louis in Buffalo. I'll never forget driving to Buffalo and walking into the stadium. I started laughing, coming from the University of Michigan.

"I said, 'This is pro ball?' I was used to playing before 103,000, 104,000, 105,000 people, and now there were 36,000 people moving like jack-in-the-boxes, to the left, then the right so they could see.

"Must have been a quarter before I stopped laughing and saying, 'This is pro ball?'"

Once upon a time Ralph Wilson had season tickets for the Lions' games in his hometown of Detroit. The tickets went in a settlement of a divorce suit. Wilson was rooted in the game . . . and when Lamar Hunt was looking for owners to establish the AFL, Wilson volunteered. He was a charter member of The Foolish Club.

His team, with Jack Kemp throwing those jump passes and scrambling, managed to win AFL championships in '64 and '65. Then came the merger with the NFL; the fighting ended in '66. And the Bills lost the AFL championship that season to the Chiefs, 31-7, at the War Memorial Stadium, failing to make it to Super Bowl I.

It took them 24 years to get close to the Super Bowl again.

The main reason was Wilson. He changed ideologies in the middle of the 1980s, when the Bills were buried with their 2-14 concepts. Now 73, and enjoying his first Super Bowl the way Art Rooney once did, Wilson told me: "They used to write that I was a cheapskate." He laughed about it now, in Tampa. The Bills had gone and spent for such as Kelly, Bruce Smith, Bennett Thurman Thomas. They had wisely added James Lofton, regarded as a problem with other clubs. They had smartly drafted a marvelous wide receiver such as Andre Reed, on the sixth round, out of a hidden Pennsylvania school, Kutztown State.

With such talent, and more harmony in the locker room, the Bills ripped through their season with a 13-3 record. The loss to Miami, after which Smith accused his coach of surrender, did not deter the Bills. They won their next seven games—twice with stunning, multi-touchdown fourth-quarter comebacks that overcame the Broncos and the Raiders. In December, the Bills edged the Giants in the New Jersey Meadowlands, 17-13. Both quarterbacks—Kelly and Phil Simms—went down in the game. Only Kelly came back for the playoffs. The Bills crunched the Dolphins at Rich Stadium in the first playoff game, 44-34, on a snow-whitened field. Cops with horses and growling attack dogs kept the victory-starved Buffalo fans from tearing down the goalposts and trashing the stadium and each other, as they had in triumph during the season.

The next week the Bills played Al Davis's Raiders for the AFC championship back at Rich Stadium.

Three days earlier, American planes had dropped their first smart bombs on Baghdad. We were at war. The games went on.

Players talked about the war and compared it to the game of football. Said the Raiders' Howie Long in a penetrating TV segment: "It shows, just how in comparison, the Super Bowl is feeble. My God, I'm calling the Super Bowl feeble. But the Super Bowl is feeble compared to what's happening in the Middle East."

So the championshp game started, with NBC on alert to switch to the Middle East, live.

Using a no-huddle offense, Kelly drove the Bills to touchdowns on his first two series. It became a classic wipe-out.

Then, suddenly, NBC switched to Saudi Arabia. Arthur Kent hollered into the microphone: "Hello, New York! This is not a drill! This is Saudi Arabia! Let's go! We're firing Patriots. This is not a drill."

Moments later, the audience that had been watching a football game was watching American Patriot missiles firing out to intercept Scud missiles. The listeners could hear air raid sirens from a desert battleground halfway around the world.

"There goes a Patriot," said Kent from Saudi Arabia.

And in Buffalo, the Bills kept scoring. When NBC returned to football, the Bills had scored another touchdown. Then they scored another, and at halftime they led, 41-3.

NBC broke away again in the second half for a Pentagon briefing and a report that five Patriots had been fired and two Scuds had been destroyed.

In Buffalo, the game back on TV, the Bills finished destroying the Raiders. The final score was 51-3 and the Bills were going to the Super Bowl.

◆ ◆ ◆

At Super Bowl XXI, Phil Simms had turned in a bravura performance in the Giants' victory over the Broncos—and Raul Allegre had satisfactorily done the placekicking. They were veterans; Parcells could rely on them on a team that he and GM George Young had rebuilt after a post-Super Bowl collapse to 6-9 in '87.

Now in '90, Allegre went down with a groin pull in the Giants' third game. He was done for the season. Young shopped for a replacement kicker and found Matt Bahr, who had been dropped by the Browns at the start of the season. Bahr had been the Steelers' kicker as a rookie when they won their fourth ring at Super Bowl XIV. After that, he traveled the placekicker's standard itinerary—from the Steelers to the 49ers to the Browns. And, when he was out of work, his career presumably finished, to the Giants.

The Giants won their first 10 games. So did the 49ers. The two teams were scheduled to play each other in Monday Night Football in game number 12. Just as the media overkill reached its dizziest, each club lost its game number 11. Then in game 12 the 49ers delivered another loss to the Giants, 7-3, at Candlestick Park, before a yawning TV audience. Two games later, the Giants lost again, this time to the Bills; they also lost Simms, the top-rated passer in the league, when he damaged his foot.

Hostetler and Bahr were an unlikely entry for a club with notions about the playoffs. One was a hardly-ever-used quarterback, the other a wayfaring kicker. But the Giants won their final two games, with field goals by Bahr providing the spread in both, and they finished the season 13-3. Then, with Hostetler throwing two TD passes, they beat the Bears, 31-3, in the first playoff game.

The Giants returned to San Francisco to play the 49ers for the NFC championship on the Sunday after the war had started. Montana was going for "one for the thumb," a fifth Super Bowl.

Again the Giants and 49ers struggled against each other. It was 3-3 in the second quarter when CBS interrupted its football telecast. Dan Rather reported that Dharhan was under Iraqi Scud attack for the second time that day. A figure in a gas mask and an anti-gas attack suit appeared on the screen to provide the details from Saudi Arabia. Back to San Francisco, and the teams were tied 6-6 at the half.

In the third quarter, Joe Montana rediscovered his magic and passed 61 yards to John Taylor for a 13-6 San Francisco lead. Bahr kicked his third field goal to slice it to 13-9. In the fourth quarter, Bahr missed one. Then Hostetler went down with a crunched knee.

Moments later, Montana went down too, hit in the back by the rushing Leonard Marshall. The four-time Super Bowl hero was flat on his back in agony. Then he was on his hands and knees, a clump of grass and dirt wedged into his face mask in a graphic picture.

Hostetler came back after missing one series. On his gimpy leg, he had trouble advancing the Giants. Stuck with fourth and two, the Giants moved into punt formation. Parcells made his decision—the ball was snapped to Gary Reasons, the up back. The 49ers were fooled silly. Reasons ran 30 yards, and then Bahr kicked his fourth field goal to cut the Giants' deficit to 13-12.

Montana could not come back. But if the 49ers could hold for the final six minutes, or score again, they would play in their fifth Super Bowl. Steve Young went in at quarterback and the 49ers ran the ball. Luck was with them, and when Roger Craig fumbled, it was ruled his knee was down and the 49ers kept possession. The 49ers seemed to have an aura of invincibility about them. Then Craig fumbled again, hit by Erik Howard. The ball popped into the air, and Lawrence Taylor caught it before it hit the grass.

Hostetler trudged back onto the field. This was Joe Montana's sort of situation, 2:36 left, the clock running out, his team behind. But it was the Giants and Hostetler with the ball. Hostetler led the Giants downfield, to the 49ers' 24. With four seconds on the clock, the Giants took their last time-out. The Giants at the bench were seen in prayer.

Matt Bahr's kick was good from 42 yards, his fifth field goal, and the Giants were champions, 15-13. They were in the Super Bowl. The pictures of Joe Montana on his hands and knees with grass stuck in his mask detailed the story of the 49ers.

"This game is very ephemeral," said Bahr, who had kicked field goals for all the Giants' points. "You see players come and go all the time. And not just kickers, who are almost gypsies in football, but everyone."

"Whew, what a game," Dan Rather said when CBS switched back to war coverage. Then he informed America that 10 Scud missiles had been launched on Saudi Arabia that Sunday.

◆ ◆ ◆

Through the years, the NFL had attached ersatz patriotism to its Super Bowls. The flyovers. The flying of the flags. The reenactment of the Battle of New Orleans.

Now, at Friday noon, Paul Tagliabue addressed us with his State of the NFL press conference. Yes, the commissioner said, the Super Bowl would go on, unless there was a terribly dramatic situation in the war. The simple translation of his statement was: If ABC was forced to switch to war coverage, the Super Bowl would have to be postponed. Television paid and the NFL sold its decision-making right to ABC for Super Bowl XXV.

"After President Kennedy's assassination, we played without television and were criticized for it," Tagliabue told the massed media. "We could play this game without television and be criticized for it. We want an audience to watch our game."

Tagliabue said something else at this press conference: "The Super Bowl has become the winter version of the Fourth of July celebration."

I think he wanted all of us to stand up and salute.

◆ ◆ ◆

The same day, a Super Bowl fan from long ago issued a public statement. Said George Bush: "Somebody asked me a while back about the Super Bowl. 'Do you think we ought to cancel the Super Bowl because of this situation?' One, the war is a serious business and the nation is focused on it. But two, life goes on. And . . . the boys and men and women in the Gulf, they want to see this game go on and they're going to get great instant replays over there. . . ."

And so, the Super Bowl went on.

It went on with patriotic fervor and with Giants' fans and Bills' fans waving American flags and with anti-terrorist security and with nobody complaining about the checkpoints. It went on with a display of American technology and ingenuity: scalpers communicating from the downtown hotels to their partners outside the stadium via cellular telephones. It went on with the blimps hovering in the distance. Airspace had been cleared for a quarter mile at least, with aircraft forbidden to fly above the stadium because security people remembered *Black Sunday* as well as the dogfights of banner-trailing airplanes at Tampa's previous Super Bowl. It went on with tickets priced at $150, some of which were fetching sums eight times that. And it went on in the early evening, to catch the prime-time TV audience, an audience not certain whether Saddam Hussein might choose this place to make a terrorizing statement.

The ticket holders crushed into mobs at the perimeter gates of Tampa Stadium. Cameras were forbidden. Food buckets were opened and searched. Some sandwiches were confiscated, perhaps because they were suspected of being made with dynamite, or perhaps because the concessionaires had swung a deal that would result in higher hot dog sales. Cars with official credentials were stopped and their trunks were opened and searched. Nobody seemed to mind.

Once outside the perimeter, I hunted for the press gate. Usually, it was a walk through. I found the end of the line and waited. It took 40 minutes before I reached the frisking checkpoint. Then I was inside, set to cover my 25th Super Bowl. I felt very safe.

So did the players. They, too, had their Walkman musicmakers and camcorders checked before they were allowed into the stadium to play in the Super Bowl.

"America the Beautiful" was played, and the crowd waved flags and chanted in unison: "USA, USA, USA."

Then Whitney Houston sang "The Star-Spangled Banner" in a fervent, emotional voice. Okay, my eyes turned wet in the press box. A Super Bowl first for me. It hardly bothered me later when I learned that Whitney had sung the anthem into a recording device days before—and that was what caused me to emote in the press box.

Four F-15 Air Force jets streaked above the stadium in a Rozellian flyover. This time the crowd cheered.

The Bills were favored by a touchdown because they had Kelly and the Giants did not have Simms, because the Bills were supposed to be the best team now in the NFL and they were playing the Giants, not the 49ers.

Kelly came out with the no-huddle gimmick that had caused such trouble for the Raiders. But the Giants were ready—Parcells had six defensive backs on the field. So it was that Kelly was limited to two short completions to Reed, and Buffalo had to punt.

Then Hostetler, with two passes to Howard Cross and Mark Ingram, moved the Giants to the Buffalo 11. Bahr kicked a 28-yard field goal for a 3-0 Giants' lead.

The Bills came charging back. Kelly launched a deep pass up the left side. The ball was tipped by Perry Williams, one of the DB defenders, and plopped into the hands of James Lofton, to the Giants' eight. But the defense halted Kelly at the five. Scott Norwood tied the score, 3-3, with a 23-yard field goal.

With Kelly working three short passes to Reed inside the defenders and a pass to Thurman Thomas, the no-huddle Bills made a drive. They reached the one. Don Smith scored from there. The Bills were ahead, 10-3.

A few minutes later the Giants were pinned back at their seven. We were wondering where Bruce Smith had been when, suddenly, there he was, crashing into the end zone after Hostetler. Hostetler tripped. Smith nailed him for a safety and went into an exuberant war dance. The Bills were in front, 12-3.

Less than four minutes remained in the first half when the Giants started at their 13. Hostetler passed six yards to Bavaro, and Ottis Anderson ran for 18. Hostetler passed again, for 22 yards to Ingram. Then Dave Meggett ran for another 17. Two-minute warning. The drive resumed with the Giants at the 24. Hostetler got them to the 14. And there, with Bahr preparing for another field goal try, Hostetler hit Stephen Baker on third and 10 with a TD pass. It was 25 seconds before the half—and the Giants had altered the flow of the game.

The Giants were behind 12-10 at halftime as ABC switched to a war update. The captive fans in Tampa Stadium were forced to watch a show with an all-child cast of 2,000 put together by Disney, plus listen to some screeching by the New Kids on the Block. Mickey Mouse had not gone to war.

Then the NFL, with the tradition of 25 years of Super Bowls, unleashed a batch of dangerous doves.

The Giants got the ball again to start the second half. This time it was at their 25. Four times the Giants seemed stopped on third down. In this sequence, however, Hostetler passed 11 yards to Meggett for one first down; Anderson ran 24 yards for another; Hostetler, off the bootleg, passed 14 yards to Ingram on a third-and-13 for another; and Hostetler passed nine yards to Cross for another. When Anderson scored the touchdown on a one-yard plunge, the Giants had used up 9 ½ minutes of the third quarter. They were ahead 17-12—the Bills with their gimmick offense had managed to work one play in more than 13 minutes of elapsed time. The Giants had gone 87 and 75 yards.

Something else was clear in the Giants' scheme of ball control. Bruce Smith, the self-anointed best defensive player in football, had disappeared. Jumbo Elliott, the Giants' left tackle, had Smith neutralized.

The fourth quarter began with the Giants protecting their five-point lead. Kelly had taken the Bills to the Giants' 31 on a 19-yard pass to Kenneth Davis. On the first play of the final quarter, Kelly made an inside handoff to Thomas. Thomas broke two tackles and scooted to a touchdown. With Norwood's PAT, the Bills had regained the lead, 19-17.

One more time the Giants started deep, at their 23. Now Hostetler hit Bavaro for 17 yards on another third-down play and connected with Bavaro again for 19 yards. He passed to Ingram for 13, and quickly the Giants were at the Bills' 14. They got to the three. Then Bahr, the midseason pickup, kicked a 21-yard field goal. The Giants were ahead again, 20-19, with more than seven minutes to play.

The Bills were foiled once, then got another chance. They started with 2:16 to play from their own 10. Kelly smartly worked the ball eight yards upfield on a scramble. Then Thomas broke for 22 yards. The clock was inside two minutes now. A couple of short passes and another scramble by Kelly got the ball to the Giants' 40 with 29 seconds left. Then Thurman Thomas ran again, for 11 yards, to the 29. The Bills were out of time-outs. Kelly killed the clock with eight seconds left. The Giants took their third time-out to allow Scott Norwood to think about history.

Only once before in the 24 previous Super Bowls had there been a moment matching this one—with the kicker, the clock, the try for victory. Jim O'Brien had made the kick then for the Colts in Super Bowl V. But that Super Bowl had been flawed by 11 turnovers. In this one, neither team had coughed up the ball on a fumble, neither quarterback had thrown an interception.

America waited on hold. At last Norwood paced off his footwork for the 47-yard attempt that could win the Super Bowl for Buffalo. Frank Reich knelt to hold the ball.

The snap was fine. The hold was fine. Norwood kicked the ball—and missed, wide right, the way Booth Lusteg had missed once. Wide right. The Giants danced in celebration, 20-19 victors. It had been a classic Super Bowl, with tight and safe security on an evening when America was fighting a war.

TAMPA—This is a very curious game, this pro football.

John Elway, who once fancied himself in the same class as Terry Bradshaw, is 0-and-3 in Super Bowls. Francis Tarkenton, the most productive passing quarterback in the glorious history of the NFL, likewise was 0-and-3 in Super Bowls. The legendary John Unitas never was a winning quarterback in a Super Bowl although he played in two.

But Jeff Hostetler, this roustabout quarterback, this career bench-warmer, is a Super Bowl victor—just like Joe Montana, and Bart Starr and Roger Staubach and Bradshaw and Jim Plunkett and Joe Namath himself.

Jeff Hostetler, the quarterback with the shy grin and the shaggy mustache, the guy from the Western Pennsylvania mill territory. The guy who says: "They keep telling me I can't."

But he can. And Sunday he did. As the emergency backup to onetime Super Bowl winner Phil Simms, groggy himself at times, Hostetler guided the Giants to their 20-19 victory over Buffalo in Super Bowl XXV. He did it with aplomb and style.

"I heard so many guys say that I'd never be able to do it," Hostetler told the Super Bowl press after his bravura performance. "And thank the Lord, it's done and nobody can take it away."

What he did was complete 20 of 32 passes for the Giants. . . . He ran this methodical, unspectacular offense . . . and it commanded the ball for 40½ minutes, and thus controlled the game.

There were no gimmicks for the Giants. They huddled up on every play.

"We opened it up a little as the game went on and things started to work," said Hostetler. "Our offensive line then took over."

His quoted statements are about as flashy as his football style.

This is a guy who passed his first four seasons in pro football as a backup quarterback, watching Simms play every down in every game. For four years. He came up, as a third-round draftee of West Virginia in 1984, and didn't get into a game until 1988. Then his job was pretty much restricted to holding for the placekicker.

. . . Then, he beat Joe Montana, the four-time Super Bowl winner, by all of two points.

Sunday, he beat Jim Kelly, the newest quarterback master in pro football, by all of one point.

Following is a list of the dates on which Jerry Green's articles and columns excerpted in this book originally appeared in the Detroit *News:*

Chapter 1	January 15, 1967
Chapter 3	January 7, 1969; January 9, 1969; January 13, 1969
Chapter 4	January 7, 1970
Chapter 5	January 15, 1971
Chapter 6	January 11, 1972
Chapter 7	January 18, 1973
Chapter 8	January 7, 1974; January 14, 1974
Chapter 10	January 19, 1976
Chapter 12	January 16, 1978
Chapter 13	January 22, 1979
Chapter 14	January 14, 1980
Chapter 15	January 12, 1981
Chapter 16	January 14, 1982; January 25, 1982
Chapter 17	January 26, 1983
Chapter 19	January 20, 1985; January 21, 1985
Chapter 20	January 23, 1986; January 25, 1986; January 26, 1986
Chapter 21	January 22, 1987; January 24, 1987
Chapter 22	January 25, 1988
Chapter 25	January 25, 1991; January 27, 1991; January 28, 1991

Select Bibliography

Anderson, Dave. *Countdown to The Super Bowl*. New York: Random House, 1969.

Blount, Roy Jr. *About Three Bricks Shy of a Load*. Boston: Little Brown and Company, 1974.

Bradshaw, Terry, with Dave Diles. *Terry Bradshaw: Man Of Steel*. Grand Rapids: Zondervan, 1979.

Detroit News, Archives.

The First Fifty Years, New York: Simon and Schuster, NFL Properties, 1969.

Henderson, Thomas "Hollywood," and Peter Knobler. *Out Of Control: Confessions of an NFL Casualty*. New York: Pocket Books, 1987.

Horrigan, Jack, and Mike Rathet. *The Other League, AFL*. Chicago: Follet Publishing Company, NFL Properties, 1970.

Klein, Dave. *The Sporting News Super Bowl Book*. St. Louis: The Sporting News, annual.

Klobuchar, Jim. *Will The Vikings Ever Win the Super Bowl?* New York: Harper & Row, 1977.

Kramer, Jerry. *Lombardi: Winning is Not the Only Thing*. New York: World Publishing Company, 1970.

Neft, David S., and Richard M. Cohen. *The Sports Encyclopedia, Pro Football*. New York: St. Martin's Press, 1988.

O'Brien, Michael. *Vince*. New York: William Morrow, 1987.

Perkins, Steve. *Next Year's Champions*. New York: World Publishing, 1969.

Sahadi, Lou. *Broncos! The Team that Makes Miracles Happen*. New York: Stein and Day, 1978.

_____. *Super Sundays I-XII*. Chicago: Contemporary Books, 1978.

Schaap, Dick, ed. *Instant Replay: The Green Bay Diary of Jerry Kramer*. New York: New American Library, 1968.

The Sporting News Football Register. St. Louis: The Sporting News, annual.

Wiebusch, John. *Lombardi*. NFL Properties, Follet, 1971.

Zimmerman, Paul. *Dr. Z's Great Moments in Super Bowl History*. New York: Sports Illustrated, 1989.